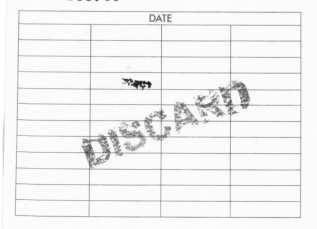

DATE			

MATHEMATICAL DISABILITIES
A COGNITIVE NEUROPSYCHOLOGICAL PERSPECTIVE

MATHEMATICAL DISABILITIES
A COGNITIVE NEUROPSYCHOLOGICAL PERSPECTIVE

edited by

GÉRARD DELOCHE
Institut National de la Santé
et de la Recherche Medicale, Paris

XAVIER SERON
University of Louvain, Belgium

LEA

LAWRENCE ERLBAUM ASSOCIATES, PUBLISHERS

1987   Hillsdale, New Jersey   London

Lawrence Erlbaum Associates, Inc., Publishers
365 Broadway
Hillsdale, New Jersey 07642

Library of Congress Cataloging-in-Publication Data

Mathematical disabilities.

Bibliography: p.
Includes index.
1. Acalculia. 2. Mathematical ability—
Physiological aspects. 3. Neuropsychology.
I. Deloche, Gerard. II. Seron, Xavier.
RJ496.A25M38 1987   616.8′5   87-429
ISBN 0-89859-891-5

Printed in the United States of America
10 9 8 7 6 5 4 3 2 1

Contents

Contributors

A.L. Benton • 504 Manor Drive - Iowa City, Iowa 52240

F. Boller • Neurology and Psychiatry, Medical Center - Veterans Administration, University Drive C, Pittsburgh, Pennsylvania 15240

C.J. Brainerd • Department of Psychology, The University of Alberta, Edmonton, Alberta T6G 2E9 (Canada)

A. Caramazza • Department of Psychology, The Johns Hopkins Hospital, Baltimore, Maryland 21218

G. Deloche • Inserm U.84 - 47, Boulevard de l'Hôpital, F-75651 Paris Cedex 13 (France)

E. Gonzalez • Department of Psychology, University of Toronto, Toronto, M5S 1A1 (Canada)

J. Grafman • Vietnam Head Injury Study, Department of Clinical Investigations, Walter Reed Army Medical Center - Washington, D.C. 20307

W. Hartje • Abteilung Neurologie der Medizinischen Fakultät an der RWTH Aachen, Pauwelstrasse D-5100 Aachen (West Germany)

D. Holender • Laboratoire de Psychologie Expérimentale, Université Libre de Bruxelles, Avenue Adolph Buyl, 117 - B-1050 Bruxelles (Belgium)

P.A. Kolers • Department of Psychology, University of Toronto, Toronto, M5S, 1A1 (Canada)

M. McCloskey • Department of Psychology, The Johns Hopkins University, Baltimore, Maryland 21218

R. Peereman • Laboratoire de Psychologie Expérimentale, Université Libre de Bruxelles, Avenue Adolph Buyl, 117 - B-1050 Bruxelles (Belgium)

X. Seron • Unité de Neuropsychologie Expérimentale de l'Adulte (NEXA), Avenue Hippocrate, 54/5480, B-1200 Bruxelles (Belgium)

P. Spiers • Beth Israel Hospital S-120, Behavioral Neurology Unit, 330 Brookline Avenue, Boston, M.A. 02215

E.K. Warrington • Psychology Department, The National Hospital, Queen Square, London WC1N 3BG (U.K.)

Introduction

Interest in mathematical cognition is not new in psychology. However, as Ginsburg (1983) has noted after a silent period of more or less 30 years, it was rediscovered in the 1970s under the influential work of the Genevan School. In particular, Piaget's work on conservation, including conservation of number, has profoundly influenced developmental psychologists who, working first in the Piagetian theoretical framework, began to discover a broader set of topics in mathematical cognition. In developmental psychology, the field is still expanding and presently covers a wide range of topics, including perceptual mechanisms in the discrimination of quantities, language processing in counting, and decoding of mathematical notational systems, procedural knowledge in calculation and problem solving, and cultural differences and social factors in numerical and mathematical skills (see for reviews: Brainerd, 1982; Carpenter, Moser, & Romberg, 1982; Ginsburg, 1983).

During the same period, however, no such evolution occurred in neuropsychology, and, except for some recent studies, very little has been published on acalculia and number processing disorders. However, a more general theoretical evolution occurred in neuropsychology, mainly due to increasing collaboration between clinical and experimental neuropsychologists, on the one hand, and cognitive psychologists, on the other. This interpenetration has been especially significant in the fields of language breakdown, acquired reading disorders, and memory impairment. One of the results of this dialogue has been a progressive shift of interest in the examination and interpretation of the pathological data. Instead of being collected only as symptoms to be organized in neurologically pertinent syndromes, the deficits began to be considered as relevant information for the elaboration of functional, psychologically motivated theory. This ongoing evolution has also deeply modified the methodological approaches to neuropsychological disorders and the so-called single-case-study paradigm for the observation of intra-subject functional dissociation has become one of the most powerful tools of neuropsychology in the study of cognitive functioning (Marin, Saffran, & Schwartz, 1976; Shallice, 1979).

The objective of this book is to promote a similar evolution in the neuropsychology of calculation and number processing deficits and thus to introduce clinical and experimental neuropsychologists as well as developmental and cognitive psychologists to recent research and theoretical approaches that are of particular interest for the neuropsychological approach to mathematical cognition. The reader will thus find chapters written by contributors issued from different areas of psychological research. There are also critical reviews of existing data and original reports of experimental work. Such a patchwork of contributions and topics is unavoidable, given the newness of the interest in mathematical cognition in neuropsychology.

The first chapter addresses the central theoretical and methodological issues raised by the investigation of brain behavior relationships in the particular case of calculation skills. Paul Spiers argues that the evaluation of calculation disorders provides a unique opportunity to study such general questions, but that the whole conceptual framework is presently inadequate, due to the previous lack of uniformity in assessment methods, the deficiency of theoretical constructs and the insufficiency of normative and developmental data. In order to overcome these shortcomings, Spiers proposes considering the localization question in terms of several discrete neural functional components organized into an integrated network, on the one hand, and in terms of formal component aspects involved in calculation skills, on the other. Nevertheless, as Spiers notes, such a correspondence between the elements of the two systems is complex because the components in the network may be involved in different levels of the cognitive functions. Finally, these operational principles are exemplified by the detailed presentation of a new taxonomy of calculation errors based on theoretical grounds and substantiated by empirical data.

In Chapter 2, Esther Gonzales and Paul Kolers consider the fundamental question of whether the cognitive operations enhanced by subjects when performing mental arithmetic are carried out in some general mental space independently of the characteristics of the notational system in which they are presented, or whether such mental operations depend upon the symbolic forms that express them and in which particular skills have developed through practice. The issue is particularly relevant to the theoretical setting of neuropsychological investigations since it refers to the debate between the proponents of the "unitary" view of symbolic function abilities and those of the parallel and more specialized skills, the consequence of brain damage being an undifferentiated loss of performance in the former case or dissociated according to task requirements in the latter. By critically reviewing the models of a common representation space (spatial metaphor "number line," analog and discrete models) and by presenting some of their own and other relevant experimental data, the authors argue for the existence of individual cognitive skills, contextually dependent developed. The implications of such a point of view are obvious, especially regarding the need to evaluate the role of the different notational systems (digit, alphabetic, phonetic forms, etc.) in the patient's impaired or preserved processing of the different operations. Although such a perspective was suggested by Grewel (1952, 1969), it has only recently begun to receive attention in the neuropsychological literature (see Chapters 7 and 8 of this book).

In the next chapter, Daniel Holender and Ronald Peereman present a thorough and thoughtful analysis of studies contrasting different types of number notational systems. They consider that a major distinction must be made between multiple- versus single-digit numbers in cognitive functioning. In the first case, the relevant factor should be the precise nature of the structural principles underlying the surface notations and determining more or less severe constraints on the sequential organization of lexical primitives into well-formed, unambiguous number codings. In the case of single-symbol number processing, the critical feature would be the nature, either logographic or phonographic, of the symbol surface form, as suggested by the widespread but controversial left visual field advantage in the processing of logograms.

Holender and Peereman offer an in-depth analysis of the data (including their own) from a variety of experiments (numerical comparison judgments, lexical decisions, naming, etc.) presented in the central field or the lateral hemifield conducted with normal and brain-damaged subjects. The picture that emerges from this review of single-digit differential processing according to the nature of the notational system and hemispheric specialization is illuminating. It is argued that, since the reliable effects found in numerical comparisons (symbolic distance, serial position) similarly occur in the two kinds of script and since lateral hemifield presentations to normal subjects show a reliable right visual field advantage independent of the type of script, the hypothesis of right hemisphere superiority for logograms is not substantiated in the case of isolated digits. A critical analysis of the methodological tools led the authors to consider that some classical experimental paradigms are inadequate for disentangling the interactions of the components involved in such seemingly basic tasks. Finally, the authors suggest that some brain-damaged patients can probably offer very fruitful investigation opportunities, provided the "pure" form of the syndromes and the question of the relationship between pathological and normal data are taken into account.

In Chapter 4, Charles Brainerd provides an experimental and theoretical rationale for evaluating the respective contribution of working-memory components in mental arithmetic. His approach to children's performance in simple mental addition and subtraction problems is fully described, from the experimental paradigms used in five experiments to the structure of stochastic models of the working memory and the actual quantitative estimations of parameters that independently characterize input variables (encoding, storage of traces) and transformation variables (retrieval, processing). Contrary to the classic emphasis on processing, the results indicate that children's developmental improvements in calculation are highly dependent on input and, more particularly, on encoding accuracy, which is of obvious importance in developmental psychology. This study also addresses some highly critical issues in the domain of acquired calculation disorders. First, the role of the working memory as a source of difficulty, particularly with auditory presentation of mental arithmetic problems, clearly deserves much more consideration than hitherto. Second, Brainerd's analyses are based on both error and success data, thus accounting for the entire corpus, which most processing studies restricted to correct response latencies fail to do. As already pointed out by Spiers, this approach seems especially valuable in the field of the study of brain-damaged patients, who produce significant error percentages and sometimes long and variable reaction times.

Arthur Benton approaches the question of the functional relations between lesion localization and mathematical disabilities by considering the particular picture of the Gerstmann syndrome. Since the three hypotheses that have been proposed to account for this syndrome (basic deficit of finger agnosia, disorder in spatial thinking, or impairment in symbolic thinking) correspond to interpretations of the three classic types of acalculia (anarithmetia, spatial acalculia, and aphasic acalculia, respectively), and because of the highly specific localizing value that some attribute to the Gerstmann syndrome, such an approach appears promising. In this respect, the anatomo-clinical data available are reviewed and discussed, together with a detailed report and analysis of a case of anarithmetia presenting short-term visual memory impairments. It is, however, concluded that no evidence can be found of a particular form of acalculia that could characterize the Gerstmann syndrome, that the taxonomy of acalculias needs to be specified by more precise definitional criteria, especially in the case of spatial acalculia, and that the so-called developmental Gerstmann syndrome is of questionable utility as a behavioral description.

In Chapter 6, W. Hartje presents and discusses the general issue of the spatial component that is supposedly intrinsically attached to arithmetical skills. Phenomenological considerations derived from developmental studies and empirical evidence derived from the co-occurrence of calculation disorders and spatial deficits are first reviewed. Hartje then focuses on written arithmetic. A fine-grained classification of the spatial errors that may be found in this activity is proposed and tentatively related to different types of spatial impairments. A detailed review of the literature, especially the earlier German authors, indicates that there is ample evidence of associations between spatial impairments and spatial acalculia but that the former does not constitute a necessary or a sufficient condition of the latter. Moreover, no unequivocal correspondence appears between the different spatial error types and the signs of spatial deficits. Similar conclusions are provided by the reports of the recent studies (including Hartje's contribution) that used more sophisticated statistical tools (hierarchical, cluster, principle component analyses) to correlate arithmetical tasks with tests differentially loaded in spatial, verbal, or other factors. Finally, it is argued that more evidence must be collected before the question can be resolved of whether there is involvement of a specific spatial component in mental arithmetic even when the task does not require visuo-spatial or spatial constructional activities. It is suggested that experimental investigations contrasting mental and written calculation might well be fruitful.

In Chapter 7, Gérard Deloche and Xavier Seron outline a comprehensive computational model of number transcodings between the phonographic and the digital notational system based on the theoretical conceptualization of the formal structural characteristics of the two written codes and justified by the analysis of a large corpus of data collected from aphasic subjects. Previous work is reviewed that suggests the framework for interpreting actual individual transcoding errors as being produced by identifiable variants of the correct procedures, highlights the role of the linguistic structure of the verbal coding system in such erroneous responses, and supports the neuropsycholinguistic relevance of a categorization of alphabetic number lexical primitives according to stack notions. The model expands the focus of research by incorporating these concepts into a multicomponent number production system featured in close relationship to the hypothesized lexical organization of the particular symbolic domain. It is argued that this approach overcomes the defects of taxonomic descriptions and, in view of the systematicness often found in the performance of aphasics, does in fact provide the framework for a cognitive theory of number processing that can contribute to the knowledge of normal mechanisms, to the diagnosis and explanation of pathological disorders, as well as to the scientifically justified foundation for therapeutic techniques (see Seron & Deloche, in press, for the last point).

In Chapter 8, Xavier Seron and Gérard Deloche report on their investigations of aphasics' performances in producing the standard sequence of number words. Since the progressive mastery of the counting word series by children is known to influence the elaboration of basic numerical principles and the development of more efficient processing strategies in arithmetic tasks and since normals are sometimes found to rely on the number sequences as a backup procedure, it is argued that some calculation impairments could stem from disorders in the performance of such simple and perhaps automated activity. Aphasics' skills in experiments contrasting the notational systems (oral counting, alphabetic or arabic digital writing) and varying the degree of automation (counting by ones, twos, or fives) are reported. The global and structural analyses of aphasics' failures indicate the relevance of type of script as a source of difficulty and as a determinant of error types. The findings thus favor the approach that considers the particular features of the symbols to be manipulated as inherent in the specifications of the mechanisms operating on them. In the case of verbal counting, a model is thus proposed based on the linguistic analysis of the verbal lexicon into primitives categorized into three stacks (units, teens, and decades) and handled by procedures dealing with stack characteristics (class, position, values). This theoretical model is found to provide a logical explanation for aphasics' data and a new framework for the reassessment of developmental errors as well. Given the aphasics' difficulties observed in producing the verbal sequence of counting words, the question of such a disruption as a possible source of error in arithmetic processes that had progressively acquired some independence relative to the verbal sequence skill that originally accompanied their development is an appropriate subject for further research.

The approach illustrated by Alfonso Caramazza and Michael McCloskey in the next two chapters is also concerned with specifying the basic component properties and their general architecture in a model of the normal cognitive system involved in arithmetic skills. The variety of patterns of impaired performance found in the examination of collections of single cases would serve as the empirical basis for inferences about the structure of the model from which they would receive, in turn, more adequate and well-articulated interpretations, provided that a theoretical basis could independently justify the whole system. A distinction is drawn between a number-processing system that comprises those mechanisms for comprehending and producing numbers and a calculation system that deals with the arithmetic knowledge of number facts and the procedures required for performing specific calculations. In Chapter 9, the relevant dimensions of the main subcomponents of normal number processing are derived by considering the set of dissociations observed in various patients as the experimental signs demonstrating that the corresponding mechanisms are represented independently in the system to be modeled. Such an approach thus supports a general parceling between number comprehension and production, between single (lexical) and multisymbol (syntactic) number form processing, and between the different scripts. McCloskey and Caramazza then focus on the spoken verbal number production part of their model and speculate on its fine structure into a lexicon also organized into three functionally distinct classes, syntactic number frames, and base-10 semantic representations. This constitutes the framework for their analysis of the erroneous reading aloud of arabic numbers by three patients. This model can be fruitfully compared with that of Deloche and Seron for transcoding mechanisms (Chapter 7) whatever the difference in modality tasks. Both sets of authors address the same problem. In Deloche and Seron's model the transcoding mechanisms operate without the intervention of a semantic component, whereas semantic processing is required as input to the number-processing system in McCloskey and Caramazza's model. Applying the same component reasoning to the detailed investigation of patterns of calculation impairments through individual subject's performance similarly provides the main features of a model of the normal calculation system grossly articulated into numerical and operational signs processing table fact retrieval and calculation procedures

(Chapter 10). Finally, Caramazza and McCloskey discuss the methodological issues raised by studying whether the cognitive mechanisms that correspond to some identified impaired number or calculation processing stages may be general or specific to the arithmetic sphere.

Chapter 11 presents two single-case reports of Elisabeth Warrington's acalculic patients. The first one is an elegant illustration of the cognitive approach to the analysis of calculation deficits and its contribution to the study of the normal processing system. The preserved impaired abilities of the patients are fully documented in a large variety of numerical and computational tasks. The calculation disorder did not stem in language, memory, constructional, number, or basic operation principles knowledge. Situated in the general framework viewing arithmetic skills as a complex multicomponent system, and discussed in reference to different models of normal activity, the findings are interpreted as a specific impairment of the particular functional subsystem responsible for the accurate retrieval of stored table facts. Failure is thus identified as an instability in gaining direct access to the special semantic category of number facts that may sometimes have to be reconstructed through backup counting procedures. The second case is a brief report of a patient whose oral calculation impairment could be attributed to difficulties in comprehending individual spoken numbers. Such investigations clearly demonstrate the utility of single-case analysis in the disentangling of the architecture of the normal calculation cognitive system and, conversely, the benefit that the evaluation of patients may derive from the consideration of experimental studies of normals.

The last chapter presents a survey of cross-cultural studies on calculation considered as an alternative source of inferences contributing to the componential analysis of this cognitive system. Jordan Grafman and François Boller argue that such a closed semiotic system is particularly well-suited to receive broad explanatory power from investigations contrasting different types of information processing demands upon representational tools, fact memory, lexical access, and algorithmic and heuristic procedures required for adequate calculation. The differential role of the notational system, culture, and education on the arithmetical ability and proficiency of children and adults is studied in illiterates and non-Western (Africa, Asia) normal subjects, and a rudimentary model of the cognitive operations necessarily involved in calculation is outlined. The general principles that emerge are classified into genetically derived skills such as magnitude estimation, culturally linked abilities like counting, and education-bound strategies (for instance the schematic aspects of arithmetic procedures). It is thus shown that cross-cultural studies of this kind are relevant to our understanding of acalculia since those skills that appear determined genetically may be hypothesized to be more basic than others to the cognitive system as a whole and thus more resistant to brain injury. Finally, further research on preserved impaired calculation abilities of non-Western or illiterate adults is clearly of interest.

REFERENCES

Brainerd, C. J. (Ed.). (1982). *Children's logical and mathematical cognition.* New York: Springer Verlag.

Carpenter, T. P., Moser, J. M., & Romberg, T. A. (1982). *Addition and Subtraction: A cognitive perspective.* Hillsdale: Lawrence Erlbaum Associates.

Ginsburg, H. P. (Ed.). (1983). *The developmental mathematical thinking.* New York: Academic Press.

Grewel, F. (1952). Acalculia. *Brain, 75,* 397–407.

Grewel, F. (1969). The acalculias. In P. J. Vinken & G. Bruyn (Eds.), *Handbook of clinical neurology* (pp. 181–194). Amsterdam, North Holland.

Marin, O. S., Saffran, E. M., & Schwartz, M. F. (1976). Dissociations on language in aphasia: Implications for normal function. *Annals of the New York Academy of Sciences, 280,* 868–884.

Seron, X., & Deloche, G. (Eds.). (in press) *Cognitive approaches in neuropsychological rehabilitation.* Hillsdale, NJ: Lawrence Erlbaum Associates.

Shallice, T. (1979). Case study approach in neuropsychological research. *Journal of Clinical Neuropsychology, 1,* 183–211.

1 Acalculia Revisited: Current Issues

Paul A. Spiers
Behavioral Neurology Unit
Beth Israel Hospital

DEDICATION

This chapter is dedicated to the memory of Professor Henry Hécaen. Professor Hécaen's leadership in the study of acalculia was well-known. He felt this topic needed revival and was generous enough to invite me to join him for such an endeavor in Paris in 1979. His abundant enthusiasm for neuropsychology was contagious and reflected in the energy with which he pursued his own research and the interest with which he followed the work of others. His scholarship and the breadth of his historical knowledge were impressive and readily available to those who wished to learn from him. He was a teacher, a scientist, and one of the foremost neuropsychologists of our time. He was also a proud grandfather, fiercely Breton, and a warm, encouraging host to a young graduate student.

INTRODUCTION

The careful examination of calculation ability in cases of brain damage provides a potentially fruitful context in which to study higher cortical functioning. Several detailed case reports of patients with calculation disorders have appeared in the neurological literature and a number of studies have attempted to investigate the parameters of these deficits using large groups of subjects. Despite these efforts, no clear statement of the relationship between calculation ability and brain functioning currently exists. In large measure, this is due to a lack of uniformity in the various methods employed to examine patients with calculation disorders. Specific computational stimuli have rarely been described and the actual errors produced by patients are almost never reported. This has led to the premature development of simplified classification schema and widely held but relatively naive assumptions regarding the localization of calculation skills that are incompatible with methodological and theoretical standards in modern neuropsychology. It is for these reasons that this volume is so timely.

Before interest in this topic can be rekindled, however, several questions need to be answered. Foremost among these is whether calculation should even be independently classified as a cognitive function. Second, it would seem important to know why enthusiasm for the study of calculation has foundered. Where did the investigation of this phenomenon go wrong, and how can it be brought back into the mainstream of neuropsychological research? Finally, how are we to understand the neural mechanisms underlying calculation? Some elementary hypotheses regarding the biological basis of this cognitive activity are sorely needed if research on calculation and its disorders is to move in a constructive direction. In this chapter, an attempt is made to address some of these issues.

HISTORICAL PROBLEMS

Almost without exception, research in this area has ignored the patient's actual calculation performance. Although it is absurd to imagine the study of aphasia without any consideration of the characteristics of aphasic speech, this has been precisely the state of affairs that has existed in the study of acalculia. Only a handful of investigators have considered the errors produced by patients as they attempted to solve calculations and no real attempt has ever been made to describe or classify patients' calculation errors in terms of a theoretical conceptualization of the number system (Grewel, 1952, 1969). Terms have been applied repeatedly without any consensus regarding their definition. *Spatial dyscalculia,* for example, has a different meaning for Krapf (1937) than it does for Kleist (1934) or for Hécaen Angelergues, and Houllier (1961), not one of which is related to Luria's (1967, 1973) concept of a quasi-spatial deficit as the basis of acalculia. Potential correlations between specific types of errors and particular lesion sites have been ignored by certain authors (cf. Bresson, DeSchonen, & Tzortzis, 1972) or obviated by the etiology of injury in other cases (cf. Singer & Low, 1933; Strub & Geschwind, 1975). Perhaps most important, however, the methods used to assess patients' calculation abilities have differed widely from study to study. Consequently, it is not known whether such parameters as carrying and borrowing, zero and identity operations, or the complexity of computations have been systematically varied. Presently there is no calculation examination that incorporates theoretical concepts regarding the calculation process, consists of items of graded complexity to reflect various error tendencies already described in the literature, and upon which adequate normative data have been collected. Clearly, this makes it difficult to evaluate and compare results from one study to another unless detailed descriptions are provided of the methods of investigation. This has generally been the exception rather than the rule.

A FEW GOOD EXAMPLES

The most encouraging work on acalculia can be found historically in the work of Singer and Low (1933), Benson (1969, 1972), Grewel (1952, 1969), Lindquist (1935, 1936), and Hécaen et al. (1961). More recently, reports by Deloche and Seron (1982), Grafman, Passafiume, Faglioni, and Boller (1982), and Warrington (1982) deserve consideration. Although none of these provides a prototype for the investigation of acalculia, a brief critical review of these studies not only reveals some encouraging developments, but also serves to illustrate the issues that face future research in this area.

In the first of these papers, Deloche and Seron (1982) examined the ability of Broca's and Wernicke's aphasics to transcode numbers from their numeral form (i.e., five hundred and twenty-one) into the corresponding digit sequence (521) and considered whether errors on this task differed by type of aphasia. They described their patients' performance in detail and categorized their observations in terms both of characteristic failures and of what they believed to be the processes operating to produce these errors. Unfortunately, Deloche and Seron did not attempt to adapt their schema to any of the existent terminology or compare their findings to any of the error types already reported in studies of number reading and writing. They also organized portions of their error analysis around theoretical linguistic processes rather than around features of the number system and its format for digit notation (Grewel, 1952, 1969). As such, there is some overlap between their various types of errors when these are viewed from a number system perspective. For example, their "serial order," "stack," and "transcoding of thousands and hundreds" errors all involve violations of the place-holding system in various ways. The "stack position errors," in particular, appear to be simply digit paragraphic substitutions of the type reported by Benson and Denckla (1969).

Regardless of perspective, however, it is clear that there is a difference in the distribution of errors that are more common to each type of aphasia, with the Broca's errors resulting primarily from grammatical difficulties and the Wernicke's difficulties centering primarily around the sequential organization of the numerals. Although Deloche and Seron felt that this pattern suggested a parallel between the dissolution of linguistic skills and digit transcription difficulties in the number system, they did not speculate on the nature of the relationship underlying this observation. However, it would seem likely that the similarity between the deficits observed in the linguistic and number realms is due to the functional specialization of the anatomical structures that have been damaged. For each type of aphasia, the lesioned areas responsible for these distinct patterns of deficits probably subserve particular aspects of a wide variety of cognitive activities that happen to include language and calculation. Unfortunately, Deloche and Seron did not present the lesion sites for their sample or attempt to relate these to the types of errors observed. They also did not report on their patients' calculation performance, though clearly the errors they described could result in computational failures during calculation operations. They did note, however, that their patients generally did well on the transcoding task. Apparently, then, there were no actual number alexics or agraphics in this population, which, presumably, contained few patients with occipital lesions. Finally, Deloche and Seron point out that in no instance was any patient's production of a random nature. Errors could always be identified upon careful investigation to reflect in some way a deficit in one of the two semantic systems under investigation.

In contrast to Deloche and Seron, Grafman et al. (1982) focused their study on the calculation performance of 76 patients with right or left hemisphere, anterior or posterior lesions who had no alexia or agraphia for numbers. The sample was administered a battery of calculations spanning all four operations, and their responses were scored for what Grafman et al. choose to call "quantitative" and "qualitative" criteria. The former was simply a total error score and the latter was an application of Benton's Visual Retention Test (VRT) categories to the patients' solutions. Grafman et al.'s definitions for the application of the VRT error categories are somewhat vague. Furthermore, they assigned a severity value, ranging from 1 to 5, to these qualitative errors. It would seem difficult, however, to decide how severe an instance of perseveration or omission might be. The severity judgments may have been based on the graphomotor features of the patients' errors, but no criteria are provided by the authors for such decisions, and it would still seem improbable that severity ratings could be consistently applied to misplaced, omitted, or perseverated items. Finally, Grafman et al. reorganized these qualitative error types into three categories, which they labeled *spatial configuration, form,* and *attention.* Unfortunately, they do not provide the defining characteristics for these categories, do not discuss the rationale underlying each one, and fail to discuss the selection criteria by which the VRT error types were assigned to each category.

In light of these factors, Grafman et al.'s error categories may actually have confounded rather than improved their analysis. Even had they decided that previously reported error categories were insufficiently robust, it might have been preferable for Grafman et al. to adopt Grewel's (1952, 1969) terminology for calculation errors, which is at least based on the structure of the number system, rather than borrow a set of error types from a different context. The disappointing aspect of Grafman et al.'s categories is that it resulted in a lack of description of their patients' actual calculation performance. In fact, Grafman et al. remark that many of the patients' errors could not easily be classified in terms of their system, which stands in marked contrast to observations by other authors that patients' errors can always be identified to bear some relation to the number system. Grafman et al. also did not report the incidence of anarithmetia or spatial dyscalulia among their patients, which would have provided a useful test of Hécaen et al.'s (1961) earlier localization hypotheses.

These difficulties notwithstanding, Grafman et al.'s findings are of great interest. In fact, they found a significant left hemisphere effect for the quantitative scores and a significant left posterior lesion effect for the qualitative scores. Both of these effects were sufficiently robust to withstand covariate analyses, using the patients' age, education, and scores on the Token Test, the Crosses Test, a test of constructional apraxia, and the Raven's Progressive Matrices. Furthermore, the left posterior effect was still apparent even when the VRT error types were regrouped into the spatial configuration, form, and attention categories. Grafman et al. conclude that even though visuoconstructional and language skills undoubtedly contribute to intact calculation performance, left posterior lesions are particularly prone to produce impaired calculation abilities independent of these disorders. They also feel their findings are generally compatible with Henschen's (1920, 1926) hypothesis that the angular gyrus in the left hemisphere has particular significance for calculation. Finally, they wisely observe that future investigation in this area is likely to be fruitful only if a more standardized assessment tool can be developed that systematically examines levels of difficulty in calculation and makes it possible to analyze qualitative deficits.

Finally, Warrington (1982), in a thorough and thoughtful case report, set out to systematically examine the parameters of one of the component functions of the calculation process. Her patient was a 61-year-old, right-handed physician who presented with headache, expressive, receptive, and nominal speech deficits, a right homonymous hemianopsia, and acalculia. The patient had a left posterior parieto-occipital haematoma demonstrated on CT Scan but improved spontaneously without intervention over the course of 2 weeks. General intellectual functioning (as measured by the Wechsler Adult Intelligence Scale), language comprehension, naming, reading, and verbal memory all returned to normal, but the patient had a persistent inability to retrieve basic number facts.

Oral addition, subtraction, and multiplication operations were systematically investigated with digits between 1 and 19. The patient often knew the approximate answer or was aware that it should be an odd or even number almost immediately but could not reliably access the exact solution. At times, he reverted to counting by ones or twos in order to reach an answer and was invariably correct if permitted to calculate slowly and check his solution. Warrington also demonstrated that the patient's response latencies as a function of the minimum addend, minuend, or multiplicand (Groen & Parkman, 1972) were significantly different in comparison to those obtained from a control sample of five other physicians in their sixties. These findings corroborated the patient's observation that this portion of his calculation process was no longer "automatic." The patient was not entirely acalculic, but his error rates for the various types of verbally presented computations ranged between approximately 2% and 24%, in comparison to an error rate of zero for the control physicians, and were susceptible to deterioration by altering the order of presentation of digits. It is noted, however, that the patient never made errors that suggested a failure to perceive the direction of the operation (i.e., his sums were never smaller than one of the addends) and, in fact, that he gave concise, accurate verbal definitions for each of the calculation operations. Furthermore, he had no deficit in number reading or writing, in quantity estimation, in giving approximate answers to large computations, in estimating sociocultural numerical facts (e.g., the height of the average British woman, how many persons fit on a double-decker bus), in the time taken to determine which was the greater of two numbers, and in retrieving facts from various numerical contexts (e.g., inches in a foot, temperature at which water boils). He could also perform decimal and fraction conversions and could analyze and apply the correct sequence of operations required by arithmetic word problems (WAIS subtest), though in both of these contexts his computational difficulties interfered with adequate timed performances.

In order to assess the impact of the patient's deficit on written calculation, Warrington administered a timed battery of computations developed by Hitch (1978a). The patient showed relative impairment in comparison to a control sample of lower educational background on addition with and without carrying, subtraction with and without borrowing, multiplication and division tables, and long multiplication and division. Unfortunately, Warrington did not report or specifically describe the patient's errors on these tasks. This would have been of great interest in determining the impact of a specific deficit in basic number fact retrieval on more complex operations in the face of apparently intact algorithms and procedural rules for the execution of these computations. Presumably, the patient did not forget carries or borrows, misalign columns, or make any other types of error that are probably related to different components of the calculation process.

In her discussion, Warrington clearly refutes any notion that this patient's calculation disorder could be attributed to deficits in language, constructional ability, or fundamental number knowledge. Furthermore, the rules of the calculation operations per se were intact. What is evidently demonstrated by this case, according to the author, is the possibility of obtaining a dissociation between arithmetical processing in general and accurate retrieval of specific computational values.

Warrington is also the only contemporary author in this field to consider her results in light of recent experimental work on the calculation process of normals. She correctly points out that the study of acalculia provides a unique test for theories of normal computational skills. One such theory is the "retrieval-counting" model of addition proposed by Groen and Parkman (1972), which states that analysis of basic addition response times reflects direct access to information stored in memory. If this is true, then all information entries are equipotential and "retrieval" of any specific semantic entry, or number fact, requires essentially a constant amount of time. When direct access fails, the subject may revert to "counting." This involves proceeding from the larger addend and then increasing the number of units until the increments equal the minimum addend, thus yielding a correct solution, a process frequently observed in children's computations. Warrington relates this model to her patient's inconsistent and increased response latencies, compensatory counting strategies, and threefold increase in error rate when computations were presented with the minimum addend first. She concludes that her patient's calculation deficit represented a failure in direct semantic entry access for number facts. She proposes that the entries themselves were undamaged and that the patient had a normal calculation strategy with faulty access based on the variability in his performance. Although this is an interesting speculation, it certainly could have been tested easily and directly by presenting a multiple-choice response format (Benson & Denckla, 1969). Presumably, if the patient's acalculia were due solely to faulty access of number facts rather than to any actual loss, then the response latencies obtained in a multiple-choice paradigm should be equivalent to those of the controls as the correct semantic entry would only require a recognition rather than a retrieval response.

Warrington's study stands out for the thoroughness with which the patient's various numerical and computational skills were evaluated, the detailed experimental investigation into the parameters of the component deficit that was undertaken, and the manner in which these results were brought into perspective relative to theories of normal computational ability. The only truly disappointing aspect of Warrington's report is that she did not describe her patient's actual written computational failures. She also does not compare her findings to recent case studies or investigations of calculation disorders and does not attempt to classify her patient in terms of existing hypothetical hierarchies or schemas concerning the breakdown of the calculation process. Her patient clearly refutes the notion that calculation difficulties are always secondary to language or constructional deficits (Collignon, Leclerq, & Mahy, 1977), appears in some respects to be similar to the case presented by Mazzuchi, Manzoni, Mainini, and Parma (1976), and adds to the weight of evidence that the left hemisphere plays a special role in the mediation of those acquired abilities that constitute the fundamental calculation process.

Although valuable contributions have obviously been made in the recent literature on acalculia, there is still no consensus regarding what is meant by this term and what its implications are for our understanding of brain functioning. This sorry state of affairs can be attributed to two major factors. First, it is not clear what is being studied. Is calculation a "higher cortical function" or simply a "performance"? If it is a function, where is it localized, or is it localizable? Second, the operational principles guiding the investigation of this phenomenon have clearly not been equal to the task. In fact, it would seem more apropos to ask whether such principles even exist and, if not, then how should this topic be studied?

IS CALCULATION A LOCALIZABLE FUNCTION?

The status of calculation as an independent "function" has essentially been debated since cases of disruption in the calculation process were first reported. The position espoused by early faculty psychologists (phrenologists) was clear. Calculation, like affiliativeness, inhabitiveness, and all other human traits, was one of an aggregate of organs whose location could be determined from palpation of the overlying skull because each organ developed in proportion to its relative power. Opposing this view was the work of Flourens (1794–1867) who had demonstrated that the disruption of function observed in pigeons and chickens after lesions to the brain varied in severity according to the mass, not the locus, of the tissue ablated. The cerebral hemispheres were, therefore, essentially equipotential (Lashley, 1929). However, Broca's (1865) and Wernicke's (1874) demonstrations that different patterns of language dysfunction were associated in more than one case with the same distinct cortical lesions disputed the validity of equipotentiality. Marie (1906) later attempted to revive the holistic view when he argued that all cognitive deficits observed after brain damage, including speech or calculation difficulties, were simply specific forms of a generalized intellectual dysfunction. Henschen certainly took the position that calculation was an independent function and assumed, in fact, that he had not only demonstrated its independent status but also generally identified the "calculation centre." Peritz, Sittig, and Lewandowsky and Stadelmann had adopted a similar perspective before Henschen, Kleist would reaffirm it, and even Berger's (1923) classification of primary and secondary acalculias implicitly assumed the existence of calculation as a higher cortical function.

Goldstein (1923) openly challenged these assumptions, at first suggesting that calculation deficits varied with the different forms of aphasia and then proposing that some general problem in visual representation was responsible. Certainly, this was most compatible with Gestaltist views; however, Goldstein would later write (1948) that two areas of the brain were critical to the performance of calculation, thereby indirectly implying its independent status. Head (1926) argued that calculation deficits did not appear to vary with distinct lesion sites in the manner observed for aphasia but the actual cases he reported, in fact, suggest the opposite. However, he did not take a stand on whether acalculia was to be considered a defective performance or a disrupted function. Other authors similarly failed to challenge the status of calculation as a function, implicitly acknowledged it by the nature of their research on acalculia, or completely ignored the issue even though they examined such patients. In contrast, Guttman (1936) addressed this question directly in his paper on developmental calculation disorders. According to Guttman, calculation deficits are due to some disruption in the fundamental processes of quantity and magnitude estimation that become perturbed as a result of structural or functional anomalies in the visual centers of the brain. This is the common denominator of all acalculias, and calculation is therefore only a secondary performance based on these more fundamental principles, processes, or "functions."

Perhaps the most reasonable position to be advanced on this topic was that proposed by Lindquist (1936). Based on his own case material and a review of the literature, Lindquist concluded that different cognitive factors and different cerebral regions were clearly responsible for the variety of acalculias that had been described up to that time. Consequently, he reasoned that it should be possible to identify distinct types of acalculia associated with specific lesion localizations, in the same fashion that different types of aphasia had been described. Hécaen et al. (1961) openly agreed with Lindquist in discussing their findings and concluded that calculation was a performance, presumably manufactured from the integration of various separate functions. Grewel's (1969) perspective is similar, though it stresses the components of the calculation system per se as parameters that have a bearing on the types of deficits observed and, by implication, on how calculation is organized and effected within the brain. Mazzuchi et al. (1976), Grafman et al. (1982), and others have essentially accepted the multiple-function view of calculation though without considering its theoretical implications. Collignon et al. (1977) have argued that careful investigation of associated abilities in patients with acalculia reveals that the calculation deficit can always be attributed to disruption in some more instrumental function, such as language or constructional praxis, and should therefore always be considered a secondary performance. However, recent factor-analytic studies with normal subjects (Furneaux & Rees, 1976, 1978) have yielded separate factors for mathematical inference and mathematical knowledge, neither of which seems to be dependent on general intelligence (g) or verbal skills. This suggests that mathematical ability, at least statistically, is an independent cognitive function.

Clearly, there is no unitary acalculia that can be specifically lateralized and localized. However, it is probably the case that the calculation system may be disrupted in a particular number of ways for which there may be corresponding specifiable lesions. By this definition calculation is a "performance" inasmuch as it is the product that results from the integrated interaction of various structures and processes within the nervous system. However, it is probably also a "function," at least in the same sense that we consider language to be a higher cortical function. Certainly, there is no unitary aphasia or single lesion that produces a generalized language disturbance. Rather, this "function" is differentially disrupted by compromise in its various neural substrates that produce different patterns of language errors. Recent studies, such as those reviewed earlier in this chapter, where calculation tasks have been analyzed in greater detail, suggest that such differential patterns of error also exist in the performance of patients with calculation deficits.

Recent writings on the concept of localization of function generally support such an approach. Benton (1981) has defined cerebral localization as "the identification of the neuronal mechanisms within the brain that are responsible for the mediation of defined behavioral capacities. These mechanisms are never located in a single discrete neural aggregate but are always defined by the dynamic sets of interrelationships among neuronal aggregates. Lesional localization consists of identifying those specific junctures within a system of interrelationships that derange the system with sufficient severity to impair its mediating functions" (p. 55).

In a similar vein, Mesulam (1981) has recently articulated a more detailed perspective for the analysis of cerebral localization in higher cognitive functions that would seem appropriate to the study of calculation. Based on a review of neuroanatomical, neuropsychological, and clinicopathological studies of directed attention and unilateral neglect, Mesulam proposed a "network approach" for understanding the relationship between major cortical and subcortical regions as they interact to control this cognitive function. The application of a network analysis to the study of calculation provides an interesting reformulation of this "function" as well.

The centrist or localizationist position (Exner, 1881) would argue, as did Henschen (1920), that there is a unitary calculation center. Although this seems absurd in light of the materials reviewed here, modern variations on this theory are implicit in much of current neuropsychological research and tend to be expressed as a parceling out of a given function into separate smaller functions, each with its own center or localization. For calculation this would mean that the spatial algorithms are located in one cerebral center, column alignment in another, table values in a third, number reading in yet a fourth, and so on. All that is then required is a CT Scanner with which to identify the lesions corresponding to these centers. At the opposite extreme would be the holistic, equipotentiality argument (Lashly, 1929) that calculation may be disrupted secondary to a lesion almost anywhere in the brain. However, this is contradicted by evidence suggesting that lesions in the posterior aspect of the left hemisphere are far more likely to produce calculation deficits and deficits of greater severity than lesions at any other site.

In contrast to the centrist or equipotential views, a network approach would conceptualize calculation in terms of several component processes. These are as yet undefined and may or may not correspond to component aspects of the number/calculation system (Grewel, 1969). Although each process may have a distinct localization in a certain site, it is also interconnected with all of the other sites required to constitute the integrated network subserving calculation and may be mediated at different levels within the nervous system. Lesions at different sites might, therefore, be expected to give rise to different types of error, whereas lesions at different levels may give rise to variability in the performance of certain components of the calculation process. The network approach differs from the parcelated centrist position in that each site may also contribute the component process it is capable of performing to functions other than just calculation, and because each site relies on more fundamental mechanisms and structures, such as those underlying arousal or visualization, in order to ensure its intact functioning.

For example, portions of the left temporal lobe are involved in the sequencing and analysis of auditory input at several levels of organization for various components of language comprehension. Certain areas may process sounds into words and then, in conjunction with other sites, analyze the order of those words for meaningful sequences. However, these same neural substrates probably also help to constitute sounds into digits, contribute to the correct sequencing of these digits to form numbers, and, at yet another level, may partially determine the sequence or order in which those numbers are manipulated to correctly complete a calculation. The angular gyrus, meanwhile, appears to contribute the spatial component of the algorithms for structuring and executing calculations. Lesions here give rise to anarithmetia or true acalculia for complex written operations of the type described by Gerstmann (1942) and Hécaen et al. (1961). Interestingly, such lesions often also give rise to agraphia, suggesting that the angular gyrus may also provide the spatial programs for the transposition of language into its written form. Although neither language nor calculation is strictly localized in either the temporal lobe or the angular gyrus, components of both functions partially overlap at such sites. Similarly, the retrieval of table values, such as 4×3 or 7×8, which appear to be automatically accessed from semantic storage (Ashcraft & Battaglia, 1978), may be disrupted by lesions in component sites that partially control the retrieval of other semantic categories of information and may overlap with memory as well as with spatial or sequencing networks.

The network approach provides an attractive model for reformulating research on acalculia. Furthermore, it accounts for findings in this area that have in some instances shown overlapping constructional, language, and calculation deficits, whereas in other cases clear dissociations have been established between these functions. This does not imply, however, that the network approach is the only perspective from which to consider the problem of cerebral organization. Mesulam (1981) has addressed this issue directly:

> It is likely that different approaches to localization may have validity depending on the function under consideration. Thus, visual acuity within segments of the visual fields is organized in striate cortex according to the centrist point of view. In contrast, generalized attributes such as intelligence, creativity, or personality may well follow the equipotentiality model of organization. On the other hand, functions such as directed attention, language, and memory may be organized according to the network approach. (p. 320)

Clearly, calculation should be added to this last list.

One final implication of this approach to the analysis of acalculia is that different components of this network may be active in the acquisition of calculation skills than are responsible for their maintenance once learned. This is particularly relevant to Guttman's (1936) contention, based on his work with children, that it is the loss of the fundamental processes of quantity and magnitude estimation that forms the basis for calculation disorders. Although there can be no question that spatial abilities and schemas underlie the development and acquisition of number concepts (Wohlhill & Lowe, 1962), it is not clear that these schemas participate actively once the number system is learned and incorporated. This system, obviously, makes different task demands that may favor the relatively sequential processing strategies of the left hemisphere. This issue is illustrated by a recent report from Weintraub and Mesulam (1984) in which they describe a syndrome of developmental social incompetence that they characterize as a right hemisphere learning disability. Interestingly, a prominent feature of this syndrome is an increased incidence of dyscalculia. This stands in direct contrast to the conventional wisdom that acalculia is due to left hemisphere injury, which is supported in the adult literature and by reports describing a developmental Gerstmann syndrome (Benson & Geschwind, 1970; Kinsbourne & Warrington, 1963; Spellacy & Peter, 1978), as well as by the fact that dyscalculia frequently accompanies developmental language learning disabilities. The disability in each case, however, may be quite different. In the right hemisphere syndrome, the child may not be able to develop the spatial relations and schemas required to understand the concepts underlying the number system and calculation. In children with right hemisphere congenital injury, the ability to appreciate aggregates and manifolds may be disrupted, and number conservation, rather than emerging as an apparently intuitive outgrowth of development, may require laborious instruction. In the left hemisphere syndrome, on the other hand, the child may have highly developed spatial skills but may be incapable of efficiently sequencing the digits required for calculation or unable to store the necessary number facts in semantic memory. Many developmental dyslexics who can calculate report that their weakness lies in retrieving table values, in properly following the grammatical rules for number transcoding, or in inverting digits in large numbers. However, they usually have less trouble with the spatial programs or algorithms required to actually proceed through the various computation operations.

OPERATIONAL PRINCIPLES

Having argued that this "function" does indeed exist, and having now outlined some of its organizational principles, how should we proceed to investigate the manner in which the brain mediates calculation ability? Clearly, there is a need for greater uniformity of measurement, for a standardized instrument that is theoretically relevant, and for the collection of normative data on different performance parameters of the four basic calculation operations. However, given that the administration format of most tests determines the usefulness of the information they elicit as surely as their item content, the question of what methodology will be most fruitful must first be resolved. This is especially true in the evaluation of calculation where language, memory, constructional, or perceptual deficits may complicate the examination.

Based on her extensive clinical experience, Kaplan (1984) has articulated an approach to the investigation of neuropsychological problems that benefits from evolving in a clear theoretical framework, incorporates various assessment traditions in psychological testing, and provides specific methodological principles that can be applied to the evaluation of calculation disorders. Kaplan's approach is founded on Werner's (1937) observation that the ultimate result achieved by an individual in solving a problem does not constitute the only measure of that individual's competence relative to a given cognitive ability. In fact, Werner pointed out that the same achievement might come about in a number of different ways and that it was only by observing the process of solution, i.e., the manner in which the ultimate result was achieved, that one could arrive at an accurate characterization of various cognitive functions.

Kaplan expands upon this fundamental tenet in her assessment methodology, which encourages the complementary use of quantitative, actuarially developed measures in conjunction with careful descriptions of the process by which success or failure comes about on a task. Furthermore, the different types of failures that occur are recorded to determine if consistent error tendencies can be demonstrated to exist in the patient's performance. The descriptive aspects of this method have often been referred to as "qualitative analyses," in a manner that implies some highly personalized, clinician-dependent skill. However, process and error analyses clearly generate data that can be consensually, reliably, and repeatedly observed, described, quantified, and subjected to statistical manipulation. The power of the "process and achievement" approach becomes apparent rapidly in the clinic and has been demonstrated experimentally in recent work by Kaplan and her associates (Kaplan, Palmer, Weinstein, & Baker, 1981).

The patient-centered, process and achievement methodology is also most compatible with the network approach to mapping functional localization. Unlike actuarial, achievement-only techniques, Kaplan's method of assessment permits consideration of the component aspects of a function as they unfold in the patient's performance on a given task. Partially disrupted networks are often capable of producing approximate solutions to many tasks and frequently achieve what appear to be intact performances or behaviors. It is often only as a result of analyzing the process leading up to the achievement that the defective components of a cognitive function can be identified and hypotheses formulated regarding which portion of the underlying neural network is disturbed.

A good example of these principles is evident in the performance of a patient examined by the author who had a severe Wernicke's aphasia. He had difficulty in retrieving table values as well as in following the usual algorithm for multi-

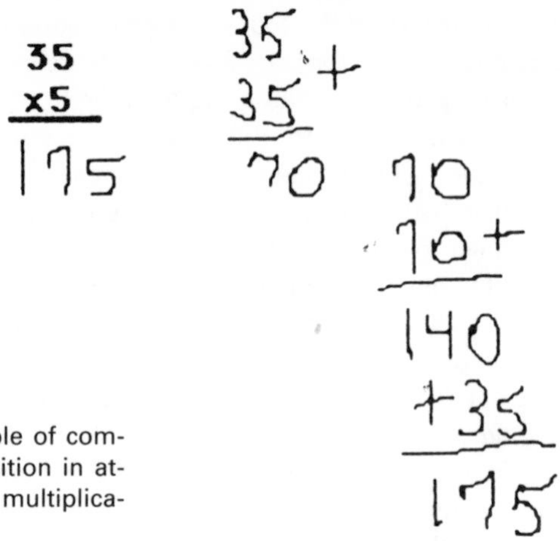

```
   35        35.+
   x5        35
  ───        ──
  175        70   70

                    70+
                    ───
                    140

                    +35
                    ───
                    175
```

FIGURE 1.1. Example of compensatory serial addition in attempting to retrieve multiplication table values.

plication but nevertheless succeeded on simple operations (Figure 1.1). When he was shown how to proceed through multiplication in the correct sequence, it was as if he were discovering the operations involved anew, and he insisted on verifying the answers the examiner obtained by performing his own multiple additions. When the patient attempted to use the normal algorithm with the examiner providing the table values, he frequently substituted addition for multiplication in the left-hand column, perhaps secondary to the imperative of adding carried digits. No difficulty was seen in number reading or writing. Although this patient fortunately articulated his process of compensation on paper, similar observations are often available when the examiner undertakes a process analysis. This patient's CT demonstrated a single lesion in the left superior temporal gyrus extending as far as the supramargynal but not to the angular gyrus laterally and to the temporal isthmus medially. He had a dense auditory comprehension deficit and a severe anomia but no agraphia, alexia, or demonstrable deficits in verbal learning when these were tested through the visual modality. The two aspects of the calculation process interrupted by this lesion were this patient's access to table values and his ability to execute efficiently the algorithms for multiplication and division, with addition and subtraction remaining intact.

Calculation is uniquely suited to study by the process-network method. The number system consists of only 10 basic units, which are combined according to a strict incremental progression. There are only four operations possible and the component steps of each operation are clearly specified. There can be no rule-exceptions to the "grammar" of these operations without the production of an incorrect or unacceptable result. Finally, there would also seem to be only a limited number of points in the calculation process where the grammatical rules can be incorrectly applied, ignored, or confounded. Consequently, it should be possible to describe specific types of errors at these different points in the process that subsequently may be found to correlate with particular lesions in the neural network subserving calculation.

ERROR ANALYSIS

Although some attempts have been made to analyze the calculation process and classify possible sources of error, these studies have generally not been concerned with the relationship of their findings to the central nervous system. For example, Brown and his associates at Clark University reported in a 1906 monograph on the "Psychology of the simple arithmetical processes: A study of certain habits of attention and association." In an ingenious paradigm, Brown gave mental and written computations $(+,-,\times,\ )$ to several of his colleagues and asked them to introspect on their cognitive process during the performance of these tasks. Brown's data were somewhat biased because all of the observations reported were formulated in terms of then prevalent theoretical models of cognition such as Ebbinghaus's laws of association. Nevertheless, Brown described several different calculation errors, including four types for addition, two for multiplication, one for subtraction, and three for division (Table 1.1).

TABLE 1.1
Types of Calculation Errors Reported by Brown (1906)

Addition	
1-Skipping tens	- producing a larger or smaller tens units than solution requires : $18 + 6 + 6 = 20/40$
2-Digit errors	- omitting a digit or adding it twice as a result of not computing in the sequence presented.
3-Forget of carry	- forgetting to continue tens digits while adding in the units column or forgetting to carry to the next column.
4-Rounding errors	- increasing or decreasing a solution by one as a result of using a rounding by tens strategy : $8 + 9 = 8 + 10 - 1 / 8 + 11 = 8 + 10 + 1$
Subtraction	
-Failure to borrow	- forgetting to reduce the tens minuend when borrowing.
Multiplication	
a-Carry	- the tens unit to be carried is forgotten when attention is turned to multiplying the next column of digits.
b-Add	- errors occur in addition as noted above as a result of focusing on the various carries that are produced by the multiplications.
Division	
1-Substitution	- Appearance in the dividend of a digit that is part of the quotient : $28 \div 4 = 4 / 8$
2-Perseveration	- Perseveration of the digit when the divisor and dividend are identical : $5 \div 5 = 5$
3-One more	- Uncertainty regarding the quotient when the quotient is one more or less than the divisor : $72 \div 8 = 8$ or 9 ?

More recently, Roberts (1968) reported four types of "failure strategies" based on his analysis of children's incorrect responses to calculation problems. Four major error tendencies emerged, which Roberts classified as wrong operation, obvious computational error, defective algorithm, or random response (Table 1.2). Engelhardt (1977) expanded on these categories by observing that there were several types of "defective algorithms" and that many of the supposedly "random responses" may have represented consistent, though incorrect, strategies. Engelhardt also adopted the heuristic position that certain failure strategies may be organized around a single conceptual component of the calculation process. In other words, a certain group of errors may result from a failure to comprehend the same fundamental rule and should therefore be considered to form a single error category. Furthermore, Engelhardt pointed out that errors may result not only from a defective conceptual component but also from confusion regarding the mechanical procedure for computation, i.e., the spatial-constructional aspects of written calculation. Engelhardt studied the calculation performance of 798 randomly selected third- and sixth-grade pupils on 84 arithmetic computation items drawn from the Stanford Diagnostic Arithmetic Test (Beatty, Madden, & Gardner, 1966). From this sample he was able to identify eight separate error types, which included basic fact, defective algorithm, incomplete algorithm, incorrect operation, inappropriate inversion, grouping, identity, and zero errors. (See Table 1.3 for definitions.) Engelhardt also examined the distribution of errors across quartiles within his sample, with rank being determined by the total number of problems correct. He found that the number of errors in a child's performance decreased with increased competence, that basic fact errors were the most common in all quartiles, and that the error type that mostly clearly determined competent performance was defective algorithm— "Apparently one of the more difficult and critical aspects of computation is executing the correct procedure" (p. 153) (i.e., executing the correct spatial-numerical combinations in the correct sequence required by the algorithm for each operation).

TABLE 1.2
Failure Strategies Described by Roberts (1968)

Wrong operation	Pupil attempts to solve a problem with an inappropriate operation.
Obvious computational error	Pupil attempts to solve a problem using an erroneous number fact.
Defective algorithm	Pupil attempts to solve a problem employing other than basic number fact errors or inappropriate operation errors.
Random responses	Pupil attempts to solve a problem in a way showing no discernible relationship to the given problem.

TABLE 1.3
Error Types described by Engelhardt (1977)

1. Basic fact error	The pupil responds with a computation involving an error in recalling basic number facts. $4 + 3 = 7 \quad 6 \times 7 = 48$
2. Defective algorithm	The pupil responds by executing a systematic but erroneous procedure. $\quad \begin{array}{r} 123 \\ \times 42 \\ \hline 186 \end{array}$
3. Grouping error	The pupil's computation is characterized by a lack of attention to the positional nature of our number system. $\begin{array}{r} 57 \\ +93 \\ \hline 1410 \end{array}$
4. Inappropriate inversion	The pupil responds with a computation involving the reversal of some critical aspects of the solution procedure. $\quad \begin{array}{r} 43 \\ -19 \\ \hline 36 \end{array}$
5. Incorrect operation	The pupil performs an operation other than the appropriate one. $2 \times 3 = 5 \quad 13 - 1 = 14$
6. Incomplete algorithm	The pupil initiates the appropriate computational procedure but aborts it or omits a critical step.
7. Identity errors	The pupil computes problems containing 0s and 1s in ways suggesting confusion of operation identities. $5 \times 1 = 1$
8. Zero errors	The pupil computes problems containing 0s in ways suggesting difficulty with the concept of zero. $3 \times 0 = 3$

Engelhardt's observations have potentially important implications for under-standing the development of calculation ability and may take on particular significance in a neuropsychological context. First, it is clear that errors or approximate solutions observed in the ontogenesis of certain higher cortical functions may parallel the deficits seen after central nervous system injury (Kaplan, 1968). Second, it has been noted that particular structures within the nervous system mature at different rates and that regions of the frontal and parietal lobe are among the last to be completely myelinated. Finally, it has already been shown that defective algorithm errors are most common in anarithmetic patients whose lesions are in the dominant parietal lobe (Benson & Weir, 1972; Hécaen et al., 1961). Even though Guttman (1936) speculated on the existence of such relationships almost half a century ago, Engelhardt's observations create the necessary link between clinicopathological studies of acalculia and the developmental literature on arithmetic achievement. Engelhardt potentially extended this link in a subsequent study when he attempted to investigate whether the types of computational errors exhibited by children might be related to cognitive style. Engelhardt (1978) classified a sample of children as either analytic or nonanalytic and as either impulsive or reflective according to their performance on the Pick Two Pictures (Wilson, Cahen, & Begle, 1968) and Matching Familiar Figures (Kagan, 1965) tests. Although he found that nonanalytic and impulsive subjects committed more errors and more types of errors, there were no clear correlations between different error types and the cognitive style groupings. However, Engelhardt did note that more complete information could have been obtained by intensive interviews of subjects as they performed computations rather than focusing solely on the endpoint when an incorrect result was obtained. Essentially, then, he suggested the need for a process analysis. Furthermore, he warned that children who consistently commit the same types of computational errors are probably not careless or lazy but rather that these tendencies reflect their cognitive style. Another obvious implication, however, is that they may reflect the stage of development and differentiation of this function at the level of the nervous system. Consequently, in attempting to account for cases where certain error tendencies persist, the possibility of a defective neural substrate should probably be the leading hypothesis.

Although the neurological and developmental speculations that emerge from Englehardt's research are of obvious interest, his error categories are much more important for the purposes of this chapter. Clearly, they represent an operationalized method for the study of calculation that is entirely compatible with the process-network approach. Furthermore, when Englehardt's categories are slightly expanded, they readily give rise to the framework for an error analysis of calculation disorders. This is presented in Table 1.4, and is based on a detailed examination of the existing literature on acalculia recently conducted by the author.

A brief examination of this table reveals that a great deal more is already known about acalculia from an error analysis perspective than might initially be suspected. Another feature that clearly emerges is that the breakdown of calculation abilities is related not only to the structure of the number system and the grammar required for the manipulation of digits, but also to the algorithms required for successful computation and calculation. Furthermore, the nervous system's attempts to compensate for deficits in these processes is readily apparent in the nature of the errors that patients produce. More detailed discussion of this error classification is obviously behond the scope of this chapter and would be premature at this time given that the validity of these error categories remains under investigation. In the meantime, it may serve as a context within which relevant parameters of the calculation process may be explored in greater detail and which can be expanded to incorporate new error categories or modified to accommodate new findings.

TABLE 1.4
Error Analysis Classification

Error type	Description
Place-holding errors	
1. Number value	Inability to distinguish the larger of two numbers due to a disturbance in the patient's appreciation of units, tens, hundreds, etc. (e.g., 465 vs. 645)
2. Number expansion	Expansion of tens, hundreds, or thousands place-holding representation in number writing without actually violating the place-holding values of the digits. (5,614 written as 5000600104)
3. Mirror reversal	Digit sequence is written, copied or repeated in reverse (564 is written 654)
4. Partial reversal	Same as (3) but only one set of digits is involved in the reversal (5614 is written 5641)
5. Transposition	Digit sequence within a number is altered violating place holding values (6325 is 6523)
Digit errors	
1. Simple substitution	The place-holding value of the various digits is maintained but an incorrect digit is present as a result of a paralexia, paraphasia or paragraphia. In this instance, the patient may or may not arrive at a correct solution as a function of whether the substituted digit is incorporated into the computation.
2. Perseverative computational	A digit is substituted from another number present in the problem and is usually incorporated into the computation yielding an incorrect solution. (25×12 performed as 25×15)
3. Perseverative solution	A digit is substituted from another number in the problem into the number given as the solution. ($17 \times 3 = 57$)
4. Omission	Failure to use a number or digit present in the problem in the process of computation leading to an incorrect solution. (This is often a leftmost digit suggesting a neglect error.)
Borrow and carry errors	
1. Neglect of carry	The patient fails to use a verbalized or clearly indicated carry in the process of computation.
2. Defective carry	All the digits of an intermediate solution are written and the higher place-holding digits are not carried, though they still may be added to the next column in computation. 237 + 175 31112
3. Incorrect placement	Though the carry is made, it then is added to the wrong column.

(continued)

TABLE 1.4 (*Continued*)

Error type	Description
4. Wrong carry	The patient carries and adds to the next column the smaller rather than the larger place-holding digit from the sum of the previous column.
5. Zero carry/borrow	Confusion of the borrowing or carrying process if there is a zero in the problem.
6. Neglect of borrow	The leftmost or higher place-holding digit is not reduced after a clearly verbalized or indicated borrow.
7. Defective borrow	1. Adding the borrowed amount to the lesser place-holding digit. 2. Borrowing from a lesser to a greater place-holding digit.
Basic fact errors	
1. Table value	Not due to a Digit Error. Retrieval of an incorrect table value. Solution would often be correct for the next higher or lower multiplicator ($7 \times 8 = 64$). Patients often compensate for this by serial addition, finger counting, or by using rounding-up strategies.
2. Zero/identity	Basic fact errors that appear only when a 0 or 1 is present in the problem being computed.
Algorithm errors	
1. Incomplete	Patient initiates the correct operation but fails to carry out all of the steps required to arrive at a solution and leaves the problem or some intermediate step incomplete.
2. Incorrect alignment	The elements of the problem are not spatially disposed on the page in a manner that will lead to correct execution of the problem.
3. Spatial	Misalignment of columns in the intermediate steps of multidigit multiplication or division leading to addition or subtraction of incorrect intermediate products.
4. Incorrect sequence	The patient proceeds from left to right or in some inconsistent manner through the problem, perhaps with correct computations, but the sequence in which they are carried out leads to incorrect carries, borrows, and intermediate products.
5. Subtraction inversion	The minuend and subtrahend are reversed in the act of computation. ($15 - 6 = 11$)
6. Inappropriate	The problem is spatially disposed on the page in the manner of another operation (typically multiplication substituted for division).
7. Substitution	The patient executes an operation other than the one asked for by the problem. For example, a multiplication is added or subtracted instead of multiplied.

(*continued*)

TABLE 1.4 (*Continued*)

Error type	Description
8. Confounded	Partial substitution of different operations within the same problem. For example, one column is added and the other multiplied but each correctly computed for the operation applied to it.
9. Defective	Anarithmetia. The patient uses incorrect, inconsistent, or idiosyncratic procedures or fails to access any correct computational strategy.
Symbol errors	
1. Loss of symbols	The patient cannot produce the four computation signs upon request or in writing down a problem that has been dictated, but this has no apparent effect on the actual execution of the correct operation.
2. Substitution	An incorrect sign is written by the patient, which then may result in the execution of a different operation from that requested, but this is usually computed correctly.
3. Rotation	A special case of substitution. This involves the perceptual similarity between the addition and multiplication signs where one is easily rotated 90° and becomes the other (+ rotated gives ×). This substitution may or may not affect the operation that is then executed.

CONCLUSION

In this chapter, the status of calculation as a "function" has been examined and a heuristic, theoretical perspective for the study of acalculia, the process-network approach, has been proposed. Several examples of recent research on the number system and calculation disorders have also been reviewed and their assets and liabilities discussed. Finally, the outline of a tentative classification for calculation and number system errors has been presented. The question that remains, however, is whether the future of research into calculation disorders will live up to its promise. Apart from language, calculation is perhaps the only culturally determined, semantic system that the majority of the population is expected to acquire and master. Consequently, calculation represents a valuable medium for the investigation of brain-behavior relationships. For example, are cognitive activities such as calculation mediated by specific neuronal populations in the component structures that constitute a given network, or are different patterns of connections between these structures elicited by different cognitive activities, with time-sharing principles governing the overlapping use of these neuronal populations? The development of new techniques in neuroradiology for high resolution imaging of relatively brief and subtle alterations in metabolic activity may soon permit us to answer such questions. However, this will only be possible if a greater uniformity of terminology and methodology can be achieved in the literature on acalculia. This, in turn, depends upon more standardized and systematic investigation of patients with calculation disorders.

Although changes of the type advocated here often come about slowly, the time has come to recognize that even a rudimentary examination of calculation requires more than a few simple mental computations. First, some exploration of the patient's facility in manipulating digits and numbers must be carried out such that an appreciation of the place-holding system is demonstrated. Second, the retrieval of basic number facts and table values should be determined to be intact. Finally, a sample of both written and oral computations should be given for each of the four basic operations. This should include problems of graded complexity so that the rules governing zero and identity computation, carrying and borrow-

TABLE 1.5
Calculation Disorders Screening Examination

Mental Computation
The following items are read aloud to the patient and the patient is encouraged to verbalize any intermediate computations.

$2 \times 3 =$	$3 \times 6 =$	$4 \times 7 =$	$6 \times 9 =$	$7 \times 8 =$
$22 + 13 =$	$16 + 27 =$	$18 / 3 =$	$28 / 4 =$	$34 - 23 =$
$38 + 54 =$	$4 \times 11 =$	$17 \times 3 =$	$8 - 5 =$	$14 - 9 =$
$150 / 25 =$	$43 \times 2 =$	$71 - 4 =$	$26 - 17 =$	$42 - 25 =$

Written Calculation
The following items are dictated to the patient, who is asked to write down and execute each one on a piece of 8 1/2 × 11″ unlined paper presented with the 11″ border on the horizontal axis. If either of the more difficult problems is failed, the patient is dictated the simpler items, which may pinpoint more clearly the source of error.

$1249 + 6574 =$	$64 + 86 =$
	$48 + 75 =$
$589 + 243 + 163 =$	$28 + 37 + 56 =$
$732 - 686 =$	$78 - 25 =$
	$52 - 35 =$
$6204 - 530 =$	$500 - 349 =$
$45 \times 39 =$	$12 \times 3 =$
	$56 \times 9 =$
214×35	$23 \times 12 =$
$1422 / 12 =$	$168 / 8 =$
	$968 / 6 =$
$38467 / 27 =$	$9684 / 12 =$

ing processes, and the algorithms for multidigit operations are all appropriately sampled.

A brief examination format that provides most of the features just described is presented in Table 1.5. These items were developed in collaboration with the late Professor Henry Hécaen, who pioneered research in this area and always maintained an abiding interest in this topic. They have been used to screen patients for calculation disorders both at his Unite in Paris and at our own Unit in Boston since 1980. On average, this examination requires less than 10 minutes to administer and is fairly sensitive in eliciting many of the errors outlined in Table 1.4. Patients identified by this screening can then be tested more comprehensively. What has been apparent thus far is that calculation disorders, characterized by a consistent error tendency in some portion of the computation process, are extremely common in patients referred for neurological consultation, even though acalculia may not be part of their presenting complaint.

In conclusion, it should be apparent that acalculia needs to regain its status in the mainstream of neuropsychological research. Clinicians and researchers must become more sensitive to the occurrence of calculation disorders, and this can only be achieved by more thorough examination of this function both at the bedside and in the laboratory. Once this has been accomplished, the methods of analysis used in modern cognitive psychology and in the rapidly evolving human neurosciences must be brought to bear on this area of investigation. In short, acalculia needs not so much to be revisited as rediscovered.

ACKNOWLEDGMENTS

The author wishes to thank Dr. Edith Kaplan, without whose teaching, inspiration, and mothering this work would not have been possible; Dr. Arthur Benton who has encouraged and promoted my interest in this area; Dr. Harold Goodglass who initially wrote to Prof. Hécaen on my behalf; and Dr. Gail Hochanadel who suffered the writing, re-writing, typing, editing, and rewriting of more manuscripts on acalculia than should ever see the light of day, who offered helpful and incisive criticism on all of them, and remained supportive and encouraging throughout. Finally, I gratefully acknowledge the Canada Council for Social Sciences Research which provided the financial support for this work.

REFERENCES

Ashcraft, M. H. & Battaglia, T. (1978). Cognitive Arithmetic: Evidence for retrieval and decision processes in mental addition. *Journal of Experimental Psychology: Human Learning and Memory, 4,5,* 527–538.

Beaty, L. S., Madden, R., & Gardner, E. F. (1966). *Stanford Diagnostic Arithmetic Test* (Level II) New York: Harcourt, Brace & World.

Benson, D. F., & Denckla, M. B. (1969). Verbal paraphasia as a source of calculation disturbance. *Archives of Neurology, 21,* 96–102.

Benson, D. F., & Geschwind, N. (1970). Developmental Gerstmann syndrome. *Neurology, 20,* 293–298.

Benson, D. F., & Weir, W. F. (1972). Acalculia: Acquired anarithmetia. *Cortex, 8,* 465–472.

Benton, A. L. (1981). Focal brain damage and the concept of localization of function. *in* C. Loeb (Ed.), *Studies in cerebrovascular disease* (pp. 47–56). Milano: Masson Italia Editori.

Berger, H. (1923). Klinische Beitraze zur Pathologie des Grosshirns. I. Mitterlung: Herderkrankungen der Prafrontalregion. *Archiv. fur Psychiatrie, 69.*

Bresson, F., DeSchonen, S., & Tzortzis, C. (1972). Etude des perturbations dans des performances logico-arithmetiques chez des sujets atteints de diverses lesions cerebrales. *Langages, 7,* 108–122.

Broca, P. (1865). Sur la faculte du langage articule. *Bulletin de la Societe Anthropologie, 6,* 337–393.

Brown, C. E. (1906). The psychology of the simple arithmetical processes: A study of certain habits of attention and association. *American Journal of Psychology, 17,* 1, 1–37.

Collignon, R., LeClerq, C., & Mahy, J. (1977). Etude de la semologie des troubles du calcul observes au cours des lesions corticales. *Acta Neurologique Belgique, 77,* 257–275.

Deloche, G., & Seron, X. (1982). From three to 3: a differential analysis of skills in transcoding quantities between patients with Broca's and Wernicke's aphasia. *Brain, 105,* 719–733.

Engelhardt, J. M. (1977). Analysis of children's computational errors: a qualitative approach. *British Journal of Educational Psychology, 47,* 149–154.

Engelhardt, J. M. (1978). Cognitive style and children's computational errors. *Perceptual and Motor Skills, 46,* 323–330.

Exner, S. (1881). *Untersuchungen uber Localisation der Functionen in der Grosshirnrinde des Menschen.* Vienna: Braumuller.

Furneaux, W. D., & Rees, R. (1976). Dimensions of Mathematical abilities. *Occasional Publications Series, 1,* (Brunel U., Dept. of Education)

Furneaux, W. D., & Rees, R. M. (1978). The structure of mathematical ability. *British Journal of Psychology, 69,* 507–512.

Gerstmann, J. (1942). Syndrome of finger agnosia, disorientation for right and left, agraphia, and acalculia. *Archives of Neurology and Psychiatry, 48,* 890–913.

Goldstein, K. (1923). Die Topik der Grosshirnrinde in Ihrer Klinischen Bedentung. *Deutsche Zeitschrift fur Nervesheilkunde, 77.*

Goldstein, K. (1948). *Language and language disturbances.* New York: Grune & Stratton.

Grafman, J., Passafiume, D., Faglioni, P., & Boller, F. (1982). Calculation disturbances in adults with focal hemispheric damage. *Cortex, 18,* 37–50.

Grewel, F. (1952). Acalculia. *Brain, 75,* 397–407.

Grewel, F. (1969). The acalculias. In P. J. Vinken & G. Bruyn (Eds.), *Handbook of clinical neurology,* Amsterdam: North Holland, vol. 3.

Groen, G. J., & Parkman, J. M. (1972). A chronometric analysis of simple addition. *Psychological Review, 79,* 329–343.

Guttman, E. (1936). Congenital arithmetic disability and acalculia. *British Journal of Medical Psychology, 16,* 16–35.

Head, H. (1926). *Aphasia and kindred disorders of speech.* Cambridge University Press: London.

Hécaen, H., Angelergues, R., & Houllier, S. (1961). Les varietes cliniques des acalculies au cours des lesions retrorolandqiues: Approche statistique du probleme. *Revue Neurologigue, 105,* 85–103.

Henschen, S. E. (1920). Klinische und Pathologische Beitrage zur Pathologie des Gehirns. Stockholm: Nordiska Bokhandeln.

Henschen, S. E. (1926). On the function of the right hemisphere of the brain in relation to the left in speech, music and calculation. *Brain, 49*, 111–123.

Hitch, G. J. (1978a). The numerical abilities of industrial trainee apprentices. *Journal of Occupational Psychology, 51*, 163–176.

Kagan, J. (1965). *Matching Familiar Figures Test*. Cambridge, Ma: Author, 1965.

Kaplan, E. (1968). *Gestural representation of implement usage: An organismic-developmental study*. Doctoral Dissertation, Clark University.

Kaplan, E. (1984). Process and achievement revisited. *In* S. Wapner & B. Kaplan (Eds) *Toward a holistic developmental psychology* Hillsdale, NJ: Lawrence Erlbaum Associates.

Kaplan, E., Palmer, E. P., Weinstein, C., & Baker, E. (1981). *Block Design: A brain-behavior based analysis*. Presented at the International Neuropsychological Society, Bergen, Norway.

Kinsbourne, M., & Warrington, E. (1963). The developmental Gerstmann syndrome. *Archives of Neurology, 8*, 490–501.

Kleist, K. (1934). *Gehrinpathologie*, Leipzig: J. Baruth, 1934. Uber akalkulie, *Archives Suisses de Neurologie et Psychiatrie, 39*, 330–334.

Lashley, K. S. (1929). Brain mechanisms and intelligence. Chicago: University of Chicago Press.

Lindquist, T. (1935). De L'acalculie *Acta Medica Scandinavica, 37*, 225–271.

Lindquist, T. (1936). De L'acalculie *Acta Medica Scandinavica, 38*, 217–277.

Luria, A. R. (1973). *The working brain: An introduction to neuropsychology*, London: Penguin-Allen Lane.

Luria, A. R., & Tsvetkova, L. S. (1967). *Les troubles de la resolution de problemes*. Paris: Gauthier-Villars.

Marie, P. (1906). Revision de la question de l'aphasie: L'aphasie de 1801 a 1866; essai de critique historique sur la genese de la doctrine de Broca. *Sem. Med., 48*, 565–571.

Mazzuchi, A., Manzoni, G. C., Mainini, P., & Parma, M. (1976). Il problema dell'acalculia: Studio di un caso. *Rivista Neurologica, 46*, 2, 102–15.

Mesulam, M.-M. (1981). A cortical network for directed attention and unilateral neglect. *Annals of Neurology, 10*, 309–325.

Roberts, G. H. (1968). The failure strategies of third grade arithmetic pupils. *Arithmetic Teacher, 15*, 442–446.

Singer, H. D., Low, A. A. (1933). Acalculia: a clinical study. *Archives of Neurology and Psychiatry, 29*, 467–498.

Spellacy, F., & Peter, B. (1978). Dyscalculia and elements of the developmental Gerstmann syndrome. *Cortex, 14*, 197–206.

Strub, R., & Geschwind, N. (1975). Gerstmann Syndrome without aphasia. *Cortex, 10*, 4, 378–387.

Warrington, E. K. (1982). The fractionation of arithmetical skills: A single case study. *Quarterly Journal of Experimental Psychology, 34A*, 31–51.

Weintraub, S., & Mesulam, M.-M. (1983). Developmental learning disabilities of the right hemisphere: Emotional, interpersonal and cognitive components. *Archives of Neurology, 40*, 463–468.

Werner, H. (1937). Process and achievement: a basic problem of education and developmental psychology. *Harvard Educational Review, 7*, 353–368.

Wernicke, C. (1874). *Der aphasische symptomenkomplex* Breslau: Cohn & Weigert.

Wilson, J. W., Cahen, L. S., & Begle, E. G. (Eds.) (1968). *NLSMA reports: No. 1, Part A, X population test batteries*. Stanford: School Mathematics Study Group of Stanford University.

Wohlwill, J., & Lowe, R. (1962). Experimental analysis of the development of conservation of number. *Child Development, 33*, 153–167.

2 Notational Constraints on Mental Operations

Esther G. Gonzalez
Paul A. Kolers
University of Toronto

Deficits in calculating ability, as in other mental abilities, have often been associated with specific cortical or other neurological functions. Dyslexia, prosopagnosia, and acalculia are among the failings that come to mind as having aroused the interest of neuropsychologists and cognitive psychologists. Neuropsychologists are often more interested in associating particular impairments with particular lesions; our approach, as cognitive psychologists, is concerned with the mental operations that may underlie particular performance. Mathematical operations, by requiring particular mental manipulations, are an especially clear way to study some aspects of such performance. In the following pages we discuss some aspects of mental arithmetic and the cognitive operations that compose it and, in doing so, are especially concerned to describe the role that particular forms of symbolization or notation play therein.

Perhaps the dominant current notion regarding cognitive skills is that they are carried out in some mental space and in some mental language, a "mentalese." Context-free or general mental operations are the hallmark of many modern investigations, particularly those that take as a model the functioning of digital computers and analogize mental operations to the sequential characteristics of computer programs. In this light the activities range from the formalist "production systems" popularized by Newell (1980) and others to the context-free computations of similarity metrics (Tversky, 1977). Mental arithmetic, although on a less sophisticated level of description, falls within the same framework. Many investigators assume that the operations of mental arithmetic are carried out in some mental space and can be described wholly in formalist terms. It is worthwhile to discuss some of the assumptions that characterize this work as a way of trying to specify what some of the operations of mind might be.

THREE MODELS OF MENTAL ARITHMETIC

People study mental arithmetic because it is a fairly simple task that almost everyone can perform, and because the operations are seemingly so transparent that their study will illuminate other characteristics of mental procedures. A survey of the literature suggests that three classes of models can be identified as offering descriptions of the underlying operations; they are called analog, counting, and network models.

Analog Models

The notion of the number line is fundamental to numerical analysis; it supposes that numbers extend from some value to some value (minus infinity to plus infinity, in theory) and that in performing the operations of mental arithmetic, especially in addition and subtraction, people actually use features of the number line. Relating his own work to that of Moyer and Landauer (1967), who also proposed that people think with numbers as analogues of spatial extents, Restle (1970) proposed that people adding two numbers together might mentally transport one section of the number line to another. For example, in one test people were obliged to say whether 5 + 7 was larger or smaller than 14, pressing one button if they thought the sum was larger and another button if they thought the comparison term was larger. In another task the same sum was compared to 25. Restle found that people responded more quickly the greater the numerical distance between the sum of two numbers and the number with which they were compared. On a wholly computational model that compared the quantities numerically, it should take no longer to compare 12 to 25 than to compare it to any other number. Restle's finding that the speed of the comparison varied with the numerical distance between the numbers suggested that something other than purely computational procedures was involved; in particular, a spatial or analogue representation of the number line. Restle went further to discuss the idea that regions or segments of that line were actually transported mentally to make the comparison, an idea also found in the work of Moyer and Landauer (1967).

Moyer and Landauer displayed two numbers side by side and required people to press a left button if the number on the left was the larger and a right button if the one on the right was larger. Their finding was that the time to respond was in direct proportion to the ratio made by dividing the larger number, L, by the difference between the larger and smaller numbers, $(L - S)$, expressed in logarithms. That is, $RT = \log (L/(L-S))$. This test was in turn an explicit extrapolation to the number domain of the inference derived by Welford (1960, 1976) from the ergonomic literature on reaction time. He reported that in general the time to make a discrimination between objects depended on their distance apart. An important point to notice is that Welford's claims were concerned with distinctions between classes of physical objects, such as lights on a panel, cards to be sorted, or lines to be judged for their length; in the extrapolations by Moyer and Landauer (1967) and by Restle (1970) the underlying dimension was also explicitly assumed to be spatial, but mental, not physical. Welford's account assumed a stable ordering among the classes in terms of fineness of discrimination, a spatial metaphor; this Restle translated into "regions" or fields of reference. For example, the number line was assumed to have regions, as in the locutions "in the region of 100" or "in the region of 500," and so on.

The spatiality underlying the metaphor of distance found another translation in work on mental imagery and the "symbolic distance effect"; in that work, speed of reaction was tested for questions regarding the relative size of objects such as horse/dog, elephant/ant (Moyer, Bradley, Sorensen, Whiting, & Mansfield, 1978) or of numbers (Henik & Tzelgov, 1982; Hinrichs, Berie, & Mosell, 1982), and the speed of responding was found to be associated with the difference in size of the things compared. Restle's (1970) claim for spatial cognition has been amplified in some of Shepard's claims (1981) that space is the fundamental basis of cognition, and provides the base for much else besides measurement and quantitative comparison. Other claims regarding the mental representation of space and spatial relations in the domain of mental imagery have been discussed, pro and con, by Kolers and Smythe (1979), Kosslyn (1980), and Shepard and Cooper (1982). The spatial metaphor may be, however, not the necessary basis of cognition, but one alternative, a strategy rather than a fundament (Kolers, 1983). Claims for spatial representation as a necessary basis underlying mental arithmetic or numerical comparison may be too narrowly selective.

Counting Models

Masses and quantities in the large may be compared in a wholistic way, but it is difficult to tell small differences apart that way, as every taxonomist knows. Rather than in spatial analogues, a model proposed by Parkman and Groen (1971) is made to assume that people add quantities in terms of discrete numerical elements. Thus, a person adding two numbers is assumed to reference the larger of the two and then to increment a mental counter the number of times specified by the numerical value of the smaller. The smaller, the minimum addend or MIN, thus supplies the action, and the proposal is called the MIN model. It was said to account reasonably well for the variations that characterized differences in time to respond to simple additions. One prediction from the MIN model is that ties, (that is, sums where the difference between the addends is zero, such as 3 + 3 or 5 + 5) should take equal amounts of time. That result was reported by Parkman and Groen (1971).

The contrast with analogue models is multiform. One difference is that between analogue and digital representation, the one model dealing in terms of spatial extents and the second in terms of discrete quantities. Another difference is in the proposal regarding ties. Ties in Restle's (1970) account were said to be operated upon by multiplication rather than addition; the sum 8 + 8, for example, was said to be resolved by multiplication as 2 × 8. The effect of ties on speed of response that Parkman and Groen reported does not hold for multiplication. Miller, Perlmutter, and Keating (1984) found in a production task that the time to perform an addition or a multiplication of equals increased with an increase in the size of the sum or product.

Differences in task requirements may actually underlie many of the results found in studies of mental arithmetic, as we mention again later. Not many arithmetically adept adults are likely to add two numbers by incrementing the larger the number of times specified by the smaller, for example, as is claimed by the MIN model. Many children are likely to do so, however. Svenson in particular claimed that that is the favored way for children. An implication of Svenson's (1975) work is that any novice adder may use a counting model even if few experienced adults do. Indeed, Warrington (1982) found that this strategy may also be used by some acalculic patients whose deficits prevent them from "accessing" arithmetic facts such as the sums of simple additions. Many experienced adders seem to have learned pair bonds, however, so that 4 + 3 or 9 + 2 are no longer computed but are output as overlearned items. In this respect, simple addition may be more like simple multiplication in respect to "table lookup" than it is to computation. (An interesting account of some aspects of children's arithmetic, from a developmental perspective, is in Gelman & Gallistel, 1978.) Task requirements may differ in other respects also. Many experiments use verification procedures and measure the time the subject requires to report whether a simple equation is true or false. Other experimenters use production methods and measure the time required for a person to supply the right-hand side of a simple arithmetic equation, and his or her accuracy in doing so. Pressing a button, or signaling in related ways, has been found in other tasks to yield different functions from those obtained with production methods (Kolers & Paradis, 1980). Thus, the influence of the relations underlying the variables or the composition of the reaction varies according to the way the person uses the information supplied by the experiment. Rather than some purified mental state, the behavior measured reflects both the means of acquisition of information and the nature of the produced reaction.

MIN models suffer from several drawbacks. The model seems to be restricted to simple addition of positive integers, leaving little if any way to account for the addition of a negative and a positive number or even of two negative numbers. (Analogue models need only move a marker or rotate the number line to achieve these ends.) Neither MIN models nor analogue models have been particularly concerned with multiplication, although Parkman (1972) made some efforts in this direction. In formal arithmetic, multiplication is of course merely successive addition but, Parkman's effort excepted, few investigators assumed that people perform mental multiplication that way. Indeed, Miller et al. (1984) assume that multiplication is due to memorized pairs, as others do, too, making multiplication something other than addition. Winkelman and Schmidt (1974) point out that people are often delayed in responding in a simple addition task when the terms verified yield the erroneous result by multiplication; for example, $3 + 4 = 12$ takes longer to reject than $3 + 4 = 9$, presumably because $3 \times 4 = 12$. Multiplication and addition related, counting models are said to be deficient in not noting the relation.

One final point concerns the complementary activities. Both analogue and counting models must assume that subtraction is the inverse or complement of addition. Whether relations obtained in experiments on addition are to be found also in measurements of subtraction seems not to have been widely examined (Shoben, Cech, & Schwanenflugel, 1983; Young & O'Shea, 1981).

Network Models

Even more removed than the preceding from the idea of implicit manipulation of spatial objects, network models assume that mind contains ordered pairs of numerical items, derived from extensive experience with their manipulation. We are all familiar with the multiplication table, and many of us learned to manipulate single digits by memorizing their products. Asked how much 7×4 is, trained people respond "directly" with the answer rather than having to compute it. The same sort of table lookup or direct report of overlearned stimulus-response relationships may well characterize simple addition also, so that adding $17 + 25$, say, is accomplished by recalling the practiced pair $15 + 25$, to whose sum 2 is added. Many practiced pairs, particularly centered around fives and tens, are likely to develop by the time of adulthood—or were likely to, before the arrival of the now ubiquitous small electronic calculator. Network models try to formalize some of these relations, and some others as well.

The fundamental idea of a network is that it is composed of nodes or stations and paths connecting them. If the nodes are assumed to be numerals expressing quantities, then connected pairs should be mutually facilitatory. Ashcraft and Stazyk (1981) found that simple sums such as $3 + 6 = 9$ were verified faster after tests of sums such as $4 + 5 = 9$ than after other sums. The argument was that the quantity 9 in this case was facilitated in retrieval or primed by its prior elicitation. In other cases the time required to achieve the sum was found to increase with an increase in the numerical size of the components. Ashcraft and Battaglia (1978) specifically challenged the counting models of Parkman and Groen, for example, by proposing that the time needed to verify an equation increased with the sum, or with the square of the sum, of the numbers added.

Implicit in the claim of network models is the assumption that some representation of numbers, or of the quantities they betoken, is laid out in a mental space and that the time for signals to travel such graphs indexes the distance apart of the components. Such a continuous or analogue representation of network stands in contrast to the idea of a random lookup table in which any pair of terms would be accessed as readily as any other pair, or be accessed with speed proportional to frequency or recency of prior lookup. The simple analogue models of Restle, among others, assumed that the mind represented quantity in some attributed mental space; network models seem to have internalized the analogue idea of such a space and proposed that operations are carried out upon this mental entity much as they would be if the objects and the space they occupied were external to a person. (Kolers and Smythe, 1984, referred to the confusion of physical events and mental events as the confusion of consensual symbol systems with personal symbol systems.) According to some authors local regions of the network may become especially practiced, and others remain unused; thus the analogue nature of the network would take on shortcuts, lumps, or other perturbations. We do not consider it unfair to point out that with the introduction of sufficient local perturbations, one can account for almost any result. However, it is not clear that much is gained by a proposal that the networks of mind have properties that they would have if the mind's objects were manipulated in physical space.

Still another claim made for network models asserts that people store numerical knowledge of the world in analogy to the way they store other sorts of knowledge. Stazyk, Ashcraft, and Hamann (1982) put the issue in such terms when they write about some earlier work by Ashcraft and Stazyk (1981): "addition facts [or multiplication facts] are stored by adults in a network structure functionally organized as a printed addition [multiplication] table. In such a table the sum [product] of any two numbers is stored at the intersection of a column and row and is assumed to be accessed by a process of spreading activation" (p. 322). They make some subtle distinctions between this view and the notion of mental arithmetic as due to table lookup, one difference being that table lookup is explicitly a matter of finding the intersection of column and row, whereas a network can be somewhat more elaborate. For example, there is little if any reason in a table lookup model to predict facilitation of the resultant by another problem. If the task is to verify $3 + 7 = 10$, say, the immediately prior occurrence of $5 + 5 = 10$ is facilitatory (Ashcraft & Stazyk, 1981). This facilitation is said to be consistent with the activation of some general or abstract notion of ten used in the two examples, whereas in a table lookup procedure access to the common result, *10,* is through different row and column headings in the two problems and is therefore not consistent with facilitation. Moreover, table lookup is unlikely to accommodate successfully relationships between different mental operations on arithmetic. If all instances were merely the retrieval of stored packets found at intersections of mental column and row, then only the procedures using the particular path to a particular column and the particular row might be facilitated by priming. Network models, in contrast, may claim a general spreading activation across procedures due to semantic relations binding the constituents; Miller et al. (1984) report finding significant positive correlations ($r = .77$) between times to perform addition and multiplication, for example.

Stazyk et al. (1982) go on to make some strong assertions regarding the nature and utility of mental arithmetic; in particular, they make the useful point that mental arithmetic as carried out among adults may be regarded as much a matter of retrieval of factual information from memory as is any other aspect of semantic knowledge. Regrettably, by their definition of factual knowledge as a well-inculcated content of mind, the procedures of mind seem to be blocked from examination. Perhaps in fact the greatest weakness of network models is that they emphasize stored knowledge so greatly that they give little if any attention to the procedures by which the knowledge is acquired, combined, and used, or how it is modified.

The strongest claim for a network model is its ability to predict a number of RT measurements, usually in terms of the nodes or steps or stages separating the material addressed. Miller et al. (1984) have shown, however, that practice and skill greatly affect the nature of the responses made, and so suggest that experience may act to modify or restructure mental networks, the shortcuts and lumps mentioned above. With this as an outcome, the strong positive claim for networks that is based on their ability to accommodate the RT data tends to evaporate, for the networks reduce to fuzzy, imprecise, or highly variable structures.

We might even conjecture that the claims for structure made by network theorists actually confuse two issues. Network theorists seek to accommodate arithmetic knowledge in terms of a collection of facts or statements to which the person has access. In this the theorists make explicit appeal to models of semantic memory and to notions such as "spreading activation" that are found in such models. In other words, arithmetic knowledge is treated as a subset of general knowledge that a person has about the world. One might wonder, therefore, whether the fact that mind itself has structure has become confused with the need to accommodate the particulars of mental structure that are evidenced by mental arithmetic. People's knowledge of the world and their ability to orient themselves successfully in it require that the appropriate knowledge be manifested at the appropriate time; this orderly nature of knowledge is what is generally referred to as structure. Hence, to claim that mental arithmetic also is structured much as is the person's semantic knowledge is merely to assert that people know the things that they know, and know them in an orderly way. The claim for networks, therefore, is often merely a restatement of the generally observable fact of epistemological orderliness, adding nothing to this fact nor explaining mental arithmetic as a unique activity.

ALTERNATIVE PROPOSALS

Investigators seem to agree that although young children count or perform related arithmetic operations in solving simple problems, practiced adults are more likely to express arithmetic knowledge as part of their general knowledge structure. If arithmetic is but another form of knowledge, its expression should be sensitive to many of the conditions that affect knowledge representation generally. Among these is the nature of the formal representation that knowledge acquires; that is, the coding scheme or notation for knowledge.

Coding schemes are representational conventions; research with special application to studies of mental arithmetic has been carried out on two schemes especially: one on language in the context of bilingual skills, and the other on forms of notational convention.

Coding by Language

A number of authors have reported on the anecdotal account given by bilingual persons that they perform their mental calculations in the language of acquisition and practice (Kolers, 1968). Many report a ready ability to translate among sentences in the two languages they know, and a far lesser ability to perform the operations of arithmetic other than in the language of acquisition. Here, of course, practice is an important issue. The individual, in becoming bilingual, has usually practiced translation of sentences particularly; he or she has had far less occasion to practice translating arithmetic operations. The notion of specialization of skill that is implied by this account can be pressed farther: It is not uncommon at international meetings to find that a person can deliver a paper in a foreign language such as English or French or German and, perhaps, even answer questions about the paper in the same language, and yet have but the meagerest ability to carry on a general conversation in that language. The implication is that language capability is composed of a number of subskills or subdomains of representation, each with its own vocabulary, syntax, and customary forms of expression. The same sort of specialization might be analogized to musical performance: the ability to play the clarinet, however skillfully, does not by itself aid in playing the piano or violin. Basic notions of tempo, rhythmic structure, and composition may be acquired with one and transferred to the other; basic notions of quantity, equality, and relation may be acquired in learning arithmetic in one language and be transferred to another. In neither case, however, do the special skills underlying the mental operations controlling the behavior transfer; each skill is learned as an individual.

A simple experiment illustrates the specificity of skill and the fact that its expression is often element dependent. In the experiment, five groups of university students, whose native language was French, German, Arabic, Korean, or Thai, were each divided in half, and each half learned to say the alphabet backwards in their own language or in English (Kolers, 1964). The number of trials required for them to say the alphabet backwards as rapidly as they could say it forwards was tallied. In acquiring this new skill of saying the alphabet backwards, the students were performing a simple mental operation of list inversion. In the second part of the study, the students were required to learn how to say the alphabet backwards in the other language than the practiced one. That is, the students who had practiced initially in their native language now learned to say the alphabet backwards in English, and the half of each group who had learned initially in English now learned to say the alphabet backwards in their native language. If the skill of inverting a list were a general mental capability, the degree of transfer of learning from practice on one language to test on the other should be everywhere the same. In fact, the extent of transfer was related to the degree of similarity between the English alphabet and the native alphabet. The transfer was very high between English and French or German, all of whose alphabets are very similar; transfer was moderate between English and Arabic, the latter of which has initial letters of *alif, be, se,* and a middle section of *kef, lam, mim, nun;* and transfer was effectively zero between English and Korean or Thai, whose alphabets have no symbols or names of symbols in common. Mental arithmetic too requires manipulation of symbols; the experiment with alphabets suggests that skill at the manipulation will be intimately tied to the means learned for instantiating the symbols.

An observation by Hatano and Osawa (1983) reinforces this claim. They measured digit span in master users (''Grand Experts'') of the abacus and their ability to recite lists of unrelated digits backwards and forwards. The finding was of superior skills in these activities. When the experts were tested with names of fruits or with haphazard lists of alphabetic characters, their performance was not different from that of other people, however. The skills were specific to the medium of operation rather than general to mind. An instance perhaps more complex than this is the finding by Chase and Simon (1973) of the extended memory chess masters have for board positions meaningful in chess, in the absence of enhanced memory for haphazard distributions of chessmen about the board.

Languages do not even represent quantities in the same way. In English and Italian the quantity *31* is expressed as *thirty-one;* in Spanish and French, the quantity is *thirty and one;* in German it is reversed to *one and thirty.* More complicated, Parisian French for *92* is *four (times) twenty (plus) twelve,* but in Walloon it is *ninety-two.* We may wonder at this simple level whether quantities come to take on fixed labels that are fundamentally equivalent for speakers of the various languages, or whether the difference in the original forms of acquisition continue to affect later usage. By this we mean to ask whether, for example, a native speaker of French who learned *92* as *quatre-vingt-douze* regards the words merely as a label that indexes a quantity, or whether the quantity was learned as the result of operations that create a product plus a sum, with consequences that continue to be expressed in mental operations associated with the quantity.

Most of our evidence about issues of bilingual skills and notational schemes derives from anecdote or historical fact. The issues concerning bilingualism are quite complex. An old tradition, recognizing that bilingual persons were not equally adept in their two languages, devised the notion of bilingual balance, and assumed therewith that on balance a person was better at one language than at the other. On the basis of the remarks above, to be perfectly balanced, a bilingual person would have to represent in his or her second language all of the linguistic skills practiced in the first language. On this criterion no one ever attains balance. Rather, people develop special skills, some of which may be greater in one language and others greater in the other. Hence, we may ask whether a person feels more skilled to perform a task in one language or another, and then test relative competence. Taking this tack, Marsh and Makki (1976) required bilingual subjects to speak the response that resolved equations such as $7 + 3 = ?$ Their findings were that people were generally faster to respond in their preferred language than in their second language. If this experiment was intended to question the notion that arithmetic operations are carried out in some mental code or language-free mentalese, the findings tend to refute the idea. Additional evidence for the strategic or contingent nature of many responses is found in a study by McClain and Huang (1982), who presented the addends for a mental arithmetic task auditorily in three different conditions. The conditions were organized by language of presentation and of response, so that in one condition the addends were presented only in the preferred language, in a second condition they were presented in the nonpreferred language, and in the third condition the presentations were alternated haphazardly among the two languages. Responses were always to be given in the language in which the addends were presented. Much as Marsh and Makki had found, McClain and Shih Huang also found that the speed of responding was faster in the preferred language when both languages were used in one session. If the mental work were done in some metalinguistic mentalese, input and output languages should have had no effect on performance.

Numbering systems

Notions of abstraction and of codability are fundamental to many of the arguments regarding mental arithmetic, but are not restricted to it. Science generally emphasizes the common across multiple instances, but it has sometimes happened that in the rush to abstract cognitive phenomena, psychologists have not given enough attention to the instances across which abstractions are to be taken. In some treatments the assertion is made explicitly that the world comes in codable form and that mind simply responds to the presentation. The issue has been discussed in some detail by Kolers and Smythe (1984); their conclusion is that mental operations cannot be divorced from the symbols on which the operations are carried out. An experiment on mental arithmetic illustrates the claim (Gonzalez & Kolers, 1982).

For the purpose, people verified simple equations while their speed and accuracy in doing so were measured. Equations were of the form $p + q = n$, $n \leq 10$, and the variable of interest was the notational system in which p and q were written. Using arabic and roman notational systems, we can write $3 + 2 = 5$, III + II = V, III + 2 = V, and five other variations. The three illustrated can be symbolized as AAA, RRR, and RAR, respectively. On the hypothesis of a formal mental representation, a person would abstract the quantity from the symbols and perform the mental manipulation in some form of "mentalese" or abstract arithmetic. On the hypothesis that the mental operations reflect the means of representation, time to verify the equations would vary with their form.

Of course people now are more familiar with arabic notation than with roman and it could be objected that that could make a difference. To forestall criticism directed to that issue, we point out that in a control study people were trained with roman symbols between I and X (one and ten) until they were able to name them at a speed within 10% of that at which they could name arabic numerals; hence nothing of what follows depends upon differential familiarity with roman and arabic numerals.

The data for latency of response are shown as a function of MIN in Fig. 2.1, separately for positive and negative equations. Considering the positive equations first, it can be seen that responses were fastest and the slope of the lines is nearly flat for equations all three of whose terms were in arabic, or whose addends were in arabic and sum in roman. Subjects took the longest time to respond to equations all three of whose terms were in roman or whose addends were in roman and sum in arabic. In between these extremes, it can be seen that the position of the arabic terms as well as their number influenced performance. Consider all the equations with two arabic terms. They rank in RT as AAR,

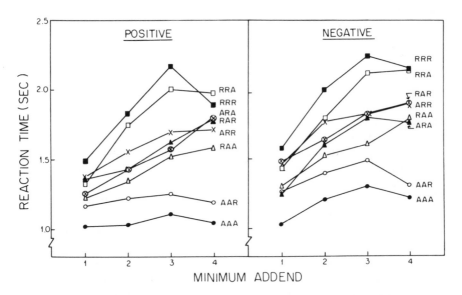

FIGURE 2.1.   Speed of reaction to verify simple arithmetic equations as a function of the size of the smaller term (Minimum Addend). The different curves are for equations whose terms were in either roman (R) or arabic (A) notation. (From Gonzalez & Kolers, 1982)

RAA, ARA, time increasing through the series; and among the series with two roman terms, the order is RAR, ARR, RRA, the complement. Allowing that the students were more familiar not only with arabic numerals as items, but with their combination in arithmetic operations, it can be inferred that mental arithmetic in these problems exercises familiar identities. The subjects know the value of 3 + 4 in arabic units, but do not know the value of three plus four in mentalese. To put it another way, the mental operations are tied to the symbols in which the quantities are expressed.

This claim has many realizations. Mayer (1982) varied the linguistic form of some simple arithmetic problems and required people to solve them when they were in algebraic notation or in natural language; the finding was that the success of solution varied greatly with the form of presentation of the problem. In the same vein Clement, Lochhead, and Monk (1981) and Clement (1982) required people to set out in algebraic relation such statements as "There were six times as many students as professors." The common error that people made was to write $6S = P$, multiplying students by the quantity, rather than the analytically correct $6P = S$. The natural language conjunction of quantity and unit quantified seemed to block proper apprehension of the mathematical relation. As Clement et al. (1981) pointed out, the grammar or rules of specification are different in natural language and in formal systems; a successful practitioner has to learn the rules of translation in going from one system to the other. Differences among formal representational systems are readily noted (Flegg, 1983; Friberg, 1984; Menninger, 1969).

Other Notations

Imaginative use of quantitative and spatial relations also affects performance. Hayes (1973) found that people reported using the spatial characteristics of numerical notation, often manipulating them in carrying out mental arithmetic. Shepard, Kilpatrick, and Cunningham (1975) applied multidimensional scaling to responses and found for a variety of notational systems that people's sense of number was tied closely to the representational conventions underlying a notation. Nickerson (1982) examined the logical structure of several numbering systems, including arabic, Mayan, cuneiform, Egyptian, and roman, comparing them for ease of use and representational efficiency, along with their formal properties of base, extensibility, compactness, and display characteristics. The examination is suggestive in respect to possible experimental manipulations, although Nickerson did not carry out any experiments. The thrust of the paper, as that also of Bertin (1980), is that quantities cannot be successfully abstracted from their representational system; people seem to use a notation as an expression of mental activity rather than as a mere means of delivering abstractable relations to mind.

Robertson (1979) points out that in initial learning children develop skills at tallying, doing implicitly the sort of arithmetic that is formalized in early roman notation (Menninger, 1969). When they go to school, the children are then required to learn base 10 notation, and to make a translation from a tally system to one that contains zero, in which place is important, where carries operate across columns, and where a decimal point is an important marker. In effect the children have to learn to quantify in a different way when they go from the one to the other system and are not always successful in making the transition. Robertson even maintains that the "new math" may actually hinder the development of arithmetic skills in that the algebraic notation used for instructions in simple arithmetic may obscure the operations of carrying and borrowing, for example.

As a final illustration of the dependence of mental operation upon symbolic form we mention the way that magnitude of quantity may exert an influence on performance. It is a classic finding of psychology that estimation of small quantities of objects is carried out expeditiously and with high accuracy, called *subitizing* (Kaufman, Lord, Reese, & Volkmann, 1949; Mandler & Shebo, 1982), but that as quantities exceed some threshold value people rely increasingly on counting, and often do rather poorly at estimating quantity. Hofstadter (1982) points out how poor we are at estimating very large quantities such as the number of people in a large crowd, the number of logs in a logjam, the number of letters in a magazine, the number of hamburgers eaten in a year in the United States. He argues that it is a deficiency of the modern mind that it cannot estimate such quantities accurately; but, however jocular this assertion, it is true that great magnitudes cause difficulties in comprehension. One need only think of the notion of infinities of different magnitude that Cantor proposed, to realize that size makes a difference to understanding.

Gonzalez and Kolers (1982) remark, "The importance of notation in facilitating or hindering thought has been commented upon by historians of mathematics, thermodynamics, and many other disciplines (Boyer, 1968; Dantzig, 1940; Rukeyser, 1942). It seems to be the case across a wide range of examples that cognitive operations are not independent of the symbols that instigate them and that 'information' is not wholly separable from its embodiment in a symbol system" (p. 319). The assertion can be extended to artforms also (Cage, 1969). The implication of these observations is that mental operations do not exist in some abstracted space and are not carried out in some abstracted metalinguistic medium, but depend for their successful use upon the specific learning that acquired them and that expresses them. There are likely to be strong implications from such results for neuropsychological investigations of mental operations.

CONCLUSION

No one needs a formal notation to keep apart the things that perception gives to mind; notations become important when the visible is transcended or its bounds exceeded. Counting based on "one, two, three, . . . many" suffices for all instances known. It may therefore be thought that our minds work differently when we count things of the visible world and when we construe entities in a mental space. Certainly the history of mathematics suggests that the modern concern with formalisms represents some fundamental change in the approach to calculation. Actually, the transition from concern with perceptible phenomena to a concern with the formal may distinguish modern science generally: It is only in the past 100 years or so that physicists and chemists have given up concern that their theories "retain the appearances" and have come to discuss their disciplines in formal terms alone.

The child's complaint, and the college student's, that mathematics is too difficult must not derive from difficulty in manipulating the perceptible objects of the environment. A high school student playing a fast game of tennis, or catching a hard-hit grounder in baseball, or going through the extraordinary contortions of a basketball game may be doing more computation in a biological framework than most other people do in mathematics in a lifetime; the same student may have difficulty with any formal system. There is something about notations and formal systems that seems to be unnatural, some aspects of mental manipulation that come with difficulty even to intellectually sophisticated people. Relating to objects of the world and relating to human constructions about worlds seem to be very different sorts of relating. One may wonder about the role that manipulative experience plays in the two cases to make reasoning about abstractions difficult.

We raise these points in a general way to identify some themes that interest us: the role of notation in cognition, the difference between mental operation carried out on perceptible objects and mental operations carried out on abstractions in a formal system, and the dependence of mental operations upon empirical experience. These themes are of general interest to cognitive psychology, and may be of specific interest in the study of operational deficits following on neurological traumas.

ACKNOWLEDGMENT

Preparation of this paper was supported by Grant A7655 from Natural Science and Engineering Research Council Canada to the second author. We also thank Chandra Ramphal for her help to its preparation.

REFERENCES

Ashcraft, M. H., & Battaglia, J. (1978). Cognitive arithmetic: Evidence for retrieval and decision processes in mental addition. *Journal of Experimental Psychology: Human Learning and Memory, 4,* 527–538.

Ashcraft, M. H., & Stazyk, E. H. (1981). Mental addition: A test of three verification models. *Memory & Cognition, 9,* 185–196.

Bertin, J. (1980). The basic test of the graph: A matrix theory of graph construction and cartography. In P. A. Kolers, M. E. Wrolstad, & H. Bouma (Eds.), *Processing of visible language 2.* New York: Plenum.

Boyer, C. B. (1968). *A history of mathematics.* New York: Wiley.

Cage, J. (1969). *Notations.* New York: Something Else Press.

Chase, W. G., & Simon, H. A. (1973). Perception in chess. *Cognitive Psychology, 4,* 55–81.

Clement, J. (1982). Algebra word problem solutions: Thought processes underlying a common misconception. *Journal for Research in Mathematics Education, 13,* 16–30.

Clement, J., Lochhead, J., & Monk, G. S. (1981). Translation difficulties in learning mathematics. *American Mathematical Monthly, 88* (4), 286–290.

Dantzig, T. (1940). *Number, the language of science.* London: Allen & Unwin.

Flegg, G. (1983). *Numbers, their history and meaning.* London: Deutsch.

Friberg, J. (1984). Numbers and measures in the earliest written records. *Scientific American, 250* (2), 110–118.

Gelman, R., & Gallistel, C. R. (1978). *The child's understanding of number.* Cambridge, MA: Harvard University Press.

Gonzalez, E. G., & Kolers, P. A. (1982). Mental manipulation of arithmetic symbols. *Journal of Experimental Psychology: Learning, Memory, and Cognition, 8,* 308–319.

Hatano, G., & Osawa, K. (1983). Digit memory of grand experts in abacus-derived mental calculation. *Cognition, 15,* 95–110.

Hayes, J. R. (1973). On the function of visual imagery in elementary mathematics. In W. Chase (Ed.), *Visual information processing* (pp. 177–214). New York: Academic Press.

Henik, A., & Tzelgov, J. (1982). Is three greater than five: The relation between physical and semantic size in comparison tasks. *Memory & Cognition, 10,* 389–395.

Hinrichs, J. V., Berie, J. L., & Mosell, M. K. (1982). Place information in multidigit number comparison. *Memory & Cognition, 10,* 487–495.

Hofstadter, D. R. (1982). Number numbness, or why innumeracy may be just as dangerous as illiteracy. *Scientific American, 1982, 246* (5), 20–34.

Kaufman, E. L., Lord, M. W., Reese, T. W., & Volkmann, J. (1949). The discrimination of visual number. *American Journal of Psychology, 62,* 498–525.

Kolers, P. A. (1964). Specificity of a cognitive operation. *Journal of Verbal Learning and Verbal Behavior, 3,* 244–248.

Kolers, P. A. (1968). Bilingualism and information processing. *Scientific American, 218* (3), 78–86.

Kolers, P. A. (1983). Perception and representation. *Annual Review of Psychology, 34,* 129–166.

Kolers, P. A., & Paradis, M. (1980). Psychological and linguistic studies of bilingualism. *Canadian Journal of Psychology, 34,* 287–303.

Kolers, P. A., & Smythe, W. E. (1979). Images, symbols, and skills. *Canadian Journal of Psychology, 33,* 158–184.

Kolers, P. A., & Smythe, W. E. (1984). Symbol manipulation: Alternatives to the computational view of mind. *Journal of Verbal Learning and Verbal Behavior, 23,* 289–314.

Kosslyn, S. M. (1980). *Image and mind.* Cambridge, MA: Harvard University Press.

Mandler, G., & Shebo, B. J. (1982). Subitizing: An analysis of its component processes. *Journal of Experimental Psychology: General, 111,* 1–22.

Marsh, L. G., & Makki, R. H. (1976). Efficiency of arithmetic operations in bilinguals as a function of language. *Memory & Cognition, 4,* 459–464.

Mayer, R. E. (1982). Different problem-solving strategies for algebra word and equation problems. *Journal of Experimental Psychology: Learning, Memory, and Cognition, 8,* 448–462.

McClain, L., & Huang, J. Y. S. (1982). Speed of simple arithmetic in bilinguals. *Memory & Cognition, 10,* 591–596.

Menninger, K. (1969). *Number words and number symbols: A cultural history of numbers* (P. Broneer, Trans.). Cambridge, MA: MIT Press.

Miller, K., Perlmutter, M., & Keating, D. (1984). Cognitive arithmetic: Comparison of operations. *Journal of Experimental Psychology: Learning, Memory, and Cognition, 10*, 46–60.

Moyer, R. S., Bradley, D. R., Sorensen, M. H., Whiting, J. C., & Mansfield, D. P. (1978). Psychophysical functions for perceived and remembered size. *Science, 200*, 330–332.

Moyer, R. S., & Landauer, T. (1967). The time required for judgments of inequality. *Nature, 215*, 1519–1520.

Newell, A. (1980). Physical symbol systems. *Cognitive Science, 4*, 135–183.

Nickerson, R. S. (1982). *Counting, computing and the representation of numbers*. Report No. 5172. Cambridge, MA: Bolt, Beranek and Newman.

Parkman, J. M. (1972). Temporal aspects of simple multiplication and comparison. *Journal of Experimental Psychology, 95*, 437–444.

Parkman, J. M., & Groen, G. J. (1971). Temporal aspects of simple addition and comparison. *Journal of Experimental Psychology, 89*, 335–342.

Restle, F. (1970). Speed of adding and comparing numbers. *Journal of Experimental Psychology, 83*, 274–278.

Robertson, J. I. (1979). How to do arithmetic. *American Mathematical Monthly, 86*, 431–439.

Rukeyser, M. (1942). *Willard Gibbs*. New York: Doubleday, Doran.

Shepard, R. N. (1981). Psychophysical complementarity. In M. Kubovy & J. R. Pomerantz (Eds.), *Perceptual organization*. Hillsdale, NJ: Lawrence Erlbaum Associates, 1981.

Shepard, R. N., & Cooper, L. A. (1982). *Mental images and their transformations*. Cambridge, MA: MIT Press.

Shepard, R. N., Kilpatrick, D. W., & Cunningham, J. P. (1975). The internal representation of numbers. *Cognitive Psychology, 7*, 82–138.

Shoben, E. J., Cech, C. G. & Schwanenflugel, P. J. (1983). The role of subtractions and comparisons in comparative judgments involving numerical reference points. *Journal of Experimental Psychology: Human Perception and Performance, 9*, 226–241.

Stazyk, E. H., Ashcraft, M. H. & Hamann, M. S. (1982). A network approach to mental multiplication. *Journal of Experimental Psychology: Learning, Memory, and Cognition, 8*, 320–335.

Svenson, O. (1975). Analysis of time required by children for simple additions. *Acta Psychologica, 39*, 289–302.

Tversky, A. (1977). Features of similarity. *Psychological Review, 84*, 327–352.

Warrington, E. K. (1982). The fractionation of arithmetical skills: A single case study. *Quarterly Journal of Experimental Psychology, 34A*, 31–51.

Welford, A. T. (1960). The measurement of sensory-motor performance: Survey and reappraisal of twelve years' progress. *Ergonomics, 3*, 189–230.

Welford, A. T. (1976). *Skilled performance: Perceptual and motor skills*. Glenview, IL: Scott, Foresman.

Winkelman, J. H., & Schmidt, J. Associative confusions in mental arithmetic. *Journal of Experimental Psychology, 102*, 734–736.

Young, R. M., & O'Shea, T. (1981). Errors in children's subtraction. *Cognitive Science, 5*, 153–177.

Differential Processing of Phonographic and Logographic Single-Digit Numbers by the Two Hemispheres

3

Daniel Holender
Ronald Peereman
Université Libre de Bruxelles

In planning the inclusion of the topic of this chapter in a book devoted to acquired mathematical disabilities. the editors must have assumed not only that the theoretical problem is interesting but also that the literature contains enough relevant data to discuss the issues. A full assessment of the differential roles played by each hemisphere in dealing with different surface forms of numbers would require the availability of results from a variety of tasks comparing different kinds of number representation. Ideally, each task should also have been investigated in the conditions resulting from the combination of different number surface forms with left and right hemifield presentations, or with left and right brain injuries. However, such is certainly not the case, and many conclusions will have to be drawn from experiments in which the requisite conditions are only partially met. The existing data further impose two restrictions on the scope of the review: Only single-digit numbers (hereafter referred to as ''numbers,'' unless otherwise specified) are considered and only nonmathematical tasks are dealt with.

Before speculating on cognitive processes and mental representations of numbers, we should have a good description and classification of what is represented in the stimulus. In spite of the restriction of this chapter to the differential processing of single-digit numbers according to their surface form, some space is also devoted to specifying the notational principles that underlie multidigit number writing. The fact that the resulting classification of symbols that will emerge is different for single-digit and multidigit numbers may highlight what we expect to find, and what has already been found, when these symbols are considered from the vantage point of the cognitive neuropsychology of number processing. The first of the five sections comprising the chapter is therefore devoted to an analysis of different types of number representations. This is followed by three sections reviewing and discussing the data from (a) numerical size comparison tasks, (b) lateral hemifield presentations, and (c) the performances of brain-damaged patients. The fifth section summarizes the main conclusions.

NUMBER REPRESENTATIONS

The arabic numeral 5, the roman numeral V, the English written word *five*, and the corresponding Chinese character are different arbitrary symbols that denote the same abstract concept: the number five. In addition to having different surface forms, these various symbols also belong to different notational systems when they are used as components of multidigit numbers. Two distinctions have to be made. One concerns the difference between numerals and number names and the other, the difference between logographic and phonographic number representations. The first distinction is better captured by characterizing multidigit number notational systems and the second is better illustrated by specifying the surface form of single-digit symbols.

Notational Systems

The first important distinction to bear in mind concerns the difference between numerals and number names. Numerals are special symbols for representing numbers visually. In many written languages they coexist with number names, which are translations of the spoken form, according to the writing system of the language. The only numerals extensively used now are arabic numerals. The universality of arabic numerals contrasts with the language specificity of number names, but the main reason for distinguishing between numerals and number names lies elsewhere: Only number names allow for a term-by-term translation of the spoken multidigit numbers. In other words, we may write and say "two hundred and thirty three," but we do not usually say "two-three-three" or "hundred-hundred-ten-ten-ten-one-one-one" when we are confronted with 233 and CCXXXIII. Hence, the rules governing the way in which numbers are transcribed differ according to notational systems.

These rules are better illustrated by Chinese number writing instead of by English or some other alphabetically written language, and by hieroglyphic Egyptian instead of roman numerals. This allows us to capture the essence of the underlying notational principle without having to deal with irrelevant and confusing features, such as the use of special words to denote the multiple of 10 in English number naming or the incorporation of a subtractive principle in the roman numeral system (e.g., IV instead of IIII). For the few following examples, let us represent the ranks of the units, tens, and hundreds by U, T, and H, respectively.

In the form of hieroglyphic Egyptian used for lapidary inscriptions, one symbol denoted the unit and a different symbol denoted each of the successive powers of 10 up to 10,000. The number 543 was written in the form, HHHHHT-TTTUUU. The only important aspect of this representation is that it is based on an additive principle. The conventional grouping of the units of the same rank and the usual order of writing were irrelevant to the understanding of the number. On a stone monument of ancient Egypt, the number would have been written right to left (instead of left to right as here) and the symbols would probably have been displayed on more than one line, but our sequence would have been unequivocally understood, even if it had been written TTHHUHTTHUHU. The same commutative principle applies to roman numerals, except that elements entering into a subtractive relation must be kept together in their conventional order.

The Chinese number-naming system is also based on an underlying additive principle, but a supplementary multiplicative principle allows for suppression of the cumbersome repetitions of the symbols belonging to the same rank. This entails a different symbol for each unit ($u1$, $u2$, . . ., $u9$). The Chinese 543 is therefore written in the form, $u5Hu4Tu3$, using five different symbols instead of the three needed in hieroglyphic Egyptian. Here too, provided the symbols entering into a multiplicative relation are kept together, permuting the terms would not transform one number into another. In this case, however, the psychological impact of doing so would be stronger, because although the order of the elements plays no intrinsic role in the representation, their usual order corresponds to their order of utterance in the spoken number. Similarly, it may be unusual to write "twenty eight and four hundred" but it clearly means 428. The Chinese number-writing principle has been called a "named place-value" notation by Menninger (1969), as opposed to the "abstract place-value" notation realized with arabic numerals. English number-name writing is also a named place value and it should be clear from what we have said that it is a pseudopositional system.

The only true positional number-writing system still in use was developed some time in the first half of the 6th century A.D. in India, whence it spread more or less rapidly to the whole world. The system uses only 10 symbols, named arabic numerals after their first principal propagators rather than after their creators. In this system the rank of the units is abstractly symbolized by the position occupied by these units in the written number. Permutations of terms are no longer allowed without changing the value of the number and the whole system works only because of the great intellectual accomplishment of symbolizing nothing by something; namely, by using zero to fill in the positions of the unemployed ranks (compare the English three thousand and twenty, in which nothing stands for the unused ranks of the hundreds and the units, with 3,020).

Aside from the Greeks' ephemeral use of a complete abstract place-value system including a zero, the only known independent invention of such a notation took place in Mesoamerica. The extent to which the Mayas really grasped the concept of zero is likely to remain controversial forever, but they undoubtedly used a symbol functionally equivalent to zero in their place-value notation of numbers (e.g., Kelley, 1976).

In Europe, widespread use of the arabic numeral place-value notation began toward the end of the 15th century, rapidly supplanting the roman numerals from then on. The most important consequence of this event is that calculation, mainly realized by means of counting boards and quite independent of number writing before this date, now became intimately bound to the arabic numeral notational system.

Much of what precedes can be found in the extensive and insightful coverage of the topic by Menninger (1969; see Flegg, 1983, for a condensed account). From an information-processing point of view, this rapid survey of the number notational systems still in use reveals three important points.

1. The arabic numerals stand alone in being the only symbols that enter into an abstract place-value notation, an inherently positional system, and in being used for purpose of calculation, a highly specialized cognitive activity of symbol manipulation.

2. Number names, whether written in an alphabetic script, such as English, or in a logographic script (see below) such as Chinese, constitute a different notational system whose purpose is mainly to provide a visual term-by-term translation of spoken numbers.

3. Unlike arabic numerals and number names, roman numerals are more concrete representations of numbers, combining some properties of tally counts with simple additive and subtractive rules. They are quite easily decoded, but they are no longer widely used, and they have never been considered an efficient medium for calculation.

Symbol Surface Forms

Number names are represented according to the writing systems in use for general writing purposes. We therefore distinguish between logographic and phonographic systems. In a logographic system the written symbols represent linguistic units of meaning; namely, morphemes. In phonographic systems the linguistic units represented by each symbol are phonological, being either syllables in syllabic systems of phonemes in alphabetic systems (see Gelb, 1963, for a history and description of the writing systems. For discussions of the psycholinguistic aspects of the written symbols and their consequences for the analysis of mental processes involved in reading, see Gleitman & Rozin, 1977; Henderson, 1984; Holender, 1987; Liberman, Liberman, Mattingly, & Shankweiler, 1980; Mattingly, 1984; Rozin & Gleitman, 1977).

In Chinese writing, the most complete logographic system ever designed and still in use today, each symbol represents one morpheme. Each morpheme is also a word, although many words are composed of more than one morpheme, and are therefore written with more than one character. Chinese characters are often called ideograms, but this terminology is misleading because few characters are actually designed on a truly ideographic principle. We call the characters *logograms* to fit the linguistic description of the unit they represent.

As already mentioned, nine symbols represent the numbers one to nine in Chinese. The first three consist of one, two, and three horizontal strokes and the others are arbitrary symbols. Thus the first three symbols are built on an ideographic, or even a pictographic, principle, representing the beginning of a stick count. Knowing that they stand for numbers, someone who cannot read Chinese at all would be able to interpret them correctly; but this is not the case with the symbols for the numbers four to nine. It is nonetheless clear that the two horizontal strokes stand for the monomorphemic word meaning *two* in Chinese and that the arbitrary symbol representing the number "six" stands for the monomorphemic word meaning *six* in Chinese. Hence, the exact nature of any of these symbols is certainly better captured by the term logogram than by any other term.

In Japan, many Chinese characters, called kanji characters, have been borrowed to be used conjointly with a syllabary. The simple syllabic structure of Japanese allows any word of the language to be written by using only the symbols of the syllabary. These symbols are called kana and they exist in two forms: hiragana and katakana. In a normal text the content morphemes (mainly nouns, verbs, and adjectives) are usually written in kanji and the grammatical morphemes are written in hiragana; foreign loan words are written exclusively in katakana.

Japanese number names are represented in kanji, the characters being exactly those used in China. Like any other words they can also be written in hiragana and katakana, but this seldom, if ever, occurs in daily life. This point should be kept in mind in interpreting the results of experiments that have exploited this possibility.

The most important point of this entire discussion is that although the 10 arabic numerals can be considered as logographic representations of the numbers zero to nine, the nine Chinese (or Japanese) logograms (zero not being represented) are not numerals, but number names. This fact has not always been correctly evaluated, either in the recent psychological literature, or by Menninger (1969) who was struck by the fact that the Chinese number symbols realize a perfect synthesis, being both numerals and number names. That this position is incorrect can be appreciated from the fact that throughout history, Chinese number names have coexisted with genuine autochthonous numerals (incorporating the Indian zero, but not the other symbols, in the 13th century). These have now been replaced by arabic numerals. Hence, the relation between Chinese characters (or Japanese kanji), denoting single-digit numbers, and arabic numerals is exactly the same as that between the corresponding English alphabetically written words and these very same arabic numerals.

This is, of course, the conclusion we reached in our discussion about number notational systems. It is clear that symbols do not lose their identity as number names or as numerals when they denote single-digit numbers. Nevertheless, in dealing with single-digit rather than multidigit numbers, processing operations should be more dependent on the surface form of the symbols than on the notational system to which these symbols belong. Therefore, in investigating the processing of single-digit numbers considered as lexical units, it is a priori more natural to regroup the symbols with respect to their surface forms irrespective of the notational system. Accordingly, in what follows, arabic numerals and Chinese or Japanese kanji number names are subsumed under the logographic category[1], and the generic term *phonographic* is applied to number names written alphabetically or in hiragana (hereafter simply referred to as kana because the katakana form has not yet been used).

Roman numerals are part of a different notational system, but their surface form can be considered as logographic.

NUMERICAL SIZE COMPARISON JUDGMENTS

A common experimental task calls on subjects to judge which of two simultaneously presented arabic numerals is the larger (less often. the smaller) numerically, with response latency as the dependent variable. Such experiments have provided a rich pattern of results revealing at least four different effects: symbolic distance, serial position, semantic congruity, and size congruity. This abundance of effects (not confined to the comparison of number numerical sizes,

---

[1]What is at issue is the distinction between semasiographic and glottographic visual messages. A glottographic message is a translation of an actual or a potential spoken utterance, each word (or morpheme) being represented in its correct position. All present-day writing systems are glottographic. A semasiographic message conveys meaning directly without being related to a unique spoken utterance. The positional system of number notation based on arabic numerals is clearly semasiographic, not glottographic. The theoretical position taken in the present chapter is that arabic numerals used in isolation may nevertheless be considered glottographic because they are in a one-to-one correspondance with words of the spoken language. As such the 10 symbols are logographic representations because nothing in their design refers to phonological segments of the words they stand for. This position departs from that of Edgerton (1941) who denied the glottographic nature of single digits on the ground that they may not always be pronounced (e.g., 2 in 2nd) or word order may sometimes be reversed (e.g., $5). Further discussion about these questions may be found in Holender (1987).

but apparent also in many other comparative judgment tasks) has recently been the subject of much theorizing (see Banks, 1977; Moyer & Dumais, 1978, for reviews). For our purposes, the main point of interest is the possibility of observing different configurations of results as a function of the surface form of the numbers. In what follows, each effect is briefly characterized and studies contrasting different types of number representations are reviewed and discussed.

Symbolic Distance Effect

The latency of the comparative judgment is an inverse function of the subtractive difference between the two numbers; for example, subjects are faster in judging that 7 is the larger in a pair like 2–7 than in a pair like 5–7 (Aiken & Williams, 1968; Banks, Fujii, & Kayra-Stuart, 1976; Buckley & Gillman, 1974; Duncan & McFarland, 1980; Moyer & Landauer, 1967; Parkman, 1971; Sekuler & Mierkiewicz, 1977). The effect is also observed when numbers are symbolized by patterns of dots (Buckley & Gillman, 1974) or with numbers written in kana and in kanji (Takahashi & Green, 1983). In the latter study, distances of 1, 3, and 5 were compared; the general trend was the same for both kinds of script, but the detailed pattern of results was slightly different in each case. With kana stimuli there was a relatively small decrease in reaction time between distances 1 and 3 and a relatively large decrease between distances 3 and 5, whereas with kanji the opposite configuration was observed, a large decrease between distances 1 and 3 and a small one between distances 3 and 5. Because only 12 out of the 36 possible pairs were studied, the effect could have arisen from an interaction between the relative coding difficulty of the pairs, symbolic distance, and type of script, rather than from a different comparison process taking place with each kind of script. This is a likely possibility in view of the absence of interaction between symbolic distance and type of script (arabic numerals vs. alphabetic number names) in the experiment of Foltz, Poltrock, and Potts (1984, Experiment 2). In this case, the complete set of 36 pairs was used.

Serial Position Effect

In the present framework, serial position refers to the position of each member of a pair of numbers relative to the boundaries of the ordered sequence of single-digit numbers. For a given symbolic distance, pairs composed of small numbers (e.g., 1–3, 2–4) are compared more rapidly than pairs composed of large numbers (e.g., 6–8, 7–9). The effect, often expressed as an increase in reaction time as a function of the increase in the smaller member of each pair, has been consistently observed with arabic numerals (Aiken & Williams, 1968; Buckley & Gillman, 1974; Parkman, 1971). As for symbolic distance, the serial position effect was also obtained with numbers symbolized by patterns of dots (Buckley & Gillman, 1974), and there was no interaction between the serial position effect and the type of script (arabic numerals vs. alphabetically written names) in the study of Foltz et al. (1984, Experiment 2).

Semantic Congruity Effect

This effect was identified by Banks, Clark, and Lucy (1975). It results from an interaction between the way the instructions are formulated with respect to the boundaries of the ordered set of numbers and the position of the pair of numbers with respect to these boundaries. With small numbers (e.g., 2–4) subjects make their comparisons more rapidly under the instruction "choose the smaller" than under the instruction "choose the larger." Conversely, with larger numbers (e.g., 6–8) decisions are reached more rapidly under the instruction "choose the larger" than under the instruction "choose the smaller." The semantic congruity effect has been observed twice with arabic numerals (Banks et al., 1976; Duncan & McFarland, 1980). Although the effect has not yet been investigated with other number representations, it is unlikely that the outcome of such a study would show differential effects according to the surface form of the numbers. One reason for this is that in judging the size of two objects or the intelligence of two animals, the semantic congruity effect has been found to be independent of the representation of the referents as pictures or as alphabetically written names (Banks & Flora, 1977).

At present, the picture that emerges from contrasting logographic and phonographic representations of numbers in numerical comparison judgments is incomplete, but quite consistent. As regards the symbolic distance and serial position effects there is no evidence that the task is performed differentially according to the surface form of the stimuli, and with respect to the semantic congruity effect the relevant information is not yet available. For the size congruity effect, to be described next, the results are more contradictory; this is also the case for experiments using lateral hemifield presentations in numerical size comparisons. In order to draw some tentative conclusions from these data a more detailed analysis will be necessary than has sufficed for the three effects discussed before.

Size Congruity Effect

This effect, labeled by Banks and Flora (1977), was first observed by Paivio (1975) in a size comparison task involving objects represented either by pictures or by words. It appeared in a Stroop-like situation in which an irrelevant dimension, the relative physical size of each member of a pair of stimuli, was combined orthogonally with the relative real sizes of the referents. In a congruent trial the stimulus referring to the larger object was also physically larger than the other. In an incongruent trial the stimulus referring to the larger object was physically smaller. Neutral trials in which both members of the pairs of stimuli were the same physical size were also included. Paivio observed a size congruity effect with pictures, the mean response latency being 89 ms faster for congruent than for incongruent trials. The most striking result was that there was no congruity effect at all when the same referents were represented by words instead of pictures. As regards number comparisons, this Stroop-like task was first used by Besner and Coltheart (1979) who obtained results parallel to those of Paivio; namely, a large size congruity effect with arabic numerals and no effect at all with the alphabetical representations of the numbers. Subsequent experiments confirmed the result with arabic numerals, but were discrepant with the initial study in showing a large size congruity effect with alphabetical number names as well (Besner, Davelaar, Alcott, & Parry, 1984; Foltz et al., 1984; Peereman & Holender, 1984). The size congruity effect was also observed with numbers written in kanji whereas kana numbers showed ambiguous results (Takahashi & Green, 1983).

Table 3.1 summarizes the main results of the experiments published so far, except for some forthcoming data of the second author (Peereman, in preparation). In addition to presenting the mean reaction time for each type of trial (congruent, neutral, and incongruent), the table also splits the congruity effect into facilitation and interference effects. The facilitation effect is obtained by subtracting the mean latency of congruent trials from the mean latency of neutral trials, whereas subtracting the latter from the mean latency of incongruent trials yields the interference effect. A few more procedural details are worth describing before we discuss the results. In some experiments the numbers were presented side by side, to left and right of a fixation point, and responses were made on a left and right response key (Besner & Coltheart, 1979, logographic condition; Foltz et al., 1984; Henik & Tzelgov, 1982). The other experiments used numbers displayed above and below a fixation point, and responses were made either on two vertically aligned response keys (Besner & Coltheart, 1979, alphabetic condition; Takahashi & Green, 1983) or by activating a forward-backward switch (Peereman & Holender, 1984; Peereman, in preparation,). Only one study used the complete set of 36 pairs generated by using the numbers 1 to 9 (Foltz et al., 1984), whereas the others used only a small subset of these pairs, from 4 to 12 according to the experiment. In addition to central presentations, Peereman and Holender (1984) also included lateral ones and Peereman (in preparation) contrasted the usual manual response with a vocal response, the naming of the larger number.

The left side of Table 3.1 shows the results with logographic scripts, i.e., kanji numbers in the experiment of Takahashi and Green (1983), and arabic numerals in all the other cases. The main results can be summarized as follows.

1. There is a large overall size congruity effect (sum of the facilitation and interference effect in Table 3.1) in each experiment. The magnitude of the effect tends to increase with the increase in the absolute level of performance.

2. Both the facilitation and the interference effects are substantial in each experiment (except for a very small facilitation effect in the experiment of Besner

TABLE 3.1
Size Congruity Effect in Numerical Size Comparison Judgments

Authors	Experiment or condition	Logographic					Phonographic				
		C	N – C	N	I – N	I	C	N – C	N	I – N	I
Henik & Tzelgov, 1983[a,b]	Exp. 1	588	36	624	72	696	—		—		—
Besner & Coltheart, 1979[a]		531	11	542	44	586	800		—		800
Foltz et al., 1984	Exp. 2	564	21	585	56	641	749	13	762	33	795
Peereman & Holender, 1984	Central field	472	28	500	61	561	719	5	724	32	756
	Left field	481	42	523	54	577	717	38	755	22	777
	Right field	472	56	528	49	577	704	41	745	14	759
Peereman, in preparation	Manual response	520	32	552	70	622	749	35	784	21	805
	Vocal response	568	34	602	92	694	751	17	768	27	795
Takahashi & Green, 1983[a,c]		752	38	790	65	855	1076	-22	1054	41	1095

Note. C = congruent, N = neutral, I = incongruent.
[a] Data estimated from a graph.
[b] First session only.
[c] Data pooled over sessions 1 and 2.

and Coltheart). With central presentations, the magnitude of the facilitation effect is in the range of 20% to 60% of the magnitude of the interference effect. With lateral presentations (Peereman & Holender, 1984), the ratio of the two effects is closer to 1.

3. The kanji numbers used by Takahashi and Green (1983) behave in pretty much the same way as the arabic numerals used in the other experiments, except that response latencies are much longer than with arabic numerals, probably because kanji numbers are not widely used.

The right side of Table 3.1 shows the results for phonographic scripts, the syllabic kana writing in Takahashi and Green's report, and alphabetic writing in all the other cases. The most prominent aspects of the results are the following.

1. Overall response latencies are in the range of 200 to 250 ms longer than with logographic numbers. The absence of a congruity effect, reported by Besner and Coltheart (1979), is not confirmed in subsequent experiments, although the effect tends to be a bit smaller than with logographic numbers. There is no systematic relation between the absolute level of performance and the magnitude of the size congruity effect.

2. With central presentations, much of the size congruity effect is due to the interference caused by incongruent trials, congruent trials provoking almost no facilitation or even a detrimental effect (Takahashi & Green, 1983). With lateral presentations, the opposite tendency is observed; that is, strong facilitation effects and weak interference effects (Peereman & Holender, 1984).

3. Kana numbers (Takahashi & Green, 1983) are responded to much slower than alphabetic numbers, but this form of representation is almost never used outside the laboratory. There is also a reversal in the facilitation effect.

The most important point to discuss is the discrepancy between the absence of a congruity effect with alphabetic numbers in the experiment of Besner and Coltheart (1979) and the presence of such an effect in the two other experiments (Foltz et al., 1984; Peereman & Holender, 1984). Foltz et al. interpreted the difference between their results and those of Besner and Coltheart as due to their use of a repeated-set design instead of the fixed-pair design of the conflicting experiment. In a repeated-set design each item (the number 1 to 9) is paired equally often with each other item, whereas only a small subset of these pairs is used repeatedly in a fixed-pair design (12 pairs repeated 20 times and 9 pairs repeated 10 times in the logographic and alphabetic conditions of Besner and Coltheart, respectively) and each item is paired with only a few other items (one, two, or three in Besner and Coltheart's experiment). It is argued that there is an increasing probability of bypassing the comparison stage as a function of the increase in the number of repetitions in the fixed-pair design: Subjects may respond on the basis of specific response-pair associations established during the experiment. This accounts for the lack of a size congruity effect in Besner and Coltheart's fixed-pair design and the presence of such an effect in Foltz et al.'s repeated-set design. Moreover, the prediction was nicely supported in a study using names of objects (Experiment 1 of Foltz et al.) and the fixed-pair design of Paivio (1975, six pairs repeated eight times, each item being paired with only one other item); no size congruity effect was observed. However, with an infinite-set design in which 48 different pairs were presented only once, as if they were drawn from an infinite set of pairs, a strong 115-ms size congruity effect was obtained, which reduced to 49 ms after three further presentations of the set. Recently, Besner et al. (1984, p. 127) also alluded to the observation of a size congruity effect in using a larger set of alphabetic numbers than in the original experiment of Besner and Coltheart (1979). There is, however, one result that is clearly at odds with this interpretation. In our alphabetical condition (Peereman & Holender, 1984), only four different pairs were repeated 72 times, each of four numbers being paired with only two other numbers. This should have maximized the chances of bypassing the comparison stage, thereby suppressing the size congruity effect, but this did not happen.

A further assumption is needed to account for the fact that the repeated-set design does not suppress the size congruity effect when arabic numerals are used instead of alphabetic number names. Foltz et al. (1984) suggested that because pictures or arabic numerals provide much shorter latencies than their spelled names, retrieving and comparing the size information could be faster than re-trieving the appropriate previously learned response in the former than in the latter case. This is a completely ad hoc interpretation. In addition, it cannot explain why, in a fixed-pair design, Takahashi and Green (1983) observed a very strong size congruity effect with kanji numbers in spite of the fact that the absolute level of performance was equivalent to that of Besner and Coltheart (1979) in the alphabetic condition (see Table 3.1). In such a case, according to Foltz et al.'s interpretation, the retrieval of previously associated responses should have been faster than the size retrieval and comparison process, leading to no size congruity effect.

For other tendencies revealed in Table 3.1, such as the smaller congruity effect with phonographic than with logographic script and the different ratios between the facilitation and the interference effect with each kind of script, no unequivocal conclusion can be drawn at present. The problem is that the situation is a little too complicated. Several confounding factors whose roles are not well understood could be responsible for these effects. Moreover, none of them might give any interesting hint toward a possible differential role of the surface form of the stimuli in the operations needed to perform the numerical size comparison judgment. Let us mention two such confounding factors.

1. The relative salience of the irrelevant dimension affects the magnitude of its influence on the decision about the relevant dimension (Besner & Coltheart, 1976; Dixon & Just, 1978). In the present context, the salience of the irrelevant

dimension may well be influenced by the factors affecting the judgment of dissimilarity between rectangles, because, roughly speaking, the areas occupied by arabic numerals or by uppercase number names are rectangular in shape. The psychophysics of dissimilarity judgments between rectangles varying in shape and area (Krantz & Tversky, 1975; Wender, 1971; Wiener-Ehrlich, 1978) is surprisingly complex, no simple dimensional structure emerging from the data. There are two ways in which the data discussed in this section could be affected by these psychophysical factors. First, the difference between the physical size of two arabic numerals can simply be more conspicuous than that between two multiletter words, leading to a stronger size congruity effect in the former than in the latter case. Second, the speed with which a dissimilarity judgment can be made, or for our purposes, the speed with which the difference in size becomes compelling, should depend on the magnitude of the physical difference, at least within a certain range. This could be responsible for subtle differences between the magnitude of the interference and facilitation effects according to type of script.

2. From our experience with the task, we know that the magnitude of the congruity effect and the relative magnitudes of the facilitation and interference effects vary considerably between different pairs of numbers, especially with the alphabetical representation. Having used only a small subset of pairs in our experiments, it is hard to find any systematic factor underlying either the intra-surface form or the intersurface form variability. We nevertheless suspect that some pairs are more easily encoded than others, thus affecting the time at which the information becomes available for performing the comparison operation. This could, of course, generate different patterns of results between experiments using different subsets of pairs.

These two confounding factors emphasize the role that the relative time course of processing both the relevant and irrelevant aspects of the pairs of stimuli might play in the determination of the size congruity effect, independent of the comparison process itself. Of course, this could be systematically studied, but we then run the risk of completely losing sight of the real goal of this research, which is precisely to investigate whether or not the surface form of the stimuli affects the numerical size comparison operations, not to untangle the complexity of Stroop-like situations.

Hemifield Presentations

The rationale for using hemifield presentations of stimuli is explained in the next main section of the paper. Suffice it to say here that a relatively better perfor-mance for stimuli displayed in one hemifield than in the other is generally interpreted in terms of a contralateral hemispheric superiority for a particular class of stimuli or for a particular experimental task. The investigation of lateral presentations of numbers for comparison of their numerical magnitudes has led to a perplexing picture, because every possible outcome has been reported. Katz (1980, 1981) found a left visual field (LVF) advantage; Besner, Grimsell, and Davis (1979). a right visual field (RVF) advantage; and Peereman and Holender (1984), no difference between fields.

The opposite field advantages of Katz (1980, 1981) and Besner et al. (1979) can be explained by the difference in the exposure durations that were used. A short exposure duration, 50 ms in Katz's experiments, could engender a RVF advantage that has little to do with either the specific material presented or the specific task performed, but is determined rather by the nature of the available visual information (see Sergent, 1983a, 1983b). According to Sergent, the right hemisphere is more efficient than the left in extracting the relevant information from low spatial frequencies than from high spatial frequencies, and vice versa for the left hemisphere. Physical parameters such as very short exposure duration, large stimulus size, and large eccentricity should favor processing on the basis of low spatial frequencies, therefore increasing the odds of finding a LVF advantage whatever the type of stimulus. On the other hand, long exposure durations, such as the 150 ms used by Besner et al. (1979), generally lead to a RVF, which was indeed observed in this particular study. Notice, however, that the authors strongly favored an interpretation of their field advantage in terms of a left hemispheric superiority for performing the comparison process rather than for encoding the stimuli.

Why then, using a relatively long exposure duration of 120 ms, did Peereman and Holender (1984) fail to show any laterality effect? There is no ready interpretation for the discrepancy between their results and those of Besner et al. (1979). However, some tentative suggestions can be made.

The combination of left and right presentations with responses that are also spatialized along the left-right dimension may generate the compatibility effect first reported by Simon (Craft & Simon, 1970; Simon & Rudell, 1967). Asking their subjects to press a right key at the sound of a high tone and a left key at the sound of a low tone (Simon & Rudell, 1967), or to associate the right key with a red bulb and the left key with a green bulb (Craft & Simon, 1970), Simon and his collaborators observed that the right-side response was made faster if the stimulus was presented in the right hemispace rather than in the left hemispace, and conversely for the left-side response. This compatibility effect has been described as a tendency to react toward the source of stimulation. It is genuinely a semantic congruity effect similar to that of Banks et al. (1976), discussed earlier, because the coding of responses in terms of left and right entails an unavoidable influence of the coding of stimulus location in the same terms, thereby facilitating or interfering with the response according to the congruency or incongruency of stimulus and response positions. This compatibility effect has also been observed with lateralized presentations of pairs of numbers. Besner et al. (1979) found that right-index responses were shorter for displays presented in the RVF than in the LVF and vice versa for left-index responses. The same was true for the relation between the rightmost or leftmost finger and the visual field when two fingers of the same hand were used to make the response (Katz, 1981). However, with bimanual responses Katz (1980, Experiment 1) failed to find the effect, a surprising outcome in view of the usual robustness of the phenomenon.

Figure 3.1 illustrates what happens when the side of presentation affects each response in an opposite direction through one factor—compatibility—and in the same direction through another factor—the presumed hemispheric superiority. In Besner et al.'s experiment, the RVF advantage, which is very strong for the right response, gives way to a small (nonsignificant) LVF advantage for the left response. Similarly, in Katz's (1981) experiment, the LVF advantage, which is

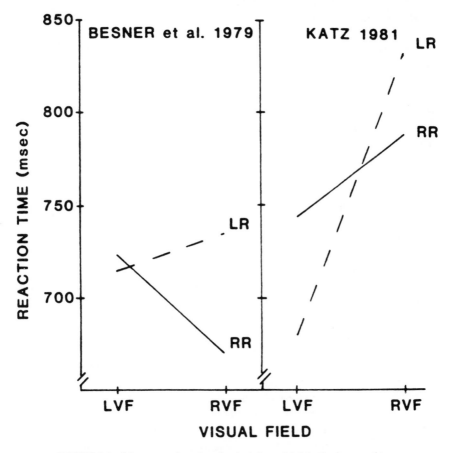

FIGURE 3.1   Mean reaction time for judging which is the larger of two numbers as a function of visual field (LVF = left visual field, RVF = right visual field) and response side (LR = left response, RR = right response) in the experiments of Besner et al. (1979) and Katz (1981). The data were estimated from graphs.

very strong for the left response, is considerably reduced for the right response. The explanation of this phenomenon goes as follows, taking Besner et al.'s results as the basis for the reasoning. For the right response, compatibility and the assumed left hemispheric superiority add their effects to enhance performance with RVF presentations and to impede performance with LVF presentations, thereby inducing a large field difference. For the left response, the advantage of the stimulus being presented in the LVF due to compatibility is counteracted by the disadvantage of being first channeled to the wrong hemisphere, whereas the benefit of the RVF presentation due to left hemispheric superiority is counterbalanced by the cost of being on the wrong side in terms of compatibility, thereby reducing, and even reversing, the field advantage.

The existence of a compatibility effect that interacts in a complex manner with a laterality effect, presumably linked to hemispheric superiority, is an obstacle to the study of this phenomenon per se. It would therefore be better to get rid of the compatibility effect, by suppressing the left-right polarity of the response, presenting the pairs of numbers vertically and replacing the left-right responses with forward-backward responses, exactly the procedure used by Peereman and Holender (1984). If the left hemisphere is really better than the right in performing the comparison process, as Besner et al. (1979) believed, it should be so whatever the spatial disposition of the numbers in the pair, and the ensuing RVF should show up uncontaminated by the compatibility effect. However, as we have already pointed out, the LVF advantage disappeared altogether when we followed this procedure. Thus, the factor that combined with compatibility to determine the pattern of results found by Besner et al. (see Fig. 3.1) was not a left hemisphere superiority for the task, but something else.

What else? We do not know, but we suggest looking to other forms of compatibility that almost certainly play a role when left-right polarized displays and responses are involved in the comparison of the numerical magnitude of numbers. For instance, in deciding which number is the larger, the response is faster if the larger number is on the right side of the pair (e.g., 3–7) than with the opposite configuration (7–3). This effect was as large as 30 ms in the experiment of Aiken and Williams (1968), using 18 pairs among the 36 possible, and 20 ms in Experiment 2 of Banks et al. (1976), using 21 pairs. However, the effect was null in Banks et al.'s Experiment 1 involving only 6 pairs, suggesting possible interactions with specific characteristics of the pairs.

A last point should be stressed. Peereman and Holender's (1984) experiment is the only one fulfilling the requirements of this chapter for numerical size comparisons; that is to say, it is the only study that combines factorially the type of script (arabic numerals and their French alphabetic names) with the side of presentation. It is clear from Table 3.1 that there is no field advantage whatever the type of script, a conclusion that can probably be safely accepted. Whether there is evidence for a differential influence of the type of script on the comparison process cannot be answered on the basis of these data because, as remarked in the preceding subsection concerning the size congruity effect, several possible confounding factors must be controlled before any reliable conclusion can be reached.

LATERAL HEMIFIELD PRESENTATIONS

Rationale Underlying the Approach

From the standpoint of understanding how numbers represented logographically or phonographically are processed, the study of laterality should be considered as one of the tools for analysis of processing operations into components. However, the extent to which the method succeeds in doing so depends on a number of difficult, unsettled issues.

In vision, provided gaze fixation is controlled, it is a matter of anatomical fact that a stimulus displayed laterally in the LVF or in the RVF is first channeled to the contralateral hemisphere and that its access to the homolateral hemisphere depends on its transit through the interhemispheric commissures. The most common interpretation of a better performance in one hemifield than in the other is in terms of a greater ability of the contralateral hemisphere to perform the task. In other words, a given hemifield advantage is almost automatically translated into a contralateral hemispheric superiority. Two points are worth stressing. First, even if a task is fully lateralized (i.e., can be accomplished by only one hemisphere), this need not entail better performance in terms of response latency or accuracy for contralaterally displayed stimuli (see G. Cohen, 1982, for an excellent discussion of this point). Second, besides hemispheric superiority, a number of factors can determine a hemifield advantage. This point has been repeatedly stressed by Bryden (1978, 1982, see also Bertelson, 1982, for a similar case). Our venture at interpreting the contradiction between the results of Besner et al. (1979) and Peereman and Holender (1984) as resulting from a combination of different compatibility effects is a good example of such an alternative approach.

Be that as it may, the logic underlying the study of lateralized presentations of different types of script implies that the results of an experiment should show some kind of interaction between hemifield and type of script. Three different interactive patterns could emerge: (a) opposite visual field advantages for each type of script, (b) no field advantage for one type of script and a field advantage for the other, (c) different degrees of field advantages in the same direction for both scripts. The first pattern is called a nonordinal interaction because each level of one factor (RVF vs. LVF) has an opposite effect on each level of the other factor (type of script). The third pattern is an ordinal interaction because the laterality effect has the same direction for each level of the other factor. The second pattern, in which there is no significant field advantage for one type of script, is a special case of either the first or the third pattern. Among these three possible interactive patterns, the first is certainly the most appealing because it takes the form of a double dissociation between the field advantages and the two kinds of stimuli, and because a nonordinal interaction cannot be removed by a nonlinear transformation of the dependent measure. The existence of such an interaction is therefore relatively independent of the choice of the dependent measure.

Claims for opposite field advantages in processing phonographic and logographic scripts arose from the initial observation of a RVF advantage in the identification of kana words (Hatta, 1978) or nonwords (Endo, Shimizu, & Hori, 1978; Sasanuma, Itoh, Mori, & Kobayashi, 1977), and of a LVF advantage in the identification of kanji words (Hatta, 1977a, 1977b, 1978). Since then, the RVF advantage for processing kana words has been clearly confirmed. Moreover, kanji words composed of more than one character are also better processed in the RVF. For single Chinese or kanji logograms the results are more contradictory because all possible outcomes—RVF, LVF, or no field advantages--have been reported. In spite of this, there is still a widespread tendency to consider that the bulk of the evidence favors the hypothesis of a right hemispheric superiority for the processing of single characters (see Coltheart, 1983, for a recent example). From our reading of that literature, we believe that too many confounding factors could have flawed most of these results for the existing data to be conclusive. If a conclusion is nonetheless to be drawn, we would argue that a right hemisphere superiority for logographic processing is extremely unlikely (see Peereman & Holender, 1985); a view shared by Leong, Wong, Wong, and Hiscock (1985) and by Paradis, Hagiwara, and Hildebrandt (1985).

Review of the Data

The best way to characterize the investigation of lateral differences in the processing of numbers is to say that the data are scarce, the procedures diverse, and the results quite consistent. Most experiments have been concerned exclusively with arabic numerals, although two have included alphabetically written numbers. Let us distinguish between those studies using response latency and those relying on response accuracy as the dependent variable, reviewing the latter first.

Hines, Satz, Schell, and Schmidlin (1969, Experiment 3) inaugurated a series of experiments in which three pairs of numbers were successively presented: One member of each pair was displayed at fixation point, the other either 3° to the left or 3° to the right of fixation. In any particular trial, the lateral member of each pair was always on the same side. (A fourth centrally placed number was temporally interpolated between the third pair and recall in two subsequent studies [Hines & Satz, 1971, 1974].) The task of the subjects was first to recall all the central numbers, and then to recall the lateral ones, only trials with 100% correct central identification being taken into account. The results always showed an overall better recall for right than for left numbers. Further examination showed the RVF advantage to be confined to the first two pairs of a trial, the last pair showing no field advantage. These data are generally disqualified on the ground that the central task in itself can generate a RVF independent of the nature of the stimuli (see Bryden, 1982, for a discussion of this long-standing debate). These data also involve a mixture between perceptual and memory processes without allowing us to disentangle their respective contributions to the RVF advantage, if any.

However, if both members of each pair of stimuli are laterally displayed one in the LVF simultaneously with the other in the RVF (rather than one laterally, the other centrally), a weak LVF advantage may be observed. This effect was not significant in Experiments 1 and 2 of Hines et al. (1969), but reached significance in Experiment 4 of Hirata and Osaka (1967). This LVF advantage could result from the strategy of report, rather than from the nature of the stimuli, the left member of each pair being generally reported before the right one.

Carmon, Nachshon, and Starinsky (1976) reported a higher percentage of recall for two- or four-digit numbers (represented by arabic numerals) in the RVF than in the LVF with fifth- and seventh-grade children. First- and third-grade children were tested only with two-digit numbers, and showed no field advantage. Hatta and Dimond (1980) also reported better RVF recognition of six-digit numbers with adult Japanese and English subjects. However, this RVF advantage might be caused by the combinatorial process involved in forming multidigit numbers rather than by the logographic nature of the representation.

Yet, Besner, Daniels, and Slade (1982, Experiment 1) obtained a very large RVF advantage with single-digit arabic numerals, right presentations leading to 80% correct responses and left presentations to only 40%. In their second experiment, they tested Japanese and Chinese subjects with both kanji numbers and arabic numerals. This time the 14% RVF advantage for arabic numerals was less pronounced than in Experiment 1. Overall performance with kanji numbers was much lower than with arabic numerals, but a 16% RVF advantage was again observed. It is a pity the authors limited their material to the numbers 4 to 9. Remember that in kanji, the first three numbers are concrete representations of the quantity they denote, being composed of one, two, or three horizontal strokes, whereas the other numbers are arbitrary symbolic representations, like arabic numerals. It would have been interesting to compare the laterality effect in the two cases.

We should point out that the extent to which the huge laterality effect obtained in these experiments was caused by physical characteristics of the displays is not known. Given the importance of visual parameters in determining visual field advantages (Sergent 1983a, 1983b), this point is worth stressing. Most studies resort to stimuli physically smaller than the arabic numerals, subtending $5.9° \times 8.5°$, $4.6° \times 5.7°$, and $2.0° \times 3.3°$, in Besner et al.'s Experiment 1 and than the $10.6° \times 10.6°$ stimuli of their Experiment 2. These stimuli were centered 8.8° to the left or right of fixation. The exposure duration was individually adjusted to yield an overall performance of 50% to 60% correct responses, mean durations being 32, 44, and 56 ms for small, medium, and large stimuli in Experiment 1, and 54 ms in Experiment 2. Finally, a 50-ms patterned mask immediately followed stimulus presentation, which is also unusual.

We now turn to studies in which response latency was the dependent variable. Naming latencies for arabic numerals showed no field advantage in the experiment of Gordon and Carmon (1976) and a small, but significant, 10-ms RVF advantage in Experiment 3 of Geffen, Bradshaw, and Wallace (1971). Procedural differences between experiments inspire no special comments. The main parameters of the task were, for Gordon and Carmon (1976) and Geffen et al. (1971), respectively, 7 and 4 different stimuli, exposure durations of 100 and 160 ms, stimulus visual angles of 2° and 0.5°, and eccentricities of 3° and 4°.

With two-choice manual response tasks involving only two arabic numerals, a significant 13-ms RVF advantage was found by Geffen et al. (1971, Experiment 5) and a similar but not significant 14-ms advantage was reported by G. Cohen (1975) in her cued condition. Cohen mixed three different representations of the numbers 4 and 5: arabic numerals, their English names presented vertically, and the corresponding patterns of dots found on a die. Subjects were either cued or not cued about the specific representation to be used on each trial. Under precuing, number names yielded a slightly greater RVF advantage (20 ms) than arabic numerals, and dots showed a nonsignificant 12-ms LVF advantage. Without cuing, there was no field difference, whatever the type of stimuli.

Classification tasks also yield a small RVF advantage with arabic numerals. Geffen, Bradshaw, and Nettleton (1973) used a many-to-one stimulus response mapping in a go-no go task involving four numbers and one vocal response. Two arabic numerals called for the response "bong" and two others required no response. This yielded a 16-ms RVF advantage. In a number-nonnumber classification modeled on the classical lexical decision task, Peereman and Holender (1985) showed a significant 13-ms RVF advantage and a significant 26-ms advantage in the same direction for alphabetically written number names, the interaction between visual field and type of script being nonsignificant.

Tasks involving more complex decisions than those just described have been almost exclusively concerned with numerical size comparison judgments (Besner et al., 1979; Katz, 1980, 1981; Peereman & Holender, 1984); they were reviewed and discussed in the preceding main section. There is only one more study to mention. Hatta (1983, Experiment 1) orthogonally varied the numerical size and the physical size of each member of laterally displayed pairs of arabic numerals, asking his Japanese subjects to perform a congruity judgment. An overall 29-ms RVF advantage ensued. A 47-ms RVF advantage also showed up when the same task was performed with the kanji logograms denoting million units (Experiment 3). By contrast, in judging the congruity between the relative physical size of pairs of logograms and the relative physical sizes of the referents (Experiment 2), the subjects showed a 26-ms LVF advantage. The author interpreted his results as evidence that the comparative judgment is based on different types of mental representation in dealing with kanji object names and with numbers, but that in this latter case, the surface form of the stimuli (arabic numerals vs. kanji words) is immaterial.

Interpreting the Results

There is nothing to indicate that opposite visual field advantages for each kind of script, the first possible pattern of results mentioned above, will ever be found in contrasting numbers written logographically and phonographically. On the contrary, both surface forms lead to RVF advantages. If the LVF sometimes reported with single Chinese logograms is valid, then arabic numerals belong to a small class of logograms behaving differently as regards laterality, as is also suggested by the results of Hatta (1983).

To date, there has been no report of a significant ordinal interaction between visual field and type of script, but the prospect of finding one is quite good. With arabic numerals and simple tasks like naming or categorizing, a RVF of 10 to 15 ms is typically found; this is the lower bound for the effect to be statistically significant. On the other hand, Peereman and Holender (1985) pointed out that the magnitude of their RVF advantage (26 ms) for numbers written alphabetically was more substantial and well within the range of the large RVF advantages typically reported in lexical decisions involving larger classes of words. Hence, there would be nothing very unexpected if a statistically more powerful study in the future came up with a significant ordinal interaction indicating a larger RVF advantage for alphabetic number names than for arabic numerals, both RVF advantages being significant.

Let us assume that the ordinal interaction has indeed been found. What, and how much information would then have been gained regarding logographic and alphabetic number processing? To answer this question, we will be obliged to integrate laterality research into the broader framework of mainstream information-processing analysis—a highly desirable, but so far unfulfilled accomplishment (Allen, 1983; Bertelson 1982). Bertelson optimistically closed his recent analysis of laterality research with the words "Progress can be expected, provided laterality research is conducted as an integral part of the study of human cognition" (1982, p. 203). Taking a few steps in this direction, in search of an answer to the question asked at the outset of this paragraph, we came up with a more distressing conclusion (Peereman & Holender, 1985). An analysis similar to that leading to this conclusion is now presented.

The aim of the analysis is to show how the ordinal and nonordinal interactions described in the rationale for the approach can be interpreted in the relatively constrained framework of a stage analysis of reaction time. The two basic assumptions are as follows:

1. Response latency can be decomposed into a series of additive component durations corresponding to different stages of processing. For additivity to hold, the processing stages should be strictly serial, each stage starting only when the

preceding stage has provided an output. Under these constraints, any modification of the duration of one particular stage under the influence of any factor (i.e., hemifield of presentation) should be reflected in the response latencies. This is one of the assumptions underlying Sternberg's (1969, 1984) additive factor method, one of the most popular methods of analyzing processing into components.

2. Hemispheric specialization is relative rather than absolute: Each hemisphere can perform the task, but one is more efficient than the other. This is more reasonable than the alternative assumption of absolute hemispheric specialization (only one hemisphere can perform the task), which would imply that the difference in latency between visual fields is due to the time needed to transfer information from one hemisphere to the other when the stimulus is displayed on the wrong side. This alternative is unlikely because it would entail a relative constancy across experiments in the magnitudes of the difference between response latencies in the two fields, which is hardly the case (G. Cohen, 1982).

Within this framework, the simplest possible account for the presence of an interaction, either ordinal or nonordinal, between visual field and type of script requires the addition of two specific assumptions. (1) All processing stages are neutral with respect to laterality save one, or at maximum two—let us call them Stages A and B—which can be either neutral or lateralized according to circumstances. In the neutral state of a stage the operations performed during that period take the same mean amount of time in each hemisphere. If a stage is lateralized, the corresponding operations are performed faster in one hemisphere than in the other one. (2) We cannot exclude a priori the possibility that (a) both Stage A and Stage B are lateralized on the same side for both types of stimulus, (b) that each stage is neutral for one type of stimulus and lateralized for the other, or (c) that the two stages are lateralized in opposite directions for each type of stimulus. Within these constraints, each pattern of interaction can be realized in three extreme ways according to the following principles. In each of the three cases, the ordinal interaction is labeled 1 and the nonordinal, 2.

A. Only Stage A is lateralized, Stage B is neutral.

1. Stage A is left-lateralized for both kinds of number representations, but the magnitude of the RVF advantage depends on the surface form of the stimuli, being larger for alphabetical number names than for arabic numerals.

2. Stage A is left-lateralized for alphabetical number names and right-lateralized for arabic numerals.

B. Stage A is left-lateralized for both scripts and produces the same degree of RVF for both scripts.

1. Stage B is neutral for arabic numerals and left-lateralized for alphabetical number names; hence, Stage B adds its RVF advantage to that of Stage A, producing the required interaction.
2. Stage B is neutral for alphabetical number names and right-lateralized for arabic numerals. Stage B produces a LVF advantage sufficient to supersede the RVF caused by Stage A.

C. Stage A is neutral for alphabetical number names and Stage B is neutral for arabic numerals.

1. Both stages are left-lateralized when dealing with their specific stimulus type. It just happens that the RVF advantage due to Stage B is larger than that produced by Stage A.
2. Stage A is right-lateralized for arabic numerals and Stage B is left-lateralized for alphabetical number names.

Within the constraints defined, one can easily find the different possible interpretations corresponding to the third interactive pattern, in which only one type of script shows a visual field advantage. Similarly, the different possibilities corresponding to an absence of interaction can also be worked out.

In performing a similar analysis (Peereman & Holender, 1985), we showed that a significant ordinal interaction is no more informative than a nonsignificant interaction. We now extend this conclusion by showing that the favorite nonordinal interaction is no more informative than the ordinal. Using the simplest possible model for the organization of processing operations, and looking at the interaction between visual field and stimulus type, we always come up with three different possible interpretations. In other words, laterality as a tool for analyzing processing into components simply fails to do its job. One can, of course, retort that nobody ever pretended to disentangle these various alternatives by using the laterality approach. The point would be well taken, but then what is the purpose of presenting all these beautiful phonograms and logograms in the left or in the right visual field? To avoid such criticisms researchers using the laterality methodology should be more explicit about their goals than they usually are.

NUMBER PROCESSING AFTER BRAIN INJURY

The discussion of the data provided by brain-damaged people is divided into two parts. In the first, all patients have lesions affecting different language areas of the left hemisphere. The patients display a variety of aphasic troubles, including alexia with agraphia. Potentially, the investigation of these patients can teach us something about the way different notational processing systems can break down, but the respective roles played by each hemisphere in determining the preserved aspects of performance cannot be ascertained. In the second part of the discussion, data concern the partial or total disconnection of the right hemisphere from the left. These data can potentially tell us something about the competence of the right hemisphere in dealing with different representations of single-digit numbers.

Number Processing with Lesions Located in the Language Areas

What is clear from the fragmentary information available is that the ability to read single- and multidigit numbers represented by arabic numerals can be somewhat preserved in patients unable to read letters and words in the alphabetic code. From the anatomo-clinical study of 183 retrorolandic brain-injured patients, Hécaen, Angelergues, and Houillier (1961) concluded that the frequency with which letter or digit reading breaks down is different according to the site of lesion; this could indicate that partially different functional subsystems are indeed involved in each case. The same authors also mentioned 16 patients who, as a group, showed a relatively stronger inability to identify mathematical signs than arabic numerals. A fully selective loss of this competence has been reported in two patients by Ferro and Botelho (1980). Unfortunately, they did not investigate the patients' ability to identify the written names of the mathematical signs.

We have found one patient-group study in which the ability to process different number surface forms was investigated (Dahmen, Hartje, Büssing, & Sturm, 1982). These authors selected three groups of 20 patients, each group corresponding to a different pathology—Wernicke's aphasia, Broca's aphasia, and right-sided retrorolandic lesion. These groups varied in their identification performance for numbers (chosen in the set 1 to 25), but showed no difference according to the type of representation (arabic numerals or their German names). The mean numbers of correct identifications (out of 20) for arabic numerals and number names were 13.3 and 12.0, 16.2 and 14.8, and 19.7 and 18.0, for Wernicke's aphasics, Broca's aphasics, and patients with a right-side lesion, respectively. The same was true in a numerical size comparison task in which the patients had to point to the larger number in pairs of numbers. For arabic numerals and number names the mean numbers of correct responses were 8.7 and 8.6, 14.2 and 14.3, and 16.2 and 15.9, for Wernicke's aphasics, Broca's aphasics, and patients with a right-side lesion, respectively. Three points should be stressed. First, the difference in performance between Broca's and Wernicke's aphasics is in the direction expected on the basis of the overall differences exhibited by these patients in terms of language comprehension. Second, the results of the comparison task confirm the trend we observed with normal subjects in being unaffected by the surface form of the numbers. Third, unlike the identification process, the comparison process seems to require the integrity of the right hemisphere as indicated by the difference in performance in each task in the group of patients suffering from a right-side lesion.

Most of the data reviewed so far are based on the comparison of the mean performances of groups of patients. Caramazza (1984) has recently pointed out that such an approach is ill-suited for addressing the issue of the analysis of cognitive processes because the patients included in a given group could differ greatly in terms of the mechanisms underlying their performance. The remaining data come either from single cases or from very small, relatively homogeneous groups of patients, whose individual symptomatology is generally available.

The few single-case studies to mention in closing this subsection all concern Japanese patients who offer the additional interest of being able to show a dissociation between the processing of two forms of logographic script (kanji words and arabic numerals). One such aphasic patient was described by Sasanuma and Monoi (1975). He was severely impaired in language comprehension, whether spoken or written. His most prominent symptom was his greater ability to read aloud kana than kanji words, though with little comprehension in either case. This dissociation is extremely rare in Japanese aphasics, most of whom show a differential ability to process each kind of script being better with kanji than with kana words (Sasanuma, 1974a, 1975). Aside from that, the patient was able to carry out arithmetical operations, and he could read and understand arabic numerals.

The other Japanese patients are alexics with agraphia. Strictly speaking, the syndrome consists of a selective impairment in reading and writing, unaccompanied by any trouble in spoken language comprehension and expression. However, this ideal definition almost always overstates the true state of spoken language performance. It would be closer to reality to say that the most prominent syndrome coexists with mild aphasic troubles (e.g., Hécaen & Kremin, 1976). In these cases, reading impairment is always stronger in kana than in kanji. Yamadori (1975) reported one such patient who was severely impaired in calculation and in number reading. Yamadori also summarized two other reports published in Japanese (Kotani, 1935; Ohashi, 1965, cited by Yamadori, 1975) concerning two other cases of alexia with agraphia accompanied by strong calculation impairments.

Sasanuma (1974b) described a case of alexia with transient agraphia. The patient's reading in both kana and kanji was strongly deficient, performance in kanji being a little better than in kana. "Reading of digits, both Arabic and Chinese was impaired also" (Sasanuma, 1974b, p. 93), but less than for kana and kanji. The patient was good at mental calculation, but written calculation was hampered by his reading problem. Six months later almost all symptoms other than alexia had disappeared, but nothing more specific was stated.

Because of his preservation of mental calculation, the patient of Sasanuma (1974b) is sometimes considered as a counterexample to the observations of Yamadori (1975). Such cannot be the case because it is extremely unlikely that the two patients suffered from the same pathology. Yamadori's patient was alexic with agraphia, whereas the patient of Sasanuma presented all the symptoms of an alexia without agraphia (see next subsection) in which preservation of mental calculation is typical (e.g., Geschwind, 1965; Symonds, 1953).

To sum up, most patients with lesions affecting the language areas of the left hemisphere show various degrees of disintegration of their mathematical abilities and a poor ability to read arabic numerals.

Number Processing by the Disconnected Right Hemisphere

For theoretical reasons that become apparent as we proceed, it is convenient to examine successively the data from patients having one of the following characteristics: (a) alexia without agrahia, (b) section of the splenium (posterior part) of the corpus callosum, (c) commissurotomy, and (d) hemispherectomy.

Alexia without Agraphia.   An ideal patient with alexia without agraphia cannot read, but can write spontaneously and to dictation, without being able to reread what he or she has written. Such a patient has no trouble in spoken language expression or comprehension, but has some difficulties in visual object naming and a strong impairment in color naming; mental calculation is preserved. The classical account of the syndrome by the pioneer neurologists, as revived and specified by Geschwind (1965), describes isolation of the intact left angular gyrus from each occipital visual cortex. This condition is caused by (a) destruction of the left visual cortex or of the connections between the left visual cortex and the left angular gyrus and (b) destruction of the splenium of the corpus callosum, which cuts off from the left hemisphere the visual information reaching the right intact hemisphere. The essence of the trouble is, therefore, the disconnection of intact language zones from the visual world (but not from the auditory or somatosensory world). Logically, the lesions should entail an incapacity to name any visual scene; this is not the case, although it is partially realized by some difficulty in object naming and a very poor ability to name colors. The supplementary hypothesis needed to account for the preserved ability to name objects is that objects can be recognized (but not named) in the right hemisphere and that it is this interpreted information, not the visual information, that is transmitted to the left hemispheric language areas through the intact anterior portion of the corpus callosum. We assume that the right hemisphere is unable to provide verbal responses (see below). By extension, any reading performance preserved (e.g., for arabic numerals) should reflect right hemisphere competence in processing the information. The same rationale is used by Coltheart (1980, 1983) in his attempt to account for deep dyslexic's preserved reading competence (the etiology of this syndrome is different from that of alexia without agraphia).

The recent literature has usually described four of the six alexic patients of

Hécaen and Kremin (1976) as displaying the symptomatology required to fit the ideal model. They all performed better in dealing with arabic numerals than with single letters or single words. Close examination of the constellation of symptoms displayed by these patients reveals that their classification is problematic: Part of their deficit could well be due to some lesion in the language area of the left hemisphere as well. Lack of space precludes any full analysis of this very complex question here. Only a brief account sufficient to make the point is presented, but it should be kept in mind that including of a patient in one of the subgroups of Table 3.2 is often tentative because we generally lack the decisive anatomo-clinical data to remove the uncertainty. For example, the inclusion of Stengel, Vienna, and Edin's (1948) two patients in the group consisting of close to ideal cases would be disputed by Oxbury, Oxbury, and Humphrey (1969).

Table 3.2 includes many of the cases of alexia without agraphia reported in the literature published in English between 1948 and 1976. All the tabulated cases are bad at reading words, and most of them are relatively better at reading arabic numerals than letters. They can be further differentiated on the basis of several features, among which four have been selected for the present discussion. These features are (a) presence or absence of a right hemianopsia, (b) color-naming performance, (c) spelling performance, and (d) mental calculation performance. Spelling is evaluated either by the ability of a patient to spell and to recognize orally spelled words or by his use of a spelling strategy in attempting to read words. A good mental calculation performance indicates that very simple arithmetic operations can be performed. Here follows the description of the groups.

Group 1: These patients are close to the ideal model in showing an anatomically verified (Cumming, Hurwitz, & Perl, 1970; Geschwind & Fusillo, 1966) or presumed brain infarction (Benson, Brown, & Tomlinson, 1971, Cases 1 to 3; Holmes, 1950; Kreindler & Ionăşescu, 1961; Oxbury et al., 1969, Case 1; Sasanuma 1974b; Stengel et al., 1948). The infarction is of the left occipital lobe (responsible for the hemianopsia) and of the splenium, both caused by some pathology of the left posterior cerebral artery. The 11 patients show a very consistent pattern of results. They all exhibit the right hemianopsia expected from their lesion in the left visual cortex. When investigated, spelling and mental calculation are always good and color naming is always bad except in one case (Cumming et al., 1970). Even the last case does not cast doubt on the homogeneity of this group of patients because the dorsal part of the splenium was preserved in this patient; this could allow for a transfer of the visual color information from the right occipital lobe to the left angular gyrus (see Greenblatt, 1973, for further discussion of this point). It is clear that the case of Sasanuma (1974b) reviewed in the preceding subsection fits perfectly well in this group of patients. It could be tentatively concluded that the right hemisphere of these patients has a much better abilit to identify arabic numerals than letters or phonographically written words.

Group 2: The four cases included in this group are remarkable for their lack of

TABLE 3.2
Tentative Classification of Cases of Alexia Without Agraphia
Reported Between 1948 and 1976

Authors	Patients	Hemianopsia	Spelling	Mental calcul.	Color naming	Word naming	Letter naming	Single digit naming
		Group 1: Close to ideal cases with minimal additional deficits						
Stengel et al., 1948	1	yes	good	good	bad	bad	medium	good
	2	yes	good	good	?	bad	good	good
Holmes, 1950		yes	good	good	bad	bad	bad	good
Kreindler & Ionăşescu, 1961		yes	?	good	bad	bad	medium	good
Geschwind & Fusillo, 1966		yes	?	?	bad	bad	bad	good
Oxbury et al., 1969	1	yes	?	?	bad	bad	medium	good
Cumming et al., 1970	1	yes	good	good	good	bad	bad	good
Benson et al., 1971	2	yes	good	good	bad	bad	medium	good
	3	yes	good	?	bad	bad	medium	?
		yes	good	good	bad	bad	good	?
Sasanuma, 1974b		yes	good[a]	good	medium	bad	—	medium
		Group 2: Close to ideal cases with potential additional deficits						
Ajax, 1967	1	transient	good	good	good	medium	good	good
Goldstein et al., 1971		no	?	good	good	bad	bad	medium
Heilman et al., 1971	1	no	good	medium	bad	bad	bad	?
Greenblatt, 1973		no	?	good	good	bad	good	good

	Group 3: Nonideal cases with attested additional lesions						
Warrington & Zangwill, 1957	yes	good	bad	bad	bad	medium	good
Ajax, 1964	1	yes	good	good	good	medium	good	good
Kinsbourne & Warrington, 1964	no	bad	medium	bad	bad	good	good
Caplan & Hedley-Whyte, 1974	yes	good	bad	bad	bad	bad	bad
D. N. Cohen et al., 1976	yes	?	medium	medium	bad	good	?
Group 4: Hécaen and Kremin's (1976) presumably nonideal cases		b	b	b	c	c	c
Hécaen & Kremin, 1976 — CRO	yes	good	bad	good	20%	100%	100%
DEL	yes	good	bad	medium	6%	86%	100%
SAL	yes	good	medium	good	12%	70%	82%
CLI[d]	yes	medium	bad	medium	0%	0%	32%
BLA[e]	Quadr. sup.	?	medium	good	30%	20%	92%
MAG[e]	Quadr. sup.	good	good	good	85%	100%	100%

Note. An ideal case is characterized by (a) a destruction of the left visual cortex or of the connections between the left visual cortex and the left angular gyrus and (b) a destruction of the splenium of the corpus callosum.

[a] Spelling of kana characters.
[b] From Table 1 (p. 298).
[c] Percent correct from Figs. 4 to 9 (pp. 305–308).
[d] Mild agraphia.
[e] Strong agraphia.

right hemianopsia, indicating an intact left visual cortex. This can be related to the etiology of their trouble, which is different from that of patients in Group 1. The cause of the alexia was either a surgical removal of a vascular anomaly (Ajax, 1967, Case 1), a carbon monoxide intoxication (Goldstein, Joynt, & Goldblatt, 1971), a head trauma (Heilman, Safran, & Geschwind, 1971, Case 1), or a tumor (Greenblatt, 1973). In the last case anatomical analysis of the brain showed that the tumor had destroyed the splenium of the corpus callosum and part, but not all, of the connections between the intact left visual cortex and the left angular gyrus. One can tentatively hypothesize that the connections needed to transmit color information to the left angular gyrus were also preserved in two of the other patients. If this were indeed the case, these four patients, showing good spelling and good mental calculation, could be considered examples of the ideal model of alexia without agraphia as good as those of Group 1. However, it seems unlikely, in view of the etiologies of these alexias, that the brain damage was really so selectively localized. We cannot preclude the possibility that the language areas have been more or less affected as well, rendering those cases potentially less conclusive than those of Group 1 with respect to the assessment of right hemisphere competence in number identification.

Group 3: The patients in this group are certainly the least appropriate for our purposes because their left occipital lesion extended to the parietal lobe as well and because we generally do not know whether the splenium was lesioned or not (Ajax, 1964, Case 1; D. N. Cohen, Salanga, Hully, Steinberg, & Hardy, 1976; Kinsbourne & Warrington, 1964; Warrington & Zangwill, 1957). The patient of Caplan and Hedley-Whyte (1974) had an anatomically verified lesion of the left occipital cortex and of the splenium, but she suffered from additional small left parietal lesions. This can explain why this patient had dyscalculia, finger agnosia, and left-right confusion. The heterogeneity of performance in this group contrasts with the homogeneity of performance of Group 1 patients, which could support the idea either of a pathology different from that of alexia without agraphia, or, at least, of the existence of supplementary problems compared with the ideal model. Therefore, these data cannot safely be used to infer anything about right hemisphere competence.

Group 4: This group includes the six alexics studied by Hécaen and Kremin (1976). It is immediately apparent that all six patients would fall in our third group, even though three of them are generally considered as ideal cases of alexia without agraphia (CRO, DEL, SAL). CLI, who is slightly agraphic, is generally assimilated to the nonagraphic patients, whereas BLA and MAG are dissociated from them on the basis of their strong agraphia. It is clear that none of these patients presents the profile of those of Group 1 in having good spelling and mental calculation and poor color naming. Within the group of four patients with a right hemianopsia, only SAL is attested as suffering from a lesion of vascular origin sufficiently selective to affect only the occipital lobe. Although his performances depart from those of patients in Group 1, he is the only one whose inclusion in this group might be defended.

In summary, we can probably safely rely on the patients of Group 1 in attempting to assess the right hemisphere ability to process visual symbols semantically. Some other cases are probably valid as well, but we have enough patients in Group 1 to adopt a conservative position, excluding all others from further discussion.

Section of the Splenium of the Corpus Callosum.   The logic of the interpretation of alexia without agraphia implies that, under LVF tachistoscopic presentations, a patient whose only lesion is a section of the splenium of the corpus callosum should exhibit exactly the same reading performance as an alexic without agraphia. To our knowledge, only six such cases have been reported, three of them being examined at a time at which the hemifield presentation technique was not well developed. All six cases had their splenium severed in the process of removing a subcortical small tumor. The patient of Trescher and Ford (1937) could not recognize letters presented in the LVF (for what duration?), but other symptoms, such as a left-hand astereognosis, did not guarantee that the splenium section was the only damage suffered by the patient. The two patients studied by Maspes (1948) did not present any hand astereognosis (for wooden letters). Letters and arabic numerals presented for 1 or 0.5s were very well recognized in the RVF, but not in the LVF, as expected. Three similar Japanese cases have been reported in the recent literature (Sugishita, Iwata, Toyokura, Yoshioka, & Yamada 1978). With RVF brief presentations (66 ms), oral reading and comprehension of both kana and kanji words were almost perfect. With LVF presentations, performance was poorer, being at chance level for kana, but somewhat better than chance for kanji. Moreover, performance improved relatively more with kanji than with kana when the same material was retested two or three times at intervals of several months. Unfortunately, numbers were not tested.

Sugishita et al. (1978) interpreted their results as showing that the right hemisphere can understand the logographic kanji better than the phonographic kana; this is consonant with the better recognition of arabic numerals than of letters or alphabetically written words by alexics without agraphia. It is unfortunate that Maspes (1948) did not systematically investigate the difference in performance for letters and arabic numerals. Sugishita et al. also assumed that the vocal response was given by the left hemisphere, not by the right one. This implies that, however accurately identified the LVF stimuli were, naming could not have been achieved at all if the corpus callosum were completely sectioned. This brings us to the next stage in our review.

Commissurotomy.   The initial investigation of patients having undergone a complete section of the interhemispheric commissures revealed the very poor language competence of the right hemisphere in most cases (see Gazzaniga, 1970). However, two patients of the California series (L.B. and N.G.) and three patients of the East Coast series (P.S., J.W., and V.P.) show a considerable right hemisphere language comprehension (both spoken and written). In addition, within 2 years following commissurotomy, P.S. and V.P. have developed the ability to access speech from the right hemisphere (see Gazzaniga, 1983). All these patients have a complete section of the corpus callosum and the hippocampal commissure. Most patients of the California series, including L.B. and N.G., also have a section of the anterior commissure, whereas most patients of the East Coast series, including P.S., J.W., and V.P., do not.

Recognition performance for letters and arabic numerals was investigated in six patients of the California series by Teng and Sperry (1973). In one condition, pairs of letters or of arabic numerals were presented either in the LVF or in the RVF, calling for a verbal report. With RVF presentations 86% of the letters and 80% of the digits were named correctly, whereas with LVF presentations these scores dropped to 13% and 35%, respectively. Notice that one patient, N.W., made 100% errors with LVF presentations of both letters and numerals and that L.B. reported only 22% of letters, but 80% of arabic numerals from the LVF. In another experiment involving fewer numerals (Gazzaniga & Hillyard, 1971), L.B. described a strategy of enumerating the numbers and stopping when the response popped out, which the authors found compatible with the idea that the response was actually generated in the left hemisphere through cross-cuing with the right hemisphere. This strategy should be easier to use with single-digit numbers than with letters because the set is smaller in the former than in the latter case. Whether L.B. or the other often-tested patients used in Teng and Sperry's (1973) experiment were using a similar strategy is not known, but it cannot be ruled out. Hence, these data are not strong enough either to challenge the hypothesis of the muteness of the right hemisphere, or to provide unequivocal evidence of a greater intrinsic ability of this hemisphere to deal with arabic numerals than with letters.

Gazzaniga and Smylie (1984) tested two of the right hemisphere language-proficient patients of the East Coast series, V.P. and J.W. Both patients showed errorless performance in multiple-choice pointing to numbers presented to the right hemisphere (LVF). V.P. was also able to read these numbers aloud perfectly well, whereas J.W. was completely unable to do so. Both patients showed extremely poor performance in carrying out simple arithmetic operations with the right hemisphere.

The data of Gazzaniga and Smylie (1984) are compatible with the idea that the left hemisphere normally subserves calculation (see preceding subsection) and that the right hemisphere can identify numbers. However, multidigit number identification in probably better in these two patients than in most patients showing the ideal symptomatology of alexia without agraphia. The extent to which these data can be generalized to the entire population of commissurotomized patients, and, a fortiori, to normal people, is debatable (see Gazzaniga, 1983, and Zaidel, 1983, for somewhat opposite views on this question).

Hemispherectomy. The last logical step in this story is to assess the number-processing ability of a completely isolated right hemisphere, the left hemisphere having been removed completely (actually the left cortex, the left subcortical structures being almost entirely preserved).

Gott (1973) described such a patient who underwent a left hemispherectomy at the age of 10 years because of malignancy. She had already undergone brain surgery at the age of 8 for removal of a tumor in the left ventricule. When she was tested 2 years after the hemispherectomy, she showed good comprehension of spoken language but very poor verbal expression (mainly single words or short stereotyped sentences) and very poor reading of single words. She was unable to name a single letter presented visually or to choose above chance (30% correct) which of four visually displayed letters was the one just spoken by the experimenter, but she performed much better in this task when arabic numerals were used instead of letters (80% correct). When Zaidel (1976) tested her one year later, using a similar procedure, she was a little better in pointing to a spoken multidigit number (out of six) than to a spoken letter.

The description given by Hillier (1954) of the performance of his patient is more anecdotal. After three surgical interventions in the left hemisphere during the preceding 15 months, a complete hemispherectomy was finally performed. The patient was 14 years old at the time of the first intervention. Each intervention left him with severe aphasic troubles, indicating that language functions were subserved by his left hemisphere. However, after hemispherectomy, he was described as having good comprehension of spoken language and an ability to say some words and to read single letters.

However poor the verbal performance of these two patients may appear, it is nevertheless much better than would have been expected if the right hemisphere were completely unable to subserve any linguistic function. Due to the youth of the patients, no generalization of this conclusion is allowed because the plasticity of the nervous system is probably still important at that age. This plasticity is now well documented in patients who have undergone hemidecortication because of infantile hemiplegia, accompanied by intractable seizures. It is clear that if the illness starts before the age of one year the healthy hemisphere, whether right or left, subserves all the functions normally shared between two hemispheres (McFie, 1961). In these cases it requires subtle testing with tasks varying in complexity to show that patients retaining their left hemispheres are relatively better at complex syntax comprehension than those retaining their right hemispheres (Dennis, 1980a; Dennis & Kohn, 1975), whereas the opposite relation between relative levels of performance holds for complex spatial tasks (Kohn & Dennis, 1974). Hence, behind the tremendous plasticity shown by each hemisphere in developing functions for which it is usually less proficient, there seems to be an irreducible difference in processing ability as well.

At the other extreme, two adults with left hemispherectomy (performed to remove tumors developed during adulthood) revealed extremely poor verbal ability, but not its complete lack (McFie, 1961). Between the age of one year and some unknown upper limit, the brain seems to keep some of its initial plasticity, allowing each hemisphere to develop abilities for which it is normally not very proficient (McFie, 1961). The two patients just described (Gott, 1973; Hillier, 1954) were probably still in this phase.

A thorough examination of the linguistic abilities of the left and right hemispheres has been undertaken by Dennis and her colleagues (Dennis, 1980b; Dennis, Lovett, & Wiegel-Crump, 1981; Dennis & Whitaker, 1976) on one case of right hemidecortication and two cases of left hemidecortication, performed before the age of 5 months. The examinations published to date took place when the children were between 9 and 14 years old. One fascinating finding of these studies is that equal performances in decoding written words can be mediated by different mental representations. The child retaining his left hemisphere shows a good awareness of the phonological structure of language: His reading draws on morphophonological properties of English orthography, and he reveals a tacit knowledge of rules that map writing onto speech when he reads new or unfamiliar words. None of these abilities is displayed by the two children retaining their right hemispheres. Yet with known words, their reading performance is equivalent to that of the child retaining his left hemisphere. Only with unknown words does their performance disintegrate; this shows that their word knowledge is not based on a morphophonological representation, so that they cannot exploit English orthographical principles to decode new words. These findings are remarkably well in line with the ideas developed by Mattingly (1972, 1984) concerning the relation between proficient reading and the availability of morphophonological representations of words in the mental lexicon. This author has also stressed that spoken language comprehension is probably less dependent on the existence of such representations than is reading (Mattingly, 1984). This claim is supported by the failure of Dennis and Whitaker (1976) to demonstrate differences in the abilities of left and right hemidecorticate children in their ability to deal with the phonemic and semantic aspects of spoken language. We may also note that a capacity for syntactic processing was much greater in the child retaining his left hemisphere than in the other two children. This is consonant with other data mentioned earlier (Dennis, 1980a; Dennis & Kohn, 1975).

Conclusions

The most important point of this section is the contrast between the disintegration of calculation and arabic numeral reading caused by lesions in the language areas of the left hemisphere and the relative preservation of these abilities by patients showing a disconnection between intact language areas and the visual cortex.

The only point left for discussion is the interpretation of the better identification of arabic numerals than of letters by the 11 alexics without agraphia of Group 1, those for whom the presumption of a pure disconnection syndrome is most likely to be correct. All these patients had their language functions located in the left hemisphere, they did not display any known cerebral brain disorder before their alexia, and the syndrome was caused by brain lesions in adulthood. Hence, these patients are the best suited for the assessment of the ability of the right hemisphere to deal with visual symbols.

A first possible explanation of the better performance with arabic numerals than with letters is that it is simply easier to discriminate 1 visual symbol out of 10 possible visual configurations than 1 out of 26 possibilities. We find this extremely unlikely. Both sets of symbols have evolved from the need to allow efficient reading. They incontestably succeed in doing so, especially under the temporally unlimited viewing conditions typical of the neuropsychological examination.

Far more likely is that performance is determined by the extent to which the right hemisphere can process the meaning of different stimuli. In essence, this amounts to proposing exactly the same schema of interpretation as that used by Geschwind (1965) to explain the differential ability to name objects and colors. Remember that the two basic assumptions are that (a) only the left hemisphere can generate a naming response. and (b) although visual information reaching the right hemisphere cannot be transmitted to the left hemisphere because the splenial route is sectioned, the information can be transferred, once it has been given a semantic interpretation, through the anterior intact portion of the corpus callosum. Hence, the solution of the problem should be sought by analyzing the nature of the semantic information conveyed by letters and arabic numerals.

The meaning of a letter is determined by the phonological unit of the spoken language to which it refers and by its relation with other similar units. In other words, the meaning of a letter is defined in terms of properties that the right hemisphere is unable to process, even when it has developed an idiosyncratic language competence, due to complete loss of the left hemisphere (Dennis et al., 1981). A fortiori, a right hemisphere that has never faced the problem of associating sounds to letters should be even less able to extract their meaning. This entails that, beyond the untransmittable visual information, there is simply no other form of information that can be conveyed to the left hemisphere. In this vein, the very poor performance of alexics without agraphia in reading and understanding phonographically written words argues for the hypothesis that word recognition is mediated by letter or syllable (kana) recognition.

By contrast, arabic numerals have a meaning in a symbolic system that has nothing to do with phonology. There is therefore no reason why the right hemisphere could not generate a semantic representation of the digit and transfer it to the other side, a task it seems able to perform with objects as well. This explanation is consonant with the better ability of the right hemisphere to interpret kanji logograms than kana phonograms (Sasanuma, 1974b; Sugishita et al., 1978).

In concluding this section it is worth specifying the exact scope of the interpretation of the right hemisphere's better performance with arabic numerals than with letters. Arabic-numeral reading in alexia without agraphia is not always perfect, and this points to the fact that, though feasible, the task is nevertheless strained. The inefficiency of the procedure is also demonstrated by the fact that the reading of multidigit numbers is rarely preserved. This would not be the case if transmission of the component numerals to the left hemisphere were more efficient. At present, we do not know whether the poor naming performance is caused by inadequacy of the semantic representation generated in the right hemisphere, or by the poor ability of the corpus callosum in transmitting interpreted rather than raw sensory information, or both. A final point worth emphasizing is that although we may conclude from the performance of brain-damaged patients that the right hemisphere has some ability to process arabic numerals, we may not conclude that it is superior to the left hemisphere in doing so.

SUMMARY AND CONCLUSIONS

Let us take the different points in the reverse order to their presentation in the chapter.

1. With respect to brain-injured patients, the fact that (a) number processing is strongly, but perhaps not fully, dependent on the integrity of the language areas of the left hemisphere and (b) these areas can be disconnected from the visual information reaching the right hemisphere allows us to assess the differential ability of this hemisphere to deal with various surface forms of numbers and of other types of visual information. Hemifield presentation of stimuli is a useful technique in this framework. An understanding of how the information is processed will require both the general progress of the analytical power of cognitive psychology as a whole and the comprehension of the basic modes of processing of each hemisphere in particular.

2. As for lateral hemifield presentation of stimuli to normal subjects, we may doubt whether the technique will help us to achieve either or both of the requirements just mentioned, at least insofar as one adopts a multicomponental view of processing. The analysis of the problem presented at the end of the third section is, of course, not the only one possible. However, it is based on the simplest and most tractable view of processing we have, and this casts serious doubt on the ability of the approach to fare better in more complex theoretical frameworks. The results show a RVF advantage for both logographic and phonographic number representations. Whether this pattern of results should be considered at odds with claims for a LVF advantage in the processing of logograms in general depends on the validity of this assertion, which is still controversial.

3. As regards numerical size comparison judgments, two of the basic effects—symbolic distance and serial position—were found to be independent of

the surface form of the stimuli in experiments published to date. By inference from related data we hypothesized that such will also prove to be the case for a third effect—semantic congruity—for which the information is still lacking. The Stroop-like task leading to a size congruity effect has been judged too complicated to provide useful, nonparadigm-bound information, a conclusion that extends to hemifield presentations for the reasons just invoked. The strategy of research illustrated in this approach could, of course, be extended to cover a variety of questions about the basic knowledge associated with single-digit numbers. One can, for instance, use the same paradigm in comparison judgments related to the odd versus even, prime versus nonprime, multiple of two versus nonmultiple of two questions. The task need not be an explicit comparison between two numbers; it can also take the form of judging whether a single number possesses the property under investigation.

4. Three points should be made about the discussion of number representations.

First, concerning multidigit number processing, it seems appropriate to distinguish between arabic numerals and number names irrespective of the surface form of the latter. The facts that arabic numerals belong to a different, more abstract notational system and that they are also intimately bound to mathematical activities make them a priori distinct from number names. The irrelevance of the surface form can be further emphasized by predicting that Japanese (or Chinese) aphasics would show the same difficulty in transcoding multidigit numbers written in one logographic form into another logographic form (arabic numerals into kanji words and vice versa) as occidental aphasics have in transcoding these same numbers represented logographically (arabic numerals) into alphabetically written number names, and vice versa (Deloche & Seron, 1982; Seron & Deloche, 1984).

Second, as soon as one focuses on the processing of single-digit numbers, the characteristics of the notational system of which the number representations are the elements cease to play a prominent role, whereas the nature of the surface form of the numbers now becomes the important variable. We should expect that access to the stored knowledge associated with these elements would be influenced by factors affecting the reading of any kind of word. From this point of view it is, therefore, appropriate to regroup the symbols into a logographic and a phonographic category, irrespective of the underlying notational system. With normal subjects, we expect the surface form of the number to affect the speed with which their conceptual knowledge is accessed, but we expect the characteristics of this knowledge, as revealed by the pattern of interactions between different variables, to be the same irrespective of the surface form of the numbers. As far as the available evidence goes, this belief is not yet contradicted (cf. conclusion 3).

Third, single-digit number processing by adult brain-injured people could lead to a more complex picture. One should consider two cases. If, on the one hand, the language areas of the left hemisphere are intact, but disconnected from the visual cortex (ideal cases of alexia without agraphia or LVF presentations with section of the splenium of the corpus callosum), the right intact hemisphere could translate the visual numbers into interpreted representations transmissible to the left hemisphere, provided the numbers are represented logographically (one should also allow for the possibility that the right hemisphere may learn to process the small set of phonographic numbers as if they were logograms). In this case, a task could be performed according to the normal synergic activity of the hemispheres of an intact brain, leading to a performance qualitatively equivalent to that of normal subjects, save for some eventual loss in efficiency. If, on the other hand, the language areas of the left hemisphere are injured and if the task can be performed at all, then performance should be at least partially determined by right hemisphere competence in dealing with numbers. A performance qualitatively different from that of normal subjects could then be considered an index of the idiosyncracy of the right hemisphere's knowledge of numbers. The nature of the right hemisphere competence could then be studied in commissurotomized patients, provided the cognitive capacities of the right hemisphere of these severely epileptic people could be considered representative of those of normal subjects.

ACKNOWLEDGMENTS

This chapter was written while the first author was a guest at Haskins Laboratories, New Haven, CT. We are grateful to Michael Studdert-Kennedy for his thorough comments and his suggestions for style improvement of an earlier version. Thanks are also due to Noriko Kobayashi for providing information about number writing in Japan and to Nancy O'Brien for editing the manuscript. This work has been partially supported by NIH grant HD-01994 to Haskins Laboratories, by the Belgian "Fonds de la Recherche Fondamentale Collective" (F.R.F.C.) under convention 2.4505.80 (with P. Bertelson), by the Research Council of this University, and by the Ministry of Scientific Policy (Action de Recherche concertée "Processus cognitifs dans la lecture"). The sojourn of the first author in the United States was supported by the University and partially subsidized by a NATO grant for scientific research. Requests for reprints should be sent to Daniel Holender, Laboratoire de Psychologie expérimentale, 117 avenue Adolphe Buyl, C.P. 191, B-1050 Brussels, Belgium.

REFERENCES

Aiken, L. R., & Williams, F. N. (1968). Three variables related to reaction time to compare single-digit numbers. *Perceptual and Motor Skills, 27,* 197–206.
Ajax, E. T. (1964). Acquired dyslexia. *Archives of Neurology, 11,* 66–72.

Ajax, E. T. (1967). Dyslexia without agraphia. *Archives of Neurology, 17,* 645–652.

Allen, M. (1983). Models of hemispheric specialization. *Psychological Bulletin, 93,* 73–104.

Banks, W. P. (1977). Encoding and processing of symbolic information in comparative judgments. In G. H. Bower (Ed.), *The psychology of learning and motivation* (Vol. 11, pp. 101–159). New York: Academic Press.

Banks, W. P., Clark, H. H., & Lucy, P. (1975). The locus of the semantic congruity effect in comparative judgments. *Journal of Experimental Psychology: Human Perception and Performance, 1,* 35–47.

Banks, W. P., & Flora, J. (1977). Semantic and perceptual processes in symbolic comparisons. *Journal of Experimental Psychology: Human Perception and Performance, 3,* 278–290.

Banks, W. P., Fujii, M., & Kayra-Stuart, F. (1976). Semantic congruity effects in comparative judgments of magnitudes of digits. *Journal of Experimental Psychology: Human Perception and Performance, 2,* 435–447.

Benson, D. F., Brown, J., & Tomlinson, E. B. (1971). Varieties of alexia. *Neurology, 21,* 951–957.

Bertelson, P. (1982). Lateral differences in normal man and lateralization of brain functions. *International Journal of Psychology, 17,* 173–210.

Besner, D., & Coltheart, M. (1976). Mental size scaling examined. *Memory and Cognition, 4,* 525–531.

Besner, D., & Coltheart, M. (1979). Ideographic and alphabetic processing in skilled reading of English. *Neuropsychologia, 17,* 467–472.

Besner, D., Daniels, S., & Slade, C. (1982). Ideogram reading and right hemisphere language. *British Journal of Psychology, 73,* 21–28.

Besner, D., Davelaar, E., Alcott, D., & Parry, P. (1984). Wholistic reading of alphabetic print: Evidence from the FDM and the FBI. In L. Henderson (Ed.), *Orthographies and reading* (pp. 121–135). Hillsdale, NJ: Lawrence Erlbaum Associates.

Besner, D., Grimsell, D., & Davis, R. (1979). The mind's eye and the comparative judgment of number. *Neuropsychologia, 17,* 373–380.

Bryden, M. P. (1978). Strategy effects in the assessment of hemispheric asymmetry. In G. Underwood (Ed.), *Strategies of information processing* (pp. 117–149). London: Academic Press.

Bryden, M. P. (1982). *Laterality: Functional asymmetry in the intact brain.* New York: Academic Press.

Buckley, P. B., & Gillman, C. B. (1974). Comparisons of digits and dot patterns. *Journal of Experimental Psychology, 103,* 1131–1136.

Caplan, L. R., & Hedley-Whyte, T. (1974). Cuing and memory dysfunction in alexia without agraphia: A case report. *Brain, 97,* 251–262.

Caramazza, A. (1984). The neuropsychological research and the problem of patient classification in aphasia. *Brain and Language, 21,* 9–20.

Carmon, A., Nachshon, I., & Starinsky, R. (1976). Developmental aspects of visual hemifield differences in perception of verbal material. *Brain and Language, 3,* 463–469.

Cohen, D. N., Salanga, V. D., Hully, W., Steinberg, M. C., & Hardy, R. W. (1976). Alexia without agraphia. *Neurology, 26,* 455–459.

Cohen, G. (1975). Hemisphere differences in the effects of cuing in visual recognition tasks. *Journal of Experimental Psychology: Human Perception and Performance, 4,* 366–373.

Cohen, G. (1982). Theoretical interpretations of lateral asymmetries. In J. G. Beaumont (Ed.), *Divided visual field studies of cerebral organisation* (pp. 87–111). New York: Academic Press.

Coltheart, M. (1980). Deep dyslexia: A right hemisphere hypothesis. In M. Coltheart, K. Patterson, & J. C. Marshall (Eds.), *Deep dxslexia* (pp. 326–380). London: Routledge & Kegan Paul.

Coltheart, M. (1983). The right hemisphere and disorders of reading. In A. Young (Ed.), *Functions of the right cerebral hemisphere* (pp. 171–201). London: Academic Press.

Craft, J. L., & Simon, J. R. (1970). Processing symbolic information from a visual display. Interference from an irrelevant directional cue. *Journal of Experimental Psychology, 83,* 415–420.

Cumming, W. J. K., Hurwitz, L. J., & Perl, N. T. (1970). A study of a patient who had alexia without agraphia. *Journal of Neurology, Neurosurgery, and Psychiatry, 33,* 34–39.

Dahmen, W., Hartje, W., Büssing, A., & Sturm, W. (1982). Disorders of calculation in aphasic patients—Spatial and verbal components. *Neuropsychologia, 20,* 145–153.

Deloche, G., & Seron, X. (1982). From one to 1: An analysis of a transcoding process by means of neuropsychological data. *Cognition, 12,* 119–149.

Dennis, M. (1980a). Capacity and strategy for syntactic comprehension after left or right hemidecortication. *Brain and Language, 10,* 287–317.

Dennis, M. (1980b). Language acquisition in a single hemisphere: Semantic organization. In D. Caplan (Ed.), *Biological studies of mental processes* (pp. 159–185). Cambridge, MA: MIT Press.

Dennis, M., & Kohn, B. (1975). Comprehension of syntax in infantile hemiplegics after cerebral hemidecortication: Left-hemisphere superiority. *Brain and Language, 2,* 472–482.

Dennis, M., Lovett, M., & Wiegel-Crump, C. A. (1981). Written language acquisition after left or right hemidecortication in infancy. *Brain and Language, 12,* 54–91.

Dennis, M., & Whitaker, H. A. (1976). Language acquisition following hemidecortication: Linguistic superiority of the left over the right hemisphere. *Brain and Language, 3.* 404–433.

Dixon, P., & Just, M. A. (1978). Normalization of irrelevant dimensions in stimulus comparisons. *Journal of Experimental Psychology: Human Perception and Performance, 4,* 36–46.

Duncan, E. M., & McFarland, C. E., Jr. (1980). Isolating the effects of symbolic distance and semantic congruity in comparative judgments: An additive-factors analysis. *Memory and Cognition, 8,* 612–622.

Edgerton, W. F. (1941). Ideograms in English writing. *Language, 17,* 148–150.

Endo, M., Shimizu, A., & Hori, T. (1978). Functional asymmetry of visual fields for Japanese words in Kana (syllable-based) writing and randon shape-recognition in Japanese subjects. *Neuropsychologia, 16,* 291–297.

Ferro, J. M., & Botelho, M. A. S. (1980). Alexia for arithmetical signs: A cause of disturbed calculation. *Cortex, 16,* 175–180.

Flegg, G. (1983). *Numbers: Their history and meaning.* New York: Schocken Books.

Foltz, G. S., Poltrock, S. E., & Potts, G. R. (1984). Mental comparison of size and magnitude: Size congruity effects. *Journal of Experimental Psychology: Learning, Memory, and Cognition, 10,* 442–453.

Gazzaniga, M. S. (1970). *The bisected brain.* New York: Appleton-Century-Crofts.

Gazzaniga, M. S. (1983). Right hemisphere language following brain bisection. *American Psychologist, 38,* 525–537.

Gazzaniga, M. S., & Hillyard, S. A. (1971). Language and speech capacity of the right hemisphere. *Neuropsychologia, 9,* 273–280.

Gazzaniga, M. S., & Smylie, C. S. (1984). Dissociation of language and cognition. *Brain, 107,* 145–153.

Geffen, G., Bradshaw, J. L., & Nettleton, N. C. (1973). Attention and hemispheric differences in reaction time during simultaneous audio-visual tasks. *Quarterly Journal of Experimental Psychology, 25,* 404–412.

Geffen, G., Bradshaw, J. L., & Wallace, G. (1971). Interhemispheric effects on reaction time to verbal and nonverbal visual stimuli. *Journal of Experimental Psychology, 87,* 415–422.

Gelb, I. J. (1963). *A study of writing.* Chicago: University of Chicago Press.

Geschwind, N. (1965). Disconnexion syndromes in animal and man: Part I. *Brain, 85,* 237–294.

Geschwind, N., & Fusillo, M. (1966). Color-naming defects in association with alexia. *Archives of Neurology, 15,* 137–146.

Gleitman, L. R., & Rozin, P. (1977). The structure and acquisition of reading I: Relations between orthographies and the structure of language. In A. S. Reber & D. L. Scarborough (Eds.), *Toward a psychology of reading: The proceedings of the CUNY conference* (pp. 1–53). Hillsdale, NJ: Lawrence Erlbaum Associates.

Goldstein, M. N., Joynt, R. J., & Goldblatt, D. (1971). Word blindness with intact central visual field. *Neurology, 21*, 873–876.

Gordon, H. W., & Carmon, A. (1976). Transfer of dominance in speed of verbal response to visually presented stimuli from right to left hemisphere. *Perceptual and Motor Skills, 42*, 1091–1100.

Gott, P. S. (1973). Language after dominant hemispherectomy. *Journal of Neurology, Neurosurgery, and Psychiatry, 36*, 1082–1088.

Greenblatt, S. H. (1973). Alexia without agraphia or hemianopsia. *Brain, 96*, 307–316.

Hatta, T. (1977a). Lateral recognition of abstract and concrete Kanji in Japanese. *Perceptual and Motor Skills, 45*, 731–734.

Hatta, T. (1977b). Recognition of Japanese Kanji in the left and the right visual fields. *Neuropsychologia, 15*, 685–688.

Hatta, T. (1978). Recognition of Japanese Kanji and Hirakana in the left and the right visual fields. *The Japanese Psychological Research, 20*, 51–59.

Hatta, T. (1983). Visual field differences in semantic comparative judgments with digits and Kanji stimulus materials. *Neuropsychologia, 21*, 669–678.

Hatta, T., & Dimond, S. J. (1980). Comparison of lateral differences for digit and random form recognition in Japanese and Westerners. *Journal of Experimental Psychology: Human Perception and Performance, 6*, 368–374.

Hécaen, H., Angelergues, R., & Houillier, S. (1961). Les variétés cliniques des acalculies au cours des lésions rétrorolandiques: Approche statistique du problème. *Revue Neurologique, 105*, 86–103.

Hécaen, H., & Kremin, H. (1976). Neurolinguistic research on reading disorders resulting from left hemisphere lesions: Aphasic and "pure" alexias. In H. Whitaker & H. A. Whitaker (Eds.), *Studies in neurolinguistics* (Vol. 2, pp. 269–329). New York: Academic Press.

Heilman, K. M., Safran, A. & Geschwind, N. (1971). Closed head trauma and aphasia. *Journal of Neurology, Neurosurgery, and Psychiatry, 34*, 265–269.

Henderson, L. (Ed.). (1984). *Orthographies and reading.* Hillsdale, NJ: Lawrence Erlbaum Associates.

Henik, A., & Tzelgov, J. (1982). Is three greater than five: The relation between physical and semantic size in comparison tasks. *Memory & Cognition, 10*, 389–395.

Hillier, W. F. (1954). Total left cerebral hemispherectomy for malignant glioma. *Neurology, 4*, 718–721.

Hines, D., & Satz, P. (1971). Superiority of right visual half-fields in right-handers for recall of digits presented at varying rates. *Neuropsychologia, 9*, 21–25.

Hines, D., & Satz, P. (1974). Cross-modal asymmetries in perception related to asymmetry in cerebral functions. *Neuropsychologia, 12*, 239–247.

Hines, D., Satz, P., Schell, B., & Schmidlin, S. (1969). Differential recall of digits in the left and right visual half-fields under free and fixed order of recall. *Neuropsychologia, 7*, 13–22.

Hirata, K., & Osaka, R. (1967). Tachistoscopic recognition of Japanese letter materials in left and right visual fields. *Psychologia, 10*, 7–18.

Holender, D. (1987). Synchronic description of present-day writing systems: Some implications for reading research. In J. K. O'Regan & A. Lévy-Schoen (Eds.), *Eye movements: From physiology to cognition.* Amsterdam: Elsevier Science Publisher (North Holland).

Holmes, G. (1950). Pure word blindness. *Folia Psychiatrica, Neurologica et Neurochirurgica Neerlandica, 53*, 279–288.

Katz, A. N. (1980). Cognitive arithmetic: Evidence for right hemispheric mediation in an elementary component stage. *Quarterly Journal of Experimental Psychology, 32*, 69–84.

Katz, A. N. (1981). Spatial compatibility effects with hemifield presentation in a unimanual two-finger task. *Canadian Journal of Psychology, 35*, 63–68.

Kelley, D. H. (1976). *Deciphering the Maya script.* Austin, TX: University of Texas Press.

Kinsbourne, M., & Warrington, E. K. (1964). Observation on colour agnosia. *Journal of Neurology, Neurosurgery, and Psychiatry, 27*, 296–299.

Kohn, B., & Dennis, M. (1974). Selective impairments of visuo-spatial abilities in infantile hemiplegics after right cerebral hemidecortication. *Neuropsychologia, 12,* 505–512.

Krantz, D. H., & Tversky, A. (1975). Similarity of rectangles: An analysis of subjective dimensions. *Journal of Mathematical Psychology, 12,* 4–34.

Kreindler, A., & Ionăşescu, V. (1961). A case of 'pure' word blindness. *Journal of Neurology, Neurosurgery, and Psychiatry, 24,* 275–280.

Leong, C. K., Wong, S., Wong, A., & Hiscock, M. (1985). Differential cerebral involvement in perceiving Chinese characters: Levels of processing approach. *Brain and Language, 26,* 131–141.

Liberman, I. Y., Liberman, A. M., Mattingly, I. G., & Shankweiler, D. (1980). Orthography and the beginning reader. In J. F. Kavanagh & R. L. Venezky (Eds.), *Orthography, reading, and dyslexia* (pp. 137–153). Baltimore, MD: University Park Press.

Maspes, P. E. (1948). Le syndrome expérimental chez l'homme de la section du splénium du corps calleux: Alexie visuelle pure hémianopsique. *Revue Neurologique, 80,* 100–113.

Mattingly, I. G. (1972). Reading, the linguistic process and linguistic awareness. In J. F. Kavanagh & I. G. Mattingly (Eds.), *Reading by ear and by eye* (pp. 133–147). Cambridge, MA: MIT Press.

Mattingly, I. G. (1984). Reading, linguistic awareness, and language acquisition. In J. Downing & R. Valtin (Eds.), *Language awareness and learning to read* (pp. 9–25). New York: Springer-Verlag.

McFie, J. (1961). The effects of hemispherectomy on intellectual functioning in cases of infantile hemiplegia. *Journal of Neurology, Neurosurgery, and Psychiatry, 24,* 240–249.

Menninger, K. (1969). *Number words and number symbols: A cultural history of numbers.* Cambridge, MA: MIT Press.

Moyer, R. S., & Dumais, S. T. (1978). Mental comparison. In G. H. Bower (Ed.), *The psychology of learning and motivation* (Vol. 12, pp. 117–155). New York: Academic Press.

Moyer, R. S., & Landauer, T. K. (1967). Time required for judgments of numerical inequality. *Nature, 215,* 1519–1520.

Oxbury, J. M., Oxbury, S. M., & Humphrey, N. K. (1969). Varieties of colour anomia. *Brain, 92,* 847–860.

Paivio, A. (1975). Perceptual comparisons through the mind's eye. *Memory & Cognition, 3,* 635–647.

Parkman, J. M. (1971). Temporal aspects of digit and letter inequality judgments. *Journal of Experimental Psychology, 91,* 191–205.

Paradis, M., Hagiwara, H., & Hildebrandt, N. (1985). *Neurolinguistic aspects of the Japanese writing system.* New York: Academic Press.

Peereman, R. (in preparation). *Size congruity effects with logographically and alphabetically written numbers.*

Peereman, R., & Holender, D. (1984). Relation entre taille physique et taille numérique dans la comparaison de chiffres écrits alphabétiquement et idéographiquement. *Psychologica Belgica, 24,* 147–164.

Peereman, R., & Holender, D. (1985). Visual-field differences for a number-nonnumber classification of alphabetic and ideographic stimuli. *Quarterly Journal of Experimental Psychology, 36A,* 197–216.

Rozin, P., & Gleitman, L. R. (1977). The structure and acquisition of reading II: The reading process and the acquisition of the alphabetic principle. In A. S. Reber & D. L. Scarborough (Eds.), *Toward a psychology of reading: The proceedings of the CUNY conference* (pp. 55–141). Hillsdale, NJ: Lawrence Erlbaum Associates.

Sasanuma, S. (1974a). Impairment of written language in Japanese aphasics: Kana versus Kanji processing. *Journal of Chinese Linguistics, 2,* 141–158.

Sasanuma, S. (1974b). Kanji versus Kana processing in alexia with transient agraphia: A case report. *Corte., 10,* 89–97.

Sasanuma, S. (1975). Kana and Kanji processing in Japanese aphasics. *Brain and Language, 2,* 369–383.

Sasanuma, S., Itoh, M., Mori, K., & Kobayashi, Y. (1977). Tachistoscopic recognition of Kana and Kanji words. *Neuropsychologia, 15,* 547–553.

Sasanuma, S., & Monoi, H. (1975). The syndrome of Gogi (word-meaning) aphasia: Selective impairment of Kanji processing. *Neurology, 25,* 627–632.

Sekuler, R., & Mierkiewicz, D. (1977). Children's judgments of numerical inequality. *Child Development, 48,* 630–633.

Sergent, J. (1983a). Role of the input in visual hemispheric asymmetries. *Psychological Bulletin, 93,* 481–512.

Sergent, J. (1983b). The effect of sensory limitations on hemispheric processing. *Canadian Journal of Psychology, 37,* 345–366.

Seron, X., & Deloche, G. (1984). From 2 to two: An analysis of a transcoding process by means of neuropsychological evidence. *Journal of Psycholinguistic Research, 13,* 215–236.

Simon, J. R., & Rudell, A. P. (1967). Auditory S-R compatibility: The effect of an irrelevant cue on information processing. *Journal of Applied Psychology, 51,* 300–304.

Stengel, E., Vienna, M. D., & Edin, L. R. C. P. (1948). The syndrome of visual alexia with colour agnosia. *Journal of Mental Science, 94,* 46–58.

Sternberg, S. (1969). The discovery of processing stages: Extension of Donder's method. *Acta Psychologica, 30,* 276–315.

Sternberg, S. (1984). Stage models of mental processing and the additive-factor method. *Behavioral and Brain Sciences, 7,* 82–84.

Sugishita, M., Iwata, M., Toyokura, Y., Yoshioka, M., & Yamada, R. (1978). Reading of ideograms and phonograms in Japanese patients after partial commissurotomy. *Neuropsychologia, 16,* 417–426.

Symonds, C. (1953). Aphasia. *Journal of Neurology, Neurosurgery, and Psychiatry, 16,* 1–6.

Takahashi, A., & Green, D. (1983). Numerical judgments with Kanji and Kana. *Neuropsychologia, 21,* 259–263.

Teng, E. L., & Sperry, R. W. (1973). Interhemispheric interaction during simultaneous bilateral presentation of letters or digits in commissurotomized patients. *Neuropsychologia, 11,* 131–140.

Trescher, J. H., & Ford, F. R. (1937). Colloid cyst of the third ventricule. *Archives of Neurology and Psychiatry, 37,* 959–973.

Warrington, E., & Zangwill, O. L. (1957). A study of dyslexia. *Journal of Neurology, Neurosurgery, and Psychiatry, 20,* 208–215.

Wender, K. (1971). A test of independence of dimensions in multidimensional scaling. *Perception and Psychophysics, 10,* 30–32.

Wiener-Ehrlich, W. K. (1978). Dimensional and metric structures in multidimensional stimuli. *Perception and Psychophysics, 24,* 399–414.

Yamadori, A. (1975). Ideogram reading in alexia. *Brain, 98,* 231–238.

Zaidel, E. (1976). Auditory vocabulary of the right hemisphere following brain bisection or hemidecortication. *Cortex, 12,* 191–211.

Zaidel, E. (1983). A response to Gazzaniga: Language in the right hemisphere, convergent perspectives. *American Psychologist, 37,* 542–546.

4 Sources of Working-Memory Error in Children's Mental Arithmetic

Charles J. Brainerd
University of Arizona

INTRODUCTION

In most information-processing accounts of how children solve mathematical and scientific problems, principal interest attaches to the nature of the processing operations that find solutions. Some familiar illustrations include serial-retrieval models of transitive inference (for a review, see Breslow, 1981), Euclidean models of mental rotation (for a review, see Kail, 1985), and rule-sampling models of conservation (for a review, see Brainerd, 1982). It is mental arithmetic, however, that provides the prototype example of processing-oriented research in cognitive development.

The task that students of mental arithmetic have traditionally set for themselves is to describe the operations that subjects use to generate responses from stored representations of numbers. Most of this work has centered upon mental addition, though some research on mental subtraction (e.g., Groen & Poll, 1973) and mental multiplication (e.g., Parkman, 1972) has also been published. In the standard design, children of different ages (or adults) are administered problems of the form $m + n = k$, where m, n, and k are all fairly small integers and $m \geq n$. These problems are normally presented in arabic notation on either a memory drum or a CRT. Two presentation methods are commonly used. On selection tasks, the items are of the form $m + n = ?$ and the subjects must select the value of k from a small set of alternatives. On recognition tasks, the items are of the form $m + n = k?$ and the subjects must indicate whether or not the stated value of k is the correct sum. Response latency is the dependent variable in both situations. As the theoretical objective is to model solution processes, only correct response latencies are usually analyzed.

Two leading theories have emerged. One is an iterative model proposed by Groen and Parkman (1972). The other is a fact-retrieval model that originally evolved from some adult studies by Ashcraft and Battaglia (1978) and has been vigorously developed in subsequent child research by Ashcraft and his associates (e.g., Ashcraft, 1982; Ashcraft, Hamann, & Fierman, 1981). On $m + n$ problems, the iterative model assumes that a sum is found by setting a mental "counter" to the value of m and then stepping the counter n times. The correct sum is merely the counter reading after n increments. A point often overlooked is that this model implicitly assumes the existence of a second counter, a "keeping-track" register that is originally set to 0 and is also incremented whenever the first counter is stepped. The solution algorithm, then, is (a) set the first counter to m and the second counter to 0; (b) step the counters in units of 1 until the value of the keeping-track register is n; and (c) read out the value in the first counter as the solution. If the average time to increment the counters by 1 unit is L, the iterative model anticipates that correct-response latency will be a linear, increasing function of n—i.e., the plot of latency against n will be a straight line whose slope is L.

In contrast, Ashcraft's model assumes that mental arithmetic is mediated by traces of number facts, which are ostensibly stored in long-term memory analogues of two-dimensional tables. On $m + n$ problems, the tables have m values as row (or column) headings, n values as column (or row) headings, and k values as cell entries for appropriate m and n headings. An interesting feature of these tables is that they are foreshortened at their "high" ends: The psychological distance between consecutive m or n values is greater for smaller numbers than for larger numbers. The fact-retrieval theory also allows for the possibility that some cells in a table may be empty. When confronted with an addition problem, subjects first attempt to solve it by scanning a relevant fact table. The scanning algorithm is an intersection search operation that enters the table simultaneously at the mth row (or column) and the nth column (or row). The scanning operation moves "down" the column and "across" the row until intersection occurs. The value of the intersection is then read out as the solution. But if the cell is empty, the subject falls back to Groen-Parkman iteration. Unlike Groen and Parkman's theory, the fact-retrieval model predicts that correct response latency will be more closely related to the value of k than to the value of n and that latency will be a nonlinear function of k.

My own work has differed from these classical efforts in three respects. First, I have been less concerned with mental arithmetic per se. I have, instead, exploited mental arithmetic as a convenient paradigm for elucidating general principles of cognitive development. Second, rather than restrict attention to processing, I have sought to expand the focus of research to other components of working memory. In the cognitive development literature, it has become routine to speak of a working-memory system of some sort as mediating performance on thinking and reasoning problems. To solve most problems, it is assumed that children must (a) be capable of encoding certain types of traces into working memory (e.g., traces of critical background facts, traces of the experimenter's questions), (b) be capable of holding these traces in storage long enough to find a solution, (c) be capable of using these traces as retrieval cues to search long-term memory for processing operations, and (d) have appropriate processing software in storage that will convert these traces to solutions. Although all four components are presumably involved in answering mental arithmetic items, the bulk of the literature deals with questions about d to the relative exclusion of $a-c$. Third, since my main concern is with development, the emphasis in specific studies has been upon error-success data, not latencies. There are some well-recognized difficulties with using latencies as measures of cognitive development, though these problems are not necessarily insuperable (cf. Kail, 1985). In particular, the need to restrict analysis to correct response latencies leaves out of account the fact that children, especially younger children, often show high error rates on mental arithmetic tasks. This means that a large percentage of responses may go unanalyzed in a given study. To reduce this percentage, investigators are compelled either to simplify such tasks drastically or to study only older children. These difficulties do not normally arise with error-success data.

The remainder of this chapter consists of two main sections. Theoretical ideas form the substance of the first section, which begins with a synopsis of the basic paradigm that has been used in my experiments and continues with a description of some elementary working-memory concepts. Next, a simple stochastic model that guided an earlier series of experiments is discussed. The aim of this first model was to provide independent estimates of two types of working-memory failures in children's mental arithmetic, namely, breakdowns on the input side (encoding and/or storage failures) and breakdowns in transforming stored traces into numerical outputs (retrieval and/or processing failures). Finally, a more comprehensive model is outlined that delivers independent measurements of the two input variables and the two transformational variables. Experimental results are reported in the second section. First, I summarize findings from previous studies in which the simplified model was applied to protocols of kindergarten and first-grade children. I then report some additional experiments in which the expanded model was applied to protocols of children from the same age range.

THEORETICAL PERSPECTIVES

Concepts and Procedures

The principal objective of my research has been to gain leverage on working-memory factors other than processing accuracy that contribute to children's mental arithmetic performance. I have been interested, more especially, in the contributions of encoding failure, storage failure, and retrieval failure. When children are asked to execute a mental calculation in everyday conversation, often as an oral exercise, any one of these factors might ultimately cause errors. Children might be incapable of encoding accurate traces of information such as "four" or "plus," into working memory (encoding failure) in the first place, or they might be unable to retain such traces long enough to solve the problem (storage failure), or they might be unable to use these traces to locate appropriate processing operations (retrieval failure). Of course, errors may also occur when processing operations are retrieved and applied to stored traces (processing failure).

Our fact library on cognitive development contains ample evidence that encoding, storage, and retrieval failures are all involved in young children's performance on logical and scientific reasoning problems. Much of the early literature, for instance, was concerned to show that errors on tasks such as conservation and class inclusion are more a matter of inability to comprehend relational terminology than of poor logic (e.g., Siegel, 1978, 1982). Comprehension difficulties of this sort are fairly straightforward cases of encoding failure. Children's inability to retain previously encoded information has also been implicated in their reasoning errors. Here, the richest source of evidence comes from overlearning studies of transitive inference. On the standard version of this task, where children must retain premise information in working memory, errors routinely occur until the middle elementary grades. In a classic experiment, Braine (1959) showed that these errors virtually disappear when children receive extensive pretraining on the premises. This effect is also obtained when knowledge of relational terminology is controlled, which seems to rule out encoding explanations. For present purposes, the interesting feature of overlearning is that it should eliminate storage failures by transferring the relevant information from a system of restricted capacity (working memory) to a system of very large capacity (long-term memory). Finally, there is comparable evidence implicating retrieval failures in children's reasoning. For example, I have reported some experiments on probability judgment that converged on retrieval failure as the major source of reasoning errors (Brainerd, 1981, 1983a). Specifically, it was found that these errors were normally a consequence of using rules that operate on irrelevant information (e.g., response alternation and stimulus perseveration rules), even though rules that operate on correct information (e.g., relative frequency rules) were known to be available in long-term memory. Overlearning studies also bear upon the incidence of retrieval failures. Some errors do occur on these tasks, though the rate is typically below 10%. Because the premise information has been trained to a strict acquisition criterion, encoding and storage failures are controlled. The fact that the correct response rate is so high shows that extremely accurate processing operations are available. Hence, it seems reasonable to interpret the residual errors as retrieval failures (Brainerd & Kingma, 1984).

For reasons that have been itemized elsewhere (Brainerd, 1983b), the usual procedure for presenting mental arithmetic problems is not well adapted to the

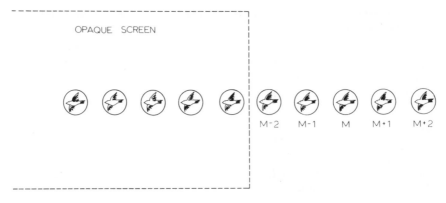

FIGURE 4.1. Sample stimulus for Experiments 1–5.

task of disentangling the role of working-memory variables in children's reasoning. I have used a modified paradigm in my experiments that is briefly described with the aid of Figure 4.1

To begin with, children are shown a stimulus containing a row of familiar objects (birds in Fig. 4.1). The number of objects falls somewhere above the normal subitizing range (10 birds in Fig. 4.1). The child does not know the precise number because a portion of the array is always occluded (see opaque screen in Fig. 4.1). Second, the child is given a number corresponding to one of the visible objects (e.g., the experimenter points to the second-from-last bird in Fig. 4.1 and says "This is bird number M"). Third, the experimenter has the child perform a simple addition or subtraction problem by pointing to some object other than the one whose number has been given and asking the child to supply its number. For example, the experimenter might point to the last bird in Fig. 4.1 ($M + 2$ addition item) or to the fourth-from-last bird in Fig. 4.1 ($M - 2$ subtraction item) and ask, "What number is this bird?" Fourth, after some but not all of the arithmetic problems, a recall probe is administered to determine whether or not the child remembers the number of the target object (i.e., bird No. 8 in our example).

Model 1: Factoring Input Variables from Transformational Variables

Although the ultimate objective is to disentangle all four theoretical variables, it would be helpful as a preliminary step if independent measurements could be obtained for groups of variables. In this connection, it proves to be possible to factor the two input variables (encoding/storage) from the two transformational variables (retrieval/processing) with simple tasks of the sort that have just been described. When children are administered an arithmetic item with a short-term memory probe, four events are possible: They may answer the arithmetic item correctly and recall the target numeral (*AM*), or they may answer the arithmetic item correctly and not recall the target numeral (*AM̄*), or they may answer the arithmetic item incorrectly and recall the target numeral (*ĀM*), or they may answer the arithmetic item incorrectly and not recall the target numeral (*ĀM̄*). If large numbers of such tasks are administered, the probability of each of the four events can be estimated, both for individual children and for groups of children. These probabilities can, in turn, be expressed as functions of the behavior of different working-memory variables, which serves as the basis for obtaining measurements of these variables.

First, consider the probability of answering both the arithmetic and short-term memory items correctly, *p(AM)*. In terms of our theoretical variables, there are three distinct ways in which this joint event could occur. First, the child might encode the information correctly, retain it in storage for whatever time it takes to solve the problem, retrieve the necessary processing operations from long-term memory, and process the contents of working memory correctly. Let *I* be the probability that neither input variable fails and let *T* be the probability that neither transformational variable fails. Second, both of the input variables might function correctly (which would permit the number *M* to be recalled), one of the transformational variables might fail (with probability 1 − T), but the child might still guess the correct answer on the arithmetic item. (Because the correct answer is always a small integer, the guessing probability is presumably nonzero on all problems.) Let the probability of a correct guess be *g*. Third, one of the input variables might fail (with probability 1 − *I*), but the child might guess correctly on both the arithmetic item (with probability *g*) and the short-term memory probe (with probability *g*). Combining the three paths to the *AM* event gives the following expression for the probability of this event

$$p(AM) = IT + I(1\text{-}T)g + (1\text{-}I)g^2. \tag{1}$$

Next, consider the probability of answering the arithmetic item correctly but failing to recall the target numeral, *p(AM̄)*. Because an error occurred on the short-term memory probe, one of the input variables must have failed (with probability 1 − *I*). Consequently, the child must have guessed correctly on the arithmetic item (with probability *g*) but guessed incorrectly on the probe (with probability 1 − *g*). The expression for *p(AM̄)*, then, is

$$p(A\bar{M}) = (1-I)(1-g)g. \tag{2}$$

Third, consider the probability of recalling the target numeral but answering the arithmetic item incorrectly, *p(ĀM)*. Here, there are two possible paths. (a) Both input variables may function correctly (with probability *I*), one of the transformational variables may fail (with probability 1 − *T*), and the child may guess incorrectly on the arithmetic item (with probability 1 − *g*). (b) One of the input variables may fail (with probability 1 − *I*), the child may guess incorrectly on the arithmetic item (with probability $1 - g$), and guess correctly on the probe (with probability g). The resulting expression for $p(\bar{A}M)$ is

$$p(\bar{A}M) = I(1-T)(1-g) + (1-I)(1-g)g. \tag{3}$$

Last, consider the probability of making an error on both the arithmetic item and the short-term memory probe, $p(\bar{A}\bar{M})$. As with $p(A\bar{M})$, the fact that there is an error on the probe means that one or both of the input variables must have failed (with probability $1 - I$) and that the child guessed incorrectly (with probability $1 - g$). The child must have also guessed incorrectly (with probability $1 - g$) on the arithmetic item. So, the expression for $p(\bar{A}\bar{M})$ is

$$p(\bar{A}\bar{M}) = (1-I)(1-g)^2. \tag{4}$$

Estimates of parameters I, T, and g, all of which are probabilities of theoretical events, can now be obtained from the parameters $p(AM)$, $p(A\bar{M})$, $\mathrm{p}(\bar{A}M)$, and $p(\bar{A}\bar{M})$, all of which are probabilities of empirical events. The essence of the procedure is as follows. Note, first, that Equations 1–4 constitute a system of four equations involving certain parameters whose values are known from data (the empirical probabilities) and certain other parameters whose values are unknown because they are probabilities of theoretical events. Actually, there are only three equations, not four, because any one of the four empirical probabilities can be calculated by subtracting the other three probabilities from unity. Although none of the theoretical probabilities are known, each can be estimated by performing some simple algebra. As all three of these probabilities appear in the equations, they define a system of three equations in three unknowns. Thus, one can estimate I, T, and g by simply inserting data estimates for the empirical probabilities and then solving the system of equations for each of the theoretical probabilities in turn. The actual procedure is somewhat more complicated and involves the theory of maximum likelihood (see Brainerd, 1983b, Appendix). However, the key fact is that a system of equations that contains certain parameters whose values are known from data can be solved to obtain estimates of parameters that measure working-memory variables.

Model 2: Factoring, Encoding, Storage, Retrieval, and Processing

We now examine a slightly more complicated version of the probed mental arithmetic task that yields measures of all four working-memory variables. The paradigm is the same as before, except that two arithmetic problems are administered before each short-term memory probe. That is, children are first given a target numeral to remember (bird number M in Fig. 4.1), this is followed by an arithmetic problem ($M\pm1$ or $M\pm2$ in Fig. 4.1), this is followed by another arithmetic problem ($M\pm1$ or $M\pm2$ in Fig. 4.1), and finally they are asked to recall the target numeral. This procedure generates eight joint data events—

namely, A_1A_2M, $\bar{A}_1A_2M$, $A_1\bar{A}_2M$, $A_1A_2\bar{M}$, $A_1\bar{A}_2\bar{M}$, $\bar{A}_1A_2\bar{M}$, $\bar{A}_1\bar{A}_2M$, and $\bar{A}_1\bar{A}_2M$, where i denotes a success on any one of the three items and $\bar{i}$ denotes an error. Assuming that large numbers of these tasks are administered, the probabilities of the eight joint events can be estimated from data.

As with Model 1, it is possible to represent each of these probabilities as a function of the probability of various working-memory events. This, in turn, allows the latter probabilities to be estimated by solving systems of equations that involve these latter probabilities as unknown variables and the empirical probabilities as known variables. In Model 2, there are five unknowns to be estimated: Let E be the probability that the original target numeral (bird number M in Fig. 4.1) was correctly encoded into working memory; let S be the probability that a trace of the target numeral is still in storage when an arithmetic problem is posed; let R be the probability that a computational operation can be retrieved that produces numerical responses when applied to such a trace; let P be the probability that such a processing operation produces a correct response; let g be the probability of a correct guess on arithmetic problems whenever encoding, storage, or retrieval has failed, and let g be the probability of a correct guess on short-term memory problems whenever encoding or storage has failed. Two simplifying assumptions are made about these variables. First, because the initial arithmetic item (A_1) immediately follows the presentation of the target numeral, it seems reasonable to suppose that a trace of this numeral must still be stored in working memory if it was correctly encoded in the first place. In other words, storage failure only operates between the time of the presentation of the first arithmetic item and the presentation of the probe, and such failures are primarily consequences of interference from processing on the two mental arithmetic problems. Second, it is assumed that the probabilities of storage, retrieval, and processing failures are the same on the first and second arithmetic problems. This assumption also seems reasonable as long as the relative difficulty of A_1 and A_2 is counterbalanced.

With Model 1, we saw that there are multiple theoretical routes to two joint empirical events. Explicitly, there were three paths to AM and two paths to $\bar{A}M$. With Model 2, things are considerably more complex, as would be expected from the larger number of theoretical processes that are being measured. There are multiple routes to all eight of the empirical events and the number of distinct paths is large in each case: There are 11 paths to A_1A_2M, 7 paths to $A_1A_2\bar{M}$, 7 paths to $A_1\bar{A}_2M$, 6 paths to $\bar{A}_1A_2M$, 5 paths to $A_1\bar{A}_2\bar{M}$, 4 paths to $\bar{A}_1A_2\bar{M}$, 4 paths to $\bar{A}_1\bar{A}_2M$, and 3 paths to $\bar{A}_1\bar{A}_2\bar{M}$. As it would be tedious to list all 47 paths, I simply exhibit the routes to the most complicated event, A_1A_2M, and the least complicated event, $\bar{A}_1\bar{A}_2\bar{M}$. Some general principles are then noted that permit rapid derivation of the paths for the other events. The remaining paths are exhibited with derivations left to interested readers as an exercise.

First, consider the probability of a correct response on both arithmetic problems followed by correct recall of the target numeral, $p(A_1A_2M)$. There are four paths that assume that the target numeral was correctly encoded in the first place (with probability E), was retained in storage during the first arithmetic problem (with probability S), and was retained in storage during the second arithmetic problem (with probability S). Because a trace of the target is still in storage, correct recall occurs with probability one on the short-term memory probe. However, there are four ways that correct responses could have been generated on the two arithmetic problems: (a) Retrieval and processing might have both been successful on each item (with probability R^2P^2); (b) retrieval and processing might have both been successful on A_1 (with probability RP) but retrieval may have failed and been accompanied by a correct guess on A_2 (with probability $(1-R)g$); (c) retrieval and processing might have both been successful on A_2 (with probability RP) but retrieval may have failed and been accompanied by a correct guess on A_1 (with probability $(1-R)g$); (d) retrieval might have failed on both arithmetic problems and been accompanied by a correct guess each time (with probability $(1-R)^2g^2$). There are four more paths that assume that the target numeral was correctly encoded (with probability E), was retained in storage during A_1 (with probability S), but was lost from storage during A_2 (with probability $1 - S$). Because a trace of the target numeral was no longer available at the time of probe administration, correct probe responses are always guesses, but the paths to correct A_1 and A_2 responses again vary: (e) Retrieval and processing might have been successful on both arithmetic problems (with probability R^2P^2); (f) retrieval and processing might have been successful on A_1 (with probability RP) but retrieval might have failed and been accompanied by a correct guess on A_2 (with probability $(1-R)g$); (g) retrieval and processing might have been successful on A_2 (with probability RP) but retrieval might have failed and been accompanied by a correct guess on A_1 (with probability $(1-R)g$); and (h) retrieval might have failed on both A_1 and A_2 and been accompanied by a correct guess each time (with probability $(1-R)^2g^2$). Note that except for the assumption about storage failure during A_2, paths e–h are the same as paths a–d. There are two additional paths that assume that encoding was correct (with probability E) and the storage failed during A_1 (with probability $1 - S$). Because a trace of the target numeral was not available on either A_2 or M, a correct guess must have been made on both items (with probability g^2). On A_1, however, either (i) retrieval and processing both are successful (with probability RP) or (j) retrieval fails and a correct guess is made (with probability $(1-R)g$). Finally, (k) the target numeral may not be correctly encoded (with probability E) but the child may guess correctly on all three items (with probability g^3). Combining these 11 routes to A_1A_2M produces the following expression for $p(A_1A_2M)$ in terms of working-memory variables

$$p(A_1A_2M) = ES^2(R^2P^2 + 2RP(1-R)g + (1-R)^2g^2) +$$
$$ES(1-S)g(R^2P^2 + 2RP(1-R)g + (1-R)^2g^2) + E(1-S)g^2(RP +$$
$$(1-R)g) + (1-E)g^3. \tag{5}$$

We turn now to the probability of errors on both arithmetic items followed by an incorrect recall on the short-term memory probe, $p(\bar{A}_1\bar{A}_2\bar{M})$. Since recall on the probe is unsuccessful, a trace of the target numeral is no longer in storage at the time the probe is administered. There are three ways in which this might occur in conjunction with errors on the two arithmetic problems. First, the target numeral might have been correctly encoded at the outset (with probability E), retrieval might have failed and the child guessed incorrectly on A_1 (with probability $(1-R)(1-g)$), the trace might have remained in storage during problem A_1 (with probability S), retrieval might also have failed and the child guessed incorrectly on A_2 (with probability $(1-R)(1-g)$), the trace might have been lost from storage during problem A_2 (with probability $1 - S$), and the child may have guessed incorrectly on M (with probability $1-g$). Second, the target numeral might have been correctly encoded at the outset (with probability E), retrieval might have failed and the child guessed incorrectly on A_1 (with probability $(1-R)(1-g)$), the trace might have been lost from storage during problem A_1 (with probability $1 - S$), and the child may have guessed incorrectly on both A_2 and M (with probability $(1-g)^2$). Third, the target numeral may not have been correctly encoded (with probability $1 - E$) and the child may have guessed incorrectly on all three items (with probability $(1-g)^3$). Therefore, the expression for $p(\bar{A}_1\bar{A}_2\bar{M})$ in terms of working-memory processes is

$$p(\bar{A}_1\bar{A}_2\bar{M}) = ES(1-S)(1-R)^2(1-g)^3 + E(1-S)(1-R)(1-g)^3 + (1-E)(1-g)^3. \tag{6}$$

The expressions for the remaining six probabilities are exhibited in Table 4.1. Some general principles whereby these expressions are derived are apparent from the two examples. (a) If the target numeral has not been correctly encoded, then responses on both arithmetic problems and short-term memory probes, whether successes or errors, are guesses, where guessing includes systematic responses based on irrelevant contextual factors. (b) If the target numeral is in storage when a probe is administered, it is recalled with probability one. (c) If the target numeral is in storage when an arithmetic problem is administered, a correct response can occur if retrieval and processing both succeed or if retrieval fails and the child guesses correctly. (d) If the target numeral is in storage when an arithmetic problem is administered, an error can occur if retrieval succeeds and processing fails or if retrieval fails and the child guesses incorrectly. (e) Whenever a correctly encoded target numeral is lost from storage, all subsequent responses, on both arithmetic problems and short-term memory probes, are guesses.

The situation with respect to empirical probabilities and theoretical probabilities in Table 4.1 is analogous to that in Equations 1–4. That is, we have a system of equations in which there are certain variables whose values are known from data and there are other variables that we wish to measure. The circumstances are slightly more complex than before because the number of known

TABLE 4.1
Theoretical Expressions for Empirical Probabilities in Model 2

Empirical	Theoretical
$p(A_1A_2M)$	$ES^2[R^2P^2 + 2RP(1 - R)g + (1 - R)^2g^2]$ $+ ES(1 - S)[R^2P^2 + 2RP(1 - R)g + (1 - R)^2g^2]$ $+ E(1 - S)[RPg^2 + (1 - R)g^3]$ $+ (1 - E)g^3$
$p(A_1A_2\bar{M})$	$ES(1 - S)[R^2P^2(1 - g) + 2RP(1 - R)g(1 - g) + (1 - R)^2g^2(1 - g)]$ $+ E(1 - S)[RPg(1 - g) + (1 - R)g^2(1 - g)]$ $+ (1 - E)g^2(1 - g)$
$p(A_1\bar{A}_2M)$	$ES^2[RP(1 - R)(1 - g) + (1 - R)^2g(1 - g)]$ $+ ES(1 - S)[RP(1 - R)(1 - g)g + (1 - R)^2g^2(1 - g)]$ $+ E(1 - S)[RPg(1 - g) + (1 - R)(1 - g)^2g] + (1 - E)g^2(1 - g)$
$p(\bar{A}_1A_2M)$	$ES^2[RP(1 - R)(1 - g) + (1 - R)^2(1 - g)g]$ $+ ES(1 - S)[RP(1 - R)(1 - g)g + (1 - R)^2g^2(1 - g)]$ $+ E(1 - S)(1 - R)g^2(1 - g) + (1 - E)g^2(1 - g)$
$p(A_1\bar{A}_2\bar{M})$	$ES(1 - S)[RP(1 - R)(1 - g)^2 + (1 - R)^2g(1 - g)^2]$ $+ E(1 - S)[RP(1 - g)^2 + (1 - R)g(1 + g)^2]$ $+ (1 - E)g(1 - g)^2$
$p(\bar{A}_1A_2\bar{M})$	$ES(1 - S)[RP(1 - R)(1 - g)^2 + (1 - R)^2g(1 - g)^2]$ $+ E(1 - S)(1 - R)g(1 - g)^2 + (1 - E)g(1 - g)^2$
$p(\bar{A}_1\bar{A}_2M)$	$ES^2(1 - R)^2(1 - g)^2 + ES(1 - S)(1 - R)^2(1 - g)^2g$ $+ E(1 - S)(1 - R)g(1 - g)^2 + (1 - E)g(1 - g)^2$
$p(\bar{A}_1\bar{A}_2\bar{M})$	$ES(1 - S)(1 - R)^2(1 - g)^3 + E(1 - S)(1 - R)(1 - g)^3 + (1 - E)(1 - g)^3$

variables (any seven of the eight empirical probabilities) is larger than the number of unknown variables (the five theoretical probabilities). Because the numbers of known and unknown variables were equal with Model 1, one could merely solve a set of three simultaneous equations to obtain unique estimates of the unknown variables. With Model 2, on the other hand, any subset of five of the seven equations will produce estimates of the unknown variables. Because there are several subsets of this sort, it is possible to obtain somewhat different estimates for different subsets. It is desirable, therefore, to use estimates that are averages of the estimates for the various subsets of equations. This is normally accomplished via computer search using an optimization program of some sort.

EXPERIMENTAL RESULTS

Model 1

I now summarize findings from four experiments in which the first model was used to factor the respective contributions of encoding/storage difficulty and retrieval/processing difficulty to the mental arithmetic performance of kindergartners and first graders. I begin by summarizing two studies with kindergartners (Experiments 1 and 2). Two further studies with kindergartners and first graders (Experiments 3 and 4) are then discussed.

Experiments 1 and 2.   The purposes of these two experiments were, first, to measure the relative contributions of encoding/storage difficulty and retrieval/processing difficulty to mental arithmetic and, second, to gather some preliminary evidence as to the validity of the parameters that ostensibly measure these two sources of difficulty. The former question was addressed by simply estimating Model 1's parameters using data from mental addition problems that had been accompanied by short-term memory probes (Experiment 1) and data from mental subtraction problems that had been accompanied by short-term memory problems (Experiment 2). Parameter validity was investigated by studying the effects of certain manipulations on the input parameter, I, and the transformation parameter, T, respectively. If I actually measures encoding/storage, then one would expect that it should react to treatments that affect the difficulty of encoding the target numeral. One such treatment is to present the target numeral in ordinal versus cardinal formats: It has been known for some time that children, especially young children, are more apt to understand the positional (ordinal) meaning of a numeral than the numerousness (cardinal) meaning (e.g., Brainerd, 1973). Also, if T actually measures the difficulty of retrieving and executing arithmetical operations, it should react to manipulations that affect the difficulty of arithmetical calculations. Here, an obvious manipulation is to study mental addition versus mental subtraction: Children typically find subtraction problems to be more difficult than formally equivalent addition problems.

The subjects in Experiment 1 were 58 four- and five-year-olds drawn from preschools and kindergartens, and the subjects in Experiment 2 were 64 four- and five-year-olds drawn from the same sources. Experiment 1 was concerned with mental addition. The children in this study were administered a total of 20 addition items of the type described earlier. All problems were of the form $M + 1$ or $M + 2$. There were 10 $M + 1$ problems and 10 $M + 2$ problems in all. The correct answer was always an integer that was less than or equal to 10. Recall probes for the target numeral M were administered after 4 of the $M + 1$ problems and after 4 of the $M + 2$ problems. For half of the children, both the addition items and the memory probes were presented in ordinal language. A cardinal language format was used for the other half of the children. A sample of an addition item and a memory probe in both language formats is presented in Table 4.2.

Experiment 2 was similar to Experiment 1, except for the fact that the subjects were different and that the arithmetic problems involved subtraction. These children received 20 subtraction problems of the type described earlier. Half of the problems were $M - 1$ and half were $M - 2$. As in Experiment 1, the correct answer was always an integer less than or equal to 10. Also as in Experiment 1, 4 of the $M - 1$ problems and 4 of the $M - 2$ problems were accompanied by a

TABLE 4.2
Sample Addition Problems, Subtraction Problems, and Short-Term
Memory Probes for Experiments 1-4

	Type of Encoding	
Type ot Item	Ordinal	Cardinal
Addition:		
7 + 1	if this bird is bird number seven, what number is this bird (+1)?	If there are seven birds up to this one, how many birds are there up to this one (+1)?
7 + 2	If this bird is bird number seven, what number is this bird (+2)?	If there are seven birds up to this one, how many birds are there up to this one (+2)?
Probe	What number is this bird (7)?	How many birds are there up to this one (7)?
Subtraction:		
7 − 1	If this bird is bird number seven, what number is this bird (−1)?	If there are seven birds up to this one, how many birds are there up to this one (−1)?
7 − 2	If this bird is bird number seven, what number is this bird (−2)?	If there are seven birds up to this one, how many birds are there up to this one (−2)?
Probe	Same as addition	Same as addition

recall probe for M. An ordinal language format was used on both subtraction problems and probes for half the children, and a cardinal language format was used on both subtraction problems and probes for the other half of the children. A sample subtraction item and probe are given in both language formats in Table 4.2.

The estimates of Model 1's parameters appear in Table 4.3 for these experiments. Preliminary analyses showed that $M + 2$ problems were not more difficult than $M + 1$ problems and that $M − 2$ problems were not more difficult than $M − 1$ problems. Hence, the estimates in Table 4.3 are for the pooled data of the two types of problems. However, the estimates are reported separately by experiment and language format. I summarize the results on parameter validity first before considering the relative contributions of encoding/storage versus retrieval/processing.

Essentially, we wish to know whether I and T behaved in a manner that is consistent with the hypothesis that they measure encoding/storage difficulty and retrieval/processing difficulty, respectively. Comparisons of each parameter between language conditions and for addition versus subtraction appear to be in

TABLE 4.3
Estimates of Model 1's Parameters
for Experiments 1–4

	Parameter		
Data set	g	I	T
Experiment 1:			
Positional	.229	.526	.670
Numerosity	.051	.281	.691
Experiment 2:			
Positional	.233	.519	.495
Numerosity	.032	.288	.432
Experiment 3:			
First grade:			
Positional	.367	.721	.730
Numerosity ...	.241	.470	.701
Preschool:			
Positional	.245	.491	.691
Numerosity ...	.111	.309	.642
Experiment 4:			
First grade:			
Positional	.344	.769	.531
Numerosity ...	.178	.512	.586
Preschool:			
Positional	.150	.541	.419
Numerosity ...	.009	.263	.456

agreement with this hypothesis. Concerning language, the use of ordinal versus cardinal language does not affect the nature of the computation that is to be carried out, though it may affect children's comprehension of the numbers. Consequently, this manipulation should affect input difficulty without affecting transformational difficulty. Consistent with this reasoning, I was much larger for ordinal addition problems than for cardinal addition problems in Experiment 1, and it was much larger for ordinal subtraction problems than for cardinal subtraction problems in Experiment 2. Language format did not seem to affect T in either experiment, however. Last, language format had a reliable effect on guessing accuracy in both studies, with more accurate guesses occurring under the ordinal format. This latter result is quite reasonable if ordinal language is generally more comprehensible to children. Concerning addition versus subtraction, this manipulation affects the nature of the computation that must be carried out, but it does not affect the intrinsic comprehensibility of the numerical information. Hence, it should affect T but not I if the interpretation of what these parameters measure is correct. It can be seen in Table 4.3 that this result was obtained. With ordinal language, the estimate of T was larger for addition problems than for subtraction problems, but neither I nor g was affected. The same pattern was observed with cardinal language.

The second question concerned the relative contributions of failures in encoding/storage operations and retrieval/processing operations to mental arithmetic. According to the model, the probability that any given arithmetic error is due to input failure is $(1-I)g(1-g) + (1-I)(1-g)^2$ and the probability that any given arithmetic error is due to transformational failure is $I(1-T)$. These are merely the expressions for the proportions of input-based and transformation-based arithmetic errors that result when the Equations 1–4 are manipulated algebraically. When the parameter estimates in Table 4.3 are inserted in these expressions, the percentages of errors due to input failures in the various conditions of these experiments were 67.8% for the ordinal addition items (Experiment 1), 88.7% for the cardinal addition items (Experiment 1), 58.5% for the ordinal subtraction items (Experiment 2), and 80.8% for the cardinal subtraction items (Experiment 2). Thus, it seems that input failure was a consistently more potent source of errors than transformational failure. Because the arithmetic items in these experiments were administered immediately after the target numeral M was presented, it seems likely that the storage failure rate for correctly encoded numerals would be very low and, therefore, that most of the input failures were probably encoding failures. If this supposition is correct, the data appear to be telling us that for young children at least, the major difficulty in mental arithmetic is getting the critical information properly encoded into working memory, not processing the information.

Experiments 3 and 4.   The next two experiments were more developmental in orientation. Since the first two experiments provided positive signals on parameter validity and delivered rather clear findings on encoding/storage versus retrieval/processing, it seemed reasonable to use the model to measure age changes in the working-memory variables. The principal goal was to assess the relative impact of age changes in input failures and transformational failures on developmental improvements in the accuracy of mental arithmetic. A secondary aim was to determine the replicability of the main results of the first two experiments. Recall here that the results of principal interest were, first, that the parameters I and T were affected by manipulations designed to affect encoding difficulty (language format) and processing difficulty (addition versus subtraction), respectively, and, second, that a larger proportion of children's mental arithmetic errors were due to input failure than to transformational failure. Concerning the former result, the input parameter I was larger with ordinal language than with cardinal language but the transformational parameter T was not affected by language, and the transformational parameter was larger with addition problems than with subtraction problems but the input parameter was not affected by problem type. Concerning the latter results, input-based errors were roughly 20% more frequent than transformation-based errors when problems were presented ordinally, and they were roughly 80% more frequent than trans-formation-based errors when problems were presented cardinally. A straightfor-ward developmental prediction from these results is that age changes in the input-failure rate will be more closely connected to improvements in mental arithmetic than age changes in the transformation-failure rate.

This prediction was tested by comparing children who differed both in age and in their amount of exposure to formal arithmetic instruction. The younger children in each experiment were from the same age level as in Experiments 1 and 2. The older children were first graders who had already received a few months of instruction in addition and subtraction. The younger children, howev-er, had not had any systematic exposure to arithmetic. The subjects in Experi-ment 3 consisted of a sample of 60 four- and five-year-olds drawn from pre-schools and kindergartens and a sample of 60 first graders. In Experiment 4, there were 55 four- and five-year-olds and 55 first graders.

The procedure in Experiment 3 was identical to that in Experiment 1: Each child received 20 addition items ($10 M + 1$ problems and $10 M + 2$ problems), 8 of which were accompanied by short-term memory probes, with ordinal lan-guage for half the children and cardinal language for the other half. The pro-cedure in Experiment 4 was identical to that in Experiment 2: Each child received 20 subtraction items ($10 M - 1$ problems and $10 M - 2$ problems), 8 of which were accompanied by short-term memory probes, with ordinal language for half the children and cardinal language for the other half.

In Experiment 3, preliminary analyses showed that older children performed better than younger children on both addition problems and probes, that ordinal presentation produced better addition and probe performance than cardinal lan-guage, and that children performed better on the short-term memory probes than on the addition problems. In Experiment 4, preliminary analyses showed that older children performed better than younger children on both subtraction prob-lems and probes, that ordinal language produced better subtraction and probe performance than cardinal language, and that children performed better on the short-term memory probes than on the subtraction problems. The results of main interest, the estimates of the three parameters of Model 1, are shown by experi-ment, age level, and language format in Table 4.3. As before, there was no evidence that ± 2 problems were harder than ± 1 problems, so the estimates in Table 4.3 are for the pooled data of the two problem types.

Insofar as replication is concerned, the results on parameter validity agreed with those in the first two experiments. In Experiment 3, it can be seen in Table 4.3 that the language manipulation affected the input parameter for addition but the transformational parameter for addition did not react to this manipulation. Similarly, in Experiment 4, it can be seen that I was larger with ordinal presenta-tion than with cardinal presentation, but T was not affected by language format. It can also be seen that the guessing parameter was somewhat larger for ordinal language than for cardinal language in both studies. Turning to the processing manipulation (addition versus subtraction), the results were also similar to Experiments 1 and 2. Combining across language formats, the average differences in the addition and subtraction retrieval/processing failure rates across language formats were .24 for the 4- and 5-year-olds and .17 for the first graders. In contrast, the average differences in the addition and subtraction input-failure rates across language formats were not reliable for either age level. In short, then, there was again presumptive evidence that Model 1's interpretations of parameters I and T are reasonable.

Also as in Experiments 1 and 2, input failure appeared to be responsible for a larger proportion of addition and subtraction errors than transformational failure. Using the expressions given earlier, together with the parameter estimates in Table 4.3, the calculated proportions for younger children's arithmetic errors attributable to input failure were 74% (ordinal language addition), 85% (cardinal language addition), 56% (ordinal language subtraction), and 84% (cardinal language subtraction). The corresponding percentages for the first graders were 55% (ordinal language addition), 74% (cardinal language addition), 30% (ordinal language subtraction), and 84% (cardinal language subtraction). Note that older children's performance on subtraction problems that were presented in ordinal language was the only instance in which input-based errors seemed to be less common than transformation-based errors.

Finally, we come to the issue of whether input failures or transformational failures contribute more to the development of mental arithmetic. Here, there are two questions about the parameter values in Table 4.3 that are relevant. First, are the estimates of I and T always larger for older children than for younger children? If it turns out that in some conditions only one of the parameters differs between ages, then naturally that parameter makes more important contributions to development. Second, in those conditions where both I and T differ between age levels, are the changes in one parameter greater than the changes in the other? Both types of data tended to show that input failures were a more important locus of development than transformational failures.

In Experiment 3, the estimate of I for older children was larger than for younger children with both ordinal and cardinal addition items. However, the estimate of T did not vary reliably between age levels for either ordinal or cardinal addition items. With addition, therefore, the transformation-failure rate does not appear to be an important source of development, but the input failure rate is. In Experiment 4, the estimate of I for older children was again larger than for younger children with both ordinal and cardinal subtraction items. The estimate of T was also larger for older children than for younger children with both language formats. It can be seen, however, the magnitudes of the age changes were much smaller for T than for I. For the ordinal subtraction items, the older versus younger difference was .23 for I but only .11 for T. For the cardinal subtraction items, the older versus younger difference was .25 for I but only .13 for T. Although both input failures and transformational failures contributed to the development of mental subtraction, the data are consistent with those for addition in suggesting that input failure is the most important variable.

Model 2

The fifth and last experiment was also a developmental study in the sense that measurements of working-memory variables were made for two age levels. However, the expanded procedure described earlier (two arithmetic problems followed by a short-term memory probe) was used so that the parameters of Model 2 could be estimated. Further, the difficulty of the arithmetic problems that were administered ($M \pm 3$ and $M \pm 4$) was increased slightly. The subjects in the study were 94 four- and five-year-olds, who were again drawn from preschools and kindergartens, and 94 first graders. As in Experiments 3 and 4, the latter children were older first graders who had completed several months of classroom instruction in arithmetic.

Each child in this study was administered a total of 32 arithmetic problems organized into 16 $A_1 A_2$ pairs of the form described earlier. On 8 of these pairs, a recall probe for the target numeral was administered after the second arithmetic problem. The 16 $A_1 A_2$ pairs were further subdivided into four sets of problems: (a) problems in which A_1 and A_2 were both addition items; (b) problems in which A_1 was an addition item and A_2 was a subtraction item; (c) problems in which A_1 was a subtraction item and A_2 was an addition item; and (d) problems in which A_1 and A_2 were both subtraction items. Within each of these four sets, two of the problems were accompanied by a short-term memory probe and two were not. All of the addition problems were either $M + 3$ (8 items) or $M + 4$ (8 items), and all of the subtraction problems were either $M - 3$ (8 items) or $M - 4$ (8 items). As in all previous experiments, the correct solution was always an integer that was less than or equal to 10. At each age level, half of the children were administered the arithmetic problems and the probes in ordinal language and the other half were administered the same material in cardinal language. Thus, the experiment was a 2 (Age) $\times$ 4 (Problem Type: add-add, add-subtract, subtract-add, subtract-subtract) $\times$ 2 (Item Type: arithmetic or short-term memory) $\times$ 2 (Language Format: ordinal or cardinal) factorial design with repeated measures on the second and third factors. Because the procedure differed somewhat from Experiments 1–4, sample problems in both language formats are exhibited in Table 4.4.

Preliminary analyses revealed that older children performed better than younger children on addition problems, subtraction problems, and short-term memory probes. Language format affected the accuracy of children's performance on both types of arithmetic problems and on the probes, with ordinal language producing consistently better performance than cardinal language. Last, subtraction problems were more difficult than addition problems for both younger and older children.

TABLE 4.4
Sample Addition Problems, Subtraction Problems, and Short-Term
Memory Probes for Experiment 5

Type of item	Type of encoding	
	Ordinal	Cardinal
M presentation	This is bird number six.	There are six birds up to this one.
Addition:		
6 + 3	What number is this bird (+3)?	How many birds are there up to this one (+3)?
6 + 4	What number is this bird (+4)?	How many birds are there up to this one (+4)?
Probe:	What number is this bird (6)?	How many birds are there up to this one (6)?
Subtraction:		
6 − 3	What number is this bird (−3)?	How many birds are there up to this one (−3)?
6 − 4	What number is this bird (−4)?	How many birds are there up to this one (−4)?
Probe:	What number is this bird (6)?	How many birds are there up to this one (6)?

The data of primary concern, the estimates of Model 2's parameters for this experiment, are reported in Table 4.5. The estimates are shown separately by age level, problem type, and language format. As in the earlier studies, the two forms of addition problems ($M + 3$ and $M + 4$) and the two forms of subtraction problems ($M - 3$ and $M - 4$) did not differ in difficulty. I summarize the main results for Model 2 by considering developmental differences first and then considering treatment effects.

It can be seen that there are eight possible between-age comparisons of the model's five parameters in Table 4.5, namely, 4 problem types (add-add, add-subtract, subtract-add, and subtract-subtract) $\times$ 2 language formats (ordinal versus cardinal). Each of these comparisons produced basically the same developmental pattern. First, there were large and consistent differences in the encoding parameter, E; the 4- and 5-year-olds were much less likely to encode the target numeral correctly than the first graders were. Second, there were also consistent age differences in the storage parameter, S, though they were smaller than those for the encoding parameter. For all four types of pairs, the younger children were more apt to lose the target numeral from storage than the older children were. Neither of these two developmental effects interacted with problem type. As can be seen in Table 4.5, the age differences in E and S were roughly the same for add-add, add-subtract, subtract-add, and subtract-subtract problems. Third, there was a small but consistent age difference in the value of the retrieval parameter,

TABLE 4.5
Estimates of Model 2's Parameters for Experiment 5

Data set	Parameter				
	E	S	R	P	g
Younger children:					
Ordinal					
add-add	.591	.798	.906	.966	.241
add-subtract	.523	.709	.808	.926	.223
subtract-add	.579	.717	.814	.961	.242
subtract-subtract	.578	.762	.709	.922	.209
Cardinal					
add-add	.272	.649	.931	.949	.012
add-subtract	.281	.647	.857	.936	.051
subtract-add	.238	.631	.848	.884	.058
subtract-subtract	.296	.609	.803	.896	.098
Older children:					
Ordinal					
add-add	.753	.941	.987	.915	.348
add-subtract	.703	.812	.928	.865	.312
subtract-add	.718	.814	.932	.977	.391
subtract-subtract	.788	.908	.822	.928	.367
Cardinal					
add-add	.199	.813	.943	.954	.201
add-subtract	.261	.793	.940	.951	.171
subtract-add	.243	.976	.921	.927	.142
subtract-subtract	.281	.720	.954	.992	.157

R, such that retrieval was more likely to be successful for older children than for younger children. This developmental effect did interact with age: The R difference was smallest for add-add problems, somewhat larger for add-subtract and subtract-add problems, and largest for subtract-subtract problems. Fourth, there were no reliable age differences in the processing parameter, P. If a processing operation could be retrieved, whether for addition or subtraction problems, it appeared to be equally accurate for 4- and 5-year-olds, on the one hand, and for first graders, on the other hand. Fifth and finally, there were large and consistent age differences in the guessing parameter, g, such that older children made more accurate guesses than younger children did. This result also did not interact with problem type.

Turning to treatment effects, I summarize the results for problem type and language format separately. Concerning problem type, it can be seen that only the retrieval parameter, R, varied consistently across problem type. The value of R was largest for add-add problems, somewhat smaller for add-subtract and subtract-add problems, and smallest for subtract-subtract items. It seems, then, that the difficulty difference between addition and subtraction problems may simply be due to the fact that it is more difficult to retrieve subtraction operations from long-term memory than it is to retrieve addition operations. Concerning ordinal versus cardinal presentation, the effects on Model 2's parameters were more pronounced than the effects of problem type were. The parameters E, S, and g all varied across the language formats. Concerning E and S, it can be seen in Table 4.5 that both of these parameters were larger for ordinal language than for cardinal language. It was more difficult to encode and to maintain the target numeral in storage when it was presented cardinally than when it was presented ordinally. This result did not interact either with age or with problem type. However, it can also be seen that the effect of the language manipulation on E was much greater than its effect on S. Although it is harder to maintain traces of cardinal numbers in storage, language format is primarily an encoding manipulation. Last, the parameter g once again varied between the two language formats, with guessing being more accurate for ordinal presentation than for cardinal presentation.

To sum up, the most important general findings to emerge from this experiment are that the pattern of results for the expanded model were in agreement with those for Model 1 and that they serve to clarify the results for Model 1. Developmentally, we saw in Experiments 3 and 4 that age changes in mental arithmetic performance were largely confined to the input parameter, I. In agreement with this result, we saw in this experiment that the age changes in the two input parameters, E and S, were larger than the age changes in the two transformational parameters, R and P. Indeed, the processing parameter, P, did not vary with age. Thus, it appears that the developmental improvements in mental arithmetic that occur with this particular paradigm are primarily a matter of improvements on the input side of working memory and that they are more a matter of reductions in the encoding-failure rate than they are a matter of reductions in the storage-failure rate. Concerning the language format manipulation and the addition-subtraction manipulation, the results were also in agreement with earlier data. The method of linguistic presentation again affected input parameters without affecting transformational parameters. However, the fact that separate parameters were now available for encoding and storage provided evidence that ordinal versus cardinal language affects initial encoding accuracy much more than it affects subsequent retention accuracy. Guessing was affected by language in the same manner as in the first four experiments. Regarding addition versus subtraction, this manipulation continued to affect transformational parameters without affecting input parameters. Consideration of the separate parameters for retrieval and processing led to the interesting conclusion that these are mainly retrieval effects. That is, the difficulty of subtraction relative to addition may not arise so much from the fact that calculation per se is harder on subtraction items as it does from the fact that subtraction operations are harder to retrieve from long-term memory.

SUMMARY

In the preponderance of studies of children's mental arithmetic, the emphasis has been on testing hypotheses about the nature of the processing operations whereby problems are solved. Although such studies have been productive of interesting new hypotheses and data, they fail to illuminate the role of other working-memory variables in children's mental arithmetic. The emphasis on processing hypotheses also tends to lead, more or less by default, to an emphasis on developmental changes in processing operations as the major source of age changes in mental arithmetic performance.

The general thesis of this chapter has been that it is possible to make progress on assessing the influences of other working-memory variables and on measuring their respective contributions to the development of mental arithmetic by relying on some simple stochastic models. When these models are applied to a certain type of mental arithmetic paradigm, some surprising results emerge. For example, contrary to the processing emphasis in most other experiments, it seems that input variables, especially encoding accuracy, have a much larger impact on the accuracy of calculation than either retrieval or processing per se do. In addition, age changes in mental arithmetic during early childhood seem to be more directly the result of improvements in encoding and short-term retention, especially encoding, than the result of improvements in retrieval and processing.

REFERENCES

Ashcraft, M. H. (1982). The development of mental arithmetic: A chronometric approach. *Developmental Review, 2,* 213–236.

Ashcraft, M. H., & Battaglia, J. (1978). Cognitive arithmetic: Evidence for retrieval and decision processes in mental addition. *Journal of Experimental Psychology: Human Learning and Memory, 4,* 527–538.

Ashcraft, M. H., Hamann, M. S., & Fierman, B. A. (1981, April). *The development of mental addition.* Paper presented at the meeting of the Society for Research in Child Development, Boston.

Braine, M. D. S. (1959). The ontogeny of certain logical operations: Piaget's formulation examined by nonverbal methods. *Psychological Monographs, 79* (5, Whole No. 475).

Brainerd, C. J. (1973). The origins of number concepts. *Scientific American, 228* (3), 101–109.

Brainerd, C. J. (1981). Working memory and the developmental analysis of probability judgment. *Psychological Review, 88,* 463–502.

Brainerd, C. J. (1982). Children's concept learning as rule-sampling systems with Markovian properties. In C. J. Brainerd (Ed.), *Children's logical and mathematical cognition: Progress in cognitive development research* (pp. 177–212). New York: Springer-Verlag.

Brainerd, C. J. (1983a). Working-memory systems and cognitive development. In C. J. Brainerd (Ed.), *Recent advances in cognitive-developmental theory: Progress in cognitive development research* (pp. 167–236). New York: Springer-Verlag.

Brainerd, C. J. (1983b). Young children's mental arithmetic errors: A working-memory analysis. *Child Development, 54,* 812–830.

Brainerd, C. J., & Kingma, J. (1984). Do children have to remember to reason? A fuzzy-trace theory of transitivity development. *Developmental Review, 311–377.*

Breslow, L. (1981). A reevaluation of the literature on the development of transitive inferences. *Psychological Bulletin, 89,* 325–351.

Groen, G. J., & Parkman, J. M. (1972). A chronometric analysis of simple addition. *Psychological Review, 72,* 329–343.

Groen, G. J., & Poll, M. (1973). Subtraction and the solution of open sentence problems. *Journal of Experimental Child Psychology, 16,* 292–302.

Kail, R. (1985). Interpretation of response time in research on the development of memory and cognition. In C. J. Brainerd & M. Pressley (Eds.), *Basic processes in memory development: Progress in cognitive development research* (pp. 249–278). New York: Springer-Verlag.

Parkman, J. M. (1972). Temporal aspects of simple multiplication and comparison. *Journal of Experimental Psychology, 95,* 437–444.

Siegel, L. S. (1978). The relationship of language and thought in the preoperational child: A reconsideration of nonverbal alternatives to Piagetian tasks. In L. S. Siegel & C. J. Brainerd (Eds.), *Alternatives to Piaget: Critical essays on the theory* (pp. 43–68). New York: Academic Press.

Siegel, L. S. (1982). The development of quantity concepts: Perceptual and linguistic factors. In C. J. Brainerd (Ed.), *Children's logical and mathematical cognition: Progress in cognitive development research* (pp. 123–156). New York: Springer-Verlag.

5 Mathematical Disability and the Gerstmann Syndrome

Arthur L. Benton

INTRODUCTION

The concept of the syndrome that bears his name was developed by Josef Gerstmann over the course of a number of years. In 1924, he described a patient who had lost the ability to identify the fingers on her own hand, or those of other persons, although she could identify other parts of the body. Giving the name of ''finger agnosia'' to this deficit, he interpreted it as reflecting ''a circumscribed disorder of the body schema.'' In 1927, he linked finger agnosia with isolated agraphia to form what he called ''a new syndrome.'' In 1930, he enlarged the syndrome to include right-left disorientation and acalculia, thus establishing the combination of deficits that came to be known as the Gerstmann syndrome.

Gerstmann made two points when he introduced his syndrome. The first was that it was symptomatic of focal brain disease, specifically of a lesion in the territory of the angular gyrus in the left (or language-dominant) hemisphere. Second, he insisted that the syndrome was no accidental assemblage of deficits, but an internally coherent combination produced by a disorder of the body schema that specifically involved the hands. It was this partial dissolution of the body schema, represented by the nuclear symptom of finger agnosia, that was responsible for the occurrence of the other components of the syndrome, viz., right-left disorientation, agraphia, and acalculia.

That the Gerstmann combination of deficits possessed the distinctive localizing significance claimed for it was readily accepted by clinical neurologists, and the syndrome found a place in the text books as a symptom-picture indicative of focal-parieto-occipital disease of the dominant hemisphere. This belief remained unshaken for decades until Heimburger, DeMyer, and Reitan (1964) demon-

111

strated that patients with the full Gerstmann syndrome invariably had large lesions that generally involved the superior temporal and supramarginal gyri, as well as the angular gyrus, of the left hemisphere. Moreover, every patient showing the full syndrome was also aphasic to some degree. In no case was the destruction of tissue limited to the territory of the angular gyrus and in fact the angular gyrus was spared in 3 of the 23 cases showing the full syndrome. Incomplete presentations of the syndrome (i.e., one, two, or three deficits) were sometimes associated with focal lesions in the territory of the angular gyrus and sometimes with focal lesions in other areas. Moreover, patients with angular gyrus lesions who did not show any of the Gerstmann symptoms were also encountered. Thus the thrust of the Heimburger-DeMyer-Reitan study was to deny that the Gerstmann syndrome had a highly specific localizing value.

Gerstmann's idea that his syndrome was ultimately referable to a disorder of the body schema was an intriguing one. Historically, there is a close connection between the fingers and calculation, as reflected in our decimal system, and the use of the fingers for counting and calculation by young children is obvious. The hands also play a role in the development and maintenance of right-left orientation. Faulty right-left orientation among normal individuals is found almost always to be associated with ambidexterity, i.e., with an insecure establishment of unilateral hand preference. Finally, the perceptual differentiation of the fingers is significantly correlated with the execution of fine finger movements. Gerstmann's (1924) first patient showed a clumsiness in the use of her fingers, which he interpreted to be a consequence of her finger agnosia. Later an association between finger localization and finger praxis was demonstrated by Jackson and Zangwill (1952) in normal adults and by Benton (1959a) in normal children. Therefore, it was to be expected that a primary finger agnosia would produce a concomitant disturbance in writing movements.

Gerstmann's imaginative conception relating all the elements of his syndrome to a partial dissolution of the body schema was not widely accepted. The explanation favored by theoretically oriented neurologists was that all the elements of the syndrome are expressions of a fundamental impairment in spatial thinking (cf. Benton, 1977; Critchley, 1967). This explanation had the merit of accounting for the fact that other disabilities of a spatial nature, such as constructional apraxia and visual disorientation, were so frequently encountered in patients showing the full Gerstmann syndrome (cf. Benton, 1961). Another explanation of a less theoretical character interpreted the concurrence of the symptoms as meaning that the cortical centers mediating the several performances occupied neighboring sites in the occipitoparietal area. Thus, depending upon its size and locus, a lesion in this territory could produce impairment in any single performance or any combination of performances. This interpretation was in accord with the observation that incomplete combinations of the Gerstmann symptoms were shown far more frequently than was the full syndrome (cf. Benton, 1959b; Heimburger et al., 1964). Still another hypothesis, derived from the finding that in fact Gerstmann patients almost invariably suffered from some degree of linguistic defect, was that all the Gerstmann symptoms reflected an impairment in symbolic understanding or expression (Benton, 1959b, 1962; Sauget, Benton, & Hécaen, 1971).

ACALCULIA AND THE GERSTMANN SYNDROME

As the contributions to this volume make abundantly clear, *Acalculia* is a multifaceted concept encompassing a variety of impairments having to do with number operations. Certainly the more general term *mathematical disability* is more appropriate as a designation for a failure in performance that may be due to disabilities of quite different types and at different levels of information processing. In his chapter, Spiers calls attention to the efforts of neurologists to analyze acalculia into types that might possess specific neurological implications, the most notable being those of Berger (1926) and of Hécaen and his collaborators (Hécaen, 1962, 1972; Hécaen, Angelergues, & Houillier, 1961; Collignon, Leclercq, & Mahy, 1977). At the present time, Hécaen's classification of mathematical disabilities into three types—an aphasic type involving impairment in the reading, writing, and oral understanding of numbers; a spatial type involving difficulty in aligning numbers and carrying them from one column to another; and anarithmetia involving loss of computational ability—is probably most relevant to the question of the place of acalculia in the Gerstmann syndrome.

Is a specific type of acalculia characteristic of the Gerstmann syndrome? A "body schema" theory of the nature of the syndrome, which relates acalculia directly to the basic deficit of finger agnosia, would predict that a Gerstmann patient's mathematical disability should be of the pure "anarithmetic" type. From the conception that the syndrome reflects an impairment in spatial or directional thinking it follows that the component of acalculia in it should be of the spatial type. The hypothesis that Gerstmann symptoms are expressions of impairment in symbolic thinking would predict that the acalculia should be of the aphasic type.

In line with his conception that the deficit in calculation is dependent upon the nuclear deficit of finger agnosia, Gerstmann himself stated that it was the pure anarithmetic type of acalculia that is found in association with the other elements of the syndrome (Gerstmann, 1940). However, he offered no empirical data to support his statement. In contrast, both Critchley (1953) and Hécaen (1972) stated that the spatial type of acalculia is the form most likely to be encountered in patients with the Gerstmann syndrome. However, again no supportive documentation was provided by either author. Later Critchley (1967) expressed the opinion that both the spatial and aphasic types of acalculia find a place in the Gerstmann syndrome, and he added that in all probability some cases show a pure anarithmetia. In their study of finger agnosia, Kinsbourne and Warrington

(1962) described Gerstmann patients who showed features of both spatial and aphasic acalculia. Analyzing the defective arithmetic performances of two patients with Gerstmann symptoms, Benson and Denckla (1969) were able to demonstrate that their failure was due to verbal impairment rather than to a basic disability in calculation.

In summary, there is no evidence that a specific type of acalculia is characteristic of the Gerstmann syndrome. All types of the disorder—spatial, purely arithmetic, and aphasic—either have been found or have been alleged to occur within the context of other Gerstmann symptoms.

THE "DEVELOPMENTAL GERSTMANN SYNDROME"

Varying combinations of Gerstmann symptoms, most notably acalculia and finger agnosia, have been described as a form of developmental disability in children (cf. Benson & Geschwind, 1970; Kinsbourne, 1968; Kinsbourne & Warrington, 1963; Spellacy & Peter, 1978). In contrast to the typical descriptions of adult patients, dyslexia and especially spelling disability are usually considered to be a cardinal feature of the clinical picture (Hermann, 1964; Hermann & Norrie, 1958; Kinsbourne & Warrington, 1963). However, children with acalculia and finger agnosia who read quite adequately are also encountered (Benson & Geschwind, 1970; Spellacy & Peter, 1978).

The study of Spellacy and Peter (1978) provides some interesting data on specific arithmetic disability in children. Fourteen school children with poor arithmetic skills were identified in a sample of 430 children who had been evaluated for a possible learning disability. Seven children proved to have adequate reading ability and the other seven were poor in reading as well as in arithmetic, six members of each group being boys. All the children had IQs of 80 or higher. The two groups of children showed rather different profiles of performance. The pure "anarithmetic" children (i.e., with adequate reading achievement) showed poorer right-left orientation and constructional praxis but better handwriting and oral word fluency than the "anarithmetic-dyslexic" children. Both groups were poor in finger localization and a visuoperceptual task (embedded figures).

There was a striking between-groups difference in respect to hand preference. Six of the seven "anarithmetic" children were left-handed as compared to only two "anarithmetic-dyslexic" children. In consonance with observations on adult patients (Benton, 1961; Heimburger et al., 1964), it was found that children who showed all four Gerstmann deficits invariably failed other task performances, leading the authors to doubt the usefulness of the "developmental Gerstmann syndrome" as a behavioral description.

It is clear from the findings of this study that specific arithmetic disability and other Gerstmann disabilities in children can be found both in association with and independently of specific reading disability. Thus the arithmetic deficit can occur within a verbal or nonverbal context, and this suggests that no single interpretation of the origin of Gerstmann symptoms is valid for all cases. Finally, if the concept of a "developmental Gerstmann syndrome" is to be retained, it would seem useful to distinguish between dyslexic and nondyslexic forms of the syndrome.

ACALCULIA AND CEREBRAL LOCALIZATION

Because mathematical performances make demands on such a great variety of cognitive capacities, it has always been clear to all but the most naive neurologists that it would be fruitless to search for a single limited region of the brain as the "center" of calculation. Instead their approach has been to try to analyze mathematical performance into its components, establish types of acalculia, and determine whether these types are systematically related to focal disease in particular cerebral areas. Thus, Henschen (1920) implicated the third frontal gyrus in the pronunciation of numbers and the angular gyrus and surrounding territory in the reading and writing of numbers. Berger (1926) attributed primary acalculia (equivalent to anarithmetia) to lesions in the posterior region of the left hemisphere, whereas acalculia secondary to aphasic, attentional or memory disorder could be produced by lesions in diverse sites.

Anarithmetia

This designation refers to failure in performing the fundamental arithmetic operations—addition, subtraction, multiplication, division—with preservation of the capacity to read and write numbers, to align them correctly in performing written calculations, to count, and to appreciate the relative value of numbers. Subtraction and division are often more severely affected than addition and multiplication. Failure is rarely complete, with simple automatized computations (e.g., 4 + 3, 2 × 2) being performed correctly. Oral calculation may be more affected than written calculation or vice versa.

Anarithmetia is a relatively uncommon disability. Among 18 patients with acalculia, Berger (1926) found only 3 that he could classify as having a primary acalculia. It can scarcely be expected that a brain-diseased patient with anarithmetia will be absolutely free from other neurobehavioral defects, and mild impairment of one type of another can always be elicited. However, such impairment does not appear to be sufficient to account for the marked disability in performing arithmetic operations. The typical picture of anarithmetia is exemplified by the following personally examined case.

A 66-year-old righthanded woman with an educational background of 12 grades and nurse's training was admitted to the neurological service of the University of

Iowa Hospitals because of complaints of poor vision and poor memory. The neurological examination was unremarkable except for the finding of a right homonymous hemianopia. She was alert and cooperative and responded appropriately to questions and commands. However, she was rather quiet, passive, and unspontaneous and showed some word-finding difficulties in conversation. She was sent for neuropsychological assessment, the referral question being whether there was evidence of a beginning dementia or a mild aphasia.

Her behavior during the assessment was much the same as had been observed at the neurological examination. She was alert and understood questions readily but was quiet and passive. She exhibited the same mild word-finding difficulty that had previously been noted. Temporal orientation was intact and she could read a watch correctly. The WAIS Information and Digit Span tests were performed at a high-average level, but performance on the WAIS Arithmetic Reasoning test was on a borderline defective level. Right-left orientation, geographic orientation, and finger recognition were normal. Constructional praxis (three-dimensional block construction, copying designs) was intact. However, she obtained a borderline score on the Visual Retention Test requiring the reproduction of designs from memory. Aphasia testing (Multilingual Aphasia Examination) elicited quite normal performances on visual confrontation naming, the Token Test, writing to dictation, and reading aloud and for meaning. The impression from these results was that the patient was neither demented nor aphasic. However, she did show a weakness in short-term visual memory that was consistent with her complaint of poor memory. Moreover, her WAIS Arithmetic Reasoning performance was significantly poorer than her other performances. For this reason she was given a battery of simple quantitative tasks specifically designed to probe for impairment in calculation (Benton, 1966; Levin, 1979).

On oral presentation of pairs of two-digit and three-digit numbers (e.g., 511 and 389) she had no difficulty in indicating which number was larger. Similarly, on visual presentation of comparable pairs of numbers she correctly identified the larger number. She correctly read two-digit and three-digit numbers aloud and correctly pointed to numbers read aloud by the examiner. She correctly wrote numbers to dictation and from copy. She correctly estimated the number of dots presented in both regular and irregular arrangements.

In contrast to these intact performances, her oral and written calculation was defective. Simple oral additions (e.g., $4 + 2$; $14 + 5$) were done correctly but extremely slowly. Two of five oral subtractions (e.g., $19 - 7$; $17 - 8$) were failed. One of five multiplication problems (e.g., 7×4) was failed. Simple division problems (e.g., $8 \div 2$) were done correctly but very slowly. Written calculation was more severely impaired with a 50% to 75% rate of failure on relatively simple problems (e.g., $55 + 89$; $72 - 35$; 142×5; $456 \div 6$).

Given the patient's normal reading and writing of numbers, her accurate counting and her correct appreciation of the symbolic value of numbers, her difficulties in calculation may be interpreted as a "true" anarithmetia. Although written calculation was more severely affected than oral calculation, the latter was also clearly defective as compared to normative expectations. Nor could her failures in written calculation be classified as a "spatial" acalculia because if this were the case she should have had difficulty in judging which of two multidigit numbers was the larger and in estimating the number of dots displayed in diverse spatial arrangements.

Computer-assisted tomography disclosed a space-occupying mass lesion in the parieto-occipital area of the left hemisphere, which was interpreted as strongly suggestive of a malignant tumor. Surgical exploration confirmed this finding, and pathological examination identified the neoplasm as a glioblastoma multiforme.

Anarithmetia in patients with focal brain disease is associated with lesions in the posterior temporo-parieto-occipital region of the left (or language-dominant) hemisphere. Henschen (1920) placed his "center" for calculation in the left angular gyrus, but few neurologists who concerned themselves with the problem accepted this localization. For example, Berger (1926) pointed out that autopsy study of his patients with primary acalculia showed that the angular gyrus was spared in all three cases. Two of his patients had extensive temporo-occipital tumors. The third patient proved to have an enormous temporal lobe tumor that undoubtedly exerted excessive pressure on neighboring areas of the left hemisphere. Kleist (1934), on the basis of his findings on patients with penetrating brain wounds as well as on the earlier observations of Poppelreuter (1917), implicated the occipital association areas close to the angular gyrus as the crucial locus of lesions producing disturbances of calculation independently of alexia or agraphia for numbers. The findings of more recent studies (e.g., Benson & Weir, 1972; Grafman, Passafiume, Faglioni, & Boller, 1982) have been consistent with this broad localization in the posterior temporo-parieto-occipital territory of the left hemisphere.

To try to specify a more precise locus for the lesions producing anarithmetia is almost certainly a futile exercise. The importance of visual imagery and visual schemata in performing all but the most automatized calculations is recognized, and hence it is understandable that a lesion in the occipital association region that impaired these schemata could produce an anarithmetia. Moreover, as Berger pointed out, a temporoparietal lesion that isolates an intact occipital area from its forward connections would have essentially the same effect in that visual schemata could not be brought into play in computational operations. Some anarithmetic patients do not merely have difficulty in attempting multiplication or division problems but seem to have entirely lost the concept of the specific operation. Although they will attempt to perform other arithmetic operations, they are completely at a loss when a multiplication or a division problem is posed. Berger attributed this distinctive performance pattern to a lesion in the speech area of the posterior temporal lobe.

Even though anarithmetia is by definition a disorder that is not explicable in terms of aphasic disorder, its close relationship to impairment in language function is undeniable. Almost all anarithmetic patients have been noted as showing mild aphasic defects such as word-finding difficulties or occasional paraphasic responses. Thus it is not unreasonable to view anarithmetia as a particular form of linguistic impairment related to disease of the language-dominant hemisphere.

Spatial Acalculia

Early case reports generally associated this type of impairment in calculation with posterior right hemisphere disease, although spatial acalculia in patients with left hemisphere lesions was also described (cf. Critchley, 1953). The large-scale study of Hécaen et al. (1961) supported this localization in finding spatial acalculia to be 12 times more frequent in patients with right hemisphere lesions than in those with left hemisphere disease. However, it is not clear precisely how "spatial" acalculia was defined in this study and the finding that no less than 24% of patients with right hemisphere disease showed a "spatial" type of disability cannot help but raise a question about the criteria of classification that were utilized.

The recent report of Grafman et al. (1982) describes the only controlled study of the question. Patients with unilateral lesions were screened for the ability to read and write numbers and only those who performed adequately were retained in the study. Their performances on a written test of calculation were evaluated both in terms of overall level and in terms of the frequency of "spatial" errors (misplacement, distortions, size, rotations, omissions, preservations). Thus both a "quantitative" score (overall performance level) and a "qualitative" (frequency of "spatial" errors) were derived from analysis of the performances. The results were clear in indicating that patients with left posterior lesions were poorer than those with lesions in other sites in respect to both overall performance level and the occurrence of spatial errors. However, patients with right hemisphere disease were also impaired on both measures relative to control patients. Inspection of the specific types of errors that were made suggested the possibility that there might be between-hemispheric differences in this respect.

Thus the thrust of this study is to deny any specific role of right hemisphere mechanisms in acalculia of the "spatial" type and to affirm the importance of left hemisphere disease in the production of all types of impairment. But perhaps the most important implication to be drawn from its findings is that "spatial" acalculia still requires more precise analysis with respect to its defining features. Once this is accomplished, the problem of site of lesion can be addressed in a more fruitful way.

Aphasic Acalculia

Although striking exceptions to the rule are encountered, impairment in the oral understanding and expression, as well as the reading and writing, of numbers is so common among aphasic patients that it is considered to be part of the clinical picture. However, just as aphasic patients with focal lesions in different loci within the language zone of the left hemisphere show qualitatively different types of linguistic impairment, it might be expected that their defects in calculation would also differ in respect to qualitative characteristics. This expectation has been borne out by some recent studies suggesting that spatial errors are more frequent in the performances of aphasics with posteriorly localized lesions than in those with anterior lesions (cf. Dahmen, Hartje, Bussing, & Sturm, 1982) and that different types of transcoding errors are made by "anterior" and "posterior" aphasics (cf. Deloche & Seron, 1982). These pioneering studies, as well as the older report of Benson and Denckla (1969) showing how misnaming can interfere with the expression of otherwise intact computational skills in aphasic patients, offer the promise that more detailed analysis of the computational performances of aphasic patients will clarify the question of lesional localization in aphasic acalculia.

REFERENCES

Benson, D. F., & Denckla, M. B. (1969). Verbal paraphasia as a cause of calculation disturbances. *Archives of Neurology, 21,* 96–102.

Benson, D. F., & Geschwind, N. (1970). Developmental Gerstmann syndrome. *Neurology, 20,* 293–298.

Benson, D. F., & Weir, W. F. (1972). Acalculia: Acquired anarithmetia. *Cortex, 8,* 465–472.

Benton, A. L. (1959a). Finger localization and finger praxis. *Quarterly Journal of Experimental Psychology, 11,* 39–44.

Benton, A. L. (1959b). *Right-left orientation and finger localization: Development and pathology.* New York: Hoeber-Harper.

Benton, A. L. (1961). The fiction of the "Gerstmann syndrome". *Journal of Neurology, Neurosurgery and Psychiatry, 24,* 176–181.

Benton, A. L. (1962). Clinical symptomatology in right and left hemisphere lesions. In V. B. Mountcastle (Ed.), *Interhemispheric relations and cerebral dominance* (pp. 253–263). Baltimore, MD: Johns Hopkins University Press.

Benton, A. L. (1966). *Problemi di neuropsicologia.* Firenze: Editrice Universitaria.

Benton, A. L. (1977). Reflections on the Gerstmann syndrome. *Brain and Language, 4,* 45–62.

Berger, H. (1926). Ueber Rechenstoerungen bei Herderkrankungen des Grosshirns. *Archiv fuer Psychiatrie, 78,* 238–263.

Collignon, R., Leclercq, C., & Mahy, J. (1977). Etude de la sémiologie des troubles du calcul observés au cours des lésions corticales. *Acta Neurological Belgica, 77,* 257–275.

Critchley, M. (1953). *The parietal lobes.* London: Edward Arnold.

Critchley, M. (1967). The enigma of Gerstmann's syndrome. *Brain, 89,* 1983–198.

Dahmen, W., Hartje, W., Büssing, A., & Sturm, W. (1982). Disorders of calculation in aphasic patients: Spatial and verbal components. *Neuropsychologia, 20,* 145–153.

Deloche, G., & Seron, X. (1982). From 3 to three: A differential analysis of skills in transcoding quantities between patients with Broca's and Wernicke's aphasia. *Brain, 85,* 719–733.

Gerstmann, J. (1924). Fingeragnosie: Eine umschriebene Stoerung der Orientierung am eigenen Koerper. *Wiener Klinische Wochenschrift, 37,* 1010–1012.

Gerstmann, J. (1927). Fingeragnosie und isolierte Agraphie: ein neues Syndrom. *Zeitschrift fuer die gesamte Neurologie und Psychiatrie, 108,* 152–177.

Gerstmann, J. (1930). Zur Symptomatologie der Hirnlaesionen im Uebergangsgebiet der unteren parietal- und mittleren Occipitalwindung. *Nervenarzt, 3,* 691–695.

Gerstmann, J. (1940). Syndrome of finger agnosia, disorientation for right and left, agraphia and acalculia. *Archives of Neurology and Psychiatry, 44,* 398–408.

Grafman, J., Passafiume, D., Gaflioni, P., & Boller, F. (1982). Calculation disturbances in adults with focal hemispheric damage. *Cortex, 18,* 37–50.

Hécaen, H. (1962). Clinical symptomatology in right and left hemisphere lesions. In V. B. Mountcastle (Ed.), *Interhemispheric relations and cerebral dominance.* Baltimore, MD: Johns Hopkins University Press.

Hécaen, H. (1972). Introduction à la neuropsychologie. Paris: Larousse.

Hécaen, H., Angelergues, R., & Houillier, S. (1961). Les variétés cliniques des acalculies au cours des lésions rétro-rolandiques: Approche statistique du problème. *Revue Neurologique, 105,* 85–103.

Heimburger, R. F., DeMyer, W. C., & Reitan, R. M. (1964). Implications of Gerstmann's syndrome. *Journal of Neurology, Neurosurgery and Psychiatry, 27,* 52–57.

Henschen, S. E. (1920). *Klinische und anatomische Beitraege zur Pathologie des Gehirns* (Vol. 5). Stockholm: Nordiska Bokhandeln.

Hermann, K. (1964). Specific reading disability with special reference to complicated word-blindness. *Danish Medical Bulletin, 11,* 34–40.

Hermann, K., & Norrie, E. (1958). Is congenital word-blindness a hereditary form of Gerstmann's syndrome? *Psychiatria et Neurologia (Basel), 136,* 59–73.

Jackson, C. V., & Zangwill, O. L. (1952). Experimental finger dyspraxia. *Quarterly Journal of Experimental Psychology, 4,* 1–10.

Kinsbourne, M. (1968). Developmental Gerstmann syndrome. *Pediatric Clinics of North America, 15,* 771–778.

Kinsbourne, M., & Warrington, E. (1962). A study of finger agnosia. *Brain, 85,* 47–66.

Kinsbourne, M., & Warrington, E. (1963). The developmental Gerstmann syndrome. *Archives of Neurology, 8,* 490–501.

Kleist, K. (1934). *Gehirnpathologie.* Leipzig: Barth.

Levin, H. S. (1979). The acalculias. In K. Heilman & E. Valenstein (Eds.), *Clinical neuropsychology* (pp. 128–140). New York: Oxford University Press.

Poppelreuter, W. (1917). *Die psychischen Schaedigungen durch Kopfschuss im Kriege 1914–16.*

Sauget, J., Benton, A. L., & Hécaen, H. (1971). Disturbances of the body schema in relation to language impairment and hemispheric locus of lesion. *Journal of Neurology, Neurosurgery and Psychiatry, 34,* 496–501.

Spellacy, F. & Peter, B. (1978). Dyscalculia and elements of the developmental Gerstmann syndrome in school children. *Cortex, 14,* 197–206.

6 The Effect of Spatial Disorders on Arithmetical Skills

W. Hartje
Abteilung Neurologie
der Medizinischen Fakultät an der
RWTH Aachen

According to an old, though only vaguely defined notion, numerical information contains a considerable spatial component. Hence defects of numerical or arithmetical skills have sometimes been traced back to deficits in spatial orientation and perception or in the mental representation of space.

Although the notion of "numerical space" ("Zahlenraum") is well known and widely used, it is difficult to decide whether this is only a useful analogy to describe the totality of all possible numbers, or whether there is in fact an inherent spatial structure in the organization and internal representation of numbers, and possibly also of mathematical operations (Annett & Kilshaw (1982).

EARLY CONCEPTS OF DYSCALCULIA— PHENOMENOLOGICAL AND DEVELOPMENTAL ASPECTS

Early in the century, efforts to find the critical cortical localization of calculation deficits, or "acalculia" as defined by Henschen (1919), were more or less unsuccessful. Although most authors stressed the importance of lesions in the parieto-occipital region of the language-dominant hemisphere, disorders of calculation were also observed after differently localized lesions in the left as well as in the right hemisphere (Berger, 1926; Geller, 1952; Henschen, 1920).

This led several authors to attempt to clarify the nature of the process (or processes) underlying calculation from a phenomenological and developmental point of view. They aimed to disentangle a primary, central, or basic function of calculation from factors secondarily involved in arithmetical performance, and then to relate "primary" and "secondary" disturbances of arithmetical activities to the localization of the cerebral lesions producing the deficit.

Impressed by a conspicuous coincidence of calculation deficits with occipital lesions accompanied by hemianopic defects, Peritz (1918) investigated the role played by visualization or optic mental representation in the processes underlying calculation. In trying to interpret his observations, he referred mainly to the work of Bergson (1911) and Wertheimer (1912).

According to Bergson, any clear mental representation of a number necessarily implies visual imagination in space, that is, numbers are conceived of as elements of a spatial matrix. Wertheimer stressed that the value of a given number is not obtained by simply adding one plus one, and so on, if there is no knowledge of the approximate total of the added "ones." What is needed is an approximate idea of the relative position of the number with regard either to the number 1 or to other familiar and outstanding numbers or quantities (e.g., 10, 50, etc.). According to Wertheimer, no meaningful idea of a number seems possible without such "quasi-spatial" determination.

Further support for the assumption that the knowledge of number values is intimately connected with an internal visual representation is derived from observations on the development of enumeration and calculation in children. In progressing from the small numbers most conveniently represented by the fingers of both hands, they learn to arrange objects in groups of fives or tens. The processes of numeration and notation, that is, the representation of numeral quantities by words and written signs (digits, figures), are thus associated with a basically concrete visual representation of quantities and visually guided manipulations of these quantities.

Combining this largely phenomenological consideration of the psychological nature of arithmetical skills with his observation that parieto-occipital lesions involving the visual system are closely linked to acalculia, Peritz (1918) inferred that the process of calculation must always be visually based. He regarded the disorder in mental calculation as due either to an impairment of visual memory or to a deficit in the visual analysis and/or synthesis ("Vermögen des Überschauens") of numerical relations and arithmetical operations.

Although Peritz cited Wertheimer's (1912) notion of "quasi-spatial" determination of numbers, he did not consider defects of spatial visualization or visuo-spatial-constructive deficits themselves as relevant factors in dyscalculia.

This was done, however, in a most explicit manner by Ehrenwald (1931), who described a patient with a bilateral dorsal parieto-occipital lesion caused by gunshot.

The patient was not aphasic but showed a severe disability of drawing and construction, an inability to indicate with open or closed eyes the topographical position of objects, buildings, and streets, and a moderate impairment of right-left orientation on the fingers.

Reading was mildly disturbed by occasional omission of syllables or of a line. Writing showed slight literal paragraphic mistakes, perseverative intrusions of letters, and somewhat irregular horizontal lines.

The calculation deficit was characterized by a spatial disorganization. Although reading and writing to dictation of two- or three-digit numbers were correct, in a problem of written addition of two-digit numbers, for example, the patient started with summing up the left column from top to bottom, continued with the right column in an upward direction, repeatedly lost his place, and finally gave up. In writing down the intermediate results (sums of ones and tens), he frequently confused the position values of the digits. Similar failures were observed with the subtraction of two-digit numbers.

Certainly, these errors could be explained by the patient's general spatial disorder. However, mental calculation was also severely impaired. When asked, for example, to multiply 12 by 13, the patient eventually found the partial products but did not know whether these should be added or multiplied.

Following the phenomenological analysis of Bergson (1911) and Wertheimer (1912), Ehrenwald (1931) conceived of the system of numbers as an eminently spatial concept, as the "distillate of optic-kinesthetically or tactually experienced impressions from the external world, the mutual spatial relations of which remained thinkable" (p. 543).

Consequently, according to this author, every numerical and arithmetical task, written or mental, comprises performances that necessarily imply the knowledge of these spatial relations.

In view of the combination of topographical disorientation, drawing or constructional disability, and deficits in calculation, writing and reading observed in his patient, which could essentially be characterized as spatial, Ehrenwald postulated a basic defect of "ordonnance" ("ordinative Grundstörung"), i.e., a disorder in the apperception of the coordination of the elements (the matrix) of space and time. He assumed that the patient's calculation deficit was the direct consequence of this basic disturbance and suggested naming this disorder "primary acalculia."

It should be noted, however, that Ehrenwald regarded the basic "ordinative" defect as an essentially motor-executive one (i.e., without concomitant deficits in the visual-receptive or visual-gnostic realm), whereas Peritz (1918) stressed particularly the optognostic aspect of the defect.

Criticizing earlier authors for overemphasizing the sensory aspect of calculation (i.e., the internal visual representation of quantities, numerals, and operations), Krapf (1937) considered the sensorimotor or constructive-praxic component to be the most important factor in calculation defects. He refers to Kleist (1934)—though otherwise critical of him—who stated that the four common arithmetic operations are abstractions of the basic ways of "handling" any quantities of objects: adding some, taking some away, producing several times the same quantity of objects or dividing a given quantity into equal parts. In this sense, calculation is to a high degree a manipulative act ("Hantierung").

Apart from his strong emphasis on the intrinsically constructive-praxic nature of arithmetical processes, Krapf agreed with Ehrenwald's interpretation that a spatial (or quasi-spatial as used by Wertheimer) factor plays an outstanding role in disorders of calculation. Thus, both authors held that there is a defect of mentally performed spatial operations at the root of acalculia.

Summarizing the evidence from these empirical observations and phenomenological interpretations, it would appear that because calculation is a function naturally linked to spatially organized thinking and manipulation, visuo-spatial and spatial-constructional deficits are at the core of acalculia.

Although in good agreement with the generally accepted preponderance of acalculia after parieto-occipital lesions, which are known to produce visuo-spatial disorders, this concept cannot explain the full diversity of calculation deficits. Geller (1952), who conceived the basic function of calculation as an act of logical thinking defining the relationship between two numbers by a third, pointed out that there must be many auxiliary functions, disturbances of which can produce difficulties in calculation. Drawing attention again to the developmental aspect of arithmetical skills, he noted that the common procedure by which children practice calculation (counting aloud while pointing to a series of objects or digits in a left to right order; manipulating the counters of an abacus, etc.) builds up a system of combined acoustic, optic, and kinesthetic representations for each numeral, the structure of the numerical matrix being characterized mainly by spatial and motor references. With increasing practice the acoustic representations become more important and the operations with these acoustic representations or number words are performed more and more automatically.

Here the concept of calculation ability is yet broader, including oral and written language, visuo-perceptive and visuo-constructive functions, spatial orientation, memory, and other functions. Indeed, Geller regards it as unnecessary to postulate a "primary" acalculia and states that in a strict sense all defects of calculation are secondary.

Finally, returning to the notion of spatial representation of numerals and arithmetical operations, a warning should be given against using this notion as if it were a reality and not merely a useful analogy (Grewel, 1952).

Possibly, however, there is a more direct correspondence between spatial abilities and mathematical geometry. This possibility is supported by findings indicating that performance in tests of spatial ability correlates higher with performance in tests of geometry than with marks in arithmetic (Smith, 1960), and that a factor defined by a spatial ability task loads higher on geometry than on algebra and higher on algebra than on mechanical arithmetic (Barakat, 1951).

ASSOCIATION OF SPATIAL DISORDERS AND DEFICITS IN WRITTEN CALCULATION

Even though it must remain an open question whether calculation is necessarily linked with spatial visualization, spatial orientation, and spatial-constructive abilities, there are many ways in which a disorder of spatial abilities can interfere with arithmetical performance. This is most obvious in written calculation.

Hypothetical Manifestations and Error Types

Consideration of the various points or stages at which spatial disorders are liable to interfere with written calculation leads to the list shown in Table 6.1. Most of the errors described in Table 6.1 can occur either on the perceptual or on the motor-executive, constructional level. For example, a 6 may erroneously be read or written as a 9, and a digit on the left side of a complex number can be omitted during reading or writing of that number.

Although it is certainly not possible to find a one-to-one correspondence between the errors listed above and the different kinds of spatial disorders, it seems useful to relate the different error-types to those spatial disorders that presumably cause them. The most relevant spatial disorders are:

1. Gaze apraxia
2. Visual hemi-inattention
3. Topographical disorientation
4. Spatial-constructional deficits
5. Disorders of topographical memory.

The term *gaze apraxia* is used here in accordance with De Renzi (1982) to designate a disruption of learned scanning movements of the eyes. It is observed as a symptom in a variety of ocular motor disorders (for review see De Renzi, 1982; Hartje, 1972). Patients with gaze apraxia have great difficulty in reading. They may show a tendency to irregular wandering eye movements, which, on the other hand, are often combined with an inability to shift fixation voluntarily from one word to the next. Frequently the patients lose their place in the text, pick out a word or two from a line, and skip the rest or select a word from a totally different place on the page.

It is obvious that such a disorder of visual exploration of space will also produce difficulties in written calculation by irregular omission or intrusion of digits or lines and a general "losing of one's place."

In *visual hemi-inattention,* one half (usually the left) of external space is neglected.

TABLE 6.1

Various Types of Spatial Errors Likely to Occur in Written Calculation

---

- Distortion of digits in shape or spatial orientation
- Inversion of single digits
- Misplacement of digits in multidigit numbers
- Dissociation of single digits in complex numbers
- Irregular horizontal alignment of digits in complex numbers
- Irregular vertical alignment of digits or numbers in columns
- Omission of digits on left or right side of a number
- Omission or displacement of auxiliary lines (e.g., to differentiate the operator from the product)
- Starting the calculation from the wrong place
- Local errors in the process of "carrying" or "borrowing"
- Skipping rows or columns during the process of calculation ("losing one's place")
- Disregard of the local values of the decimal system in the placement of intermediate results

---

In written calculation hemi-inattention will lead to omission of digits on the left side of complex numbers or even to omission of a column of digits on the left side of the problem. In writing down the intermediate products or the number values to be "carried" for example, shifting the numbers to the right will cause errors.[1]

The term *topographical disorientation* is used here in a broad sense, including defects of spatial perception, spatial visualization, and orientation in personal space (i.e., in relation to one's own body). (The reader is referred to De Renzi, 1982, for an excellent overview.) A few examples suffice here to illustrate the pertinent deficits. On the perceptual level patients may experience difficulties in differentiating the spatial orientation of lines, geometrical forms, letters, and so forth, in two- or three-dimensional space. Deficits in spatial visualization are observed in tasks where unfolded two-dimensional patterns must be related to three-dimensional geometrical forms, or in tasks requiring the visualization of rotating objects in different planes. A defect of orientation in personal space can manifest itself in confusion between the directions left, right, top, bottom, behind, and in front.

Clearly, spatial disorders of this type can lead to inversion errors in calculation problems: 5 may be misperceived or incorrectly reproduced as 2, or 86 could

---

[1]From a formal point of view it does not make much difference whether the arithmetic operation proceeds mainly from right to left as in addition, subtraction, and multiplication, or mainly from left to right as in division. In both instances it will be the digits on the left that are neglected. In more complex multiplication problems shifts of gaze in both directions are required and complex divisions usually include subprocesses of multiplication. In reading multidigit numbers the effect of hemi-inattention may well be more pronounced than in reading words and sentences because a number truncated on the left does not appear to be incomplete (unless a particular number is expected).

be read or written as 68 or even 89. Similarly, irregular alignment of digits in rows or columns, starting an addition from the left column, misplacement of figures in the process of carrying, wrong placement of the auxiliary lines, or separating the operators from the product are all examples of errors that can be caused by defects of topographical orientation.

In differentiating between *spatial-constructional deficits* and topographical disorientation, the stress is laid on the motor-executive or praxic component. In most, if not all, cases the constructional deficit is embedded in deficits of spatial perception, visualization, and orientation (Dee, 1970). It is therefore difficult to decide whether an error is due specifically to a constructional deficit.

However, a few errors in calculation can be ascribed more readily to a constructional deficit: (1) Distortion of digits in shape or spatial orientation, leading to faulty processing of these digits in the ongoing calculation and (2) misalignment of rows and columns, leading to overlapping of numbers and illegibility.

A *disorder of topographical memory* expresses itself, for example, as difficulty in remembering the location of pieces of furniture in a familiar room, the spatial arrangement of rooms and staircases in one's office, or the spatial orientation of well-known buildings and places in familiar surroundings. It can also show up in tasks where the spatial arrangement of a series of objects has to be kept in short-term memory, or where the path through a maze must be learned and remembered.

Keeping in mind that the conventional procedures used in written calculation must be learned and are forgotten if not practiced, it appears quite possible that a defect of topographical (spatial) memory can lead to errors or failure in calculation.

Of course, the schedules to be followed in written calculation are not simply spatial but also logical. Probably only few subjects, however, would be able to solve a complex division problem by logical reasoning alone if the conventional and more or less automatized spatial patterns of processing had been forgotten. We can also speculate that a defect of spatial memory might lead to errors on a more elementary level as well, for example, when the correct position of the hundreds and tens on the left of the ones is forgotten.

It has already been noted that there is no unequivocal correspondence between the different types of calculation errors and spatial disorders. In addition, it must be pointed out that in many instances we cannot be sure whether a given error is indeed determined by spatial factors. For example, starting a complex multidigit addition with the left column could as well be due to a breakdown of logical thinking or to an impaired knowledge of the significance of the decimal system. The same is true for errors caused by misplacement of "carried" values and intermediate products. Similarly, the misplacement of digits in complex numbers (e.g., 47 instead of 74) could be interpreted as a linguistic-symbolic error.

Therefore, before an error can reliably be classified as spatial, other possibilities should be considered and, if possible, excluded. To give a fictitious example: In a complex multiplication problem each successive intermediate product is shifted by one decimal place to the right instead of to the left. This could be interpreted as a spatial error due to severe left-sided hemi-inattention. But unless other mistakes characteristic of hemi-inattention (e.g., omission of left-hand digits in reading and writing numbers) occurs at the same time, this error could as well be explained by deficient insight into the properties of the decimal system.

Clinical Observations

In the previous paragraphs the points at which spatial disorders are liable to affect arithmetical performance were discussed mainly from a phenomenological point of view, i.e., without considering whether and to what extent spatial disorders do actually interfere with calculation.

A good deal of light has been shed on this question by the work of Hécaen, Angelergues, & Houillier (1961). Based on the clinical records of 183 acalculic patients with unilateral retrorolandic lesions, these authors suggested a classification of calculation defects according to the predominance of:

1. difficulties in the reading and writing of numbers,
2. difficulties in the spatial arrangement of numbers,
3. difficulties in the execution of arithmetical operations.

The second, spatial type of calculation deficit, which is the subject of the present chapter, was described as characterized by errors in the location and arrangement of digits with respect to each other, by spatial neglect (leading to omissions), and by spatial inversions of the operational processes. It was assumed to be present in 48 of the 183 cases.

This spatial type of dyscalculia was found to be predominantly associated with the following signs of spatial disorder:

1. Spatial hemi-inattention
2. Spatial agnosia
3. Spatial type of dyslexia
4. Dressing apraxia
5. Unilateral disorders of body schema
6. Oculomotor disorders
7. Vestibular disorders
8. Constructional apraxia

The prevalence of these disorders, with spatial hemi-inattention and spatial agnosia (visual hemi-inattention and topographical disorientation in the terminology used here) ranking highest in frequency, agrees well with the assumed relationship between the various types of spatial errors in written calculation and spatial disorders as described above. (Dressing apraxia and unilateral disorder of body schema can be subsumed under the disorders of topographical disorientation and hemi-inattention [Poeck, 1982].)

It seems remarkable, on the other hand, that in a group of patients without dyscalculia (and probably also with retrorolandic lesions) a constructional-apraxic disorder was nevertheless observed in 33% of cases, oculomotor disorders in 32%, and vestibular disorders in 52%. This indicates that these disorders do not necessarily lead to a disturbance in calculation.

Because only a minor proportion of the patients without dyscalculia showed clinical signs of spatial hemi-inattention and topographical disorientation, one could be tempted to conclude that these two types of spatial disorder are almost sufficient to produce a dyscalculia of the spatial type. However, such a conclusion is not warranted by the data presented in Hécaen et al.'s paper, which only gives the frequency of spatial disorders observed in the presence of spatial dyscalculia, but not vice versa. In other words, cases were selected according to the presence of dyscalculia and not on the basis of clinical signs of spatial (and other) disorders.

The finding that constructional-apraxic symptoms were present in 94% of patients with spatial dyscalculia, and also in 68% and 61%, respectively, of patients with the two nonspatial types of dyscalculia, is probably due to the fact that constructional difficulties occur about equally often after right and left retrorolandic lesions and are frequently observed in combination with receptive disorders of language (Arena & Gainotti, 1978; Benton, 1973; Colombo, De Renzi, & Faglioni, 1976; De Renzi & Faglioni, 1967). Again, the high proportion of patients with nonspatial dyscalculia in the presence of constructional deficits points to the fact that a constructional-apraxic disorder is not a sufficient condition for the manifestation of spatial calculation defects.

The critical involvement of visual hemi-inattention in spatial dyscalculia is further supported by observations of Cohn (1961). He described typically spatial defects of written calculation in three patients with either left homonymous hemianopia or left-sided hemi-inattention on double simultaneous visual stimulation. In written multiplication the numbers were not properly arrayed and consequently could not be totaled correctly, or the patients lost their place, omitted a digit in the stepwise process of multiplication or in the notation of intermediate products, or multiplied with a "carrying" number. (The reader is referred to the original paper for the depiction and detailed description of excellent examples.) According to Cohn, the hemianopic defect itself is not sufficient to explain these errors, because patients with right-sided hemianopia did not produce similar mistakes.

It is interesting to note that one of the dyscalculic patients described by Cohn showed a remarkable topographical (right-left) disorientation—but no signs of spatial deficit in complex written multiplication.

Further evidence for the fact that topographical disorientation and constructional-apraxic deficits do not necessarily lead to spatial errors in calculation can be derived from an observation of Strub and Geschwind (1974). Their patient, whose symptoms were described as Gerstmann syndrome without aphasia, showed minor difficulties with orientation in her environment and in locating cities on a map. She failed almost completely on the WAIS block design subtest and was unable to copy or draw spontaneously three-dimensional figures. Her errors in written calculation, however, could not be explained by misalignment of numbers but rather seemed to be due to a loss of the basic mathematical concept of complex multiplication and division.

In conclusion, there is ample evidence that the spatial type of dyscalculia as it manifests itself in written arithmetic is highly associated with disorders of space exploration, spatial or topographical orientation, and constructional-praxic performance. No single one of these disorders seems, however, to be either a necessary or a sufficient condition for the elicitation of spatial dyscalculia.

RECENT STATISTICAL RESEARCH ON THE IMPLICIT NATURE OF CALCULATION DEFICITS

Grafman, Passafiume, Faglioni, and Boller (1982) endeavored to evaluate the role played by visuo-spatial disorders (and by anarithmetia as defined by Hécaen et al., 1961) in subjects with impaired calculation abilities. Subjects were given a series of written calculation problems including multidigit addition, subtraction, multiplication, and division. The scoring procedure took account, among other things, of errors of the spatial type, like misplacement, rotation, and omission of numbers. Analyses of covariance, which also included scores on two tests of visuo-spatial and constructional abilities—copying crosses and geometric figures, respectively (De Renzi & Faglioni, 1967)—as concomitant variables, revealed no clear-cut effect of constructional ability and only a minor effect of visuo-spatial ability on the patients' performance in calculation. Similarly, an analysis of the severity of the different types of errors showed that spatial errors were not the most important.

A different approach to the problem of spatial factors in arithmetical skills was chosen by Dahmen, Hartje, Büssing, and Sturm (1982). These authors tried to classify a series of elementary numerical and arithmetical tasks into two groups, reflecting to a different extent spatial and verbal components. The tasks comprised (1) simple comprehension of numbers, (2) decomposition of complex numbers into "ones," "tens," and so on, (3) vertical alignment of numbers (including decimal numbers), (4) comparison of pairs of numbers according to their numerical value, (5) identification of the correct operational sign in arithmetical problems (e.g., 3 . . . 3 = 9), and (6) solution of conventional arithmetical problems. Three of the familiar visuo-spatial tasks were included as factorial reference tests.

Three different approaches were followed in classifying the tasks. First, all tests were presented pairwise to 20 normal subjects whose task it was to determine which of the two tests they considered to have a greater "spatial component," whatever this might be. Second, on the basis of the results in the three visuo-spatial reference tests, a group of 20 patients with retrorolandic right hemispheric lesions was divided into two clusters by means of a cluster analysis, with the patients in cluster 1 performing better than the patients in cluster 2. The arithmetical tasks were then ranked according to the differences in performance between the two clusters (larger differences pointing to a larger spatial component of the respective task). Third, the test results of three groups of brain-damaged subjects (the 20 right-brain-damaged subjects, as well as 20 patients with Broca's and 20 patients with Wernicke's aphasia) were submitted to a principal component analysis. Two factors were extracted, accounting for 83.4% of the total variance.

Conjoint consideration of the results of all three approaches suggested that the task of comprehension of operational signs involved the largest and most distinct spatial component, whereas the other arithmetical tasks appeared to be mainly characterized by a numeric-symbolic component.

Comparing the performances in the two arithmetical tasks with the most distinct spatial and numeric-symbolic component, respectively, showed that the patients with right-sided retrorolandic lesions and the Wernicke's aphasics scored lower on the spatial than the numeric-symbolic task, whereas there was no such difference for the Broca's aphasics. The former groups also performed less well on the three visuo-spatial reference tests.

Thus the findings supply indirect evidence for the postulate that spatial skills (or their disorders) play an important role at least in some kind of arithmetical performance. Since none of the tasks required written calculation, this evidence could pertain to some basic process in calculation.

Considering the task with the most prominent spatial component in the study by Dahmen et al. (1982), i.e., comprehension of operational signs, one is reminded of Geller's (1952) definition of calculation as an act of logical thinking that defines the relationship between two numbers by a third one. Though this process is, of course, also required in the usual form of arithmetical problems, e.g., "3 × 3 = . . .," it appears much less automatized and less liable to a verbo-acoustical solution if the problem is presented in the form "3 . . . 3 = 9."

OBSERVATIONS ON THE CEREBRAL LOCALIZATION OF SPATIAL DYSCALCULIA

In their efforts to demonstrate the importance of visual or visuo-spatial abilities in arithmetical performance several authors have focused their attention on the association between defects in calculation and occipital or parieto-occipital lesions (Kleist, 1934; Lewandowsky & Stadelmann, 1908; Peritz, 1918). Most of the earlier authors held that it is the parieto-occipital region of the language-dominant hemisphere that is critically involved in arithmetical abilities. Later, the importance of the homologous region in the right hemisphere became more and more evident, in parallel with the discovery of the relative dominance of this hemisphere for visuo-spatial functions.

It was once again the pioneer work of Hécaen et al. (1961) that first gave a clear empirically based picture of the relationship between dyscalculia and cerebral localization. They observed a calculation disorder of the spatial type in 23.5% of their patients with right-sided retrorolandic lesions as against only 2% of patients with left-sided retrorolandic lesions, and in 17% of patients with bilateral lesions.

In a more recent study, Collignon, Leclercq, and Mahy (1977) found an almost equal proportion of spatial calculation deficits in patients with unilateral left- and right-sided cerebral lesions. It must be noted, however, that their sample was very small (11 right- and 15 left-sided cases) and that the authors gave no sufficiently clear definition of what they mean by spatial difficulties in calculation.

Indirect evidence with regard to the importance of left and right hemispheric lesions can be derived from the experimental studies of Grafman et al. (1982) and Dahmen et al. (1982). Both studies agree that posterior lesions of either hemisphere are found to lead to greater impairment of arithmetical performance than anterior lesions, and that the severest impairment is observed with left posterior lesions (associated with Wernicke's aphasia and/or visual field defects). However, whereas Grafman et al. gave only little weight to the effect of spatial deficits in the impairment of calculation (at least insofar as patients with left retrorolandic lesions are concerned), Dahmen et al. conclude that a deficiency in spatial visualization plays an important role in the impaired arithmetical performance not only of patients with right posterior lesions but also of patients with left posterior lesions (and Wernicke's aphasia).

CONCLUDING REMARKS

In trying to elaborate the involvement of spatial disorders in arithmetical performances it is helpful to distinguish explicitly visuo-spatial or spatial-constructional errors as seen in written calculation from those defects in written or mental calculation to which an implicitly spatial nature is ascribed merely on theoretical or phenomenological grounds.

There can be no doubt that severe disorders of space exploration, spatial visualization, and spatial orientation will often lead to errors in calculation. The type of error most readily identified as being due to a spatial disorder is omission of digits or even of a column of digits (mainly to the left of where the subject is just working). This corresponds very well to the observation of Hécaen et al.

(1961) that spatial hemi-inattention is frequently associated with dyscalculia of the spatial type, but only rarely with the nonspatial types of dyscalculia (i.e., anarithmetia and dyscalculia due to alexia and agraphia for numbers). It should be noted in this respect that no such dissociation is observed for the presence of visual field defects per se, i.e., without concomitant hemi-inattention.

Furthermore, marked disarray of the vertical alignment of numbers or gross dislocation of intermediate products or "carrying" numbers can generally be traced back to a disorder of general spatial orientation or ocular scanning.

However, apart from a few instances in which the spatial disarray in written calculation is obvious, only thorough observation of the ongoing process of computation (preferably including the verbalization of the various steps by the subject) allows reliable identification of spatial errors in calculation. The rareness of unequivocal examples of spatial errors in calculation in the literature is probably indicative of this difficulty.

Even if spatial deficits in written calculation are observed, the question still remains whether this implies an impairment of arithmetical skills in general. Up to now, this question has not been explored systematically, e.g., by comparison of written and mental calculation. A major obstacle lies in the fact that the average subject is not able to solve mentally the complex arithmetical problems normally used in the examination of written calculation. The solution of simpler arithmetical problems, on the other hand, is achieved by more or less automatic processes relying mainly on verbo-acoustical memory. Typically, the use of the multiplication table, which relies heavily on verbo-acoustical memory, is least impaired in most dyscalculic patients.

Perhaps the central issue of this chapter, i.e., the question whether spatial abilities are fundamental to arithmetical skills, is even more difficult to answer. The observation of spatial deficits in calculation in patients with one or the other type of spatial disorder cannot answer this question. They could be merely one possible manifestation of the spatial disorder in an activity that is, like many others, sensitive to disturbances of spatial exploration, visualization, and orientation.

The partial support for an intrinsic link between spatial and arithmetical activities provided by the results of Dahmen et al. (1982) is limited by the factor-analytic findings of Barakat (1951), showing that although proficiency in geometry has a high saturation with the spatial factor, elementary arithmetical skills are rather more closely related to memory.

The use of number-forms (i.e., spatially visualized patterns or schemata in which each numeral has a fixed place) has been taken as evidence for the importance of spatial factors in arithmetical skills (Galton, 1880; Morton, 1936). Spalding and Zangwill (1950) ascribed the arithmetical disability of a patient with impaired visual memory and topographical orientation to the concomitant impairment of the patient's visual-spatial number-form. The relevance of these observations can be doubted, however, because even in subjects possessing a number-form, the actual computational processes appear to be performed without the active manipulation of the visual image (Oswald, 1960).

Thus, whereas the detrimental effect of spatial disorders, and above all of spatial hemi-inattention on some arithmetical performance, is well established, more research is needed to answer the question whether a spatial factor is involved in every kind of arithmetical activity.

ACKNOWLEDGMENT

I wish to thank Vivien Kitteringham for her great help with the English manuscript.

REFERENCES

Annett, M., & Kilshaw, D. (1982). Mathematical ability and lateral asymmetry. *Cortex, 18,* 547–568.

Arena, R., & Gainotti, G. (1978). Constructional apraxia and visuo-perceptive disabilities in relation to laterality of cerebral lesions. *Cortex, 14,* 463–473.

Barakat, M. K. (1951). A factorial study of mathematical abilities. *British Journal of Psychology (Statistical Section), 4,* 137–156.

Benton, A. L. (1973). Visuo-constructive disability in patients with cerebral disease: Its relationship to side of lesion and aphasic disorder. *Documenta Ophthalmologica, 34,* 67–76.

Berger, H. (1926). Über Rechenstörungen bei Herderkrankungen des Großhirns. *Archiv für Psychiatrie und Nervenkrankheiten, 78,* 238–263.

Bergson, H. (1911). Zeit und Freiheit. Jena: Diederichs.

Cohn, R. (1961). Dyscalculia. *Archives of Neurology, 4,* 301–307.

Collignon, R., Leclercq, C., & Mahy, J. (1977). Etude de la sémiologie des troubles du calcul observés au cours des lésions corticales. *Acta Neurologica Belgica, 77,* 257–275.

Colombo, A., De Renzi, E., & Faglioni, P. (1976). The occurrence of visual neglect in patients with unilateral cerebral disease. *Cortex, 12,* 221–231.

Dahmen, W., Hartje, W., Büssing, A., & Sturm, W. (1982). Disorders of calculation in aphasic patients—spatial and verbal components. *Neuropsychologia, 20,* 145–153.

Dee, H. L. (1970). Visuo-constructive and visuo-perceptive deficit in patients with unilateral cerebral lesions. *Neuropsychologia, 8,* 305–314.

De Renzi, E. (1982). Disorders of space exploration and cognition. Chichester: Wiley.

De Renzi, E., & Faglioni, E. (1967). The relationship between visuo-spatial impairment and constructional apraxia. *Cortex, 3,* 327–342.

Ehrenwald, H. (1931). Störung der Zeitauffassung, der räumlichen Orientierung, des Zeichnens und des Rechnens bei einem Hirnverletzten. *Zeitschrift für die gesamte Neurologie und Psychiatrie, 132,* 518–569.

Galton, F. (1880). Visualised numerals. *Nature, 21,* 252–256; 323; 494–495.

Geller, W. (1952). Über Lokalisationsfragen bei Rechenstörungen. *Fortschritte der Neurologie, Psychiatrie und ihrer Grenzgebiete, 20,* 173–194.

Grafman, J., Passafiume, D., Faglioni, P., & Boller, F. (1982). Calculation disturbances in adults with focal hemispheric damage. *Cortex, 18,* 37–50.

Grewel, F. (1952). Acalculia. *Brain, 75,* 397–407.

Hartje, W. (1972). Reading disturbances in the presence of oculomotor disorders. *European Neurology, 7,* 249–264.

Hécaen, H., Angelergues, R., & Houillier, S. (1961). Les variétés cliniques des acalculies au cours des lésions rétrorolandiques: Approche statistique du problème. *Revue Neurologique, 105,* 85–103.

Henschen, S. E. (1919). Über Sprach-, Musik- und Rechenmechanismen und ihre Lokalisationen im Großhirn. *Zeitschrift für die gesamte Neurologie und Psychiatrie, 52,* 273–298.

Henschen, S. E. (1920). Klinische und anatomische Beiträge zur Pathologie des Gehirns. Stockholm: Nordiska Bokhandeln.

Kleist, K. (1934). Gehirnpathologie. Leipzig: Barth.

Krapf, E. (1937). Über Akalkulie. *Schweizer Archiv für Neurologie und Psychiatrie, 39,* 330–334.

Lewandowsky, M., & Stadelmann, E. (1908). Über einen bemerkenswerten Fall von Hirnblutung und über Rechenstörungen bei Herderkrankung des Gehirns. *Journal für Psychologie und Neurologie, 11,* 249–265.

Morton, D. M. (1936). Number forms and arithmetical ability in children. *British Journal of Educational Psychology, 6,* 53–73.

Oswald, I. (1960). Number-forms and kindred visual images. *Journal of General Psychology, 63,* 81–88.

Peritz, G. (1918). Zur Pathopsychologie des Rechnens. *Deutsche Zeitschrift für Nervenheilkunde, 61,* 234–340.

Poeck, K. (1982). Neuropsychologische Symptome ohne eigenständige Bedeutung. In: K. Poeck (Ed.), Klinische Neuropsychologie (pp. 167–177). Stuttgart: Thieme.

Smith, I. M. (1960). The validity of tests of spatial ability as predictors of success on technical courses. *British Journal of Educational Psychology, 30,* 138–145.

Spalding, J. M. K., & Zangwill, O. L. (1950). Disturbance of number-form in a case of brain injury. *Journal of Neurology, Neurosurgery, and Psychiatry, 13,* 24–29.

Strub, R., & Geschwind, N. (1974). Gerstmann syndrome without aphasia. *Cortex, 10,* 378–387.

Wertheimer, M. (1912). Über das Denken der Naturvölker I. Zahlen und Zahlgebilde. *Zeitschrift für Psychologie, 60,* 321–378.

7 Numerical Transcoding: A General Production Model

Gérard Deloche
Institut National de la Santé et de la Recherche Médicale

Xavier Seron
Unité de Neuropsychologie Expérimentale de l'Adulte

INTRODUCTION

This chapter is devoted to one of the so-called verbal components of acalculia, the processing of numbers in function of the system of notation used to represent the quantities. That isolating number processing as a separate cognitive domain considered as distinct from calculation abilities has some utility is evident from the neuropsychological literature and can be related to three areas of research:

1. In the semiological and classificatory approaches to acalculia, the distinction we propose between digit/number and calculation processing echoes the classic distinction between alexia/agraphia for numbers and "true acalculia" or anarithmetia (Hécaen, Angelergues, & Houllier, 1961).

2. In the neurolinguistic approaches to aphasia, the question of the dependence or the autonomy of digit-number and letter/word processing has frequently been raised.

3. In lateral difference studies, a differential implication of each hemisphere in number and language processing has often been hypothesized but remains unresolved. This issue is generally situated in the more general theoretical framework of differential hemispheric processing capabilities according to the logographic versus the phonographic surface code of the linguistic units.

This introduction is restricted to a brief examination of the most important neuropsychological data relevant to these three issues. Because the problem of a possible right hemispheric contribution to digit and number processing and to calculation is discussed in detail (at least on the level of single-digit processing)

137

in Holender and Peereman's contribution to this volume (Holender & Peereman, chapter 3), our treatment of this subject is less detailed than would otherwise be the case.

Dissociation Between Digit/Number and Calculation Processing

A dissociation between calculation disorders and alexia or agraphia for digits and numbers was suggested by Henschen (1920), on the basis of an extended group-based study (including personal cases as well as many cases collected from the literature). He pointed out that even though number reading and writing disorders were frequently associated with calculation deficits, cases of dissociations in the two directions do occur: acalculia without number alexia or agraphia, and number or digit alexia without calculation difficulties. Henschen's studies have since been questioned, and two major flaws have been observed. The first is general and methodological: the inadequacy of the group-study paradigm (gathering together cases analyzed with different testing procedures) to establish the existence of selective and separate disorders (Shallice, 1979), the general opinion being that selective functional dissociations cannot be assessed on the sole basis of variations in the distribution of errors gathered from clearly heterogeneous subpopulations of subjects. The second concerns the lack of detail in the description of the procedures used for assessing the calculation or number-processing disorders as well as the lack of precise descriptions of the disorders themselves. For example, in Henschen's review it is not clear if acalculia was established by means of oral or written tasks or if the number-reading and -writing difficulties generally referred to numbers presented in the digital code. Thus some of the dissociations could have resulted from a modality or surface-code confusing effect rather than from a true dissociation on a clearly different and identifiable component processing level.

Another historically important group study (Hécaen et al., 1961) was conducted 40 years after Henschen's. From an analysis of the distribution of errors in various arithmetic tasks and by taking into account the presence of associated disorders, Hécaen proposed distinguishing three groups of acalculic subjects: alexic/agraphic acalculia subjects, whose main characteristic is difficulty in reading and writing digits and numbers; spatial acalculia subjects, who have prominent but highly differentiated spatial difficulties in performing written calculations; and the anarithmetia subjects, who mainly have procedural difficulties in solving arithmetic operations. This classification resembles Henschen's somewhat, but because it also derives from a group-based study, Henschen's limitations are also applicable to it. However, since Hécaen et al. systematically examined the co-occurrence of alexia and agraphia for digits and numbers as well as difficulties in solving oral and written arithmetic problems, some of their data must be carefully considered. In favor of a lack of dissociation, these authors observed that the subjects presenting digit or number alexia, or digit or number agraphia, were, as a group, inferior to subjects without such disorders in written as well as in oral arithmetic operations. Given the absence of detailed description of what the arithmetic difficulties were, however, such a relationship cannot be interpreted as indicating the existence of a common underlying processing deficit. More interesting are the data that point to a possible dissociation: of the subjects with digit alexia, 20% presented no oral calculation disorders and 5% no writing calculation disorders, and, of those with digit agraphia, 8% presented no oral and 10% no written calculation disorders.

Other, less well-documented group studies also seem to favor the existence of various dissociations between number and calculation processing. In the study of Collignon, Leclercq, and Mahy (1977) dissociations were reported (but with no details) in a group of 26 unilaterally brain-lesioned subjects. There was one case of oral acalculia without number alexia, and the reverse, one case of number alexia without oral acalculia. Dissociations of intramodality tasks were also observed: two cases of written acalculia without number alexia, three cases of number alexia without written acalculia, and finally, five cases of apparent dissociation between number agraphia and written acalculia. Although they did not address this question directly, Grafman, Passafiume, Faglioni, and Boller (1982) demonstrated the presence of digit-written calculation difficulties in subjects otherwise able to write digits corresponding to a set of various tokens and to perform a magnitude comparison task on pairs of two-digit numbers. However, because the analysis of calculation errors was mainly designed to examine the incidence of spatial factors, the kind of dissociation exemplified in such cases cannot be specified. Finally, although Dahmen, Hartje, Büssing, and Sturm (1982) used five different interesting tasks (four devoted to number processing and one to elementary arithmetic operations) in testing 20 Broca's aphasics, 20 Wernicke's aphasics, and 20 right-hemispheric-lesioned subjects, the type of statistical analyses they used did not give any indication of the functional dissociations we are looking for here.

In summary, the data from these group studies are ambiguous. Although most of them point to the existence of a dissociation between number processing and calculation abilities, they contain several methodological biases as regards subject selection and classification, the methods and procedures of deficit assessment, and the description of the errors themselves.

Single-case studies are somewhat more numerous, but for some of them we have only secondhand information at our disposal (especially the review of Ajuriaguerra & Hécaen, 1960; Boller & Grafman, 1985). In 1908, Lewandowsky and Stadelman described a case of alexia for numbers that they distinguished from difficulties in reading isolated digits. Sittig's (1921) contribution was to indicate the existence of several different difficulties, some concerning number processing, like position errors when reading numbers and auditory confusion between morphologically similar number names, others being true procedural difficulties in performing arithmetic operations. Van Woerkom (1925) described a patient with a frontal lesion who, in addition to difficulties in tasks like counting, solving arithmetic problems, and comprehending the digit positional value system, presented some difficulties in writing numbers and a preserved ability to do simple addition and subtraction. However, as we lack a sufficiently clear description of the precise errors made by these patients, none of these single cases can at present be considered as providing strong evidence in favor of a dissociation between number processing and calculation.

In fact, the most interesting single-case study and the only well-documented one before the fifties is the one presented by Singer and Low (1933) about a subject who had contracted encephalitis from carbon monoxide poisoning. This subject, in addition to minor aphasic difficulties (mostly discrete anomia), constructional apraxia, a right hemineglect syndrome, and gross agraphia, presented specific difficulties in number processing and arithmetic abilities. Singer and Low's case presented no clear dissociation between number processing and calculation abilities but the analysis indicated that a more subtle dissociation has to be sought. First, the patient was clearly able to read numbers of one, two, and three digits. Difficulties arose with numbers containing three digits and zero (probably intercalar) and more than three digits. This would seem to indicate specific difficulties in dealing with *thousand,* which, as indicated later in this chapter, provokes the execution of specific transcoding rules.

More generally, the analysis of the errors indicated that they were not at random, and some could be interpreted as the result of inadequate transcoding mechanisms. Number writing from dictation was also possible for one- and two-digit numbers, and number repetition was correct, at least when the numbers were not embedded in a linguistic context or in the context of arithmetic problems. One may thus conclude that this patient was able to read, write, and repeat single- and two-digit numbers and that these abilities contrasted with severe calculation disorders, there being an inability to solve simple two-digit addition problems if the result was greater than ten and simple two-digit subtraction problems (either in the verbal or in the written modality).

Benson and Weir (1972) presented an interesting case of a patient with anarithmetia who had difficulties only with written multiplication and division. This patient could count forward and backward rapidly, and could read, write, and recognize all numbers. His calculation abilities, assessed with a formal test of computation ability problems, oral and written, and a multiple-choice paradigm, indicated no problem with addition or subtraction but almost total failure with multiplication and division. Analysis of the errors indicated that the calculation difficulties did not result from an inability to retrieve multiplication tables or from difficulties with the addition part of the multiplication procedure, but specifically with the multiplication steps of multidigit multiplication problems. Interestingly enough, these specific procedural difficulties were completely independent of the processes implied in the treatment of numbers and digits. In another interesting study, Benson and Denckla (1969) pointed out some of the "secondary effects" that transcoding problems with numbers and digits may have on calculation abilities. They presented two single-case studies of what they called paraphasia, paralexia, or paragraphia in kind when reading, writing, or repeating number names. Such transcoding errors had dramatic consequences on arithmetic calculations that varied according to the assessing procedures used. Thus their first subject for the written problem 4 + 5 said "eight," wrote "5," and chose "9" from the multiple-choice list. Their second subject having to solve 22 minus 17 repeated "22 minus 18," but gave the correct answer "5" and, when asked to write and solve the problem 4 plus 7 wrote the problem correctly, gave the answer "16" orally, and wrote the correct digit solution "11."

Even though both cases described by Benson and Denckla seemed also to present some true procedural difficulties when performing calculation (for example with carrying procedures), the main interest of their observations is that they confirm that arithmetic abilities have to be examined through the many modes of stimulus presentation and response and not as "a unitary or irreducible phenomenon." The problem is thus not to establish on a gross level the existence of processing independence when handling numbers or performing calculations, but to carefully analyze the processing component of both tasks and to determine the calculation tasks and the modality of presentation and response (written or oral) that are or are not altered by a specific digit or number-processing deficit. Finally, the orientation of neuropsychological research toward more finely grained and more theoretically motivated dissociation has been reflected in the well-documented study of Warrington (1982, and this volume), who presents a selective breakdown in arithmetic calculation due to an impaired knowledge of arithmetic facts but without number-processing deficiencies. Other illustrative data in the same direction have also been presented and discussed in the framework of information-processing models by Caramazza and McCloskey (this book).

To conclude this brief and certainly not exhaustive review of the neuropsychological literature we would note that the problem of a possible dissociation between number processing and calculation also has to be reexamined on other grounds. The main objective is presently not to establish gross dissociation but to construct detailed models of the subprocesses implied in the various number-processing tasks (transcoding from one code to another, simple or complex forward and backward counting, magnitude comparison tasks and so on) and in various arithmetic tasks (oral calculation, written digit calculation, automated arithmetic facts, arithmetic problems, and so on). It is only where such models have been clearly elaborated in a coherent theoretical framework that co-occurrence or dissociation of errors between number and arithmetic tasks would be interpretable by means of analyses of selective breakdown altering clearly identified subjacent processing components.

Number Processing, Acalculia and Related Disorders

As to the question of acalculia and its functional relations to associated disorders (mainly aphasic language disorders), a number of issues must be briefly reviewed. First, aphasics are often reported able to perform better in number than language processing. Such number sparing was found in the group study of Gardner (1974), which compared the naming performance for pictures of animals, colors, letters, and numbers. The numbers proved to be the best preserved and to have the highest in-kind substitution percentage when errors occurred. It thus seems that numbers do form a coding system relatively resistant to brain damage. Single-case studies also mention this point in alexics (Albert, Yamadori, Gardner, & Howes, 1973) in reading aloud, understanding, and writing numbers despite alexia and agraphia (but with noticeable preserved abilities to rapidly produce the number-word sequence both forward and backward without error and even to count in discontinuous series [e.g., by threes, Benson & Weir, 1972]); in showing written and auditory number comprehension even in cases of severe aphasia (Barbizet, Bindefeld, Moaty, & Le Goff, 1967; Ruffieux, Jacot-Descombes, Python-Thuillard, & Assal, 1981); and in Wernicke's aphasia with Gerstmann syndrome (Assal & Jacot-Descombes, 1984). Because the reverse pattern, digit- or number-reading impairment without alexia for letters or words also occurs (Grewel, 1973), language and numbers thus appear to be semiotic systems that possess a degree of independence. Second, the variety observed in the nature (linguistic [spatial, Hartje, this volume] etc.) of calculation disorders points to the variety of the representational tools (verbal, visual, etc.) preferentially used by individuals when performing arithmetic (Leonhard, 1979). In this respect, it is not surprising that calculation errors in the cases described by Benson and Denckla (1969) were induced by a language disorder (verbal paraphasia), but by a left-sided occipito-parietal lesion that grossly impaired the visual spatial pattern of number form commonly handled by Spalding and Zangwill's (1950) patient prior to his gunshot wound. Also relevant here are cross-cultural studies that analyze the effect of abacus training and of the verbal learning of basic addition and subtraction number facts in Japanese (Hatano, 1982) and Chinese children (Stigler, 1984; see also Grafman & Boller, this volume) as compared to the emphasis in Western countries on a more abstract approach to numbers. Comparisons of children's performances, of their preferred strategies in solving calculation problems, and of the type of errors committed have provided evidence of the differential influence of the kind of representational structure constructed for number processing in the two cultures on the management of the same base-10 system. See Gonzalez and Kolers (1982, and this volume) for a general discussion of the role of learning conditions on learned skills, and examples in Singer and Low (1933) or Lawler (1981) showing that the apparently same addition problem (75 + 26) can be handled by different procedures depending on its context (arithmetic problems presented auditorilly or in writing, or money problems involving cents). Third, and this is suggested by the last remark, there may exist a dissociation between written and oral calculation, the former being generally better preserved (Assal, Buttet, & Jolivet 1981; Gardner, Strub, & Albert, 1975; Hécaen et al., 1961).

Right Hemisphere Contribution

Because written arithmetic has always been examined in the ideographic system of arabic digits and not in the alphabetical forms corresponding to auditorilly presented numbers, the differential effect of these two notational systems may be attributable to differential hemisphere processing capacities for the ideographic/aphabetical dimension. An ability for the right hemisphere to do simple counting and enumeration of figures had already been suggested by Henschen (1926) on the grounds of the ability of this hemisphere to handle automatic processes with significant visual dimension; the arguments more recently reviewed by Coltheart (1980) emphasize the distinction between verbal and ideographic material in both pathological (split-brain subjects, alexics) and normal subjects for tachistoscopic recognition of numbers or magnitude comparisons in Stroop-like conditions. For instance, incongruence between the physical size of number symbols and their values was shown to affect numerical comparative judgments with digital but not with alphabetical English forms (Besner & Coltheart, 1979; but see Peereman & Holender, in press, for conflicting results), which was replicated by Takahashi and Green (1983), who observed an interference effect with the Japanese ideographic script (kanji) but not with syllabic script (kana). However, the proposal of the last two authors that the two ideographic systems (arabic digits and kanji) are read by the same mechanism must be considered with caution since neuropsychological data seem to indicate a double dissociation; Sasanuma and Monoi (1975) studied a patient who could read arabic numerals but not kanji characters, and the inverse was reported by Yamadori (1975). However, such arguments could, in turn, be inconclusive because, as pointed out by Besner, Daniels, and Slade (1982), the symbols used in both scripts do not have the same meanings, and thus the results might be accounted for by differential preserved or impaired processing of numbers as a specific semantic domain. Thus, at present, more experimental data have to be gathered, and the significance of the lateral difference observed has to be more clearly interpreted (see, for a more detailed discussion on some pitfalls in the lateral difference literature on digit material, the critical contribution of Holender and Peereman, this volume). The absence of any syllabic effect in latencies for naming two-digit numbers presented in arabic forms seems to favor the hypothesis of a direct recognition procedure, without a syllable-dependent implicit speech process (Henderson, Coltheart, & Woodhouse, 1973) that could be handled by right hemisphere mechanisms (however, see Klapp, 1974, for contrary results). However that may be, the right hemisphere hypothesis for ideographic or arabic script processing requires further elaboration to account for right visual field advantages found in a metalinguistic task where subjects judged the congruity between numerical magnitudes and physical sizes of arabic digits and of their kanji counterparts (Hatta, 1983) and in the verbal tasks of writing down arabic digits or naming kanji and arabic digits mixed in the same test battery (Besner, Daniels, & Slade, 1982). One must also account for the preserved ability of a right-handed subject with right cerebral damage to complete written digit series with constant increments like 1, 8, 15, 22, . . . or 27, 21, 15, . . . (Leleux, Kaiser, & Lebrun, 1979).

THE TWO MAIN CODING SYSTEMS FOR QUANTITIES: DESCRIPTION AND TRANSCODING PROCESSES

In analyzing in the light of pathological data the architecture and functioning of the processes used by normals when operating on the different systems or notations that represent quantities, one must first consider the linguistic properties and the structure of these notational systems, second, elaborate a hypothetical model of normal transcoding processes used when one passes from one notational system to another and, third, evaluate the relevance of the proposed transcoding model in function of its capacity to interpret and predict errors produced by brain-damaged subjects.

The Two Main Coding Systems of Quantities: Some Descriptive Elements

Among the different systems used to represent quantities, we restrict our analysis to the two most common: the *digital* or *arabic* code, e.g., "34," and the *alphabetic* or *numeral* code, e.g., "thirty-four." In our analysis, each code is considered as a true linguistic system having a specific lexicon (the ensemble of the symbols used), a syntax that defines the set of acceptable structures, and a semantics that attributes its meaning at each sequence.

The Arabic or Digital Notational System

The digital system has a restricted lexicon of 10 digits, 0, 1, 2, . . . , 9, and the comma ",", which is used as a separator, splitting the digit string from the right in groups of three-digit substrings. Apart from this separation rule, the only condition for a well-formed integer number is that the digit string cannot have one or more 0s at its leftmost part.[1] The signification of a digital form, its value, is obtained by the addition of the lexical value of each digit affected by a power of ten depending on the position of the digit in the string. For example, 439 has

---

[1]This rule is of course only true for numbers representing quantities. When digit strings are used with denotative and not cardinal meaning as in phone numbers, ZIP codes, and in the case of James Bond's 007, the heading 0's deletion rule is not relevant.

the value of $4 \times 10^2 + 3 \times 10^1 + 9 \times 10^0$. Thus the arabic system constitutes an autonomous notational system distinct from language. The logographic nature of the digit units as well as the better preservation evidenced by aphasics when handling quantities in the arabic system than in the alphabetic code has raised the problem of the specificity of the processes acting on the digit symbols. In lateral difference studies, this has led to hypotheses proposing a specific contribution of the right hemisphere in the processing of the digit symbols. However, as we have discussed before, almost all these studies are restricted to single-digit symbols, and their results are still controverted (see Holender & Peereman, this volume). On the level of multidigit numbers, the logographic nature of the digit symbols has to be questioned because single digits have different meanings depending on their position in the digit string. For example, the digit 2 can be transcoded by the number name *two* in 32, *twenty* in 24, and *twelve* in 12. It would thus be hazardous to generalize to the entire digital coding system the results obtained only from the particular case of single-digit forms (the lexical primitives) without account being taken of the usual case of their integration into multidigit figures.

The Alphabetic or Numeral Coding System

The French lexicon for representing quantities from 1 to 999 is composed of nine digit names called units: the words from *un* (one) to *neuf* (nine); six teen names: the words from *onze* (eleven) to *seize* (sixteen); six one-word decade names from *dix* (ten) to *soixante* (sixty); and three complex decade words of two or three words for seventy, eighty, and ninety (*soixante-dix* [70] which literally translated is sixty [plus] ten; *quatre-vingt* [80] is four [times] twenty; and *quatre-vingt-dix* [90], four (times) twenty [plus] ten); and the words *cent* (hundred) and *et* (and). To represent a number having four to six digits, only one supplementary word is needed: *mille* (thousand). In a similar way, in each supplementary three-digit substring only new words need to be added to the lexicon: million, billion, and so on.

We have suggested (see Deloche & Seron, 1982a, and Seron & Deloche, 1984) that the mechanisms that process the elements of the numeral lexicon may be conceptualized as psycholinguistic procedures operating in a stack-structured environment. By such a stack-like organization, we mean that each lexical primitive is unambiguously characterized by two sets of independent categorizing information. The stack information specifies the lexical class (among three possibilities: the unit name stack, the teen name stack, and the decade name stack) and the position information that specifies the position value class (of nine or six possibilities: 1st, 2nd, . . .). For example, *two, twelve,* and *twenty* share the same position information (2nd) but differ according to the stack information (unit, teen, and decade, respectively). *Two* and *three* differ according to their position information (2nd, 3rd) but share the same stack information (units) (see Table 7.1). On this descriptive level, the stack structure and array structure refer to the same model. However, on the functional level where lexical access issues

TABLE 7.1
Lexical Structure of English and Arabic Digit
Numerical Coding Systems

Digit Lexicon		Words Lexicon		
	Positions	Lexical Categories		
		Units	Teens	Decades
9	9th	nine	nineteen	ninety
8	8th	eight	eighteen	eighty
7	7th	seven	seventeen	seventy
6	6th	six	sixteen	sixty
5	5th	five	fifteen	fifty
4	4th	four	fourteen	forty
3	3rd	three	thirteen	thirty
2	2nd	two	twelve	twenty
1	1st	one	eleven	ten

are involved, the way the position-within-stack (or array) information is managed must be taken into account. Are the elements of a given lexical class sequentially (bottom-up or top-down) or directly addressed? Coltheart (1980) has published a review of deep dyslexic data that seem to favor serial processing from the first position to the actual position to be reached. In this chapter, we use *stack* as a generic term, without any special assumption regarding access.

The syntax of the numeral coding system is much more complicated than the syntax of the arabic system. There are different descriptions of the syntactic component. For example, Hurford (1975) treats numerals as surface structures generated by a transformational grammar that is a set of context-free rewriting rules with some well-formedness constraints 'to separate the wheat from the chaff' (p. 393): Power and Longuet-Higgings (1978) propose well-formed syntactic structures stated as strings of abstract lexical categories (the major "roles" or minor terms, of sums or products) that are associated with corresponding arithmetic formulas, a lexicon specifying the possible roles of the value of each primitive.

Number words thus seem to constitute a specific and widespread microlinguistic system of particular interest for experimental investigations because it has a restricted lexicon, a formalizable syntax, and a clear semantic component free of ambiguities. Its acquisition in children has been extensively studied and presents some peculiarities that point to the possible specificity and autonomy of the cognitive and linguistic processes that underlie number acquisition (Fuson, Richards, & Briards, 1982; Gelman & Gallistel, 1978). Such a restricted area of cognitive functioning raises the question of the specificity of the brain processes operating on numbers and, in neuropsychology, leads to the empirical question of their selective breakdown by brain damage. The issues of concern in this chapter are the neuropsycholinguistic status of the alphabetic and arabic number notational systems as well as the procedures that operate upon them. We assume, therefore, that evidence relevant to these two questions may be gathered by having aphasic subjects translate number forms from one system into the other. Indeed, aphasics provide a good opportunity to investigate the fragmentation of the complex mechanisms normally involved in processing linguistic systems, and translating is a task that may involve a wide variety of procedures.

The Transcoding Processes

Transcoding processes constitute a very large class of cognitive activities that transform a form presented in one code (the source code) into another code (the target code). Activities such as reading aloud, writing to dictation, and translating one language into another are such transcoding processes. Because numbers can be represented in the written modality by a double code (digital or alphabetic) and by a single phonemic code in the oral modality, six different transcoding situations may occur, as illustrated in the triangular schema presented in Fig. 7.1.

Some of these transcoding activities are usually assessed in the traditional acalculia test batteries, e.g., by the reading aloud of numbers written in the digital code or the writing of numbers in the digital code from dictation. In general, however, they are analyzed only quantitatively in a way that does not take into account the structural properties of the two codes except for the usual distinction between reading and writing of a single-digit string versus digits integrated into numbers (multidigit string).

All these six transcoding activities are interesting in their own right; but the

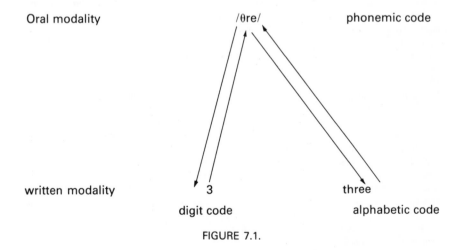

FIGURE 7.1.

simplest way of addressing the specificity of the several coding systems for quantities is, first, to restrict the analyses to the written modality in order to avoid the problems of memory traces of auditory material. Thus, our research has concentrated on experimental designs in which subjects were asked to produce alphabetic numeral forms from digit forms or the reverse in situations where both target and source codes belonged to the same written modality. Such transcoding written tasks, although the simplest to analyze, are almost always absent in the traditional acalculia investigation batteries, which usually focus on writing from dictation, reading aloud of numbers, and performing calculations.

From a cognitive point of view, the transcoding algorithms can be divided into two main classes: one that requires a semantic interpretation of the quantity represented in the source code followed by an encoding of the semantic formulae in the target code; another that simply produces the form in the target code by the procedural application of a set of rewriting rules to the lexical primitives found in the source code form.

In the latter case, no intermediate elaboration of the semantic value of the number source code form is postulated. Suggestions for the psychological relevance of such a phenomenological distinction come from the descriptions of selective reading and writing disorders where processing dissociations have been interpreted in such a theoretical framework. The transcoding algorithms we present here belong to the asemantic class, the choice being only strategic, although it is empirically justified later. Nevertheless, we leave open the possibility that semantic transcoding algorithms could be used, as some semantic errors reported in the neurolinguistic literature seem to indicate (see in Rinnert & Whitaker, 1973, the following paraphasias: three-fourths $\rightarrow$ seventy-five, or one-half $\rightarrow$ fifty.[2] In our models, the central component is made of a set of

---

[2]The main difficulty encountered in a precise description of a transcoding algorithm based on a semantic interpretation of the numbers or numerals to be transcoded lies in the precise formulation of the underlying semantic structure. From this point of view, the comparison of the semantic representations advanced in the production model of Power and Longuet-Higgins (1978) and of McCloskey and Carmazza (this book) is enlightening. In McCloskey and Carmazza's model the semantic formulas are expressed in powers of ten. The common semantic formula of the two forms "six hundred seventy-three" or 673 is thus conceived as the addition of "six times ten to the exponent two" plus "seven times ten to the exponent one" plus "three times ten to the exponent zero," whereas in the Power and Longuet-Higgins model the number forms were analyzed by a syntactical component into the underlying relations of sums and products, the end result of this analysis being the semantic formulas of the number. For 673 this would be $100 \times 6 + 70 + 3$. What is noteworthy in both these models is that they are clearly not independent of the coding system that implicitly generated them. McCloskey and Caramazza's semantic formalization is obviously derived from the digit code system organization, which is a base-10 system. Power and Longuet Higgins's formalization is more related to the linguistic lexical and syntactic organization of the word numeral system. Apart from the question of common or specific semantic representations in the case of several notational systems (see Gonzales & Kolers, this volume), such discrepancies raise the general issue of the influence of the surface code structure notation on the way the researchers conceive the underlying semantic representation of quantities.

transcoding rules that operate on each lexical unit (digit or alphabetic numeral primitive) that appears in the number form to be translated. The rules are triggered on the basis of place and of lexical specifications that result from previous processings. The place information is assumed to be controlled by a parser who normally ensures the left-to-right analysis of the number string in the source code form. Thus, the three 5s in 555 will be differentially transcribed according to their different places (5 → five hundred; 5 → fifty; 5 → five); in the reverse direction the *trois* and *cent* in *trois cent* (300) will not be processed the same way as in *cent trois* (103). The lexical information refers to the features that characterize the primitives, namely, their position values as defined in stack structures (either in digit [1, 2, 3, . . .] or in alphabetic [Table 7.1] lexical files) and, in the case of alphabetic primitives, their lexical class or stack categorization. On this lexical level, the transcoding procedures therefore have to handle lexical specifications that apply to two different notational systems (digit and alphabetic codes) but that also allow a correspondence to be made between their elements through the common dimension of the lexical position feature (e.g., 5 is bidirectionally related to the set "*five, fifteen, fifty*"). Because the lexical categorization of alphabetic primitives into stack and position-within-stack information operates on the two parameters independently, the procedures that process (in fact, receive or return, depending on the transcoding direction) the two dimensions are actually independently designed, each one handling only one parameter. Such an architecture, which maximizes the processing capacities of the whole number-transcoding mechanism, requires precise lexical primitive identification only in exceptional cases (*mille, cent, et*), whereas lexical feature analysis is generally sufficient, seems to be supported by neuropsycholinguistic evidence for the double dissociations reported in aphasic subjects along the two lexical dimensions of the alphabetic number lexicon, and makes no assumption about syntactical or semantic components.

Transcoding Algorithm: From Numeral to Digital Form

A preliminary remark is in order: The transcoding of integer numeral forms into digital forms (or the reverse) is by no means trivial, because it cannot be reduced to a simple one-to-one correspondence between lexical transcriptions of the primitives in the two notational systems. Such a context-free strategy would yield gross errors like *cinq cent trois* (503) → "51003" by the successive application of *cinq* → 5, *cent* → 100, and *trois* → 3, and in the reverse direction 503 would be erroneously transcoded *cinq zero trois* by the concatenation of the names of the digits considered in isolation.

Descriptions of a transcoding algorithm acting upon a number word string can first be restricted to the case where the word string does not contain *mille* (thousand). In such a case, the digit string to be produced may contain a maximum of three digits. We thus postulate that a frame of three digits is generated, d1, d2, d3, and that this frame is initially filled by the digit 0 at each position,

"0, 0, 0" (Rule 1). Each word of the numeral string is then processed from left to right by the application of a set of rules. These rules for French can be summarized as follows:

– If the alphabetic lexical primitive is categorized as a decade stack element, then apply Rule 2.

Rule 2: Write in d2 the digit specification that corresponds to the position value of the particular decade lexical primitive. For example, in the case of *trente*, put 3 in d2, that is, the value corresponding to the third position in the decade stack.

– If the alphabetic lexical primitive is categorized as unit, then apply Rule 3.

Rule 3: Store in working memory store (WMS) the digit specifications corresponding to the position value of the particular unit. For example, in the case of *six*, put 6 in the WMS, that is, the value corresponding to its position in the unit stack, here the sixth.

– If the alphabetic lexical primitive is identified as *cent*, then apply Rule 4.

Rule 4: Write in d1 the digit specification of 1 if the WMS is empty; otherwise load in d1 the digit specification previously stored in the WMS, and clear the WMS.

– If the alphabetic lexical primitive is categorized as a teens, then apply Rule 5.

Rule 5: Write in d3 the digit specification corresponding to the position value of the teen lexical primitive and increment by one the digit specified in d2. For example, in the case of *quatorze*, put 4 in d3 and "+ 1" in d2.

– If the string ends, then apply Rule 6.

Rule 6: Load in d3 the content of the WMS if not empty, and erase the "0" headings, if any, from the digit frame.[3]

In summary, given the two types of lexical information that generally characterize the primitives in our model of the alphabetic numeral lexicon, the stack information acts as a key word that branches to the particular transcoding rule specifying at which location of the three-digit frame (or working memory) must be stored the specifications of the digit values. The position value information is used by the rules to find out which particular digit specifications have to be stored. Among number words, there are two exceptions to this general framework: the separators (*mille, million,* etc.) and *cent,* which have not yet been incorporated into stack structures and which activate different types of transcoding rules.

This algorithm is, of course, relevant only to the French language numeral system. The algorithm for English language is actually much simpler, since teens

---

[3]Due to a peculiarity of the French numeral system, one more rule not mentioned in our algorithm is necessary for the word "and."

TABLE 7.2.
Examples

(36) Trente-six	State of the Digit Specification Frame			Working Memory Store
	d1	d2	d3	
R1 reset the digit frame	0	0	0	0
Trente-six				
Trente categorized as decade then apply R2 (3 in d2)	0	3	0	0
Trente-six				
Six categorized as unit then apply R3 (6 in WMS)	0	3	0	6
Trente-six Ø				
string ended then apply R6 (load WMS into d1); clear WMS and erase d1	0	3 3	6 6	0

may not be integrated with other primitives and since "hundred" is always preceded by a unit name (in English "one" hundred and sixty-three, unlike the French form, which omits "one": *cent-soixante-trois* is literally translated as "hundred sixty three.") The consequence of this much simpler organization of the English numeral system is a simplification of Rules 4 and 5. The algorithm for the English numeral system is presented in Appendix 1.

TABLE 7.3
This More Complicated Example Illustrates the Particular Case in French of Teen Names Incorporated into Complex Decades

(174) Cent soixante-quatorze	Digit frame			Working Memory Store
	d1	d2	d3	
R1 reset *cent soixante-quatorze*	0	0	0	0
Cent is identified then apply R4 (as WMS is empty set "1" in d1)	1	0	0	0
Cent soixante-quatorze				
soixante categorized as decade; then apply R2 (6 in d2)	1	6	0	0
Cent soixante-quatorze				
quatorze categorized as teens; then apply R5:				
4 in d3	1	6	4	0
+ 1 in d2	1	7	4	0
Cent soixante-quatorze Ø				
- string ended then apply R6	1	7	4	

TABLE 7.4
Neuf Cent Vingt Sept Mille Soixante

	d1	d2	d3				WMS
R1 reset digit frame	0	0	0				0
Neuf cent vingt sept mille soixante							
Neuf - R3 - 9 in WMS	0	0	0				9
Cent - R4 - WMS in d1	9	0	0				9
clear WMS	9	0	0				0
Vingt - R2 in d2	9	2	0				0
Sept R3 - 7 in WMS	9	2	0				7
Mille - R7 apply R6	9	2	7				0
-write "." after d3			.				
generate a new d1 d2 d3	9	2	7.	d1	d2	d3	0
R1 reset digit frame				0	0	0	0
Soixante R2 -6 in d2	9	2	7.	0	6	0	0
String ended R6■							
no deletion of heading "0" in d1	9	2	7.	0	6	0	

The generalization of the algorithm to the case of alphabetic strings that contain *mille* (thousand) requires only the addition of one new rule and must be considered the repeated application of the algorithm on the two substrings respectively situated at the left and the right side of the separator *mille*. The rule to be added may be stated as follows:

Mille identified then apply Rule 7.

Rule 7: Apply Rule 6, write "."[4] after d3; generate a new three-digit frame, and modify Rule 6 to Rule 6■ in order not to delete the heading of "0" from this second-digit frame. An example is given in Table 7.4.

Finally, alphabetic number lexical strings that contain million, billion, and so on, give rise to no additional problems, and the general algorithm may be viewed as the repeated left-to-right application of the basic algorithm each time a separator is identified in the word string.

Transcoding Algorithm: From Digital to Numeral Code

Three-Digit String. The general structure of this algorithm is very close to the preceding one; that is, it also takes advantage of the stack-like information of the alphabetic number lexicon and operates with reference to a three-digit frame in a similar repetitive way. Thus, as in the preceding section, we first illustrate the functioning of the algorithm on digit strings having a maximum of three

---

[4]In the English digital system ",".

digits (d1, d2, d3) before examining its generalization to larger digit strings. For instance, the digit string 36:

Rule A: A three-digit frame is generated: d1, d2, d3.

Rule B: Load the digit frame from the right to the left by the elements of the digit string. If there is no element at the leftmost place, set them to 0s.

d1	d2	d3
0	3	6

Rule C: If di = 0, then apply Rule D, if and only if i = 3, otherwise process di + 1.

Rule 1: Transcode d1 into a unit stack lexical primitive whose position value is specified by the position value of d1 in the digit lexicon, then add to the right of this alphabetic form the word *cent*.

Rule 2: Transcode d2 into a decade stack lexical primitive whose position value is specified by the value of d2 in the digit lexicon. In the example 3 → *trente* (thirty).

Rule 3: Transcode d3 into a unit stack lexical primitive whose position value is specified by d3. Here 6 → *six*.

Rule D: When the string ends, the transcoding operation is finished.

In view of the linguistic peculiarities of the French numeral system, the three general place-driven rules, Rules 1, 2, 3 for d1. d2, and d3, respectively, must be complicated by the the the addition of some subrules:

Rule 1_1: If *un* is produced from Rule 1, then delete it from the transcription.

Rule 2_1: If *dix* (issuing from *dix, soixante-dix,* or *quatre-vingt-dix*) has been transcoded from Rule 2, then apply Rule 3_1, instead of Rule 3.

Rule 3_1: If the d3 digit value is less than 7, delete the *dix* in the transcription and transcode d3 into a teen stack lexical primitive whose position value is specified by d3. Conversely, if the d3 is greater than 6, apply Rule 3 as usual.

Such subrules are required in order to transcode correctly figures like *1d2d3* into *cent. . .* and not into *un cent. . .* (Rule 1_1), and for the correct transcoding of the teens and the decade unit structure beyond seventy (Rule 2_1 and 3_1).

A version of the algorithm for English is presented in Appendix 2.

General Case.   When the digit string is composed of more than three digits, the ",", is a separator, and the algorithm must be applied repetitively to the different three-digit portions of the number form. The "," must be translated (according to the case) by *milliard* (billion), *million,* or *mille.* In such a way, the transcoding of, for example, 43,671, is thus done by the successive application of the algorithm on the two subsequences 43 and 671, the separator *mille* being produced between the two runs.

Theoretical Comments on Some Specific Aspects of the Transcoding Algorithm

The Repeated Runs of Three-Digit Figures.   Even if the general architecture of these algorithms cannot be justified on intuitive grounds, some considerations derived from naive observations of natural behavior may have some value in reference to the issue of the repeated processing of a three-digit frame. We could, for instance, imagine a task in which one has to read as a single integer number a non-partitioned (by ",") digit string of n-digits, such as 91274653209312. The first overt operation one is obliged to perform is to partition the string from the right to left in five substrings: 91/274/653/209/312. Then one can perform the transcoding of each three-digit substring even if one does not know the name of the separator just after the transcoding of the first two digits, 91, but one knows that the result is ninety-one (x) two hundred seventy-four billion/ six hundred fifty-three/ *million* /two hundred nine *thousand* / three hundred and twelve.[5]

The same observation can be made in the reverse direction that any educated normal subject is perfectly able to transcode "six hundred seventy-three" by 673 without having to know whether such a verbal string ends the number or if it is followed by billion, million, or thousand. In fact, as suggested by the proposed algorithm, each time a separator (thousand or million, etc.) is encountered, the first algorithm application ends and a new one is applied. In "six *thousand* one hundred seventy-three," the new algorithm has to be applied as soon as the word *thousand* is identified, and in the forms "six hundred *thousand* seventy-three," or "six hundred seventy *thousand* and three" or "six hundred seventy-three *thousand*," the displacement of thousand in the string has the main effect of modifying the place where the application of the algorithm ends and a second one is started.

Use of Number Lexical Features.   We want to make it clear that the use of notions like "stack" and "position-within-stack" must not lead the reader to erroneously conclude that the model is designed according to lexical properties that refer only to the alphabetic coding and consequently ignore, or pay insufficient attention to, the other code (digits). On the contrary, the main peculiarity of the model is precisely that it takes advantage of the fact that the same lexical feature, namely position information, is relevant to both lexicons (lexical primi-

---

[5]In French, an exercise of particular interest is to ask people to say their phone number as an integer. The difficulty resides in the fact that phone numbers are generally coded as a substring of three digits followed by two substrings of two digits, for example, 241/55/31. In many cases, people are obliged to write down their phone number and then to segment it in a three-digit string before producing it.

tives in the arabic system [digits] are characterized by their position values in the sequence 1, 2, . . . , 9 in the same way that alphabetic lexical primitives are characterized in their respective units, teens, or decades stack). Such common lexical information naturally provides the basis of bridging the two systems. It must also be noted that this central point still remains the same, whatever the precise interpretation of stack-like (bottom-up or top-down access) or array-like structure (direct access possible), because such distinctions concern the way position information is processed but not its relevance. Moreover, since the values (1, 2, . . . , 9) of the position information (1st, 2nd, . . . , 9th) in digit lexical file (1, 2, . . . ,9) or in alphabetic lexical categories (one, two, . . . , nine; eleven, twelve, . . . , nineteen; ten, twenty, . . . , ninety) coincide with digit meaning (1, 2, . . . , 9), the bridge does stand in any kind of structure in the digit lexicon. In other words, the type of information common to both lexicons and thus entered, processed, and returned by transcoding procedures may be considered at the abstract level of a formal ordinal parameter (positions in the digit and alphabetic files) or as the deep level of single-digit number meaning (digit values and verbal lexical position values).

TOWARD A PRODUCTION MODEL: FROM ALPHABETIC TO DIGIT FORMS

The number-transcoding algorithms described above constitute only some of the components of the processing mechanisms involved in such transcoding tasks. A general description of the other task components and of the entire architecture of the system is thus necessary in order to locate all the potentially relevant sources of error. We limit our presentation here to the transcoding task of transforming alphabetic written numerals into the corresponding digit forms. As a first step, we describe only the different processing components that can be logically postulated for handling such a transcoding task without specifying the details of their functioning. By using such a component information-processing approach, we need make no definitive assumptions about serial versus parallel or hierarchical versus nonhierarchical organization of these different components. At this stage, we postulate only that these different components are functionally distinct, which implies that they can be independently altered and that each one accomplishes a specific class of operations. Such a functional independence assumption does not mean that alteration or disorganization of one component processing has no effect on the others but that the other components are only affected as long as they receive information that has been incorrectly pre-processed by various altered components.

However, our model is interactive in that we postulate that, in some cases, the alteration of a component processing may be detected during the task either because the erroneous information that is passed on cannot be treated by some of the subsequent components or because logical incompatibilities have been detected by some kind of task supervisor. In such cases, one could suggest that different tactics can be generated in order to overcome impasses or to resolve logical incompatibilities. As we see later, tactics are generally employed to enhance repair mechanisms or, more simply, to reset the whole process at the point where the trouble arose. The component architecture of our number production mechanism, which models the set of operations involved in translating number forms from one notational system to the other, is thus not restricted to handling local perturbances considered independently in terms of their systemic consequences, as is usually done in neuropsychology. On the contrary, our approach provides a theoretical framework suitable for studying the dynamic adaptation of the different functional components to the abnormal conditions that may occur. Finally, the production models have been clearly featured in reference to the lexical organization assumed to structure the numeral and digital lexicons.

Four main functional components may be characterized in the complex processing of translating alphabetic number forms into their corresponding digit forms:

– A parsing process that operates from left to right on the number word string in order to discern the lexical primitives (made of one, two, or three words) by means of an alphabetic lexicon search.

– A lexical categorization/identification processing of the primitive isolated by the parsing process: The purpose of this component is to specify the parameters required to address the appropriate rules in the transcoding algorithm per se (position, stack information) and to identify the separators (million, thousand) whose recognition controls the repeated runs of the algorithm (thousand, million, etc.) or indicates termination of the process (the end of the word string).

– A transcoding process: As described in the detailed algorithm presented above, the transcoding rules are generally activated by the stack information (delivered by the lexical primitive categorization) or exceptionally by precise identification (in the case of hundred). The end-product of this component is to load the three-digit frame with the correct digit specifications (corresponding to the position information that may be obtained in the case either of rules from lexical categorization [Rules 2, 3, and 5] or from the rule itself [Rule 4], or even from calculation [Rule 5]) at the right place specified by the rule.

– A digital encoding and output process: This constitutes the actual writing of the digit forms. The arabic digit output lexicon is addressed through the specifications found in the three-digit frame.

Error Analysis According to the Production Model

We now consider the transcoding errors produced by aphasic subjects in the framework of our component model (the data have been described quantitatively elsewhere and studied in the neurolinguistic perspective of performance dissociations between Broca's and Wernicke's aphasics: Deloche & Seron, 1982b; Seron & Deloche, 1983).

Parsing Errors

Left-to-right Direction Violations.   Errors due to a selective spatial defect on the parsing level may be identified in digit strings that correspond to the correct processing by the other components of the model but operate on a permutation of the original number word string (such as *cinq cent* (500) transcoded by 105 [*cent cinq*]).

The existence of parsing errors is more easily demonstrated in the particular cases of alphabetic numeral strings when all the permutations constitute well-formed numeral strings whose corresponding digital forms are thus all different. This provides the opportunity of unambiguously tracing back the serial error performed on the original alphabetic material. For example, all the possible permutations of the three-word numeral *sept cent mille* (700,000) give other, equally legal alphabetic numeral forms that can be transcoded into five different digit strings (i.e., 1,107, 7,100, 100,007, 107,000, and 1,700). As we have observed elsewhere (Deloche & Seron, 1982b; Seron & Deloche, 1983), it seems that Wernicke's aphasics make this kind of parsing error; Broca's aphasics also produce digit strings that result from a systematic permutation of the word order of the numeral, preferentially applied to numeral forms containing *cent* and *mille* in multiplicative structures (sept *cent mille,* that is, sept times *cent* times *mille*), and they produce a digit string whose alphabetic numeral forms contain *mille* and *cent* in additive relationship (sept $\times$ *cent* $\times$ *mille* $\rightarrow$ 1,107 (*mille* plus *cent* plus sept). In other words, several order-parsing errors by Broca's aphasics seem linguistically driven, consisting in transformations of multiplicative (hierarchical) relations into additive (linear) ones.

Aside from the cases where all the permutations are legal numeral strings, one must consider cases of permutations yielding illegal numeral forms. Such illegal numeral forms may have different consequences on the application of transcoding rules. There are some cases where digital transcriptions may, nevertheless, be produced, but in other cases conflicts that occur before reaching the end of the process may have a blocking effect. For instance, the illegal numeral form "cent trois quinze" derived from the well-formed *trois cent-quinze* (315) cannot be transcribed because, within the same run of the transcoding algorithm, two rules independently address the same output position (units) in the three-digit frame (the unit *trois* [3] and the teen *quinze* [15] names). However, some three-word figures like "cent, trente, and neuf" that yield only two well-formed numerals (*cent trente-neuf* [139] and *neuf cent-trente* [930]) but four illegal numeral forms do not stop the transcoding algorithm, and moreover, it turns out that the digit strings produced from the four illegal forms correspond precisely to the two legal permutations: *trente neuf cent* and *neuf trente cent* $\rightarrow$ 930; *trente cent neuf* and *cent neuf trente* $\rightarrow$ 139. Thus, in the latter example, if serial order troubles do exist. then they cannot be traced back and precisely identified by simply considering the digit strings because several error patterns produce the same result.

Segmentation Errors.   On the segmentation process level the lexical primitives have to be isolated. In most cases, the result of such segmentation consists in picking single words—that is, a sequence of connected letters flanked by two blanks—in the string. For example, *six cent trente* has to be successively segmented into /*six*/ /*cent*/ /*trente*/. Yet, because complex decades are composed of two or three words (*quatre-vingt* [80], *soixante-dix* [70], and *quatre-vingt-dix* [90]), the parsing process must consider more than one word at a time in order to correctly segment *quatre vingt treize* (93) into two lexical primitives /*quatre vingt*/ /*treize*/, and not into three lexical primitives as /*quatre*/ /*vingt*/ /*treize*/. That complex decades raise some specific problems was clearly shown in our previous studies of error rates in French and Walloon numeral systems on the processing of 70 and 90 numeral string series. In French, where 70 and 90 are complex decades (*soixante-dix* and *quatre-vingt-dix* respectively) the error rate was .36 whereas in Walloon where both are simple one-word decades (*septante* and *nonante*) the error rate dropped to .10 which was not different from the other simple decades.

Moreover, the errors observed in transcoding these multiple-word lexical primitives did, in fact, correspond to an erroneous one-word parsing, as shown by the writing of the digit that transcribes the first word when considered alone as a one-word primitive. For instance, 22 out of the 28 errors found with *quatre-vingt* (80) began with the digit 4 for *quatre* (4), instead of 8, and most of the errors in the seventies (*soixante-dix* . . .) and nineties series (*quatre-vingt-dix* . . .) also began with 6 for *soixante* (60) or 4 for *quatre* (4), instead of 7 or 9, respectively.

Overlapping and Skipping Errors.   Each time the parsing mechanism isolates one lexical primitive from the numeral form string and passes it to other components of the system, some trace of the current place in the original word string must be maintained in order to ensure the regular left-ro-right progression in the repetition of the process. Two error sources are present here: either skipping or overlapping of one or more words (or lexical primitives) in the numeral string that are either omitted or used twice in two consecutive runs of the parsing algorithm. Examples of such errors are predominantly found in the aphasics' transcriptions of numerals that contain multiple-word lexical primitives, as in *cent quatre-vingt-trois* (183) → "123" (*cent vingt-trois* by omission of *quatre*), or in *quatre-vingt-sept* (87) → "827" where *vingt* is first correctly integrated into the two-word decade name *quatre-vingt* (80) → "8," but is then processed a second time and transcribed as a one-word decade (*vingt* [20] → "2"). Because such parsing errors do not seem to be randomly distributed but differentially affect complex structures like multiple-word substrings to be transcribed into one single digit a systematic disorder located on a higher level than more erratic positioning on the numeral word string may be indicated.

Lexical Categorization and/or Identification Errors

Because most transcoding rules are selectively activated on the basis of the particular stack information attached to the actual lexical primitives that make up a given alphabetic number form and because the procedures also manipulate the position information, the whole transcoding component thus relies heavily on categorization mechanisms dealing with these two independent lexical features. On this categorization level, errors thus consist in attributing an erroneous value to one dimension, from the set of possibilities (three for the stack information (unit, teen, decade), nine for the position information (1st, 2nd, . . . , 9th). Although the confusion may, of course, concern both lexical features, such errors are more readily identified when only one dimension is impaired (stack or position error), while the other (position or stack) is preserved.

Stack errors are easy to identify when they occur on lexical primitives presented alone, for example, when the unit name *six* (6) is transcoded either as a teens name (*seize* [16]) or as a decade name (*soixante* [60]). Such stack errors can also be clearly identified when their occurrence in a numeral string happens to produce another well-formed alphabetic numeral such as *seize* mille (16,000) → 6,000 (*six* mille), or cent *trente* (130) → *103* (cent *trois*) or *113* (cent *treize*). More complicated cases appear when the stack error would induce illegal numeral forms like *cent cinq trois* from *cent cinquante-trois* (153) by the substitution of the unit *cinq* (5) for the decade *cinquante* (50), the result being that the altered numeral string now contains two primitives to be transcoded in the same place of the digit string (unit). As already mentioned, such conflicts have to be solved by the transcoding process, which points to the dynamic of the interactions between the components of the production model to be discussed later on. Another source of difficulty in trying to trace back errors is shown by cases where several interpretations may be proposed. For instance, the erroneous *cent cinquante-trois* (153) → 163 (*cent soixante-trois*) unambiguously demonstrates a lexical error, but, unfortunately, it may be attributed equally well to a position-within-stack error (decade confusion between *cinquante* [50] and *soixante* [60]) or to a stack error (teen [*treize,* 13] for unit (*trois* [3]) and correct application of the transcoding rule (Rule 5) for teens: *cent cinquante treize* thus transcribed into the digits 1, 5 + 1, and 3).

An open question is how the categorization processes function. One may postulate that they rely on morpholexical information or on more direct procedures. Because decade and teen names are generally formed with the same root morpheme (which is the unit name sharing the same position value) concatenated to a bound morpheme that unambiguously specifies the stack (*-ty* and *-teen* for decades and teens, respectively), stack lexical primitive categorization may be obtained by a morphemic analysis that isolates and identifies the bound morpheme. Such a morphological analysis process would be similar to mechanisms dealing with language at large. Indeed, the parallels between the two materials to be operated upon seem to extend to the differential difficulties experienced by Broca's and Wernicke's aphasics. Stack confusion errors found with the Broca's aphasics were predominantly the lack of differentiation between teen and decade names, which corresponds precisely to the affix stripping often reported in such patients (sixteen or sixty → "6," like transportation → transport and other derivational errors; see Coltheart, Patterson, & Marshall, 1980). No regularities were observed in the errors made by the Wernicke's aphasics either in the substituted or in the substituting numeral stacks. Such a nonpreferential effect seems to be in line with the kind of lexical disorganizations reported in those aphasics (Zurif, Caramazza, Myerson, & Galvin, 1974). However, there are some lexical primitives whose stack categorization cannot be based on morphemic analysis. This is the case with the few exceptions where the suffix is absent (in English ten, eleven, and twelve; in French *dix* [10] and *vingt* [20]), and with multiple-decade names (*soixante-dix* [70], *quatre-vingt* [80] and *quatre-vingt-dix* [90]). Errors in the lexical processing of those primitives whose precise identification is required resulted in different erroneous digit productions depending on the nature of the lexical primitive for which they occurred.

When they concern key words that address specific rules (e.g., hundred) they lead to a change of magnitude in the digit string. For example, when, due to a morphological similarity, *cent* (hundred) is transcoded by 5 (*cinq*) or by 20 (*vingt*) as in *cent* (100) → 5 and *cent quatre* → 24 (*vingt-quatre*). They could also be observed when they occur with separators that control the end of a transcoding step and reset the repeated algorithm runs, which is, for example, the case with confusions between *mille* and *cent* as in *quatre mille cinquante-trois* (4,053) → 453 (*quatre cent cinquante-trois*).

Finally, the errors may concern stack position information. In such cases they can easily be detected in the digit string as simple digit substitutions like, for example, *cent quatre* (104) → 105 (resulting from a position error between the fourth and the fifth position in the unit stack) or *soixante-quatre* (64) → 54, which is a position error between the sixth and the fifth position in the decade stack. As we have noted elsewhere, such stack position errors were more frequently observed in Wernicke's aphasics and the confusion generally occurred between adjacent or close position values. Such a minimal distance position error has been tentatively considered comparable to the semantic verbal paraphasia that is classically encountered in Wernicke's aphasics and that also concerns semantically closely related items. Nevertheless, stack position confusion errors also occurred between remote positions, but in these cases the errors were prompted by a phonological or graphemic resemblance as in *treize* (13), *seize* (16), in *trente mille trois cent treize* (30,313) → 30,316.

Finally, some stack position errors were related to the base-10 structure of the coding system and to the mode of access to position information, in that the position value of the erroneously produced figure is regularly the ten-complement of the position of the correct form, e.g., *huit* (eight) → 2, *sept* (seven) → 3. Such cases, when they appear systematically within a given subject's productions, seem to favor the hypothesis of the structuring of the lexicon into stacks (serial-ordered files that can be processed either forward from the first element, or downward from the last) as opposed to the more general assumption of a single array structure.[6]

Transcoding Errors

Lexicalization of Individual Elements of the Numeral.
In this category of error the digit string produced seems to result from the simple concatenation of the lexical values of each numeral element. For example, *mille neuf cents* (1,900) yields the digit string 10009100 by a left-to-right successive lexicalization—*mille* → 1,000, *neuf* → 9, and *cent* → 100—. Such errors could either disassociate the decade unit couple as in *quarante-cinq* (45) → 405 or, in some cases, be restricted to only a part of the numeral elements as in *cent cinquante-trois* (153) → 10053 into which only *cent* is lexicalized.

These errors are interesting for two reasons. First, they permit some of the component processes that were spared to be clearly identified; second, they point to those processes that are undoubtedly impaired. The left-to-right parsing of the numeral element is preserved, which means that the numeral elements were all correctly picked out one after the other in a left-to-right progression, and there is no problem on the level of lexical categorization/identification. In cases of complete lexicalization strategies, what is clearly disturbed in the transcoding component is that no transcribing rules called for by stack information (here preserved) or that could be driven by some higher level structural analyzer were applied and no three-digit position frame was generated. In cases in which the lexicalization strategies are only partial, it appears that the element that has been lexicalized plays no role in the transcoding rules subsequently applied to the other elements. For example. when *mille trente-quatre* (1,034) yields the string 100034, this means not only that *mille* has been directly lexically transcribed but also that it has not played any separator role, otherwise the transcoding would have been 1000/034. Thus, *mille* was first transcoded as a separate and independent lexical unit, then *trente-quatre* was transcoded by the normal application of the algorithm rules that include the ending rule requiring the deletion of 0 in the d1 digit frame position. Such a deletion rule may not have occurred if *mille*,

---

[6]However, if the ten complement errors may indicate the erroneous lexical processing just described, they may also correspond to the faulty application of a strategy that is legal in other calculation contexts, such as counting down in subtraction. The latter case was observed in the systematic errors made by one aphasic subject who complemented the unit to ten and at the same time subtracted one from the position value of the decade figure, as in *huit cent trente neuf (839)* → *821* or *sept cent quarante deux* (742) → 738.

although lexicalized, had played a separator role in the subsequent application of the transcoding algorithms. In other words, *mille* was processed as a separator between two independent numeral forms, instead of as a separator between lexical units that belong to the same integer number.

Term-by-Term Correspondence.   In some cases like *quatre mille quatre-vingt-trois* (4,083) → 4183 or *cent deux mille six* (102,006) → 1216, each lexical primitive (of one, two, or three words) is transcribed into one single digit. Although such errors can generally be easily identified, it must be noted that there are some undecidable figures like *cent cinquante trois* (153) because the term-by-term strategy here produces a digit string that is the correct digital form. In the theoretical framework underlying the transcoding algorithm, this erroneous strategy may be interpreted as a degenerated system that makes use only of position information (in the cases of lexical primitives belonging to stack structures) and only of the transcribing rule (set a "1") specified for *mille* (thousand) and *cent* (hundred) when the two primitives have to be marked in the digit string (i.e., when not multiplicands). Thus, the digit frame and the memory store for units are inoperative, or the stack information required to address them cannot be obtained. Consequently, digit specifications are attributed to each alphabetic lexical primitive one at a time from left to right. Such errors can thus be attributed to the transcoding component when they preserve the parsing stage and the identification of *cent* and of the separators as well as position information decoding in stack lexical primitives.

The Cases of *Mille* (Thousand) and *Cent* (Hundred).   These two words play very special roles within the numerical system and in number processing that clearly distinguish them from the other lexical primitives. Their peculiarities are evidenced on several levels from linguistic analysis (Power & Longuet-Higgings, 1978), procedural models of number-transcoding operations (see previous sections in this chapter), and differential performances of aphasics (Deloche & Seron, 1982b; Seron & Deloche, 1983). First, and unlike the general lexical structure within which the primitives are characterized by position and class information, no such categorization stands for *mille* and *cent*. Second, both words are syntactical ambiguities because, when integrated into numerical forms of more than one word, they may be involved in either addition or multiplication, which corresponds, on the grammatical level, to the distinction between the usual lexical sequential relations and functors. Moreover, this distinction has been shown to be critical in the processing of agrammatic subjects. Third, the kind of transcoding procedures called for by the occurrence of *mille* and *cent* specifically concerns organizational issues (reset a three-digit frame for receiving further digit specifications or indicate which particular place in the frame must be filled in), whereas the rules operating on the other lexical primitives handle lexico-semantic information (the position-within-stack value that determines the digit to be actually written down). In other words, the transcoding procedures dealing with *mille* and *cent* generally deliver specifications relevant to the serial ordering of digits in the number forms, but rarely a digit specification per se in French (at least the ''1'' when not a multiplicand). Conversely, the procedure operating on units, teens, and decades essentially carries the particular digit codes, but in some cases the precise location where they are to be produced is not already determined (digits to appear either in the hundred or the unit place). Consequently, on a structural level, although each nonzero digit in the arabic number forms generally corresponds to one word in the alphabetic form (with the exception of the teens and complex decades), the digit traces of *mille* and *cent* may have many different forms, depending not only on their syntactical role but also on the occurrence of decades, teens, and units in their particular number surroundings. The digit string may thus either present no explicit digit counterpart as in vingt sept *mille* quatre *cent* dix neuf (27,419) or show a ''1'' in the thousand or hundred place (*mille cent* trente deux, 1,132), and/or have 0s as in *mille* quatre *cent* six (1,406), *cent* deux *mille* six (102 006) and deux *cent mille* (200,000). Finally, it is from the consideration of *cent* and *mille* that global semantic information on the magnitude of numerical forms can be most appropriately extracted because their arrangement largely determines the digit form length, and such magnitude approximations may be used by subjects to check number productions.

Lexicalization errors like *mille* neuf *cent* (1,900) → *1000 9 100,* and term-by-term correspondences where *mille* and *cent* are transcribed by the ''1'' that corresponds to their lexical trace as in trente neuf *mille* sept *cent* quarante-deux (39,742) → 39*1*7*1*42 were observed, but such strategies are not specific to these two primitives, as exemplified in the two previous sections. More interesting errors concerned different misapplications of the particular *mille* and *cent* transcoding rules. Some cases were erroneous digit frame location addressings, for instance, the decade position instead of the hundred position: mille neuf *cent* (1,900) → 1,090. In other cases, the error source seemed to be the difficulty of generating a digit string whose underlying structure contains multiplicands. The control exercised by *mille* and *cent* showed several possible ways of overcoming such problems. The multiplicator may be erased (or not transferred from the unit specification working memory to the digit frame): *huit* mille trois (8,003) → 1,003 (mille trois), mille *huit* cent dix (1,810) → 1,110 (mille cent dix); the multiplicand may be rendered selectively opaque to the transcoding process that operates on the other primitives according to term-by-term processing: quatre *mille* trois (4,003) → 43; or the relation between the multiplicator and the multiplicand may be broken down, the multiplicand acting as a separator that ends the transcription of the substring to its left and that reinitializes the transcoding algorithm to be applied to itself and the substring to its right. The latter mechanisms result in the production of 1s for *mille* and *cent*, which can be more clearly identified in transcriptions where the presence of some 0s demonstrates the reset of the three-digit frame (*deux cent quatre* (204) → 2 104) than in cases like *quatre cent cinquante-neuf* (459) → 4159 where another interpretation (term-by-term transcoding) may account for the data equally well. Such erroneous responses that can be produced by different processes thus point to the question of the criterion of interpretation choice. Decisions may be made by examination of the subject's entire corpus and by presenting items where the several hypothesized mechanisms will induce clear-cut differentiated productions. For instance, the systematic transcription of "*mille* unit 1 *cent* unit 2" figures into "unit 1 unit 2 0 0" as in *mille* quatre *cent* six (1,406) → 4,600 (quatre *mille* six *cent*) was not considered a parsing error of the serial-ordering type but the systematic computation of 1000 × unit 1100 × unit 2 because the strategy was unambiguously identified in *mille* deux *cent* quatorze (1,214) → 3400 (trois *mille* quatre *cent*) through 2000 (deux × *mille*) + 1400 (quatorze × *cent*).

Digital Encoding and Output Process Errors

Such an output component must clearly be integrated in the whole production model in order to control the final process that actually forms the digit string from the lexical specifications computed by the transcoding component. The perturbations that are likely to occur could concern the programming of individual digits whose formation might be altered in varying degrees that may or may not preserve the set of recognizable digits. However, our data base does not allow us to develop this topic further because our main interest in analyzing the errors that could occur in the parsing, lexical categorization, and transcoding components resulted in selecting patients who did not show obvious impairments on this output level. Some incidental errors that may tentatively be considered relevant here were confusions between digits that have some similarities like 5 and 3 in *quatre cent cinquante-neuf* (459) → 439 or 6 and 9 in *mille deux cent quarante-six* (1,246) → 1249. Probably due to our selection bias, we observed neither the production of unidentifiable digits nor the inclusion of nondigit symbols like the letters of the alphabet or of characters different from "." conventionally used as a separator on digit strings. However, some subjects spontaneously added monetary units (Francs, Frs.) to the end of their transcriptions.

Integrative Control of the Components of the Production Model

The component architecture of our number translating production model necessarily addresses the issue of a master scheduler to control the interactions between the several components and to solve problems that may occur during the process. Within such a structural framework, erroneous transcriptions are considered the surface manifestations of the ways the production system tried to overcome impasses encountered while handling subtasks. Despite the relatively small number of errors in our corpus, the aphasics' productions seem to be generally interpretable as resulting from variations of the normal procedures to which repairs are tentatively applied, the repairs being in turn procedures that are valid in some calculation circumstances (see Brown & Van Lehn, 1982, and Resnick, 1982, for similar conceptions in the analysis of subtraction errors produced by children or students). The systematicity of the difficulties a particular subject often demonstrates with one type of numeral figures (for instance complex decades or multiplicands), and the often unique repair strategy engendered by each particular kind of impasse, clearly support the interpretation of the performances as being due to a missing part in the original skill. Conversely, the several different erroneous transcriptions found when all the subjects are faced with the same item point to the variety of error sources and available repairs. Impasses may occur when a procedure is called without receiving the arguments in their correct number, form, or order or when processing results in contradictory events. Some examples have already been cited, like the misordering of the alphabetic lexical primitives (parsing component) or multiple-digit specifications relative to the same one-digit place (transcoding component). In such situations, the control system must provide ways of overcoming the difficulties. One reasonable procedure is to return one step backward and to retry the operations that led to the detected incorrect event. This is exemplified in transcriptions that show the blend between two successive trials, like 482 for *quatre-vingt-deux* (82) through *quatre* → 4, then *quatre* is integrated to *vingt* to form the complex decade *quatre-vingt* (80). Other repairs consist in ignoring the element that makes the item so difficult (for instance, the selective deletion of *dix* renders the complex decade *soixante-dix-huit* [78] much simpler: *soixante-huit* [68], or in adopting lexical or term-by-term transcoding strategies (*soixante-dix-huit* [78] → 60108 or 618), or in stopping the transcoding process and reinitializing it on the substring not already transcribed, as though two independent numerals were to be successively processed (*soixante-dix-huit* (78) → 6018 (note that the unit and the *dix* are integrated into a two-digit number)).

Finally, it must be stressed that both impasse detection and repair selection seem to depend in aphasics on contextual, syntactical, and semantic factors. For instance, stack errors on units (*trois* (3) → 30 [*trente*]) are more likely to occur in numeral figures like *cent trois* (103) → 130 where the decade place is empty than in *cent cinquante-trois* (153) where a conflict would occur because the digit in the same decade place would be differentially specified from two sources. It thus appears that the preserved abilities of the aphasic subjects as well as their preserved knowledge of what principles must not be violated constitute the framework of their performance constraints. As already indicated, some linguistically driven errors like agrammatics' difficulties with multiplicands may be solved by reordering the alphabetical lexical primitives in such a way as to have additive structures only (in the cases where it is compatible with grammaticality constraints as in *deux cent mille* (200,000) → 1102 (*mille cent deux*), or, when the constraints do not allow such repair procedures, by deleting the multiplicator (*mille huit cent dix* [1,810] → 1,110 [*mille cent dix*]), or the multiplicand (*mille neuf cent* (1,900) → 1,009 (*mille neuf*). Semantic, magnitude information seems likely to control the plausibility of the digital transcriptions. This is the case in aborted transcodings that respect the correct number length but, due to previous errors, have to ignore the rightmost part of the numeral form (*"cinquante cinq mille huit cent trente-neuf* (55,839) → 55803), and in the numerous four-digit transcriptions of alphabetic forms with *mille* (thousand), whatever the actual magnitude (6, 5, or 4 digits). The frequent use of fractionating of the production process over two parts of the alphabetic numeral string that present no problems in themselves may be related to the peculiarity that numeral forms may generally be truncated anywhere, the two substrings remaining well-formed numerals (with only one exception, between *quatre* and *vingt* in the complex decade *quatre-vingt* (80) followed by another primitive). Language is clearly much more constrained, from this point of view, which may be why, in part, very few aphasics could not participate in our investigations of transcoding mechanisms.

SUMMARY

After a brief review of the neuropsychological literature devoted to digit and number alexia or agraphia, we have presented two original and theoretically motivated transcoding algorithms that describe the transcoding operations when one passes in the written modality from an integrated number alphabetic string to the corresponding digit string and the reverse.

The two asemantic transcoding algorithms we have proposed have two major characteristics: first, they take advantage of the stack-like organization of the alphabetic number lexicon and of the position information organization of the lexical primitives in both alphabetic and digital number lexicons; second, they operate repetitively with reference to a three-digit frame triggered by separators (presence of thousand, million, etc., in the alphabetic code; presence of ",") on the creation of three-digit groups from the right in the digit code. Second, we have shown how one of these two transcoding algorithms from the alphabetic to the digit form could be integrated in a complete production model that specifies all the other processing components (parsing, categorization, etc.) implied in such a transcoding task. Then, we tentatively interpreted the errors produced by aphasic subjects by referring them to different processing deficits that could occur at each component level.

Finally, in order to explain either regular constraints on the occurrence of some class of errors or the existence of errors that could not be easily explained solely by a local processing deficit affecting a component in a noninteractive model, we have introduced the idea that some processing deficits may be detected during the task, either by a control supervisor mechanism or because some errors may lead to a logical, syntactical or semantic impasse. Error analysis suggested that different tactics that enhance repair mechanism or reset the whole process intervene in such cases. Such an interactive component model not only is useful in the limited domain of number transcoding tasks but also may be fruitfully applied in other neuropsychological contexts.

APPENDIX 1

An English asemantic transcoding from the numeral to the digit code.

Rule 1: Reset the three-digit specification frame.

Decade name: Apply Rule 2.
Rule 2: Write in d2 the digit specification corresponding to the position value of the particular decade lexical primitive.

Unit name: Apply Rule 3.
Rule 3: Store in the WMS the digit specifications corresponding to the position value of the particular unit.

Hundred: Apply Rule 4.
Rule 4: Write in d1 the content of WMS.

Teens names: Apply Rule 5.
Rule 5: Write in d2 the digit specifications of ''1'' and in d3 those of the position value of that particular teen name.

String ended: Apply Rule 6.
Rule 6: Load in d3 the content of WMS if not empty; erase the ''0'' headings. if any, from the digit frame.

APPENDIX 2

English transcoding algorithm from digital to alphabetical number.

Rule A: Generate a three-digit frame; d1, d2, d3.

Rule B: Load the digit frame from the right to the left by the elements of the digit string. If there is no element at the leftmost place, set them to 0s.

Rule C: If $d_i = 0$, then apply Rule D if and only if $i = 3$, otherwise process $d_i + 1$.

Rule 1: Transcode d1 into a unit stack lexical primitive whose position value is specified by the position value of d1 in the digit lexicon. Then write ''hundred.''

Rule 2: Transcode d2 into a decade stack lexical primitive whose position is specified by d2.

Rule 3: Transcode d3 into a unit stack lexical primitive whose position is specified by d3.

Rule D: When the string ends, the transcoding operation is finished.

Two subrules only:

Rule 2¹: If "ten" has been selected by Rule 2, then consider Rule 3¹ instead of Rule 3.

Rule 3¹: If d3 is not 0 then transcode d3 into a teen name whose position value is specified by d3; otherwise apply Rule D.

REFERENCES

Albert, M. L., Yamadori, A., Gardner, H. & Howes, D. (1973). Comprehension in alexia. *Brain,* *96,* 317–328.

Ajuriaguerra, J. de, & Hécaen, H. (1960). *Le cortex cérébral.* Paris: Masson et Cie.

Assal, G., Buttet, J., & Jolivet, R. (1981). Dissociations in aphasia: a case report. *Brain and Language, 13,* 223–240.

Assal, G., & Jacot-Descombes, C. (1984). Intuition arithmétique chez un acalculique. *Revue Neurologique, 140* (5), 374–375.

Barbizet, J., Bindefeld, N., Moaty, F., & Le Goff, P. (1967). Persistance de possibilité de calcul élémentaire au cours des aphasies massives. *Revue Neurologique, 116,* 170–178.

Benson, D. F., & Denckla, M. B. (1969). Verbal paraphasia as a cause of calculation disturbances. *Archives of Neurology, 21,* 96–102.

Benson, D. F., & Weir, W. F. (1972). Acalculia: Acquired anarithmetia. *Cortex, 8,* 465–472.

Besner, D., & Coltheart, M. (1979). Ideographic and alphabetic processing in skilled reading of English. *Neuropsychologia, 17,* 467–472.

Besner, D., Daniels, S., & Slade, C. (1982). Ideogram reading and right hemisphere language. *British Journal of Psychology, 73,* 21–28.

Boller, F., & Grafman, J. (1985). Acalculia. In P. J. Vinken, G. W. Bruyn, & H. L. Klawans (Eds.), *Handbook of clinical neurology* (2nd ed., Vol. 1). Amsterdam, North Holland.

Brown, J. S., & VanLehn, K. (1982). Towards a generative theory of "Bugs." In T. P. Carpenter, J. M. Moser, & T. A. Romberg (Eds.), *Addition and subtraction: A cognitive perspective* (pp. 117–135), Hillsdale, NJ: Lawrence Erlbaum Associates.

Collignon, R., Leclercq, C., & Mahy, J. (1977). Etude de la sémiologie des troubles du calcul observés au cours de lésions corticales. *Acta Neurologica Belgica, 77,* 257–275.

Coltheart, M. (1980). Deep dyslexia: A right hemisphere hypothesis. In M. Coltheart, K. Patterson, & J. C. Marshall (Eds.), *Deep dyslexia* (pp. 326–380). London: Routledge & Kegan Paul.

Coltheart, M., Patterson, K., & Marshall, J. C. (Eds.). (1980). *Deep dyslexia.* London: Routledge & Kegan Paul.

Dahmen, W., Hartje, W., Büssing, A., & Sturm, W. (1982). Disorders of calculation in aphasic patients—spatial and verbal components. *Neuropsychologia, 20,* 145–153.

Deloche, G., & Seron, X. (1982a). From one to 1: An analysis of a transcoding process by means of neuropsychological data. *Cognition, 12,* 119–149.

Deloche, G., & Seron, X. (1982b). From three to 3: A differential analysis of skills in transcoding quantities between patients with Broca's and Wernicke's aphasia. *Brain, 105,* 719–733.

Fuson, K. C., Richards, J., & Briards, D. J. (1982). The acquisition and elaboration of the number word sequence. In C. J. Brainerd (Ed.), *Children's logical and mathematical cognition* (pp. 33–92). New York: Springer Verlag.

Gardner, H. (1974). The naming of objects and symbols by children and aphasic patients. *Journal of Psycholinguistic Research, 3*(2), 133–149.

Gardner, H., Strub, R., & Albert, M. L. (1975). A unimodal deficit in operational thinking. *Brain and Language, 2,* 333–344.

Gelman, R., & Gallistel, C. R. (1978). *The child's understanding of number.* Cambridge, MA: Harvard University Press.

Gonzalez, E. G., & Kolers, P. A. (1982). Mental manipulation of arithmetic symbols. *Journal of Experimental Psychology: Learning, Memory and Cognition, 8*(4), 308–319.

Grafman, J., Passafiume, D., Faglioni, P., & Boller, F. (1982). Calculation disturbances in adults with focal hemispheric damage. *Cortex, 18,* 37–50.

Grewel, F. (1973). The acalculias. In P. J. Vinken & G. Bruyn (Eds.), *Handbook of clinical neurology,* (Vol. 4, pp. 181–194). Amsterdam: North Holland.

Hatano, G. (1982). Learning to add and subtract: A Japanese perspective. In T. P. Carpenter, J. M. Moser, & T. A. Romberg (Eds.), *Addition and subtraction: A cognitive perspective* (pp. 211–223). Hillsdale NJ: Lawrence Erlbaum Associates.

Hatta, T. (1983). Visual field differences in semantic comparative judgments with digits and Kanji stimulus materials. *Neuropsychologia, 21,* 669–678.

Hécaen, H., Angelergues, R. & Houillier, S. (1961). Les variétés cliniques des acalculies au cours des lésions rétro rolandiques: Approche statistique du problème. *La Revue Neurologique, 105,* 85–103.

Henderson, L., Coltheart, M., & Woodhouse, D. (1973). Failure to find a syllabic effect in number naming. *Memory and Cognition, 1*(3), 304–306.

Henschen, S. E. (1920). *Klinische und anatomische Beitrag zür Pathologie des Gehirns.* Stockholm: Nordiske Bofhandelen.

Henschen, S. E. (1926). On the function of the right hemisphere of the brain in relation to the left in speech, music and calculation. Brain, *49,* 111–123.

Hurford, J. R. (1975). *The linguistic theory of numerals.* Cambridge: University Press.

Klapp, S. T. (1974). Syllable-dependent pronunciation latencies in number naming: A replication. *Journal of Experimental Psychology, 102* (6), 1138–1140.

Lawler, R. W. (1981). The progressive construction of mind. *Cognitive Science, 5,* 1–30.

Leleux, C., Kaiser, G., & Lebrun, Y. (1979). Dyscalculia in a right-handed teacher of mathematics with right cerebral damage. In R. Hoops & Y. Lebrun (Eds.), *Neurolinguistics 9: Problems of aphasia.* (pp. 141–158). Lisse: Swets & Zeitlinger.

Leonhard, K. (1979). Ideokinetic aphasia and related disorders. In R. Hoops & Y. Lebrun (Eds.), *Neurolinguistics 9: Problems of aphasia* (pp. 11–77). Lisse: Swets & Zeitlinger.

Lewandosky, M., & Stadelmann, E. (1908). Uber einen bemerkenswerten Fall for Hirnblutung und über Rechenstörugen bei Herderkrankung des Gehirns. *Journal für Psychologie und Neurologie 11,* 249–265.

Peereman, R., & Holender, D. (in press). Visual field differences for a number-nonnumber classification of alphabetic and ideographic stimuli. *Quarterly Journal of Experimental Psychology.*

Power, R. J. D., & Longuet-Higgings, H. C. (1978). Learning to count: A computational model of language acquisition. *Proceedings of the Royal Society, London, 200,* 391–417.

Resnick, L. B. (1982). Syntax and Semantics in learning to subtract. In T. P. Carpenter, J. M. Moser, & T. A. Romberg (Eds.), *Addition and subtraction: A cognitive perspective.* (pp. 136–155)., Hillsdale, NJ: Lawrence Erlbaum Associates.

Rinnert, C., & Whitaker, H. (1973). Semantic confusion by aphasic patients. *Cortex, 9,* 56–81.

Ruffieux, C., Jacot-Descombes, C., Python-Thuillard, F., & Assal, G. (1984). *Why acalculic have not all gone bankrupt.* Paper presented at International Neuropsychological Society meeting in Aachen, Germany. June.

Sasanuma, S., & Monoi, H. (1975). The syndrome of Gogi (word meaning) aphasia: Selective impairment of Kanji-processing. *Neurology, 25,* 627–632.

Seron, X., & Deloche, G. (1983). From 4 to four: A supplement to "From three to 3". *Brain, 106,* 735–744.

Seron, X., & Deloche, G. (1984). From 2 to two: An analysis of a transcoding process by means of neuropsychological evidence. *Journal of Psycholinguistic Research, 13* (3), 215–235.

Shallice, T. (1979). Case study approach in neuropsychological research. *Journal of Clinical Neuropsychology, 1,* 183–211.

Singer, H. D., & Low, A. A. (1933). Acalculia: A clinical study. *Archives of Neurology and Psychiatry, 29,* 467–498.

Sittig, O. (1921). Storungen und Verhalten gegenuber Farben bei Aphasischen. *Mohatschrift für Psychiatric und Neurologie, 49,* 63–159.

Spalding, J. M. K., & Zangwill, O. L. (1950). Disturbances of number form in a case of brain injury. *Journal of Neurology, Neurosurgery, and Psychiatry, 13,* 24–29.

Stigler, J. W. (1984). Mental abacus, the effect of abacus training on Chinese children's mental calculation. *Cognitive Psychology, 16,* 145–176.

Takahashi, A., & Green, D. (1983). Numerical judgments with Kanji and Kana. *Neuropsychologia, 21,* 259–263.

Van Woerkom, W. (1925). Uber Storugen im Denken bei Aphasie-patienten. *Monatschrift für psychiatrie und Neurologie, 59,* 256–322.

Warrington, E. K. (1982). The fractionation of arithmetic skills: A single case study. *Quarterly Journal of Experimental Psychology, 34A,* 31–51.

Yamadori, A. (1975). Ideogram reading in alexia. *Brain, 98,* 231–238.

Zurif, E. B., Caramazza, A., Myerson, R., & Galvin, J. (1974). Semantic feature representations for normal and aphasic language. *Brain and Language, 1,* 167–187.

8

The Production of Counting Sequences by Aphasics and Children: A Matter of Lexical Processing?

Xavier Seron
Unité de Neuropsychologie Expérimentale de l'Adulte (NEXA), Bruxelles

Gérard Deloche
*Service de Rééducation Neurologique
Hôpital de la Salpétrière, Paris*

INTRODUCTION

In previous studies on the number-transcoding abilities of aphasics, we stressed the role of the linguistic structure of the verbal lexicon for numbers (either in alphabetically written or in phonological forms) on the logic of erroneous strategies considered in the line of the theoretical framework already set forth by Grewel (1973) and Power and Longuet-Higgins (1978) and of computational models of number processing with lexical semantic and syntactic components (Deloche & Seron, 1982a, 1982b, 1984a, and the preceding chapter; Seron & Deloche, 1983, 1984). Although these investigations documented some of the neuropsycholinguistic mechanisms involved in handling number-coding systems and their dissolution accompanying language disturbances, the present chapter considers the role of a specific ability: the production of the standard sequence of number words. Mastery of number word sequence proves critically important in the development of arithmetical skills in children. It sometimes appears as a backup procedure in adults' counting and can consequently constitute in aphasic subjects another source of linguistic error resulting in calculation disorders.

The classic Piagetian position, which attributes no special contribution of the acquisition of the verbal sequence of number words (one, two, three, . . .) in the progressive elaboration of the concept of number (Piaget & Szeminska, 1941), has been challenged by several researchers who have provided converging counter-evidence (see Fayol, 1985, for a review). In the general view that children's arithmetic skills develop through dynamic interactions between executive procedures and planning action schemata for problem solving (Riley, Greeno, & Heller, 1983), the mastery of the number word sequence has been shown to influence the acquisition of the basic numerical principles involved in calculation such as one-to-one correspondence, cardinality (Gelman & Gallistel, 1978), and conservation (Fuson, Secada, & Hall, 1983). Moreover, the various developmental levels found in children's processing of individual number words of the sequence seem to determine the variety of progressively available strategies in arithmetical tasks like enumeration (Beckwith & Restle, 1966), addition (Cohn, 1971; Fuson, 1980, 1982; Fuson, Richards, & Briars, 1982), and subtraction (Carpenter & Moser, 1982; Fuson, 1984). For instance, the primitive "counting-all" addition procedure (3 + 2 is 5 through [one, two, three, four, five] while pointing to objects or raising fingers) persists as long as the verbal sequence still functions as an unbreakable chain that can only be recited and accessed from its beginning. The more elaborated "counting-on" procedure only develops when the chain has become breakable and may be started at any point (then 3 + 2 = 5 by counting forward two words from three: three, four, five).

Development of counting algorithms thus seems closely linked to progress in arithmetic skills. In adults, it has been suggested that counting-on is a backup process used to solve addition problems in cases where direct retrieval of number facts has failed (Parkman & Groen, 1971). Counting based on covert or overt production of the sequence of number words also occurs when subjects are presented additions with letters like $K + G = R$ rather than digits (Fuson, 1982) or have to search for the smaller of two numbers in magnitude comparison tasks (Parkman, 1971).

There is thus a convincing body of evidence indicating a contribution of the number word sequence in the progressive elaboration of the different meanings and uses of number words (elements of the sequence, counting words, names of digits, cardinal values, measures in arbitrary units, ordinal positions, etc.) that results in making numbers a natural cognitive domain (Fuson & Hall, 1983; Starkey & Gelman, 1982). Before investigating whether or not aphasia can disrupt the production of the so-called automated number-word sequence, we consider the main characteristics of the fine-grain lexical structuration of counting words. Whether such a disruption could cause errors in the arithmetical processes, which have acquired increasing independence relative to the verbal sequence that originally accompanied their construction, is a matter for further research.

Number words appear to constitute an autonomous lexical domain in language. The distinction between number and non-number names is acquired very early in childhood for both comprehension and production. The intrusions seem restricted to the elements of the only other conventional sequence concurrently taught to children, the letters of the alphabet (Fuson et al., 1982; Gelman & Meck, 1983). This acquisition seems rule-governed: Children spontaneously create generative rules inferred from their morphological knowledge of the number names from 1 to 21, as shown by their production of nonstandard number forms that may ignore an orthographic exception and regularize a decade (five-ty instead of fifty), regularize a teen name (eleven-teen for eleven), or apply the repetitive process within decades to the whole string of one-word numbers from 1 to 19 (twenty-nine, twenty-ten, twenty-eleven) instead of the correct x-ty nine, $(x + 1)$-ty figures (Fuson et al., 1982; Siegler & Robinson, 1982). Insight into the lexical structure of counting words and into the psycho-linguistic procedures that organize them in the standard sequence is also provided by the distribution of the stopping points and incidental jumps in child produc-tions (Siegler & Robinson, 1982). Such series can be analyzed into three parts, a stable standard portion (the child is always correct for the first items) followed by a stable nonstandard portion (the same nonstandard substring is always pro-duced), and a final unstable portion varying from trial to trial by the same child (Fuson et al., 1982). These authors thus distinguish three developmental stages: learning the words from one to nineteen; handling the decade structure, i.e., learning the decade names and the rule for the repetitive decade unit pattern; and finally introducing hundred. The production models proposed to account for these data evolve according to the progressive modifications of number represen-tations from unidirectional forward ''next'' relations in the rote-learning stage to mixed schema involving both connections between numbers and generative rules reflecting the child's knowledge of the decimal organization of the verbal and written arabic digital systems (Resnick, 1983; Siegler & Robinson, 1982). The structure of teens would not be understood by children at the time of acquisition (Fuson & Hall, 1983); however, this point is not clear because thirteen, the first truly suffixed (Ginsburg, 1977), is considered at an end point in development (3 : 6, 4) by Fuson and Hall (1983), and the distribution of stopping points shows only three cases between 14 and 19 out of 37 stops before 20 (Siegler & Robin-son, 1982). The sequence of number words and the lexicon of numbers thus seem, like language, to be rule-governed, to appear prior to schooling, and, although depending on a supporting environment (Hatano, 1982), to possess some autonomy and specificity among verbal skills.

By adulthood, the production of the number sequence has become a highly automated verbal skill. It is sometimes used by experimental psychologists as a distractor task in order to clean out the short-term memory store and thus assure uncontaminated investigation of long-term memory processes (Nairne & Healy, 1983; Peterson & Peterson, 1959); and the insensitivity of number-naming laten-cies to the size of the memorized set of alternatives, a property that characterizes highly overlearned response codes, thus demonstrates the lexically integrated structure of numbers (Forrin, 1975).

The effect of brain damage on the production of number sequences and its possible role in acalculia does not seem to have received adequate research attention. Some indirect information on the brain mechanisms responsible for such verbal performance may be found in studies using the WADA technique (however, counting here appears only as a sign that an experimental disinhibition of one hemisphere is effective and not as a relevant issue) or in the measurement of the concomitant variations of regional cortical blood flow that show right hemisphere hyperactivity and intrahemispheric modifications of the pattern of distribution that could demonstrate the involvement of the two hemispheres when counting aloud (Larsen, Skinoj, & Lassen, 1978). Studying the changes of performance induced by electrical stimulation of the right or left thalamus on counting backwards by threes, Ojemann (1974) found errors that predominantly occurred at decade boundaries (. . . 62, 59 . . .), with a tendency for the ones place errors to be related to right stimulations whereas the tens place errors differentially appeared with left stimulations. The involvement of the right thalamus in controlling the sequence of digit names was tentatively interpreted in relation to the somesthetic associations that develop there during the early ac- quisition of numbers (Benson & Geschwind, 1969). However that may be, counting is considered the prototypical example of highly automated verbal skills in adults, and it is as such that it is included, together with other verbal recita- tions (days of the week, months of the year, letters of the alphabet), in some standard protocols for the assessment of language disorders (Minnesota Test for Differential Diagnosis of Aphasia [MTDDA], Schuell, 1965; Boston Diagnostic Aphasia Examination, Goodglass & Kaplan, 1972; and, in French, the standard language evaluation test of Ducarne, 1976, and the CRMC Montreal battery of Lecours, Rascol, Nespoulous, Joanette, & Puel, 1980). It must be noted that patients are never required to count beyond 21, and thus their ability to generate the repetitive parts of the sequence (decade unit figures) is, in fact, not investi- gated. Moreover, statistical data on the stopping points or on the kinds of errors are not available because the test is simply scored as passed or failed. A contrario information is provided by the clinical teams that simply do not include this test in their protocol because they consider it too easy and consequently without discriminative power, as in the shorter version of the MTDDA devised by Thompson and Enderby (1979), or too far from the processes involved in propo- sitional speech, as in the Aachen Aphasia Test (Huber, Poeck, & Willmes, 1984). The same line of reasoning prevailed in a group study by Alajouanine, Lhermitte, Ledoux, Renaud, and Vignolo (1964) where aphasic subjects pro- duced the sequence from 1 to 30 in a delayed auditory feedback condition that manifests an interference effect in normals. The abnormal lack of errors in the subgroup of jargonaphasics with phonemic paraphasias whereas subjects with semantic paraphasias were impaired was interpreted in favor of a role of the mechanisms controlling automatic verbal sequencing in the genesis of phonemic disorders. However, the ways in which the semantic paraphasia group erred were not explored, because failure was considered to reflect the normal performance of this subgroup. Counting skills have also been reported incidentally in some detailed single-case investigations. Whitaker (1976) described a mixed transcor- tical aphasic who could, with occasional perseverations, count up to 19. This relatively preserved ability was discussed in the same theoretical framework as the distinction between the automatic, overlearned aspect and the propositional, semantic aspect of language processes. In their remarkable monograph, Singer and Low (1933) raised the interesting problem of an acalculic patient who failed in his attempts to do addition by the counting-on strategy despite correct initialization of the procedure (7 + 5 = 8; 14 + 13 = 15; 16 + 6 = 17) and preserved counting by ones, twos, threes, and tens. Such backup mechanism proved more efficient in Warrington's (1982, and this volume) case when the subject was trying to overcome difficulties in retrieving stored number facts. Counting from one to the target item in the sequence happens to be the only way for some patients, particularly deep dyslexics (Coltheart, 1980), to read and match auditorially presented numbers (Gardner, Strub, & Albert, 1975) and to read aloud numbers (Gott, 1973) and elements of other series like letters, days, and months. The automated sequence of number words may also be an element in the explanation of the better resistance to brain damage of reading aloud and writing one-digit numbers from dictation than multidigit numbers that is encountered in some patients (Assal, Buttet, & Jolivet, 1978, 1981; Assal & Jacot-Descombes, 1984).

The points that clearly emerge from these studies directly related to the counting word series and from the consideration of the more general question of calculation in the different codings (Deloche & Seron, this volume) are, first, the prominent role of the verbal sequence of number words in developing the concept of number and the different types of number processings in some backup calculations used by normals and patients; second, the specificity of number words as an autonomous rule-governed cognitive domain different from language at large; third, the relevance of the distinction between the various forms of number notational systems as regards normal and impaired processing, with a tentative but controverted hypothesis relating the differential abilities found with alphabetic and ideographic forms to cerebral hemispheric specializations. Consequently, we investigated some French aphasics' abilities to produce a sequence in three coding systems, oral, written alphabetic, and written arabic digits. This design offers an opportunity to study the relationships between the different scripts as they emerge in function of dissociated or similar impairments. Three series (counting by ones, twos, and fives) are considered, to study the differential sensitivity of more or less automated sequences to brain damage. At a lexical level, the analysis of aphasics' erroneous productions is relevant to the evaluation of models of the structure of number lexicons (Deloche & Seron, this volume) and models of the representation of the relations between numbers in the counting sequence (Resnick, 1983; Siegler & Robinson, 1982). Of course, further research is needed to relate the kind of disorders observed in aphasics' productions of the standard number sequence to concomitant impairments in particular number-processing skills. In this way we hope to highlight one aspect of the so-called verbal component of acalculia and to document the influence of the notational code on such of a simple but rule-governed and structured activity.

EXPERIMENTAL INVESTIGATIONS: RATIONALE AND METHOD

The abilities of aphasics to produce the number sequences are assessed in a group study and analyzed by general scoring procedures common to the three notational systems used; together with special procedures related to the specific characteristics of each particular script.

Subjects

The population was composed of 18 native French speakers diagnosed as aphasics in the Neuropsychological and Neurological Departments of La Salpêtrière Hospital in Paris. There were 13 males and 5 females; the mean age at the time of examination was 38.4 years with a range of 26–70 years. The etiology was vascular in 16 and infectious in 2 cases. The mean time post onset was 1.9 years with a range of 3 months to 9 years. According to the French adaptation of the Boston Diagnostic Aphasia Examination (Mazaux & Orgogozo, 1981), the subjects were classified into Broca's (6). Wernicke's (6), conduction (3), and anomic (3) aphasics.

Experimental Procedure

The subjects were asked to count forward until they were stopped by the examiner. Three series (counts in units of ones, twos, and fives) were produced in each of three notations (oral, arabic digital, and alphabetically written). After specifying the sequence type and the coding system, the examiner always indicated orally the first number name (one, two, or five) and stopped the patient's production at 30. This point was chosen as a trade-off between the duration of the investigation and the opportunity to tap both one-word numbers (in French, the numbers from 1 through 16, and 20 and 30) and a significant portion of the presumably rule-governed two-word decade unit figures (in French, the numbers from 17 through 19 and from 21 through 29). In order to make the experimental situations between the three systems as similar as possible along external memory traces, written forms (alphabetic and arabic digits) were produced on separate sheets of paper for each item in the sequence. thus avoiding the possibility of the paper being a visible storing device that could be accessed in the course of counting (Hitch, 1978). The nine conditions were presented in the same order to the 18 subjects, first written alphabetic, then written arabic digits and, finally, oral counting. In each case, the series had to be produced first by fives, then by twos, and then by ones. The subjects worked at their own pace and were videotaped for detailed analysis of their errors, hesitations, and concomitant gestures or verbal comments.

176

Scoring Procedures

Most of the different departures from the correct conventional number sequences were classified according to a scoring system identical for the three notational forms (Table 8.1). The main categories of events recorded are local errors that involved only one item but did not disorganize the whole sequence, global errors that changed the general sequence pattern, pauses presumably indicating critical points in the structure of the production mechanisms (Goldman-Eisler, 1972), and some motor or oral accompanying behavior. Aspects of the data that are specific to the type of script, such as orthographic errors in alphabetically written numbers, are considered separately in the results and discussion sections below.

In local errors the delayed correction of a previous error was not scored as a second error; for instance, in a counting by twos, the only error was the omission of 24 in . . . 20, 22, 26, 28, 24, 30. The intrusion of nonstandard number names in aphasics' erroneous sequences was simply categorized as either a global nonconventional series, a local addition or, as in the written alphabetic counting by twos (. . . *huit* [eight], *dix* [ten], *dix-deux* [ten-two], *quatorze* [fourteen] . . .), a local substitution (the illegal decade unit form dix-deux instead of the correct teen name *douze* (twelve)). Global errors can be distinguished from local errors on the basis of the foregoing deviation of the sequence relative to the conventional string, as shown in the examples given in Table 8.1 concerning, for instance, local addition and global series change in counts by twos or fives. Silent pauses (to which filled pauses like ''uh'' were added in the oral condition) were assessed by two independent judges from the videotapes in reference to each patient's own mean production rate. Oral accompanying behavior appeared not only in written but also in oral counting. In the latter condition, the distinctions between series change (counts by ones instead of twos: one, two, three, four, . . .) and oral intermediate counting (one, TWO, three, FOUR, . . .) and oral rehearsal (. . . TWELVE, twelve, FOURTEEN, fourteen . . .) relied on intonational cues (stressed items capitalized). Miscellaneous verbal productions generally occurred in the written conditions, the correspondence between the two codes not necessarily being perfect.

RESULTS

The results in the nine experimental conditions are presented by pooling the data from the 18 aphasic subjects and by first considering the three notational systems, oral, written arabic digit, and written alphabetic forms separately. The three countings (by ones, twos, and fives) in each script are analyzed in reference to the taxonomy described in Table 8.1; they provide the data base for evaluating the relevance to the pathological dissolution of number processing, of developmental or normal production models of counting sequences. The general issue of

TABLE 8.1
Taxonomic Categories Used for Analyzing Aphasics' Performances
in Producing Conventional Number Sequences

Local errors	Involve just one item in the series, whether self-corrected or not
Omission	One number (26) is missing in a count (by 2s): . . . 22,24,28,30
Addition	There is one extra number (25) in a count (by 2s): . . . 22,24,25,26,28,30
Reduplication	An item (16) is immediately repeated in the sequence: . . .15,16,16,17 . . .
Substitution	A number (treize [13]) is replaced by another item (trois [3]): . . . onze (11), douze (12), trois (3), quatorze (14) . . .
Global errors	The general conventional structure of the number string is disrupted
Series change	Counting started (by 2s) then proceeds (by 1s): . . . 20,22,23,24,25 . . .
Series displacement	beyond some number (quatorze [14], counting starts again from another point (cinq [5]) and progresses with the correct increment: . . . treize (13), quatorze (14), cinq (5), six (6), sept (7) . . .
Nonconventional series	Scrambled numbers and/or elements of other lexical stores (letters of the alphabet) are introduced in a count (by 5s): 5,B,C, . . .
Stop	Patient stops at a number before 30 and cannot continue despite the examiner's encouragements
Pauses	Hesitations that noticeably depart from the average particular patient's counting rate
Accompanying behavior	Any motor or verbal activity that contributes to the production of the number series
Fingers	Fingers are progressively raised while counting
Oral counting from one	The production of each item (Five, Ten in written counting by fives) is preceded by the whole recitation of the number sequence from 1 to that number: one, two, . . . five; writes FIVE; one, two, . . . nine, ten; writes TEN; . . .
Oral intermediate counting	Orally counting by 1s, the patient picks up the numbers relevant to the series to be produced (5, 10, . . .): one, two, . . . five, writes 5; six, seven, . . . ten, writes 10;
Oral rehearsal	Repeats the just-delivered item (5, 10, . . .) before producing the next one (10, 15 . . .): 5, five, 10, ten, 15, fifteen . . .
Miscellaneous verbal	other oral production

the functional relationships between the three scripts is addressed in the next discussion section, which contrasts a unitary conception with a simple mechanism operating on abstract number representations shared by the different coding systems and a dissociated view with compartmentalized skills related to the several numerational codes.

Oral Counting

The quantitative results shown in Table 8.2 indicate in each of the three counting series the total observed instances of the different categories defined in Table 8.1. together with the number of items where the particular phenomenon occurred (in order to take into account multiple trials) and the number of subjects that depicted such behavior (since, by definition, the scope of global errors surpasses local points in the sequences, the number of items is not specified in this case). Transforming some of the totals of Table 8.2 into frequencies can be done by noting that there are 18 subjects and, respectively, 30, 15, and 6 numbers in the standard counts by ones, twos, and fives.

The results are first discussed from a descriptive point of view and then analyzed on a procedural level in the framework of production and lexical models.

Description of Errors. The 24 local errors, mainly substitutions (11) and omissions (10), were made by 10 subjects. The substitutions were four stack-position errors (like the teen name 16 instead of 15 in a count by fives); three stack errors, two of which in forms that do not correspond to legal number names (*vingt-quatorze* [twenty-fourteen] for 24); three cases where there was produced only one of the two words in a decade unit figure (huit [8] for *dix-huit* (18) in counts by twos), and the utterance of *mille* (1,000) instead of 10 (see Deloche & Seron, 1982a, and this volume) for the definition and a discussion of the neuropsycholinguistic relevance of stack and position errors). The 10 number omissions generally occurred in the decade unit pattern of the 20s, with no noticeable regularity. The two additions were simply the localized intrusions of odd numbers between two items in counting by twos. The forward progression of the series was reversed by seven cases of number addition or number substitution, interrupted in the two cases of non-number substitutions, unchanged in the one reduplication case, and respected in other cases. By reference to the total of counting words to be produced, local errors were rare in the three sequences (2%, 4%, and 2% respectively in counting by ones, twos, and fives).

The 19 global errors occurred in 14 erroneous series by nine subjects. There were three series changes from twos to ones counts (. . .*quatorze* [14], *seize* [16], *dix-sept* [17] . . .) and two cases from fives to tens. Among the six series displacements, two resulted from lexical errors on decade number names (*vingt* [20] for *dix* [10] in counting by twos: . . . *huit* [8], *vingt* [20], *vingt-deux*

TABLE 8.2

Oral Counting: Distribution of Errors, Pauses and Accompanying Behaviors, by Items and Patients, According to Counting Increment and Taxonomic Categories of Table 8.1

	Counting Increment								
	1			2			5		
	Total	*Items*	*Patients*	*Total*	*Items*	*Patients*	*Total*	*Items*	*Patients*
Local errors:									
Omission	6	6	4	4	4	4	—	—	—
Addition	—	—	—	2	2	2	—	—	—
Reduplication	1	1	1	—	—	—	—	—	—
Substitution	3	3	1	5	5	5	3	3	3
Global errors:									
Series change	—		—	3		3	2		2
Series displacement	2		1	3		2	1		1
Nonconventional series	2		2	—	—	—	2		1
Stop	1		1	2		2	1		1
Pauses	4	4	3	3	3	2	3	3	2
Accompanying behaviors:									
Fingers	1	1	1	15	15	1	7	7	2
Oral counting from one	—	—	—	9	8	2	5	4	2
Oral intermediate counting	1	1	1	14	14	1	11	11	3
Oral rehearsal	1	1	1	—	—	—	2	1	1
Miscellaneous verbal	—	—	—	—	—	—	—	—	—

[22], . . .), and once from a stack error (*cinq* [5] for *quinze* [15] in . . . *treize* [13], *quatorze* [14], *cinq* [5], *six* [6], . . .). The four nonconventional series produced by two subjects were either intrusions of letters of the alphabet, of non-number words bearing some morphological relations to number names (huile (oil) for *huit* [8]), or apparently random sequences of counting words that were soon stopped by the subjects. Global errors thus occurred in 26% of the series; they violated the forward direction of numbers in only three cases; series changes concerned the counting by twos and fives, but not by ones.

The 10 pauses were produced by five subjects and appeared in six cases at transitional points, i.e., just before the first number name of a lexical category (for instance the teen name *douze* [12] to be uttered after the decade *dix* [10] in counting by twos) or when the lexical pattern changed (as between the last teen name *seize* [16] and the two-word decade unit figure *dix-sept* [17]).

Finger counting was systematically used by one subject, with accompanying intermediate oral productions, in the twos and fives series. A Broca's aphasic recited the number string from one to each item in the fives count and also from one to some even numbers (from 6 to 20 in the twos series).

Table 8.3 gives the distribution of the locus of errors and pauses analyzed at the lexical level for one-word number names, categorized into units, teens, and decades, and at the structural level of decade-unit pattern, for two-word names. The locus of an error is either its place (local substitution), or the first item of the conventional series that is not produced (local omission, global stop, global series change). Pauses are attributed either to the next item (interitem filled or unfilled pauses) or to the particular item (intraword pauses).

Grouping the data of the 18 aphasics to the three counting sequences indicated virtually no trouble (2%) in the units and no special problem in their repetitive use in the decade unit structures (6%). The low error/pause percentage (7%) on decades should be considered cautiously because only the first three (10, 20, 30) were used in the range of the series investigated. The highest percentage (11%) observed in the teens rules out any interpretation that would correlate the occur-

TABLE 8.3
Distribution of Locus of Errors and Pauses in Oral, Digit, and
Alphabetic Countings According to Number Lexical Pattern

	Units	Teens	Decades	Decade-Unit
Total figures	252	180	162	324
Error and pauses				
Oral total	4	19	12	18
%	2	11	7	6
Digit total	5	4	5	6
%	2	2	3	2
Alphabetic total	16	58	21	40
%	6	32	13	12

rence of error and hesitation phenomena with the serial order of numbers in the conventional sequence, because such progressive dissolution of a one-dimensional, chain-like structure that could have been proposed to account for the unit preservation is not supported by the finding of more errors/pauses in the teens than in the category that comes next (decade unit pattern). Teen names thus seem to be processed as a truly independent lexical class. The issue of the neuro-psycholinguistic relevance of our lexical categorization may also be addressed by separate analyses of aphasics' productions considering both those portions of the counting sequence that stay within the same category (units, teens) or structure (decade-unit figures) and the transitions between such classes. Excluding the fives series because it contains only transitional points and thus offers no contrasting opportunities, there were twice as many errors and pauses between (8%) than within (4%) categories in the ones and twos counts. This finding thus specifies some critical breakpoints and confirms the importance of lexical mechanisms in the so-called automatic production of the counting sequence.

Interpretation of Errors.   Let us now discuss our results in reference to developmental models of oral counting. Interindividual performance variability and the globally low level of errors, hesitations, and accompanying behavior do not allow definitive statements, but some observations would seem valuable. One subject (conduction aphasia) failed before 10 in the three counts and rapidly stopped, her only conventional sequence production being the beginning of the series of even numbers (2, 4, 6) in counting by twos. She also produced non-number names that shared some similarity with numbers, either morphologically (phonemic paraphasias) or structurally (letters of the alphabet). A few subjects (all were Broca's aphasics) showed the primitive stage where numbers are connected through next-by-one relationships and where the string can be accessed only from the beginning of the series as shown in oral intermediate counting or in counting from one (the ''unbreakable chain'' of Fuson et al., 1982; Model 1 of Siegler & Robinson, 1982, with no particular structure except next connections; the ''number line'' of Resnick, 1983). Beyond such very severe cases, what emerges when aphasics' productions deviate from conventional sequences is the prominent role of the notion of lexical categories that structure the oral lexicon for numbers. It thus seems that the so-called prototype of automated verbal behavior should be more appropriately dissociated into specific rule-governed production mechanisms operating on the different lexical categories. If any automaticity were to be found, it would more likely concern those portions of the counting sequence that stay within a currently operative lexical pattern, not along the whole string. However. a finer fragmentation of intracategorical lexical primitive production mechanisms, which is suggested by our procedural distinction between category and position information, is required to account for series displacement that preserves the forward progression of positions, but not of values, such as *treize* (13; third, teen name), *quatorze* (14; fourth, teen name), *cinq* (5; fifth, unit), and *six* (6; sixth, unit). Our views favoring rule-based verbal procedures relative to rote learning are in line with conceptions developed by Ginsburg (1977), Siegler and Robinson (1982), and others to account for the progressive elaboration of children's knowledge of the decimal number system. However, our results seem at variance with developmental studies on one particular point, the role we assign to teens as a lexical category. According to a review by Fuson et al. (1982), there is no evidence of teens categorical knowledge when children learn the sequence. This divergence may, of course, be due to fundamental differences between acquisition steps and pathological disorders (see Caramazza & Zurif, 1978, for studies discussing the "regression" hypothesis) or to the peculiarities of the English system with nine teen names, the first two being morphologically irregular: eleven and twelve, and the French system, with only six teen names (11, 12, . . . , 16) followed by three decade unit figures. As we have already indicated in the introduction section when discussing Siegler and Robinson's (1982) data, the point is not clear in English. In fact, some support for the lexical specificity of teens can also be found in the data of Fuson et al. (1982). Rule-governed lexical production mechanisms seem good candidates to account for, first, the systematic omissions of fifteen, which is often replaced by the morphologically more regular "five-teen" by children in their stable portions of the sequence; second, the higher preservation rate of truly affixed teen numbers (13, 14, . . . , 19) than the irregular eleven and twelve; and, third the morphological regularizations of these two words into eleven-teen and twelve-teen. The existence of the lexical specificity of teens even in children must thus be examined in more detail.

Arabic Digit Written Counting

Description of Errors.   Errors, pauses, and accompanying behavior were rare in the written condition and less frequent than in the oral condition.

The 14 local errors found in nine series produced by six subjects were nine reduplications and five additions. The four global errors were series changes or displacements made by two subjects in the counting by twos sequences. There were two pauses observed in the counting by ones. Written activity was not accompanied by finger counting, but oral productions were noticed in six subjects. In two of them, subvocalizations were attested by videotape, but they could not be analyzed because they were inaudible. In three cases, the utterances were the names of the numbers they were writing, but one subject, whose three oral countings, already described, all had stopped before 10, used various forms of oral namings: two-digit numbers were either named as two independent digits not integrated into a single figure (two seven before writing 27), or the digit in unit position was the only one named (two, 22; three, 23; four, 24). Finally, it must be noted that the written productions were always well-formed integers (an isolated digit or a digit string without heading 0 or comma), and that the forward direction of number values was either respected or unchanged (local reduplications) but never reversed.

Interpretation of Errors.   Given the very high frequency of correct sequences, our analyses of the performance of aphasics on a procedural level is no more than indicative. The distributions of errors and pauses were not sensitive to the lexical categorizations relevant to oral counting because their percentages (Table 8.3) remained at nearly the same level (2%) in the four classes (units, teens, decades, decade unit patterns) as well as within categories or at lexical transitional points. If one considers the logic of the base-10 written digital system, the production of the sequences of number forms may be conceptualized as the monitoring of two counters: one, to the right (units), regularly incremented by one, two, or five depending on the particular series; the other counter, to the left (decades), being incremented by one each time the unit counter passes nine. Such a model is suggested by the already mentioned strategy of the subject who named the two individual digits of figures above 10, and by studies showing that children develop written procedures linked to arabic digital forms more or less independently of their knowledge of the underlying semantics, particularly for carrying, which is what is required in the counting task (Resnick, 1982, 1983). In such a model, the critical points where errors and pauses could be expected to occur would be the transitions to decades because, in those cases, the left-to-right writing process must anticipate on the first digit (decade) the result of a carry from the second digit (unit). However, and perhaps due to ceiling effect, the analysis contrasting decade transitions and nondecade points failed to show any significant differences.

Alphabetic Written Counting

Description of Errors.   The 20 cases of misspelled productions that did not modify the reading of number words, like *vaingt* for *vingt* (20) or *sis* for *six* (6), or the four instances of an uppercase letter at the beginning of the second member of two-word number names such as *dix-Huit* (18) were not registered as errors in written counting words sequences.[1] Errors, pauses, and accompanying behaviors were far more numerous than in the other two notational systems (Table 8.4).

Fifteen subjects were responsible for a total of 123 local errors found in 38 sequences, with the highest proportion (90%) being substitutions (they are analyzed in detail below). There were some omissions (9%) but virtually no additions or reduplications.

The nine global errors due to five subjects appeared in eight sequences. Five

---

[1]This does not mean that such errors are not interesting in their own right, but that they are irrelevant to the specific context of production-counting models considered here.

TABLE 8.4

Written Alphabetic Counting: Distribution of Errors, Pauses and Accompanying Behaviors in 18 Aphasics, According to Counting Increment and General Taxonomy of Table 8.1

	Counting Increment								
	1			*2*			*5*		
	Total	*Items*	*Patients*	*Total*	*Items*	*Patients*	*Total*	*Items*	*Patients*
Local errors:									
Omission	7	7	4	3	3	2	1	1	1
Addition	—	—	—	—	—	—	—	—	—
Reduplication	1	1	—	—	—	—	—	—	—
Substitution	61	61	13	32	32	12	18	17	9
Global errors:									
Series change	—	—	—	—	—	—	2	—	2
Series displacement	—	—	—	—	—	1	—	—	—
Nonconventional series	3	—	3	2	—	2	—	—	—
Stop	1	1	1	2	2	1	—	—	—
Pauses	1	1	1	2	2	1	—	—	—
Accompanying behavior:									
Fingers	4	4	1	1	1	1	—	—	—
Oral counting from one	5	5	1	8	8	4	2	2	1
Oral intermediate counting	—	—	—	1	1	1	—	—	—
Oral rehearsal	6	6	2	1	1	1	—	—	—
Miscellaneous verbal	79	79	11	60	59	9	14	14	7

sequences were stopped before 30 by four subjects. Two countings by fives were changed into increments of ten: 5, 10, 15, *25* , *35* and 5, 10, 15, 20, *30, 40*.

Two silent pauses occurred in one subject's counting by twos, between the teen name 16 and the decade unit figure 18, and then before the decade 20. A filled pause was introduced by another subject between 10 and 11, in his ones count.

Fifteen subjects produced 30 sequences with numerous (176) oral accompanying behaviors, 5 of which were associated with simultaneous finger countings. The 153 miscellaneous verbal productions were number words more or less systematically uttered by 13 subjects. Overall, the oral productions corresponded to the phonological forms of the expected written responses according to conventional series in 90% of the cases, and they differed from actual written numbers in 19% of the cases. Their functional relevance is addressed in more detail later on in the discussion of the relationships between oral and alphabetical written number production systems. Local and global errors preserved the forward progression of number values in 19% of the total errors, kept it unchanged (1%), interrupted it (63%) in the numerous cases of non-number names (either literal/verbal paragraphias or not well-formed arrangements of legal number lexical primitives), or finally, reversed it (17%), mainly when teens or decades were replaced by the corresponding unit names (stack errors).

Our analysis now focuses on the relatively important corpus formed by the 111 local substitution errors. These productions provide the data base for a two-way analysis intended to give information about the number-word lexicon organization and the procedures ordering counting words into alphabetic written sequences. First, errors are described on a surface level with reference to the set of lexical primitives of alphabetic numbers. Individual written production can thus be categorized into forms, first, that contained a "non-word" (i.e., a letter string that is not a legal primitive); second, that are dyssyntactic, (i.e., constitute pseudo-number names like *two-five* or *twenty-fifteen* for *twenty-five*); or third, that are well-formed alphabetic numbers substituted for the correct item in the conventional counting sequence. Next, the logic and attributes of the neuropsycholinguistic processes that could produce such particular deviations are outlined and integrated into the framework of normal production models.

Apart from the 20 simple orthographic mistakes already mentioned (and not considered errors), 46% of the 111 substitutions contained at least one non-French word. These errors were five jargonagraphic productions (*xigne huet* for *vingt huit* [28], two of which blended two-word figures (into single-letter strings without spaces between decades and units (*vignquatre* for *vingt quatre* [24]); five aborted responses (*qua* for *quatorze* [14]), seven-letter misorderings (*spet* instead of *sept* [7], and four substitutions like *trinte* for *trente* [30] involving either a letter (e.g., *i* for *e*) or a primary phonemic unit (e.g., /$\tilde{\varepsilon}$ / [in] for / $\tilde{a}$ / [en]). It must be noted that with the exception of the first two categories (10 cases) and of two occurrences of *quarte* (morphologically similar to both *quatre* [4] and *quarante* [40]), these local errors were clearly more similar to the correct number forms than to any other number elsewhere in the conventional sequence or in the number sphere as a whole. No particular systematicity was found in the occurrence of these first 21 errors, either in the lexical structure (7 on units, 8 on teens, 3 on decades, and 3 on decade unit names) or in the lexical breakpoints in the counting sequence (only six cases). Although the letter errors looked like usual literal paragraphias of aphasics (Lecours, 1966), the 12 following errors seemed to stem from an alphabetic lexical mechanism specifically responsible for the production of teen names by concatenation of root and bound (-*ze*) morphemes. In such a morphological recomposition of lexical primitives, the errors concerned the slight variations around the unit name to be integrated like the root morpheme in *deu* from *deux* (2), in *deuze* for *douze* (12) or *cinqui* from *cinq* (5) in *cinquize* instead of *quinze* (15). Two points may be noted: first, vowels were sometimes inserted between the root (for instance *six* [6]) and the bound (*ze*) morphemes, thus producing a letter string that did not grossly violate the sequential rules of French orthography (*sixeze* for *seize*); the same goal being reached by consonant deletions such as *si* from *six* (6) in *size* for *seize* (16); second, the mechanism extended to the few decade unit number words (17, 18, 19) immediately after the teens because 4 out of the 19 errors were like *huize* (from *huit* [8] and *ze*) for *dix-huit* (18) or *neuze* (from neuf [9] and *ze*) for *dix-neuf* (19). The 11 other errors were two cases of misproduction of teen names by blending a pseudo-root morpheme (*quar* from *quatre* [4] or *quarante* [40]) to the first teen name (*onze* [11] in *quaronze* for *quatorze* [14]); six substitutions of the kind of teen neoforms just described, but occurring at other places in the counting sequence than their most morphologically similar number forms (*huize* for *onze* [11], *deuze* for *quatre* [4]); two insertions of lexical primitives belonging to the digital (9 in *dix 9* for *dix-huit* [18]) or English (*one* for *un* [1]) coding systems; and one example of a unit name erroneously deduced by affix stripping from the corresponding teen form (*quin* from *quinze* [15] for *cinq* [5]) in decade unit structure (*vingt quin* for *vingt-cinq* [25]). The 60 substitution errors that were made of French words contained non-number words in only six cases that showed high morphological similarities with the correct number names, on the basis of orthography/phonology (3 cases like *tendre* [kind, tender] for *trente* [30]) and/or lexico-semantic similarity (two numeral ordinal adjectives: *sixième* [sixth] for *seize* [16]) and one noun (*huitaine* [a set of eight things] for *dix-huit* [18]). The 54 remaining errors consisted of lexical primitives of the alphabetical number system that can be classified into 26 dyssyntactic sequences; 2 two-word and 26 one-word well-formed numbers. Nonlegal two-word number forms concerned mainly teens (12 cases) that were not integrated into one single name but whose two digits were transcribed separately by the decade name (*dix* [10]) followed by the unit name (*un* [1], *deux* [2], . . . , *six* [6]) as in *dix un, dix deux, dix six* for *onze* (11), *douze* (12), and *seize* (16), respectively. There were also seven instances of omission of the arithmetical operator *et* (and) that must appear in French between 1 and 30 in only one item, "vingt-*et*-un" (21); three cases where the decade name *vingt* (20) was replaced by the corresponding unit name *deux* (2) as in *deux cinq* for *vingt-cinq* (25); or where the unit name was replaced by a teen name (*quinze* [15] in *vingt quinze* for *vingt-cinq* [25]) or by a decade name (*trente* [30] in *vingt trente* for *vingt-trois* [23]); two cases that rely on the same kind of mechanism, but without the preserved correspondence between the teen and the unit names positions (*douze* [12] for *huit* [8] in *vingt douze* for *vingt-huit* [28]); one substitution of a morphologically similar primitive (*cent* [hundred] for *cinq* in *vingt cent* instead of *vingt-cinq* [25]); and finally one miscellaneous error (*quatre quatre* [four four] for *trente* [30]). The two well-formed two-word erroneous sequences were *quarante-deux* (42) for *vingt-huit* (28) and the position-within-stack error *trente* (30) for *vingt* (20) in *trente-six* (36) instead of *vingt-six* (26). Position errors accounted for only two cases *dix* [10] for *vingt* [20], and vingt for *trente* [30]) out of the 26 one-word number substitutions. The remaining errors were 18 stack errors (four units, six teens, and eight decade names being replaced by their corresponding [same position] primitives in the other lexical categories [nine units, seven teens, and two decades]); three probable erroneous writings of teens into the decade name (*dix* [10] followed by the unit name but aborted just after the *dix* as in *dix* [10] for *douze* (12) or for *quinze* [15]); two omissions of the decade name (*neuf* [9] for *dix-neuf* [19]); and one error (*treize* [13] for *seize* [16]) that can be analyzed either as a position error within the teens stack (3rd for 6th) or as a phonemic/literal paragraphia (/ trɛ / for / SɛZ/).

Interpretation of Errors. The 111 substitution errors were thus neither scrambled letter strings unrelated to number words nor random substitutions within alphabetically written number lexical primitives. In 41 out of the 57 cases where the error was a letter string that did not belong to the number lexicon, the erroneous production could, nevertheless, be unambiguously related to the correct number form of the conventional counting sequence because it was precisely on this item that the morphological similarity between the error and the whole set of number names was the maximum. The 16 other cases included jargonaphasic productions, aborted responses, morphemic paragraphias constructed on the teen pattern (*huize, deuze*) but with position errors, and two undecidable figures. The target number was also clearly identifiable with the correct item in 19 out of the 54 substitutions within the number lexicon (nonintegration of decades and units in teen names, omissions of et [and]). Combined together, the results thus indicate erroneous responses directly linked to the expected ones in 54% of the error total. The 21 stack and 3 position errors preserved one kind of information (position and stack, respectively) while violating the other in the correct number. The 11 remaining errors were either aborted productions in the teens and the decade unit number forms just following them, or mixed errors combining two of the simple error types defined above (stack [teen for unit] and position [6th for 7th] in *vingt seize* (twenty sixteen) for *vingt-sept* [27], etc.). The detailed comparisons between each erroneous written production and, on the one hand, the correct number form in that position of the conventional counting sequence and, on the other hand, written numbers at large have thus evidenced systematic mistakes that can be logically related to troubles in processes controlling both the selection of lexical primitives according to position and category characteristics, and the generating of numbers in the range from 11 through 19 from some knowledge of teens and decade unit morphological structures. The neuropsychological relevance of our hypothesized lexical categorization of alphabetic number primitives is also supported by the nonhomogeneous distribution of local substitutions in the four classes, the units being the best preserved (5%) relative to the teens (28%), the decades (10%), and the decade unit patterns (10%). Despite the high level of errors within one category (the teens), transitional points were more often (17%) the locus of substitutions than nontransitional items (10%). Because such findings observed in alphabetic written forms, which can be generalized from the scope of substitutions to the whole range of local or global errors and pauses, are similar to the results obtained in oral counting, the question of the functional relationships between the two sequence production mechanisms must now be discussed in the broader framework of code-dependent procedures.

DISCUSSION

We first briefly summarize the main features of some developmental models designed to account for the progressive elaboration of producing the counting sequences, because the final stages of such models simulate normal adult behavior and thus provide a theoretical framework to consider the data observed in aphasic subjects. The functional relationships or independence between the procedures operating in the three kinds of number-coding systems investigated here are then discussed in the light of the errors, pauses, and accompanying behavior found in counting sequences. The particular nature of the pathology (acquired language disorders) requires that more prominence be given to the linguistic aspect of number processing than is customary in developmental models. Such a "lexical" model is briefly outlined. The conclusion thus attempts to justify the need for normal models to incorporate lexical characteristics of the notational systems. We try and situate the findings of the present study in the more general discussion on symbolic system processing (unitary views versus specialized skills). Other lexical domains where some of the procedures that can be tentatively hypothesized in the production of the so-called automatic counting sequences may prove to be of some relevance.

Developmental Models of Counting Sequence Production

The developmental models of counting sequence production have essentially been designed to account for the data observed in the oral modality, but some have integrated into their representational systems the progressive knowledge of the arabic digit written forms as a significant source of modifications. According to Fuson et al. (1982), the model should begin with an unbreakable chain of number words that can be produced only by starting from one and continuing by means of stable next connections (in the first two portions, which are followed by a nonstable portion). The final bidirectional chain should elaborate by acquiring the ability to enter the string at any point and by establishing backwards links between the items. Siegler and Robinson (1982) distinguish three developmental stages. Their Model I covers the first 20 counting words, also simply characterized as structured by next connections but without the specification of the beginning of the sequence as its only entry point. Model 2 applies to children whose counting stops between 20 and 99. A lexical categorization of words used to name numbers is introduced that allows the lexical generation of two-word numbers by picking a decade name in a "rule applicability list" and maintaining it while unit names are selected from a "digit repetition list" normally containing the first nine items of the number string from 1 to 20. The decade list is unstructured, except for 30 linked to the 9 in 29, and unit names are connected by ordinary next relations. In Model 3, next connections between x-ty decade names and the nines in ($[x-1]$-ty)-nine figures are established, together with rules for handling hundred.

Unlike Siegler and Robinson's (1982) models, where the production of the counting-word sequence is described at the level of psycholinguistic procedures operating on verbal lexical primitives, Resnick's (1983) approach focuses on number representations themselves. In the first stage, numbers are individual positions linked by next relationships on a mental number line. As a consequence of children's practice and knowledge elaboration of the written arabic digit system, a next-by-ten relation between numbers is then developed. In the final stage, the representation looks like a two-dimensional matrix with next-by-one connections in the rows and next-by-ten in the columns. Despite the different levels (verbal lexical, analogic, or digital representations) at which the procedures that ultimately produce the number sequence are supposed to operate, the models all fit more or less a number of characteristics of children's counting that concern stopping points (usually at numbers ending in 9 when engaged in the repetitive decade-unit pattern), entire decade omissions and repetitions (in the absence of stable next connections between decades), and the ability to enter the sequence at any point and to proceed at least to the end of the current decade, even if it is out of the range of spontaneous counting. Some discrepancies may, however, be noted; nonstandard number names (thirty-ten, thirty-eleven . . .), which are generated by mistakenly concatenating a decade name and a number name greater than 9, can easily be accounted for by Siegler and Robinson's (1982) Model 2 by considering that the digit repetition list lacks a reset specification beyond the 9, which remains connected to the next number (10) as in the primitive serial-ordered structure of the 20 first numbers. Resnick's (1983) number representations that do not seem to predict such data may perhaps more economically account for some jumps like . . . 2, 3, 14, 15 . . . (Fuson et al., 1982) corresponding to substitutions between ten-related numbers (14 for 4) than Siegler and Robinson's (1982) Model 3, where entire decade omissions can only occur at decade boundaries due to confusion between the multiple-next relationships that one single item in the digit repetition list, 9, has supposedly established with all decade names in the rule applicability list. Another issue concerns the nature of the next connections between the first counting words when the series can only be entered from its beginning. This empirical result found in preschoolers has been well-documented by Fuson et al. (1982), and its relevance to the study of aphasics' processing strategies is clearly shown by the counting-from-one behavior of some of our subjects.

Functional Relationships Between Production Mechanisms in Different Coding Systems

The question of the differential role of the notational systems on aphasics' performance in the production of the counting sequences may first be considered at a global level, before analyzing fine structural and procedural parallels or divergencies. As shown in Table 8.5, the digit-writing condition proved the easiest, and alphabetic sequences were the most difficult. There was no noticeable effect of counting increments, with the possible exception of oral modality.

Spearman's rank-order correlation coefficients computed between the subjects' performance in the three coding systems indicated a statistically significant relation ($r = .50$; $p < .05$) only for the two notations that share the same lexical structure, the oral and alphabetic number forms. It must thus be asked whether such systems do have common production mechanisms, a question that is tentatively answered by briefly reviewing the possible traces of each of the two coding systems in the erroneous sequences produced in the other codes.

Arabic Digit Written Counting Sequences.   The high preservation rates of aphasic performances and their lack of correlation with the other two verbal

TABLE 8.5
Distribution of Errors and Pauses Percentages
According to Notational Systems
and Counting Increments

	Counting Increment		
Coding System	1	2	5
Arabic digits	1%	4%	2%
Oral	4%	8%	11%
Alphabetic	14%	15%	19%

notational systems seem to indicate that normals may develop particular skills in handling arabic digits and that this ability can resist brain damage that produces language disorders. The preservation may be facilitated by the ideographic nature of the symbols, by their very small number (10), by the simplicity of the counting algorithm (increment units, carry when reaching 10), and by the early acquisition of written-digit-dependent procedures that are operated without a necessary reference to the semantic of arithmetic (Resnick, 1983). The specificity of arabic counting sequence production mechanisms is also supported by the eight series that were started from 0 (despite oral prompting at 1, 2, or 5), as though a unit counter had to be reset before the incrementation process becomes operative. The relative independence in reference to other coding systems is substantiated by the irrelevance to arabic digits; of verbal lexical characteristics that were significant difficulty factors in oral and alphabetic counting (lexical categorization of primitives, transitional points); by the few oral accompanying behaviors, some of which were controlled by (and did not control) the logic of the base-10 arabic digit representation (naming separately the two digits in a number as two units); and finally, by intrasubject dissociations like the two aphasics who extensively used intermediates or counting-from-one strategies in twos and fives oral counts, but performed without any error, pause, or accompanying behavior in the written-digit modality, and conversely, like one anomic subject who had local addition and reduplication errors with digits in the three series but was perfect in oral counting.

Oral Counting Sequences: A Verbal Lexical Counting Model.   Position and stack errors, on the one hand, and the differential distribution of errors and hesitation phenomena according to the categorization of verbal lexical primitives and the role of lexical transitional points, on the other hand, clearly located disorders on the level of manipulating the lexicon. It thus seemed that the production of the different counting sequences could be modeled, on a lexical level. by some conceptual knowledge of the sequence structure (units, ten, teens, decade-unit repetitive patterns) served by procedures selecting lexical primitives on the basis of class specifications (units, teens, decade names) and controlling position-within-class informations, the position values being incremented, in the units and teens files, by 1, 2, or 5 depending on the series, a kind of carry mechanism adding 1 to the position value pointing to the decade file name, and producing the reset of the unit file pointer. In such an architecture, the forward progression of number values would simply be monitored by the steady incrementation of pointers that, given the particular position information, can address lexical primitives in their respective categories. Alien letter intrusions found in children's oral counting, like 1, 2, 3, 4, 5, 6, 7, h, i, j, . . . (Gelman & Meck, 1983), may thus receive a clear procedural interpretation, the pointer value incrementation from 7 to h being preserved (h is the 8th letter), but the error being switching to the wrong lexical file (alphabet instead of numbers). Many children's errors may be reconsidered in the framework of this lexical model, which can logically structure their apparent randomness (the examples are taken from Fuson et al., 1982). Preservation of pointer value incrementation but confusion in lexical category pointing occur between units and teens (. . . 4, 15, 16 . . . or . . . 12, 3, 4. . . .), teens and decades (. . . 13, 40, 41 . . . or . . . 30, 14, 15 . . .), and units and decades (. . . 4, 50, 51 . . . or . . . 60, 7, 8 . . .). A slight variation of this erroneous process consists in keeping constant the position value (instead of the class information) but changing the lexical category (instead of incrementing the positions pointer value). Such mistakes are found between units and teens (. . . 4, 14, 15 . . . or . . . 13, 3, 4 . . .), teens and decades (. . . 14, 40, 41 . . . or . . . 30, 13, 14 . . .), and units and decades (. . . 3, 30, 31 . . . or . . . 40, 4, 5 . . .). It must be noted that the forward progression of number values is preserved in some cases (the first examples within parentheses) and is violated in others (the second examples), but in both situations, the steady progression of pointer value is respected or locally unchanged but never reversed. The notion of position values used to address the lexical primitives that are identified, in their respective classes, precisely by this position information points to the question of the different ways of gaining access to sequential files. Indeed, such an information-processing approach seems to account for some empirical findings from both children and aphasics. The most primitive method for finding an item whose serial order position is known in a sequential file is to enter the file at its beginning and to proceed until the correct number of elements (i.e., the position value) have been "recited." Such a process seems to correspond to the early unbreakable chain-like structures proposed by Fuson, Richards, and Briars to account for the inability of very young children to start counting from a prompt beyond one; it was repeatedly used by the aphasic with oral counting from one to each of the elements in twos and fives counts. When the file length is known (here, 9), another access method is to enter the file from the end and then to proceed backwards with a position value that must be the ten's complement of the original value. The following errors correspond to cases where position values were complemented and the category information was modified. The examples include units and teens (. . . 6, 14, 15 . . . or . . . 13, 7, 8 . . .), teens and decades (. . . 14, 60, 61 . . . or . . . 40, 16, 17 . . .) and units and decades (. . . 4, 60, 61 . . . or . . . 30, 7, 8 . . .). A more efficient method is direct access to sequential file elements from the key given by their position value. This seems to correspond to the progressive elaboration of the number sequence demonstrated when children can count-on from any prompt, which requires, in the lexical model, only the ability to set the pointers at other values than one.

As evidenced both quantitatively by significant correlations and qualitatively by the above analysis of oral counting at a verbal lexical level, the similarities between oral and alphabetical written countings are important. The two notational systems are, of course, different surface forms of the same "words." In the discussion of their relative dependence, it may be recalled that alphabetic writing was sometimes (in fact, often) accompanied by oral productions, but the reverse was never observed in our sample of aphasic subjects. As concerns the relation between oral counting and written alphabetic counting it must be stressed that aphasics, despite their relatively substantial number of lexical errors, almost never (only twice) uttered dyssyntactic forms like ''vingt quatorze'' (twenty fourteen), a finding that points to the existence of a set of ''critics'' controlling the grammaticality of their productions (see Brown & Van Lehn, 1982, and Resnick, 1983, for a discussion of children's procedures that assure that some minimal constraints are satisfied when they generate buggy algorithms in order to repair processing failures).

Alphabetic Written Counting Sequences.   Aphasics' errors and accompanying behaviors (mainly oral) were clearly more frequent in alphabetic notational forms than in the other two codes. The data provided evidence of both alphabetic-written-system-dependent troubles and of phenomena that could be related to oral or arabic digit notations.

As concerns the grammatical rules of the written number-coding system itself and independently of the appropriateness relative to the counting-word sequences, it must be noted that the productions were often not well-formed numbers (for instance, only 25% of the 111 local substitution errors were legal numbers). Some graphic conventions, like the space between lexical primitives, or the nonmixing of upper- and lowercase letters, were violated on occasion. Intrusions of quantity words (nouns like *huitaine* [about eight] for 18, or numeral ordinal adjectives such as *sixième* [sixth] for 16) demonstrate the relevance of the lexical hypothesis concerning the procedure handling position information and suggest a particular lexical production mechanism for teen names. This morphological reconstruction process of lexical primitives (one-word names) by concatenating a root morpheme (the name of the pointer value) and a bound morpheme (the teen indicator-*ze*) seemed to be specific to the written code because the preserved orthographic acceptability rules (by adding vowels or deleting consonants and thus producing CVC forms) and such invented pseudo-teen names were not observed in oral counting, which does not imply, of course, that such forms will never be uttered. Interestingly, the same lexical generative process extends to numbers that come immediately next teens (like *dix-huit* [18]), which received one-word teen-like forms (''huize'') instead of their conventional two-word writings.

A mediation through the arabic digit system could be traced back in the seven series that were started at zero despite the oral prompts one, two, or five, and possibly in the lexical fragmentation process that produced illegal decade unit structures instead of teens. The latter errors (''ten one'' for 11) may indeed reflect some dependence of alphabetic writing on arabic notations (one word for each digit) or, less probably because it was not observed in oral counting, the overgeneralization of the canonical decade unit pattern found in most numbers below 100. Number writings that mixed arabic digit and alphabetic lexical primitives may also be considered an example of interwoven numerical processing skills *dix 9* [ten 9] for *dix-neuf* [19]).

As we have already pointed out, the structural relationships between alphabetic and oral number notational systems are very close because their lexicons, grammars, and semantics are the same, the only difference being in the symbolic units to be assembled (letters or phonemes). Such architectural similarity has a functional correspondence indicated both macrostructurally (correlation between aphasics' performances) and in the local phenomena. Phonology seemed to play some role in the written form production system as demonstrated by the verbal paragraphias, which exhibited a high sound similarity to the correct number names, and also by the 20 cases of misspelled words that preserved print-to-sound correspondences. The lexical categorization of verbal primitives (units, teens, decades) and number name compositions (one or two words) was relevant in the two verbal production systems that were sensitive to those transitional points. The lexical model of forward counting that has been detailed in the preceding section thus seems relevant, in its main characteristics, to the conceptualization of the alphabetic number-counting sequence production in normals on the grounds of the evidence that can be deduced from the procedural analysis of aphasics' data. Besides such similarities that point to possibly common mechanisms, some specific points must be noted. For instance, the teens seem to constitute a major specific lexical problem in the alphabetic system because they are not always treated as one-word ready-made lexical primitives but sometimes reconstructed on the basis of knowledge of morphological regularities (root and bound morphemes) or fractionated into two words (ten one). The numerous (173) oral accompanying behaviors are also indicative of the connections between the two production systems. There were cases where number writing was preceded by the oral recitation of the entire counting sequence, from one to the current item, and many other cases where the oral and written forms were produced nearly at the same time, so it is difficult to say whether one determined, verified, or was just associated with the other. Nevertheless, both the presence of oral productions and their nature (correct, or not, in reference to the number that comes in the conventional sequence) were found to influence the error and pause percentages, which varied from 15% (no oral behavior) to 18% (the oral forms were not the expected ones) but fell to 11% when the oral forms were correct. Individual dissociations in the aphasics' abilities to handle the two verbal number systems are indicated by the differential distribution of unfinished sequences: the subject who stopped before 10 in the three oral series was successful in her twos and fives alphabetic written counts and stopped only at 23 in counting by ones; conversely, three subjects who reached 30 in the oral modality failed in at least one out of the three written series.

The alphabetic written production of the counting sequences does not appear, in aphasics, to be an automated process that would simply deliver number names from a store one by one in a routine order. Indeed, it may be a creative lexical mechanism that obeys a logic of its own, specific to the alphabetic notational system and not reducible to the mere writing of oral sequence forms or to the verbatim transcoding of individual digits from arabic forms. However, traces of the influence of digit and, more frequently, of oral counting processes also emerge.

CONCLUSION

Aphasic patients, as a group, often have difficulty in producing forward-counting sequences. Within the scope of our study, the most significant difficulty factor was not series increment (ones, twos, and fives) but the nature of the notational system, and more particularly its verbal (impaired, oral, or written) or ideographic (relatively preserved, arabic digits) dimension. The departures from the standard counting series indicated some degrees of specificity in coding system-dependent procedures implied in the production of the sequences and also some relationships between mechanisms in the different codes. Teen names, especially in alphabetic written forms, clearly pointed to the existence of lexical mechanisms handling morphological knowledge and category and position information. The lexical production model we proposed thus departs from classical developmental models on the role attributed to generative lexical rules relative to rote-learned chain-like structures or analog-digital number representations. Some insight into the structure of the verbal number lexicon is also provided by the findings. The categorization of lexical primitives into units, teens, and decades, which emerged from our earlier studies of number-transcoding processes in aphasics and which is consistent with number-naming latencies in normals (Henderson, Coltheart, & Woodhouse, 1973), thus constitutes the data structure where production procedures do operate. More research is required on the issue of whether the traces of relationships between the production mechanisms in the different notational systems are necessary characteristics of normal models or simply result from developing backup procedures in one system to overcome impaired processing in another code.

Our approach, which favors the integration of the lexical properties of numerational systems in the models of number manipulation skills (and thus contrasts the unitary conception of a single universal mechanism with unique number representation) is in the line of other studies. For instance, Takahashi and Green (1983) found an interaction between type of script and numerical distance or physical size in magnitude comparison judgments of numbers presented in kanji (ideographic) or kana (syllabic) forms. It was thus suggested that either the numerical representations accessed from the two scripts or the comparison procedures differed. Gonzalez and Kolers (1982, and this volume) investigated normals' performance in verifying simple equations where arabic and roman numbers were mixed. Their analysis of reaction-time data showed that symbol-processing procedures had not developed independently of the notational systems. Wapner and Gardner (1981) also rejected the strong version of the "unitary" symbol-processing approach in their analysis of subjects' (right or left hemisphere damaged) performance on a visual symbol recognition test. Indeed, these subjects adapted their strategies to the type of material, which ranged from verbal (words, phrases) to pictured objects, through trademarks, traffic signs, and numbers and to their preserved linguistic or nonlinguistic abilities, depending on their pathology. Saxe and Posner (1983) have shown the role of some dimensions—verbal or spatial (body parts) number representations, base or non-base systems, and culturally organized practices—on the elaboration of numerical skills.

In view of the prominent role of the acquisition of the counting sequence in the elaboration of arithmetical skills, the influence of the sequence production disorganizations that we have analyzed in aphasics on their calculation abilities remains to be determined. In this respect, it must be recalled that brain damage may differentially affect performances in function of the preferred premorbid individual elementary calculation strategies (Leonhard, 1979). Visuo-spatial disorders could thus pose special difficulties for those who use visual number forms and shape in their minds diagrams on which calculations are operated (Spalding & Zangwill, 1950, have described such a case of acalculia). Conversely, verbal impairments should naturally affect subjects whose calculation procedures rely on the sound of the number or on transcoding the figures into written digital forms.

The scope of the study of aphasics' performance in the counting sequence is obviously not restricted to numbers. Other domains of linear orders should be concurrently investigated so as to determine the general relevance of some of the procedures and file access methods we have discussed here (see Deloche & Seron, 1984b, for the application of position and class information to word processing in serial-ordered semantic categories).

ACKNOWLEDGMENTS

Thanks are due to Mrs. I. Ferrand and Mr. M. Frederix for technical assistance and to the clinicians, psychologists, and speech therapists of La Salpêtrière Hospital, Paris, for kindly referring subjects and providing useful help. This research was supported by grants from INSERM, from the Fyssen Foundation, and from the French and Belgian governments through Scientific Exchange Projects.

REFERENCES

Alajouanine, T., Lhermitte, F., Ledoux, M., Renaud, D., & Vignolo, L. A. (1964). Les composantes phonémiques et sémantiques de la jargonaphasie. *Revue Neurologique, 110* (1), 5–20.

Assal, G., Buttet, T., & Jolivet, R. (1978). Aspects idéographiques de l'écriture: Analyse d'un nouveau type d'agraphie. *La Linguistique, 14,* 79–101.

Assal, G., & Jacot-Descombes, C. (1984). Intuition arithmétique chez un acalculique. *Revue Neurologique, 140* (5), 374–375.

Beckwith, M., & Restle, F. (1966). Process of enumeration. *Psychological Review, 73* (5), 437–444.

Benson, D. F., & Geschwind, N. (1969). The alexias. In P. J. Vinken & G. W. Bruyn (eds.), *Handbook of clinical neurology* (Vol. 4, pp. 112–140). Amsterdam: North Holland.

Brown, S., & Van Lehn, K. (1982). Towards a generative theory of "bugs". In T. P. Carpenter, J. M. Moser & T. A. Romberg (Eds.), *Addition and subtraction: A cognitive perspective.* (pp. 117–135). Hillsdale, NJ: Lawrence Erlbaum Associates.

Caramazza, A., & Zurif, E. B. (1978). *Language acquisition and language breakdown.* Baltimore: Johns Hopkins University Press.

Carpenter, T. P., & Moser, J. M. (1982). The development of addition and subtraction problem-solving skills. In J. P. Carpenter, J. M. Moser, & T. A. Rombert (Eds.), *Addition and subtraction: A cognitive perspective* (pp. 9–24). Hillsdale, NJ: Lawrence Erlbaum Associates.

Cohn, R. (1971). Arithmetic and learning disabilities. In H. R. Myklebust (Ed.), *Progress in learning disabilities.* (pp. 322–389). New York: Grune & Stratton.

Coltheart, M. (1980). Deep dyslexia: A right hemisphere hypothesis. In M. Coltheart, K. Patterson, & J. C. Marshall (Eds.), *Deep dyslexia* (pp. 326–380). London: Routledge & Kegan Paul.

Deloche, G., & Seron, X. (1982a). From one to 1: An analysis of a transcoding process by means of neuropsychological data. *Cognition, 12,* 119–149.

Deloche, G., & Seron, X. (1982b). From three to 3: A differential analysis of skills in transcoding quantities between subjects with Broca's and Wernicke's aphasia. *Brain, 105,* 719–733.

Deloche, G., & Seron, X. (1984a). Some linguistic components of acalculia. In F. C. Rose (Ed.), *Advances in neurology: Vol. 42. Progress in aphasiology* (pp. 215–222). New York: Raven Press.

Deloche, G., & Seron, X. (1984b). Semantic errors reconsidered in the procedural light of stack concepts. *Brain and Language, 21,* 59–71.

Ducarne, B. (1976). *Test pour l'examen de l'aphasie.* Paris: Centre de Psychologie Appliquée.

Fayol, M. (1985). Nombre, numération et dénombrement: Que sait-on de leur acquisition? *Revue Française de Pédagogie, 70,* 59–77.

Forrin, B. (1975). Naming latencies to mixed sequences of letters and digits. In P. M. A. Rabbitt & S. Dornic (Eds.), *Attention and performance V.* (pp. 345–356). London: Academic Press.

Fuson, K. C. (1980). *The counting word sequence as a representational tool.* Paper presented at the fourth International Conference for the Psychology of Mathematic Education, Berkeley.

Fuson, K. C. (1982). An analysis of the counting on solution procedure in addition. In T. P. Carpenter. J. M. Moser, & T. A. Romberg (Eds.), *Addition and subtraction: A cognitive perspective.* (pp. 67–81). Hillsdale, NJ: Lawrence Erlbaum Associates.

Fuson, K. C. (1984). More complexities in subtraction. *Journal for Research in Mathematics Education, 15* (3), 214–225.

Fuson, K. C., & Hall, J. W. (1983). The acquisition of early number word meanings: A conceptual analysis and review. In H. P. Ginsburg (Ed.), *The developmental mathematical thinking* (pp. 49–107). New York: Academic Press.

Fuson, K. C., Richards, J., & Briars, D. J. (1982). The acquisition and elaboration of the number word sequence. In C. J. Brainerd (Ed.), *Children's logical and mathematical cognition* (pp. 33–92). New York: Springer Verlag.

Fuson, K. C., Secada, W. G., & Hall, J. W. (1983). Matching counting and conservation of numerical equivalence. *Child Development, 54*, 91–97.

Gardner, H., Strub, R., & Albert, M. L. (1975). A unimodal deficit in operational thinking. *Brain and Language, 2*, 333–344.

Gelman, R., & Gallistel, C. R. (1978). *The child's understanding of number.* Cambridge, MA: Harvard University Press.

Gelman, R., & Meck, E. (1983). Preschoolers' counting: Principles before skills. *Cognition, 13*, 343–359.

Ginsburg, H. P. (1977). *Children's arithmetic: The learning process.* New York: D. Van Nostrand.

Goldman-Eisler, F. (1972). La mesure des pauses: Un outil pour l'étude des processus cognitifs dans la production verbale. *Bulletin de Psychologie, 304*, 383–390.

Gonzalez, E. G., & Kolers, P. A. (1982). Mental manipulation of arithmetic symbols. *Journal of Experimental Psychology: Learning, Memory and Cognition, 8* (4), 308–319.

Goodglass, H., & Kaplan, E. (1972). *The assessment of aphasia and related disorders.* Philadelphia: Lea & Febiger.

Gott, P. S. (1973). Language after dominant hemispherectomy. *Journal of Neurology, Neurosurgery and Psychiatry, 36*, 1082–1088.

Grewel, F. (1973). The acalculias. In P. J. Vinken & G. W. Bruyn (Eds.), *Handbook of clinical neurology* (Vol. 4, pp. 181–194). Amsterdam: North Holland.

Hatano, G. (1982). Learning to add and subtract: A Japanese perspective. In T. P. Carpenter, J. M. Moser, & T. A. Rombert (Eds.), *Addition and subtraction: A cognitive perspective* (pp. 211–223). Hillsdale, NJ: Lawrence Erlbaum Associates.

Henderson, L., Coltheart, M., & Woodhouse, D. (1973). Failure to find a syllabic effect in number naming. *Memory and Cognition, 1* (3), 304–306.

Hitch, G. J. (1978). The role of short-term memory in mental arithmetic. *Cognitive Psychology, 10*, 302–323.

Huber, W., Poeck, K., & Willmes, K. (1984). The Aachen aphasia test. In F. C. Rose (Ed.), *Advances in neurology: Vol. 42, Progress in aphasiology* (pp. 291–303). New York: Raven Press.

Larsen, B., Skinhoj, E., & Lassen, N. A. (1978). Variations in regional cortical blood flow in the right and left hemispheres during automatic speech. *Brain, 101* (2), 193–209.

Lecours, A. R. (1966). Serial order in writing: A study of mispelled words in developmental dysgraphia. *Neuropsychologia, 4*, 221–241.

Lecours, A. R., Rascol, A., Nespoulous, J. L., Joanette, Y., & Puel, M. (1980). *Protocole Montréal-Toulouse.* Examen de l'Aphasie, module standard initial, version Alpha, Université de Montréal.

Leonhard, K. (1979). Ideokinetic aphasia and related disorders. In R. Hoops & Y. Lebrun (Eds.), *Neurolinguistics 9: Problems of aphasia* (pp. 11–77). Lisse: Swets & Zeitlinger.

Mazaux, J. M., & Orgogozo, J. M. (1981). *Boston diagnostic aphasia examination: Echelle Française.* Paris: Editions Scientifiques et Psychologiques.

Nairne, J. S., & Healy, A. F. (1983). Counting backwards produces systematic errors. *Journal of Experimental Psychology: General, 112*, 37–40.

Ojemann, G. A. (1974). Mental arithmetic during human thalamic stimulation. *Neuropsychologia, 12*, 1–10.

Parkman, J. M. (1971). Temporal aspects of digit and letter inequality judgments. *Journal of Experimental Psychology, 91* (2), 191–205.

Parkman, J. M., & Groen, G. J. (1971). Temporal aspects of simple addition and comparison. *Journal of Experimental Psychology, 89* (2), 335–342.

Peterson, L. R., & Peterson, M. J. (1959). Short-term retentions of individual verbal items. *Journal of Experimental Psychology, 58*, 193–198.

Piaget, J., & Szeminska, A. (1941). *La genèse du nombre chez l'enfant.* Neuchâtel: Delachaux et Niestlé.

Power, R. J. D., & Longuet-Higgins, J. C. (1978). Learning to count: A computational model of language acquisition. *Proceedings of the Royal Society of London, 200,* 391–417.

Resnick, L. B. (1982). Syntax and semantics in learning to subtract. In T. P. Carpenter, J. M. Moser & T. A. Romberg (Eds.), *Addition and subtraction: A cognitive perspective* (pp. 136–155). Hillsdale, NJ: Lawrence Erlbaum Associates.

Resnick, L. B. (1983). A developmental theory of number understanding. In H. P. Ginsburg (Ed.), *The development of mathematical thinking* (pp. 109–151). New York: Academic Press.

Riley, M. S., Greeno, J. G., & Heller, J. I. (1983). Development of children's problem solving ability in arithmetic. In H. P. Ginsburg (Ed.), *The development of mathematical thinking* (pp. 153–196). New York: Academic Press.

Saxe, G. B., & Posner, J. K. (1983). The development of numerical cognition: Cross-cultural perspectives. In H. P. Ginsburg (Ed.), *The development of mathematical thinking* (pp. 291–317). New York: Academic Press.

Schuell, H. (1965). *Differential diagnosis of aphasia with the Minnesota Test* (2nd ed.). Minneapolis: University of Minnesota Press.

Seron, X., & Deloche, G. (1983). From 4 to four: A supplement to "from three to 3". *Brain, 106,* 735–744.

Seron, X., & Deloche, G. (1984). From 2 to two: An analysis of a transcoding process by means of neuropsychological evidence. *Journal of Psycholinguistic Research, 13,* 215–236.

Siegler, R. S., & Robinson, M. (1982). The development of numerical understandings. In H. W. Reese & L. P. Lipsitt (Eds.). *Advances in child development* (Vol. 16, pp. 241–312). New York: Academic Press.

Singer, H. D., & Low, A. A. (1933). Acalculia. *Archives of Neurology and Psychiatry, 29,* 467–498.

Spalding, J. M. K., & Zangwill, O. L. (1950). Disturbances of number form in a case of brain injury. *Journal of Neurology, Neurosurgery, and Psychiatry, 13,* 24–29.

Starkey, P., & Gelman, R. (1982). The development of addition and subtraction abilities prior to formal schooling in arithmetic. In T. P. Carpenter, J. M. Moser, & T. A. Romberg (Eds.), *Addition and subtraction: A cognitive perspective* (pp. 99–116). Hillsdale, NJ: Lawrence Erlbaum Associates.

Takahashi, A., & Green, D. (1983). Numerical judgments with kanji and kana. *Neuropsychologia, 21* (3), 259–263.

Thompson, J., & Enderby, P. (1979). Is all your Schuell really necessary? *British Journal of Disorders of Communication, 14,* 195–201.

Wapner, W., & Gardner, H. (1981). Profiles of symbol reading skills in organic subjects. *Brain and Language, 12,* 303–312.

Warrington, E. K. (1982). The fractionation of arithmetical skills: A single case study. *Quarterly Journal of Experimental Psychology, 34A,* 31–51.

Whitaker, H. (1976). A case of isolation of the language function. In H. Whitaker & H. A. Whitaker (Eds.), *Studies in neurolinguistics* (Vol. 2, pp. 1–58). New York: Academic Press.

9 Cognitive Mechanisms in Normal and Impaired Number Processing

Michael McCloskey
Alfonso Caramazza
The Johns Hopkins University

INTRODUCTION

Deficits in number processing and calculation, which are collectively referred to as *dyscalculia,* occur frequently as a consequence of brain damage, and take a variety of different forms. The research described in this chapter and the next approaches the study of dyscalculia from a cognitive information-processing perspective. The aim of the research is to develop, through the analysis of patterns of impaired performance, a model specifying the structure of the normal cognitive systems for number processing and calculation, and the ways in which the systems may be damaged to produce the various observed deficits.

Our attempt to bring together the development of a model of normal cognitive processing with the study of cognitive deficits is motivated first by the assumption that cognitive impairments can be extremely informative about the structure of normal cognitive systems. In essence, we can make use of a pattern of impaired performance by asking, What must the normal system be like in order that damage to the system could produce just this pattern of performance? (See, e.g., Caramazza, 1984; Shallice, 1979, for more detailed discussions of this point.)

On the other side of the coin, the development of explicit cognitive models can contribute to the understanding of cognitive deficits. The process of interpreting and classifying deficits necessarily involves assumptions about normal processing—impaired performance is interpreted in terms of damage to one or more components of a normal cognitive system. If the conception of the normal system is vague and implicit, characterizations of deficits will be very general and somewhat arbitrary, and hence not particularly helpful in making sense of the wide variety of performance patterns that are likely to be observed. In contrast, a well-articulated model of the normal cognitive system provides a framework within which clear and detailed interpretations of deficits may be developed.

Previous research on dyscalculia has relied for the most part upon rather vague and general conceptions of the normal cognitive system (see, e.g., Boller & Grafman, 1983, Levin, 1979; for reviews). For example, the most widely adopted system for the interpretation of deficits (Hécaen, Angelergues, & Houillier, 1961) classifies impairments into three categories: *number alexia/agraphia, spatial dyscalculia,* and *anarithmetia.* This tripartite classification is based upon the assumption that normal number processing and calculation involves a number-reading and -writing ability, a spatial ability, and a calculation ability. Unfortunately, the nature of the posited abilities is left unspecified, so that it is difficult to determine how an ability is involved in various sorts of number-processing and calculation tasks, or what sorts of impairments should result from its disruption. Hence, the classification of deficits is inevitably somewhat arbitrary. In addition, the postulation of three general abilities and the consequent grouping of deficits into three categories cannot begin to account for the enormous diversity of number-processing and calculation impairments that are observed in brain-damaged patients—vast heterogeneity within each category is left unexplained. In this chapter and the next we suggest that by examining patterns of impaired performance in light of a detailed and explicit model of the normal number-processing and calculation systems, we can arrive at more adequate characterizations of the underlying deficits.

COGNITIVE MECHANISMS IN NUMBER PROCESSING AND CALCULATION

In considering the cognitive mechanisms implicated in the use of numbers, we begin with a basic distinction between the *number-processing system* and the *calculation system.* The number-processing system comprises the mechanisms for comprehending and producing numbers, whereas the calculation system consists of the facts and procedures required specifically for carrying out calculations. Figure 9.1 depicts our assumptions about the overall structure of the number-processing and calculation systems.

In this chapter we focus on the number-processing system; the following chapter considers the calculation system. In discussing the number-processing system, we first present a model specifying the general architecture of the system. Next, we consider number-processing deficits in light of this model, arguing that the observed patterns of deficits support the major assumptions of the model, and that the model provides a framework for interpreting the deficits. Finally, we suggest through the discussion of a single-case study that the detailed

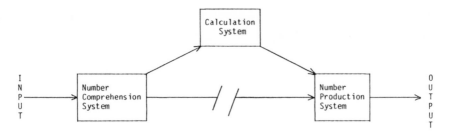

FIGURE 9.1. Schematic representation of number processing and calculation systems.

analysis of deficits can allow us not only to sketch the general architecture of the
number-processing system, but also to explore the inner workings of the various
components and how they break down.

THE ARCHITECTURE OF THE NUMBER-PROCESSING
SYSTEM

As shown in Fig. 9.1, we assume that the number-processing system comprises
two major subsystems, one for number comprehension and one for number
production. In other words, we suggest that the cognitive mechanisms for
number comprehension are distinct from those for number production. Within
the comprehension and production subsystems, we draw a number of further
distinctions, as depicted in Figs. 9.2 and 9.3. First, we distinguish the mechanisms for processing arabic numbers (i.e., numbers in digit form, such as 7,040)
from the mechanisms for processing verbal numbers (i.e., numbers in the form
of written or spoken words, such as "seven thousand forty"). According to this
view, reading the price marked on a product in a store requires the arabic
comprehension mechanisms, whereas writing a check involves both arabic and
verbal production mechanisms.

Within the arabic and verbal comprehension and production mechanisms we
draw a further distinction between lexical processing and syntactic processing
components. Lexical processing involves comprehension or production of the
individual elements of a number, such as the digit 6 or the word *forty*. Syntactic
processing, in contrast, involves the processing of relations among elements in
order to comprehend or produce a number as a whole. For example, comprehension of the verbal number "six thousand forty" requires lexical processing to
interpret the individual number words, and syntactic processing that uses word
order and meanings of words specifying powers of the number base (e.g., thousand) to determine that the number is made up of six thousands and four tens.
Similarly, production of the arabic number 725 requires lexical processing to

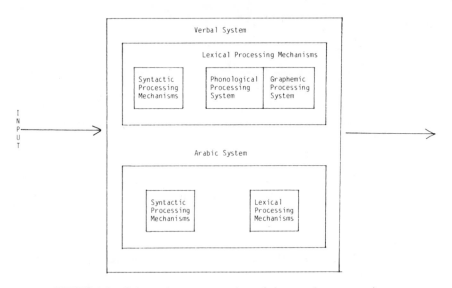

FIGURE 9.2. Schematic representation of the number comprehension subsystem.

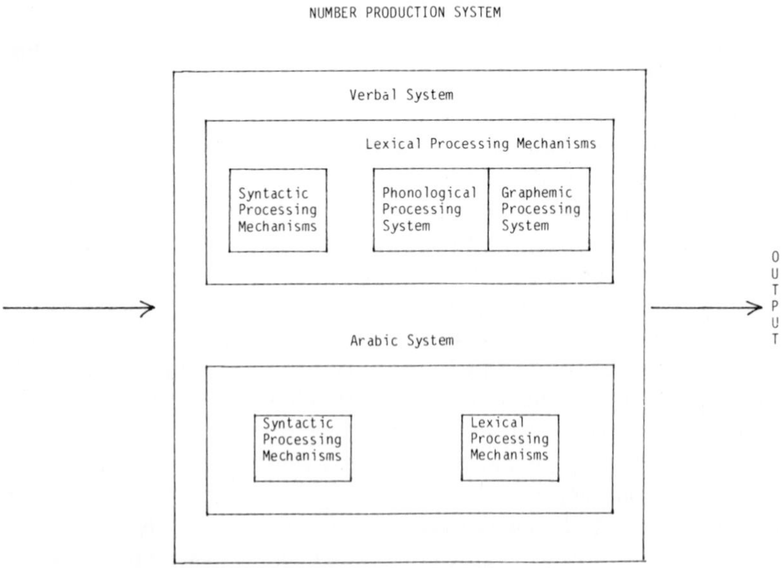

NUMBER PRODUCTION SYSTEM

FIGURE 9.3. Schematic representation of the number production subsystem.

select the appropriate digits, and syntactic processing to arrange the digits in the appropriate sequence.

Within the lexical processing components of the verbal number system we distinguish finally between the mechanisms for comprehending or producing spoken numbers (phonological processing components) and the mechanisms for comprehending or producing written numbers (graphemic processing components). Thus, for example, we assume that comprehending the written word *sixteen* implicates cognitive mechanisms different from those required for comprehension of the spoken word *sixteen*. No corresponding distinction is drawn in the realm of syntactic processing, because the syntax of spoken verbal numbers is the same as that of written verbal numbers. Further, because arabic numbers occur only in written form, we do not assume separate phonological and graphemic components for the lexical processing of arabic numbers.

NUMBER-PROCESSING DEFICITS

Number-processing deficits observed in brain-damaged patients provide strong support for our assumptions about the general architecture of the number-processing system. In this section we discuss deficits evidenced by patients we have tested, as well as deficits described in the dyscalculia literature, arguing that our model provides a framework for interpreting the deficits, and that interpretation of the deficits requires the distinctions we have drawn between production and comprehension mechanisms, arabic and verbal number-processing mechanisms, and lexical and syntactic processing mechanisms.

In interpreting a patient's performance on a task, we assume that impaired performance reflects damage to a cognitive system that was, prior to the damage, capable of performing the task successfully. In most instances, this assumption is readily justified. In the first place, the tasks we discuss (e.g., judging which of two numbers is larger, reading an arabic number aloud) require only very basic number-processing abilities. In our studies the tasks presented to patients were performed virtually without error by control subjects comparable in age and education to the patients. Further, in many cases information is available to show that a patient was capable premorbidly of performing a task (e.g., the patient successfully kept a checkbook). Nevertheless, the possibility of a premorbid difficulty with a task cannot always be completely ruled out.

The Comprehension/Production Distinction

Results from our patients, and also findings reported previously, strongly suggest that number comprehension mechanisms are distinct from number production mechanisms, and hence that number-processing deficits should be characterized in part according to whether number comprehension or number production (or both) is impaired. For example, Benson and Denckla (1969) describe a patient who appears to show intact comprehension but impaired production of arabic and verbal numbers. When arithmetic problems (e.g., 273 + 45) were presented visually in arabic form, or aurally in verbal form, the patient could consistently choose the correct answer from a multiple-choice list. This result implies that the patient could comprehend the arabic numbers in the written problems and the verbal numbers in the aurally presented problems (as well as the numbers in the multiple-choice list). Clearly, the patient was also able to perform the calculations needed to solve the problems.

However, when the patient was asked to say or write the answer to a problem, he almost always gave an incorrect response. For example, for the written problem 4 + 5, the patient said "eight," wrote "5," and chose "9" from the multiple-choice list. The excellent performance on the multiple-choice problems strongly suggests that the errors on tasks requiring spoken or written responses stem from an impairment in producing the responses, and not in comprehending the numbers in the problems, or in carrying out the calculations. Hence, the patient shows a comprehension/production dissociation in number processing, such that comprehension is intact whereas production is impaired.

Our patient V.O. shows a comprehension/production dissociation in the processing of arabic numbers. V.O.'s performance was normal on tests of arabic and verbal number comprehension (e.g., judging which of two numbers was larger). However, when presented with a written verbal number (e.g., seven thousand forty) and asked to write the number in arabic form (e.g., 7,040), V.O. performed poorly for numbers above one thousand. For example, "seven thousand forty" was written as 700040. The normal performance on verbal number-comprehension tasks suggests that the errors in writing arabic numbers from written verbal stimuli reflect an impairment in producing the arabic responses, and not a deficit in comprehending the verbal stimuli. Hence, in arabic number processing, V.O. shows a dissociation between comprehension (intact) and production (impaired). The patient described some years ago by Singer and Low (1933) shows a similar dissociation.

The Arabic/Verbal Distinction

The available data also suggest that the processing mechanisms for arabic numbers are distinct from those for verbal numbers, and hence that number-processing deficits should be characterized in part according to whether arabic or verbal processing is impaired. Our patient A.T. shows excellent performance (over 99% correct) when she is presented with a written verbal number (e.g., six thousand seven hundred five) and is asked to write the number in arabic form (e.g., 6,705). However, when written verbal numbers (or arabic numbers) are presented and A.T. is asked to read the numbers aloud, she shows a clear impairment, producing only about 80% correct responses. For example, for the stimulus number "three hundred fifty-seven," A.T. wrote 357, but read the number as "four hundred fifty-nine." Table 9.1 presents further examples of A.T.'s performance; the table shows a sequence of stimuli from one of the number lists used in testing A.T., and her arabic and verbal responses to the stimuli.

A.T.'S excellent performance in writing arabic numbers from written verbal stimuli indicates that her ability to produce arabic numbers is intact. This result also suggests that comprehension of written verbal numbers is intact. Hence, the errors in reading verbal numbers aloud cannot readily be attributed to an impairment in comprehension of the written verbal stimuli, but appear to reflect instead a deficit in producing the spoken verbal responses. Note also that these errors cannot be attributed to some peripheral production deficit (e.g., an articulation problem)—the errors take the form of incorrect number words produced in place of the correct words (e.g., "three" produced instead of "four" in response to the stimulus "four hundred fifty-seven") and hence clearly stem from imparied processing within the number-processing system. Hence, patient A.T. shows a dissociation between the production of arabic numbers (intact) and the production of spoken verbal numbers (impaired).

Arabic/verbal dissociations may also be observed in number comprehension. Patient H.Y. produced 100% correct responses in judging which of two arabic numbers was larger (e.g., 6 vs. 7; 405,034 vs. 400,534), suggesting intact arabic number comprehension. However, he performed poorly on magnitude comparison judgments for written verbal numbers (e.g., six vs. seven; four hundred five thousand thirty-four vs. four hundred thousand five hundred thirty-four),

TABLE 9.1

Examples of Patient A.T.'s Performance in the Production of Arabic
and Spoken Verbal Numbers in Response to Written Verbal Stimuli

Stimulus	Arabic Response	Spoken Verbal Response
four thousand seven hundred thirty	4730	eight thousand seven hundred thirty
two hundred seventy	270	two hundred seventy
nine thousand five	9005	nine thousand five
three hundred six	306	eight hundred six
one thousand thirty-four	1034	two thousand thirty-four
eight thousand three hundred sixty	8360	eight thousand two hundred sixty
three hundred ninety-eight	398	two hundred ninety-eight
six thousand thirty	6030	eight thousand thirty
seven thousand	7000	seven thousand
four hundred three	403	two hundred three
seven thousand sixteen	7016	seven thousand ,seventeen
six thousand three	6003	two thousand three
nine thousand six hundred eighteen	9618	nine thousand two hundred seventeen

indicating impaired verbal number comprehension. Patient K., in contrast, performed without error in judging which of two number words was larger (e.g., four vs. five), but showed near-chance performance on magnitude judgments for digits (e.g., 4 vs. 5).

The Lexical-Syntactic Distinction

If we not only consider whether performance on a task is good or poor, but also examine the *types* of errors patients make, we find clear support for the distinction between lexical and syntactic number-processing mechanisms. Our patient V.O. presents with a striking dissociation of lexical and syntactic processing in the production of arabic numbers. When verbal numbers are presented visually and V.O. is asked to write the numbers in arabic form, the individual digits in his responses are invariably correct. However, for numbers above one thousand, the order of magnitude of the response is usually grossly incorrect. For example, for the stimulus number "five thousand six hundred" V.O. wrote 5,000,600. Table 9.2 presents additional examples of V.O.'s responses. As the examples illustrate, V.O. writes arabic numbers by concatenating the arabic forms of various parts of the stimulus (e.g., "five thousand six hundred" is written by concatenating 5,000 and 600), instead of appropriately integrating the parts. Thus, V.O. shows intact lexical but impaired syntactic processing in the production of arabic numbers: He selects the appropriate digits to represent the individual magnitudes in the stimulus, but is unable to assemble these digits into an arabic number of the appropriate form.

In contrast, the number-production deficit evidenced by Benson and Denckla's (1969) patient apparently involved lexical but not syntactic process-

TABLE 9.2
Examples of the Performance of Patient V.O.
on an Number-Writing Task

Stimulus	Response
one	1
eight hundred	800
fifty thousand seven hundred two	50,000,702
nine thousand	9,000
one thousand forty	1,000,40
eighteen	18
three thousand four hundred	3,000,400
nine hundred nineteen	919
five thousand eleven	5,000,11
one hundred five thousand five hundred	100,5000,500
seven hundred twenty	720

TABLE 9.3
Examples of Errors Made by Patients A. T. and J. E.
in Reading Aloud Arabic Numbers

Stimulus	Response	
	A. T.	J. E.
5900	nine thousand nine hundred	five thousand ninety
750	seven hundred fifty	seven thousand five hundred
3108	three thousand one hundred six	three thousand one hundred eight
602	six hundred three	six thousand two
5600	five thousand six hundred	five thousand sixty
8900	eight thousand eight hundred	eight thousand ninety
8360	nine thousand two hundred sixty	eight thousand three hundred sixty
6030	six thousand thirty	six thousand three hundred
163	nine hundred sixty-two	one hundred sixty-three
1200	one thousand two hundred	one thousand twenty
1034	two thousand thirty-four	one thousand thirty-four
5097	five thousand ninety-seven	five thousand nine hundred seven

ing. The patient, in tasks requiring the production of arabic numbers or spoken verbal numbers, generated responses that differed from the correct response only in the substitution of incorrect digits or number words for the correct items. For example, the patient, asked to write "two hundred and twenty-one," produced 215, which is of the correct order of magnitude but includes incorrect digits. This pattern of performance suggests that the patient is impaired in producing the individual elements of a number (that is, the individual digits, or the individual number words), but is intact in assembling the elements into a number of the appropriate syntactic form and order of magnitude. Thus, Benson and Denckla's patient shows impaired lexical processing but intact syntactic processing in number production.

Dissociations of lexical and syntactic processing may also be observed in the production of verbal numbers. Our patients A.T. and J.E. both show impairments when they are presented with arabic numbers and asked to read the numbers aloud. Both patients show normal performance on tests of arabic number comprehension, so that their errors in reading arabic numbers aloud apparently represent deficits in production of the spoken verbal responses, and not in comprehension of the arabic stimuli. As shown in Table 9.3, however, the two patients do not make the same type of errors. Patient A.T. consistently makes errors in which the produced sequence of words differs from the correct sequence only in the substitution of one or more incorrect number words for the correct words. For example, for the stimulus 4,051, A.T. produced "three thousand fifty-one." A comparison of A.T.'s response with the correct response indicates that the word "three" was produced instead of the correct word "four":

> Correct response : four thousand fifty-one
> A.T.'s response: three thousand fifty-one

This pattern of performance suggests a lexical processing deficit. In reading a number aloud, one must retrieve stored information about the phonological forms of the to-be-spoken words. Apparently, A.T. occasionally accesses the phonological form of the wrong number word, and so, for example, may say "three" instead of "four." In other respects, A.T.'s responses are almost always correct. Thus, A.T. shows impaired lexical processing but intact syntactic processing in the production of spoken verbal numbers.

In contrast, patient J.E. presents with a pattern of performance suggesting a selective deficit in syntactic processing. For the most part, J.E.'s errors cannot be accounted for by assuming that he sometimes retrieves the wrong number word. For example, given the stimulus 4,051, J.E. said "four thousand five hundred one." This response does not represent a simple substitution of an incorrect number word for the correct word:

> Correct response: four thousand fifty-one
> J.E.'s response: four thousand five hundred one

Instead, J.E.'s errors seem to represent an impairment in assembling the individual quantities in the stimulus number into the appropriate verbal form. In the 4,051 example, J.E.'s response contains the correct individual quantities from the stimulus: 4, 5, and 1. However, in the response these quantities are not all associated with the correct power of ten. Whereas the stimulus number consists of 4 thousands, 5 tens, and 1 one, J.E.'s response represents a number consisting of 4 thousands, 5 hundreds, and 1 one. Thus, J.E. evidences intact lexical processing and impaired syntactic processing in the production of verbal numbers.

The Phonological/Graphemic Distinction

Consistent with our assumption that phonological and graphemic lexical processing mechanisms are distinct, the lexical processing of spoken verbal numbers and written verbal numbers can be dissociated. For example, our patient H.Y. performed at chance on magnitude comparison judgments for written number words (e.g., four vs. five), but showed perfect performance on magnitude judgments for spoken numbers. The deficit for written number words does not represent a peripheral visual perception problem, because H.Y. shows intact comprehension of single- and multidigit arabic numbers.

The dissociations we have described clearly support our assumptions about the general architecture of the number-processing system, and suggest that the

TABLE 9.4
Examples of Various Types of Syntactic Errors
in the Production of Arabic Numbers

Stimulus	Response
seven thousand forty	700040
forty thousand seven	407
forty-seven thousand	470000
five thousand seventeen	5,17
four hundred thirty-seven thousand	37,400
four hundred thirty-seven thousand	4370
four hundred thirty-seven thousand	4,37000

model represents a useful framework for interpreting number-processing deficits. Ultimately, however, the utility of the model will depend upon whether we can develop it in more detail, making explicit what the various components do, how they do it, and what happens when they are damaged. That the current theoretical framework is insufficiently articulated is evident both in our inability to answer such questions as, ''How is syntactic analysis carried out in the comprehension of a verbal number?'' and in our inability to provide detailed interpretations of particular patterns of impaired performance within broad categories of deficits defined by our model (e.g., lexical deficit in the comprehension of arabic numbers, syntactic deficit in arabic number production). For example, as Table 9.4 illustrates, syntactic deficits in the production of arabic numbers take many different forms. At present, we can do little more than classify the impairments as syntactic deficits in arabic number production. Although this is a nontrivial accomplishment, it does not account for the various specific patterns of observed performance by specifying how damage to the syntactic processing mechanisms leads to these patterns of performance.

To illustrate how we can begin to develop the model further through the detailed analysis of patients' performance, we describe in the next section case studies of three patients who present with similar lexical deficits in the production of spoken verbal numbers.

LEXICAL AND SYNTACTIC PROCESSING IN SPOKEN VERBAL NUMBER PRODUCTION

The three patients—A.T., R.R., and H.Y.—make lexical errors in producing spoken verbal numbers. In this discussion we focus on their performance in reading arabic numbers aloud. Examples of the patients' errors in this task are presented in Table 9.5. As can be seen from the examples, A.T. and H.Y. occasionally produce an incorrect number word in place of the correct word.

211

TABLE 9.5
Examples of Errors Made by Patients A. T., H. Y., and R. R.
in Reading Arabic Numbers Aloud

Patient	Stimulus	Response
	418	five hundred eighteen
	16	seventeen
A. T.	116	nine hundred fourteen
	1080	one thousand seventy
	32	thirty-three
	90,730	twenty thousand seven hundred thirty
	1208	one thousand six hundred eight
H. Y.	19,710	sixteen thousand seven hundred ten
	72	fifty-two
	119	one hundred seventeen
	419	three hundred fifteen
	4	one
R. R.	7253	three thousand one hundred forty-three
	39,018	forty-three thousand fifteen
	600	thirteen

R.R., however, is much more profoundly impaired—the number words in his responses are usually incorrect, and he occasionally produces syntactic as well as lexical errors. To make the nature of R.R.'s performance clearer, we present in Table 9.6 a sequence of stimuli and responses from one of the arabic number lists we asked R.R. to read aloud.

All three patients show normal comprehension of arabic numbers. It is especially notable that R.R., who is severely impaired in reading arabic numbers aloud, shows excellent performance in judging which of two single-digit or multidigit arabic numbers is larger, and in selecting a number of tokens corresponding to a digit. Hence, the patients' errors in reading arabic numbers aloud cannot readily be attributed to impaired comprehension of the arabic stimuli, but instead seem to reflect a deficit in the production of the spoken verbal responses. Furthermore, the patients' production deficits are predominantly lexical. In other words, most of the patients' erroneous responses differ from the correct responses only in the substitution of one or more incorrect number words for the correct words. Hence, the errors seem to stem from an impairment in the retrieval of the to-be-produced words.

Over several testing sessions we have asked each of the patients to read over 1,000 numbers. Analyses of their patterns of performance lead to strong inferences about the structure of the verbal number production system, and about the specific nature of the patients' deficits. In order to make clear the basis for these inferences, we must consider the patients' performance in more detail.

A word-by-word comparison of the patients' responses with the correct responses (e.g., comparing the correct response "fifty-nine" with R.R.'s response "twenty-three") reveals that the probability of producing correctly the word corresponding to a digit in a stimulus (e.g., the probability of producing "sixty" in response to the digit 6 in 362) was approximately .28 for R.R., .92 for H.Y., and .92 for A.T.

In spite of the fact that individual number words were often incorrect, the patients' responses were almost always (approximately 90% of the time for R.R., and over 98% of the time for A.T. and H.Y.) of the correct order of magnitude: single-digit stimuli elicited responses in the range zero through nine, two-digit stimuli led to responses from ten to ninety-nine, three-digit stimuli elicited responses in the hundreds, and so forth.

The errors were further constrained in that stimuli in the teens (10–19) usually elicited responses in the teens. This phenomenon occurred both for teen numbers in isolation (e.g., stimulus 16, response "eighteen"), and for teens embedded in larger numbers (e.g., stimulus 18,020 response "fourteen thousand twenty"). However, stimuli in the twenties did not tend to elicit responses in the twenties, thirties stimuli did not tend to elicit thirties responses, and so forth. Responses to stimuli in the 20–99 range were distributed throughout that range (e.g., stimulus 41, response "seventy-five").

The teens phenomenon did not occur because the patients were somehow especially accurate in processing the digit 1. The proportion of teen responses to teen stimuli was, for all three patients, significantly higher than the probability of a correct response to a 1 in a non-teen position (e.g., the 1 in 4,180, or 41). (This

TABLE 9.6
Examples of the Performance of Patient
R. R. in Reading Aloud Arabic Numbers

Stimulus	Response
4	one
81	thirty-one
207	three oh one
9	three
39,018	forty-three thousand fifteen
10	fifteen
47	forty-seven
2000	one thousand
8	one
18,042	seventeen forty-one
17	thirteen
59	twenty-three
68	thirty-six
900	three thousand
19	thirty-five

finding, incidentally, provides further support for our assumption that the patients' errors do not stem from an impairment in comprehending the digits in the arabic stimuli. If incorrect responses to a 1 in a non-teen position reflect a difficulty in comprehending the digit 1, then the patients should experience equal difficulty comprehending a 1 in a teen position. Thus, the hypothesis of a digit comprehension deficit cannot explain why non-teen responses to teen stimuli, such as "twenty-seven" in response to 17, were much less frequent than incorrect responses to a 1 in a non-teen position, such as "seventy-two" in response to 71.)

The patients' errors show, then, a clear pattern. It was not that any number word could occur as an error in the place of any other number word. When the correct word was between one and nine, the corresponding incorrect words were usually also in this range. For example, given the stimulus 3,000, the patients might say "seven thousand" or "two thousand," but were very unlikely to say "fourteen thousand" or "sixty thousand." When the correct word was in the range ten to nineteen, incorrect responses were usually also in that range. For example, in response to 18, the patients might say "twelve" or "sixteen," but almost never "nine" or "forty." Finally, when the correct word was in the set twenty, thirty, forty, . . . , ninety, the corresponding incorrect responses were usually also in that range. Thus, given 630, the patients might say "six hundred forty" or "six hundred eighty," but not "six hundred seven" or "six hundred fifteen."

Within these three sets, patients R.R. and H.Y. showed no tendency to produce incorrect responses that were close in magnitude to the correct responses. For example, given 7, they were as likely to say "three" as "six." Patient A.T., in contrast, tended to produce errors that were close to the correct responses.

The structured pattern of errors exhibited by patients A.T., H.Y., and R.R. provides a basis for inferences about the structure of the verbal number production system. In reading a number aloud, one must access stored information about the phonological forms of the to-be-spoken words. This stored information may be referred to as the phonological number-production lexicon. The pattern of lexical errors observed in our three patients strongly suggests that the production lexicon is organized into three functionally distinct classes, as shown in Table 9.7. The ONES class contains the phonological forms of the words one through nine, the TEENS class contains the phonological specifications of the words ten through nineteen, and the TENS class contains phonological information about the words twenty, thirty, forty, and so forth, up to ninety.

A person retrieving the phonological form of a number word must select the appropriate class and the appropriate item within that class. We can interpret the performance of patients A.T., H.Y., and R.R. by assuming that these patients are largely intact in their ability to select the appropriate lexical class, but are impaired (profoundly in the case of R.R., mildly in the cases of A.T. and H.Y.) in selecting the appropriate item within class. Thus, for example, in reading the

Ones	Teens	Tens
—	ten	—
one	eleven	—
two	twelve	twenty
three	thirteen	thirty
four	fourteen	forty
five	fifteen	fifty
six	sixteen	sixty
seven	seventeen	seventy
eight	eighteen	eighty
nine	nineteen	ninety

number 30, the patients usually select the TENS class, and so are unlikely to say "six" or "fifteen." However, they are impaired in selecting the appropriate item within the TENS class, and so may produce "twenty" or "seventy" instead of "thirty."[1]

The distinction among the ONES, TEENS, and TENS classes in the verbal number-production lexicon, and our interpretation of the patients' deficits in terms of this distinction, are consistent with the pattern of performance evidenced by the patients: the patients' number-reading errors respect the boundaries between the postulated classes. However, the ones/teens/tens dissociation apparent in the patients' errors is not in itself a sufficient motivation for the postulation of a ONES/TEENS/TENS distinction within the number-production lexicon. Before the distinction among lexical classes in the number-production system can be taken seriously, this distinction must be shown to have a theoretical as well as an empirical basis. In other words, it is important to demonstrate that the distinction makes sense within the context of an explicit model of the number-production process. Thus, in the following discussion we outline a verbal number-production model that incorporates the assumption of three distinct number-lexical classes.

A MODEL FOR SPOKEN VERBAL NUMBER-PRODUCTION

We assume that the input to the number-production process is a semantic representation of the to-be-produced number, in the form of a list of each quantity in the number, and the power of ten associated with that quantity. For example, given the

---

[1]Deloche and Seron (1982a,b) have also invoked the concept of number-lexical classes ("stacks" in their terminology), in classifying the number processing errors made by groups of aphasic subjects.

arabic number 6,743 to be read aloud, the input to the number production system would be a semantic representation (generated by the arabic comprehension system) something like [6]10EXP3, [7]10EXP2, [4]10EXP1, [3]10EXP0. EXP abbreviates "exponent," so that 10EXP3 means 10 to the third power; the digits in brackets indicate semantic representations of quantities. (It is conceivable that the number-production system can accept as input other forms of information in addition to semantic representations, and that the process of reading a number involves a series of comprehension and production operations applied to successive parts of the number. However, neither of these possibilities affects the arguments offered below.)

When the number-production system receives a specification of a to-be-spoken number, a number-production syntax mechanism determines from the input representation the largest power of ten in the number, and on this basis generates a syntactic frame. For example, if the arabic number 6,743 were presented to be read aloud, a syntactic frame of the sort shown below would be generated:

___(ONES)	T	___(ONES)	H	___(TENS)	___(ONES)
"10EXP3"		"10EXP2"		"10EXP1"	"10EXP0"

The syntactic frame represents a plan for the production of the to-be-spoken number. (See Garrett, 1980, for a discussion of planning structures in sentence production.) After the syntactic frame is generated, each basic quantity in the number is assigned to the appropriate slot in the frame. This filling of slots is guided by the labels beneath each slot.[2] For example, the label under the leftmost slot specifies that this slot should be filled with the quantity associated with 10EXP3. Thus, for 6,743 the filled frame would take the following form:

[6] (ONES)	T	[7] (ONES)	H	[4] (TENS)	[3] (ONES)
"10EXP3"		"10EXP2"		"10EXP1"	"10EXP0"

Each filled slot specifies a phonological form to be retrieved from the number-production lexicon. The class label (e.g., ONES) specifies the number-lexical class, and the quantity representation specifies the item within class. For example, the leftmost slot specifies retrieval from the ONES class, so that for this slot /six/will be retrieved. (We use words enclosed in slashes to represent phonological forms.) Finally, the T and H represent instructions for retrieval of the phonological forms of the words "thousand" and "hundred."

Production of the number involves the successive retrieval of the phonological forms specified by the filled syntactic frame. In the present example, the production process would yield the sequence /six/ /thousand/ /seven/ /hundred/ /forty/ /three/.

---

[2]These labels should be conceived of as syntactic category labels corresponding to the semantic values for the various powers of ten.

The retrieval process unfolds as described, except when the procedure encounters an unfilled slot (as when 7,023 is read), or when a TENS-class slot filled with a representation of the quantity 1 is encountered. We consider only the latter case here, as it is the more relevant for our purposes. We assume that when a 1 is encountered in a TENS-class slot, a special subprocedure is invoked. This subprocedure retrieves nothing from the TENS class, but instead proceeds to the next slot, and uses the quantity representation in that slot to retrieve a phonological form from the TEENS class. Consider. for example, the reading of 6,713, for which the filled syntactic frame will take the following form:

   6 (ONES)   T   7 (ONES)   H   1 (TENS)   3 (ONES)
  "10EXP3"   "10EXP2"   "10EXP1"   "10EXP0"

This frame should result in the retrieval of the sequence /six/ /thousand/ /seven/ /hundred/ /thirteen/.

It should be evident from the preceding discussion that in the verbal number-production model we have described the distinction among the ONES, TEENS, and TENS classes in the phonological production lexicon plays a central role. Hence, the model, in conjunction with the patterns of errors exhibited by patients A.T., H.Y., and R.R., provides strong motivation for the distinction among classes. It is also important to note that the model specifies unequivocally the lines along which the distinction must be drawn—the model offers no latitude in decisions about the category to which each number word should be assigned. One might, purely on the basis of intuitions about the number system, arrive at the conclusion that ones, teens, and tens number words should be distinguished. However, in the absence of an explicit model of the number production process, it is likely that in at least a few cases it will be unclear how a word should be classified. For example, an intuitive division of number words might well place the word "ten" in the tens class, with twenty, thirty, and so forth. However, the model we have described makes it very clear that "ten" is a TEEN number—its role in the production process is the same as that of the words eleven through nineteen, and quite different from the role of the words twenty, thirty, and so forth.

The number-production model not only motivates the distinction among number-lexical classes, but also provides the basis for a more detailed interpretation of the number-production deficits of patients A.T., H.Y., and R.R. We suggest that these patients usually generate the appropriate syntactic frame, fill it with the correct quantity representations, and access the appropriate number-lexical classes when retrieving the phonological forms of the to-be-spoken words. However, the patients are impaired in selecting the correct item within a class.

The production model also permits a more detailed interpretation of the deficit evidenced by patient J.E. Recall that J.E. evidences a verbal number production deficit that cannot be characterized as an impairment in the retrieval of individual number words (e.g., "six thousand three hundred" produced in response to 6,030; see Table 9.3). On the basis of the number-production model, we can go beyond simply labeling J.E.'s deficit syntactic, to suggest that J.E.'s errors stem from an impairment in assigning the individual quantities of a number to the appropriate slots in the syntactic frame, and from the occasional generation of an inappropriate syntactic frame. For example, for the number 6,030, the filled syntactic frame should take the following form:

[6](ONES)   T   ___(ONES)   H   [3](TENS)   ___(ONES)
"10EXP3"   "10EXP2"   "10EXP1"   "10EXP0"

This frame would lead to the retrieval of the sequence /six/ /thousand/ /thirty/ (given appropriate assumptions about processing of unfilled slots).

J. E., however, apparently filled the frame in the following way:

[6](ONES)   T   [3](ONES)   H   ___(TENS)   ___(ONES)
"10EXP3"   "10EXP2"   "10EXP1"   "10EXP0"

As a result, he produced "six thousand three hundred."

CONCLUSION

In this chapter we have argued that the study of number-processing deficits can shed light on the structure of the normal number-processing system, and that the development of a model of the normal system can contribute to our understanding of the deficits. On the first point we attempted to show that by considering not only whether performance on tasks is good or poor but also the pattern of performance within tasks, we can sketch the general architecture of the number-processing system, and explore the inner workings of the various components.

On the second point we suggested that our general model of the number-processing system provides a framework for interpreting the wide variety of number-processing impairments observed in brain-damaged patients. In particular, the model provides a basis for inferring what number-system components (e.g., arabic comprehension syntactic component, verbal production lexical component) are disrupted in a patient. Further, as the model is elaborated to specify the inner workings of the various components, increasingly specific interpretations of deficits become possible. The enormous diversity of number-processing impairments points clearly to the need for a detailed and explicit theoretical framework within which the deficits can be interpreted.

The development of an explicit theory is also important for several other reasons. In the first place, a well-articulated theory of normal and impaired cognitive processing is essential in any attempt to relate cognitive processes to brain mechanisms, whether in the realm of number processing or in any other cognitive domain. We cannot hope to succeed in this endeavor unless we have both a sophisticated analysis of the brain mechanisms *and* a sophisticated analysis of the cognitive processes.

Finally, an explicit model of normal and impaired cognitive processing is of central importance in the development of diagnostic tests, and in cognitive rehabilitation. Tests are designed to prove the various cognitive processes in a particular domain, to determine which are intact and which are impaired. Hence, a theoretical framework is needed to specify the component processes to be tested, and how they may be assessed. Similarly, in cognitive rehabilitation a clear understanding is needed of what cognitive processes are impaired and intact in a patient.

We suggest, therefore, that research focusing on the articulation of an explicit model of the normal cognitive system is relevant to the issues of major concern not only in cognitive psychology, but also in neuropsychology and neuroscience.

REFERENCES

Benson, D. F., & Denckla, M. B. (1969). Verbal paraphasia as a source of calculation disturbance. *Archives of Neurology, 21,* 96–102.

Boller, F., & Grafman, J. (1983). Acalculia: Historical development and current significance. *Brain and Cognition, 2,* 205–223.

Caramazza, A. (1984). The logic of neuropsychological research and the problem of patient classification in aphasia. *Brain and Language, 21,* 9–20.

Deloche, G., & Seron, X. (1982a). From one to 1: An analysis of a transcoding process by means of neuropsychological data. *Cognition, 12,* 119–149.

Deloche, G., & Seron, X. (1982b). From three to 3: A differential analysis of skills in transcoding quantities between patients with Broca's and Wernicke's aphasia. *Brain, 105,* 719–733.

Garrett, M. F. (1980). Levels of processing in sentence production. In B. Butterworth (Ed.), *Language production: Vol. 1, Speech and talk* (pp. 177–220). New York: Academic Press.

Hécaen, H., Angelergues, R., & Houillier, S. (1961). Les varieties cliniques des acalculies au cours des lesions retrorolandiques: Approche statistique du probleme. *Revue Neurologique, 105,* 85–103.

Levin, H. S. (1979). The acalculias. In K. M. Heilman & E. Valenstein (Eds.), *Clinical neuropsychology* (pp. 128–140). New York: Oxford University Press.

Shallice, T. (1979). Case study approach in neuropsychological research. *Journal of Clinical Neuropsychology, 1,* 183–211.

Singer, H. D., & Low, A. A. (1933). Acalculia (Henschen): A clinical study. *Archives of Neurology and Psychiatry, 29,* 476–498.

10 Dissociations of Calculation Processes

Alfonso Caramazza
Michael McCloskey
The Johns Hopkins University

INTRODUCTION

Calculation is a complex process involving the interaction of various cognitive mechanisms. To calculate one must be able to (a) process the numerical information, that is, perceive, comprehend, and produce numbers; (b) process the operational sign that indicates the specific calculation to be performed; (c) access arithmetic or table facts—e.g., $4 \times 9 = 36$; $8 + 3 = 11$; and (d) execute the retrieved calculation procedure. This last feature of the process implicates the application of a sequence of steps that constitute the calculation procedure, and the availability of cognitive resources (such as working memory systems) needed for executing the procedure.

A disruption to any part of this complex system will result in a calculation impairment, the particular form of impairment being determined by the locus of damage to the cognitive system. The detailed analysis of these patterns of deficits provides an important source of information concerning the organization of the normal calculation processing system. In turn, the analysis of patterns of dyscalculia in terms of an explicitly formulated model of normal processing provides a principled basis for the interpretation of impaired cognitive performance—that is, the categories of analysis of impaired performance are not to be chosen arbitrarily, but should be determined by the nature of the assumed model of the normal cognitive system.

The contention that the analysis of patterns of acquired cognitive impairments can be used to constrain and inform models of cognitive systems is not controversial. More problematical is the nature of the assumed relationship between patterns of impaired performance and normal cognitive systems and the proper form of analysis of impaired performance in order to test and further articulate models of normal cognitive systems. We take it that the primary objective of cognitive neuropsychology is to formulate hypotheses about the functional architecture of normal cognitive systems which when "lesioned" appropriately result in specific patterns of impaired performance. A proposed functional architecture of a cognitive system receives empirical support whenever an observed pattern of impairment can be explicated by hypothesizing damage to a component part or parts of the proposed architecture. Inability to articulate a hypothesis about the form of damage to the proposed functional achitecture that would result in the observed patterns of impairment would constitute disconfirmation of the proposed architecture. When considered in these terms, it is clear that the assumed relationship between impaired performance and normal cognitive systems is not, in principle, different in kind from the relationship between unimpaired performance and cognitive systems. Furthermore, the form of analysis of impaired performance considered appropriate within this framework is one in which the performance of *individual* patients constitutes the primary set of observations to be explicated. This contention is motivated by the presupposition that variation in performance among patients has to be accounted for explicitly by the proposed functional architecture and hypothesized damage to the architecture and cannot simply (in advance of an explicitly worked out theory of cognitive systems) be dismissed as irrelevant variation or noise in performance. Our approach to the analysis of calculation disorders is guided by these general principles.

In the preceding chapter, we saw an example of the application of this cognitive neuropsychological approach to the analysis of numerical processing deficits. In this chapter we use this approach to analyze the cognitive mechanisms implicated in calculation and calculation deficits.

THE ARCHITECTURE OF THE CALCULATION SYSTEM

We have already noted that calculation requires, in addition to the ability to interpret and produce numbers, three other forms of processing: (1) processing of operational symbols and words that specify the arithmetic operation to be performed (e.g., the multiplication symbol, $\times$); (2) retrieving arithmetic or table facts (e.g., $5 \times 9 = 45$); and (3) the execution of calculation procedures (e.g., find the product of the two rightmost digits in each row). The general relationship between the calculation system and the number-processing system is depicted in Fig. 10.1. In Fig. 10.2 we depict our assumptions about the three components of processing needed for the normal execution of arithmetic calculation.

A *prima facie* case can be made for the proposed general architecture of the calculation system by exploring an example. Consider the sequence of steps involved in carrying out the calculation

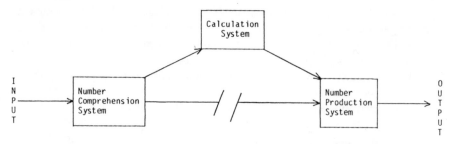

FIGURE 10.1. Schematic representation of number-processing calculation systems.

$$\begin{array}{r} 39 \\ \times\ 21 \end{array}$$

The first step, obviously, is to recognize that the operation required is one of multiplication, as indicated by the operational symbol $\times$. The second step is to retrieve the calculation procedure for multiplication, which involves a series of subprocedures. These subprocedures specify an ordered sequence of arithmetic fact retrieval ($1 \times 9 = 9$, $1 \times 3 = 3$, etc.), the proper arrangement of intermediate products and sums, the retrieval of another calculation procedure (addition), and so forth. Despite the complexity of the process, it is possible to distinguish the three major components of calculation we have identified: operational symbol processing, arithmetic facts, and calculation procedures.

CALCULATION SYSTEM

Operation Symbol/Word Processing Mechanism	Calculation Procedures	Arithmetic Fact Store

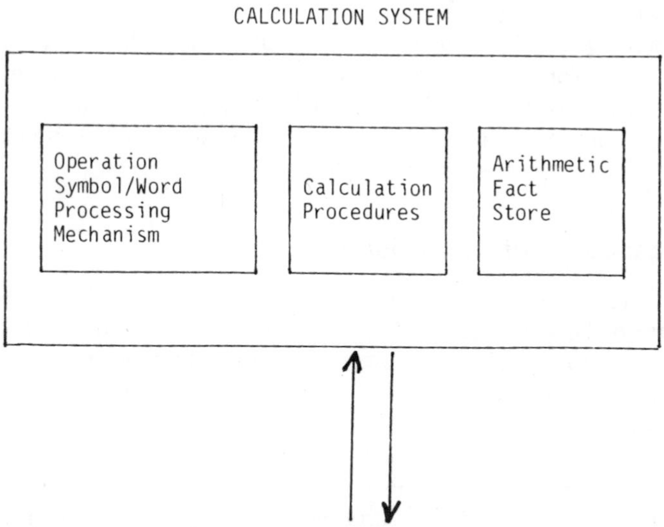

FIGURE 10.2. Schematic representation of calculation system.

At this gross level of analysis of calculation there can hardly be disagreement on the general architecture of the system—the three types of processing are clearly definitional of calculation—and, indeed, this tripartite distinction of the calculation process receives strong empirical support in the classical literature on acalculia (although calculation deficits have not usually been classified explicitly in terms of these three forms of processing). Patients have been described whose calculation performance could be construed to reflect selective deficits to each of these major aspects of calculation (e.g., Grewel, 1952, 1969). In the following we draw from our own observations of calculation deficits to motivate and further articulate the general cognitive architecture of the calculation process. Our aim here is not to describe new phenomena, but to organize and interpret mostly familiar calculation deficits in terms of a cognitive model of calculation.

Processing Operational Signs

To perform calculation successfully, one must be able to process the operational signs/words (e.g., $+$, $\div$, times) in order to retrieve specific arithmetic facts and calculation procedures. A selective deficit in processing operational signs should result in problems retrieving calculation procedures. Like previous investigators (e.g., Ferro & Botelho, 1980), we have observed patients who present with difficulties in processing operational signs independently of their ability to understand numbers, to retrieve arithmetic facts, and to carry out calculation procedures. For example, one patient (W.F.) could not match the name of an operation with its sign and carried out the wrong operation when given problems in arabic numeral form but executed the inappropriate operation correctly. This patient, when asked to pick the problem indicating addition from the set $8 - 5$, $8 + 5$, and 8×5, picked the problem indicating multiplication. Furthermore, when asked to carry out operations such as $9 + 5$, the patient would often respond with a "correct" response for the inappropriate operation—45 in this case. These data suggest that the processing of operation symbols is independent of arithmetic fact retrieval and calculation procedure processes.

The Organization of Calculation Procedures

The two major components of the calculation process, calculation procedures and arithmetic facts, can also be disrupted selectively—that is, there are patients who present with calculation deficits restricted to either the application of calculation procedures or the retrieval of arithmetic facts. We first consider various examples of procedure deficits.

Selective disruption of the calculation procedure system results in diverse patterns of deficits involving different component parts of the procedures. Some patients have difficulty with the carry and borrow operations. For instance, in Fig. 10.3 we show examples of the performance of a patient who was inconsis-

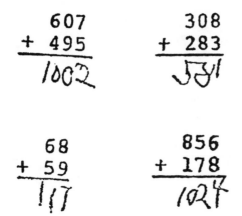

$$\begin{array}{r} 607 \\ +\ 495 \\ \hline 1002 \end{array} \qquad \begin{array}{r} 308 \\ +\ 283 \\ \hline 531 \end{array}$$

$$\begin{array}{r} 68 \\ +\ 59 \\ \hline 117 \end{array} \qquad \begin{array}{r} 856 \\ +\ 178 \\ \hline 1024 \end{array}$$

FIGURE 10.3. Examples of a patient's performance showing failure to carry consistently.

tent in borrowing and carrying. A more complex form of carry operation deficit involves the misordering of the carry step in relation to other steps in the calculation procedure. Thus, one patient (D.L.) added the carry to the multiplicand instead of the intermediate product as shown in the examples in Fig. 10.4 (e.g., $5 \times 3 = 15$, write down 5 and carry 1; add 1 to 7 and multiply by 5, which equals 40). Other patients have no difficulty with the carry operation but fail in organizing intermediate products correctly (Fig. 10.5). In this example the patient aligns the tens intermediate product incorrectly, but note that the arithmetic facts retrieved are correct. Another typical form of procedure error involves the failure to integrate intermediate products. In other words, the patient fails to carry out the complex operation of separating an intermediate product into ones and tens, writing the ones, and carrying the tens for addition to the next intermediate product. Instead, the patient writes down the full intermediate products (Fig. 10.6).

A particularly interesting type of error involves the confusion of component

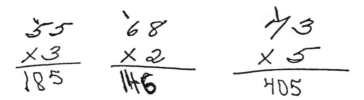

FIGURE 10.4. Examples of a patient's multiplication performance showing inappropriate carry procedure.

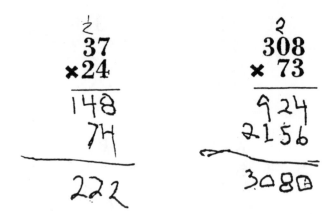

FIGURE 10.5. Examples of a patient's multiplication performance showing failure to shift the intermediate product in the second row.

steps of the procedure for one operation with component steps of the procedure for another operation: One patient uses part of the multiplication procedure in an addition problem (Fig. 10.7; left panel) whereas another does the reverse—using the addition procedure in a multiplication problem (Fig. 10.7; right panel). A more dramatic form of procedure deficit involves the inability to carry out the computational step in the prescribed sequence—in other words, a deficit involving the overall organization of the component steps of a calculation procedure (Fig. 10.8). It is important to note here that the patient does not present with difficulties in spatial alignment of figures—the difficulty appears to be one of retrieving and executing the proper sequence of multiplication procedures.

A final observation we wish to make concerning procedure deficits concerns the dissociation of processing deficits for different types of operations (e.g., addition, division, etc.). Although it would not be unexpected to find that some patients have more difficulty in carrying out division than multiplication or subtraction than addition, perhaps reflecting degrees of premorbid facility with

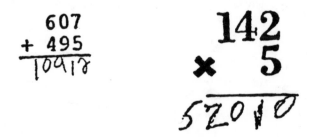

FIGURE 10.6. Examples of two patients' inappropriate treatment of intermediate sums (A) and products (B).

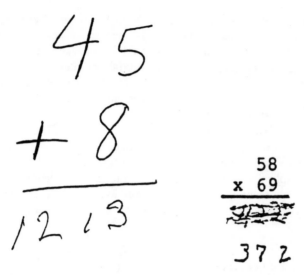

FIGURE 10.7. Examples of performance by two patients showing apparent confusion of component steps of one operation with steps of another operation.

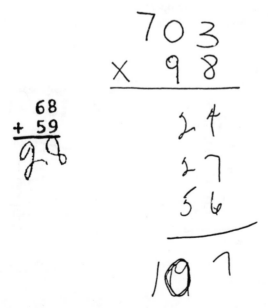

FIGURE 10.8. Examples of two patients' performance showing drastic disruption of calculation procedures.

these operations, it would be striking to find the reverse order of performance difficulty. Such a reversal would strongly suggest the possibility of selective deficits of individual operation procedures. It is interesting to note, therefore, that one of our patients presented with a specific procedure deficit in multiplication in the presence of a normal ability to divide (Fig. 10.9). This result suggests that individual operation procedures are represented independently in the calculation procedure system.

The data reviewed support unequivocally the existence of an independent cognitive system that represents and executes calculation procedures. This conclusion is motivated by the fact that particular forms of calculation performance deficits are explicable in terms of disruption to *just* calculation procedures. In other words, by assuming the selective disruption of an independent calculation procedure system, we can explain the patterns of dyscalculia presented in this section.

The Arithmetic Fact System

There are relatively clear indications in the literature that the other major component of calculation, the arithmetic fact system, can be disrupted selectively. Most recently, Warrington (1982) has described in detail a patient who presented with difficulties in accessing arithmetic facts but who seemed to appreciate the basic concepts of arithmetic operations. We have studied a patient, M.W., who could carry out the various arithmetic operations, but who presented with a distinctive impairment in retrieving arithmetic facts. As can be seen in Fig. 10.10, M.W. could carry out the multiplication procedure flawlessly except that he occasion-

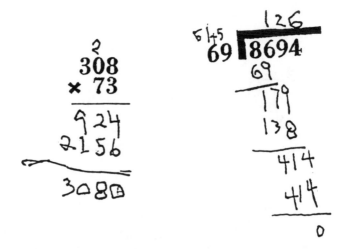

FIGURE 10.9.   Examples of a patient's performance showing intact performance in division and impaired performance in multiplication.

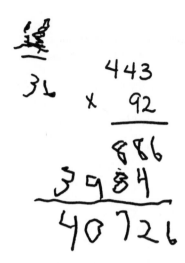

FIGURE 10.10. Example of patient M.W.'s multiplication performance
showing intact calculation procedure and impaired fact retrieval.

ally retrieved an incorrect arithmetic fact. Thus, 9 × 3 was 24, and being unable
to retrieve the product of 9 × 4, solved the problem by adding 9 × 2 to 9 × 2—a
correct decomposition of the 9 × 4 problem. It is clear from these examples that
M.W. not only is able to retrieve the procedure for multiplication, but appreci-
ates the significance of the component steps in relation to the overall operation.

We have studied in some detail M.W.'s arithmetic fact retrieval performance
focusing in particular on the multiplication facts. In Table 10.1 are shown the
percentage of errors for each multiplication fact for the numbers 1 to 10. (A dash
indicates perfect performance.) Thus, for example, he always responded cor-

TABLE 10.1
Percentage of Errors on Basic Multiplication Facts for Patient M. W.

	1	2	3	4	5	6	7	9	9	10
1	—	—	—	5	—	—	6	7	—	—
2		9	7	—	—	10	8	—	13	—
3			7	—	—	11	8	10	31	—
4				12	—	8	20	27	5	—
5					—	—	40	10	36	—
6						—	19	7	48	—
7							13	59	3	—
8								62	23	—
9									44	—
10										—

Note. Dash indicates perfect performance.

rectly to 5 × 5, but was incorrect 40% of the time for 5 × 7 or 7 × 5. There are several important features to note in this table. First, the fact retrieval deficit is more severe for some facts than others. M.W. had great difficulty retrieving the product of 8 × 8, and 7 × 8 or 8 × 7 but not 6 × 8 or 8 × 6 and 7 × 9 or 9 × 7. Second, if we consider only the ones and tens facts it is clear that M.W. had no difficulty processing the numbers from 1 to 10 and that, therefore, the specific facts deficit cannot be attributed to a number-processing impairment. As a further precaution against this possibility, other experimental manipulations were introduced, such as giving M.W. two piles of chips that he was supposed to count and then give the product of two numbers. In all cases it was clear that M.W.'s difficulty to retrieve arithmetic facts was independent of number-processing performance.

Further evidence in support of the view that M.W.'s dyscalculia reflects a selective disruption of retrieval of arithmetic facts is provided by the analysis of his errors. Of the 106 errors he made, 97 were within-table errors, that is, the numbers he gave as responses were products in the 1 to 10 times table; for example, a response of 49, but not 46, to 9 × 6 or 5 × 3, or the multiplication of any two one-digit numbers, would be considered a within-table error because 49 is a product in the 1 to 10 multiplication tables. Furthermore, the error responses almost always (85% of the time) were products involving one of the two multiplicands. For example, given as a stimulus 6 × 7, he produced the responses 30, 63, 54, and 36, which are in the 7 or 6 times table. Finally, incorrect responses were usually close in magnitude to the correct responses (e.g., 7 × 8 = 49 or 72 or 48 or 63). This pattern of errors is consistent with the view that the locus of deficit is at the level of the address or retrieval mechanism for arithmetic facts.

In short, M.W.'s performance suggests a selective impairment of the arithmetic fact system: The pattern of spared and impaired functions clearly indicates that he can execute calculation procedures normally except for the retrieval of specific arithmetic facts. This pattern of performance provides the complementary dissociation to procedural dyscalculia in which the calculation procedure system is disrupted selectively.

GENERAL VERSUS SPECIFIC DEFICITS

We have shown that by testing a patient with tasks chosen on the basis of a model of normal number processing and calculation, we can make inferences about what stages of processing are disrupted. Consider, for example, a patient who shows poor performance on pencil-and-paper multiplication of single-digit numbers. According to our model, pencil-and-paper multiplication involves, in addition to peripheral perceptual and motoric processing, comprehension of the numbers in the problem, comprehension of the operation sign, retrieval of multiplication facts, and production of the retrieved number. Assume that we find normal performance on tests of arabic number comprehension and production, and on tests of operation sign comprehension. Assume further that the subject's deficit on the multiplication task consists of the frequent production of incorrect responses that are multiples of one of the multiplicands in the problems (e.g., 6 × 4 = 18, 8 × 7 = 64). On the basis of these results, we could infer that the patient has a deficit in the stage of processing that retrieves stored arithmetic facts.

However, once we have specified the disrupted stage(s) of processing, the question remains whether the disruption represents damage to a cognitive mechanism specific to that processing stage, or instead to a mechanism that is more general in nature. For the patient with a deficit in arithmetic fact retrieval, we may ask whether the deficit involves damage to some cognitive mechanism specific to arithmetic fact retrieval, or disruption of some cognitive structure or process that is implicated not only in the retrieval of arithmetic facts, but also in the retrieval of other sorts of stored information.

In previous discussions of dyscalculia, the general versus specific issue has been raised repeatedly in regard to several different types of deficits. For example, many researchers have attributed various forms of calculation impairment to a general spatial processing deficit (e.g., Collignon, Leclercq, & Mahy, 1977; Hécaen, Angelergues, & Houillier, 1961; Krapf, 1937; Luria, 1966). Similarly, it has often been assumed that some or all number-processing deficits are manifestations of generalized language disorders (e.g., Benson & Denckla, 1969; Benson & Weir, 1972; Berger, 1926; Collignon et al., 1977; Dahmen, Hartje, Bussing, & Sturm, 1982). Unfortunately, previous treatments of the general/specific issue have not been entirely adequate. In the first place, the nature of the posited general deficits has usually not been specified in sufficient detail. Before a general-deficit hypothesis can be evaluated, it must be set forth explicitly in terms of damage to some component of a clearly specified normal system. The claim that a calculation deficit reflects a general spatial processing impairment, or that a number-comprehension deficit reflects a general language impairment, is too vague to be meaningful. One must specify in detail the nature of the general mechanism presumed to be disrupted, how damage to the mechanism could produce the observed pattern of performance on number tasks, and what sorts of non-number deficits are expected given the hypothesized disruption.

As an example of the need to make hypotheses explicit, consider the concept of *spatial dyscalculia*. This concept reflects the widely held view that a general spatial processing disorder is frequently the cause of a calculation impairment. However, the nature of the spatial processing system that is presumed to be damaged, the ways in which the presumed disruption of the system impairs calculation, and the other deficits that should result from the spatial disorder have not been specified. Instead, a deficit has typically been labeled spatial dyscalculia whenever some aspect of the spatial arrangement of numbers in a calculation is incorrect.

In some instances, deficits labeled spatial dyscalculia do not seem consistent with any reasonable construal of the notion of a general spatial disorder. Consider the examples of one of our patient's performance shown in Fig. 10.5. In these examples, the intermediate products are not aligned properly: 74 and 2156 should be shifted one column to the left. However, it is unlikely that the errors reflect a general spatial impairment that renders the patient unable to align numbers. The intermediate products are perfectly aligned—the alignment is simply incorrect. Further, the alignment of the digits in the sums of the intermediate products is perfect. This example points up the pitfalls involved in the use of vague notions like "spatial disorder" instead of a specific description of the nature of the presumed deficit.

We do not intend to imply that spatial disorders are never implicated in calculation impairments. Our point is simply that it is incumbent upon researchers who offer spatial deficit hypotheses to specify these hypotheses in sufficient detail that they may be evaluated.

A second point to be made about the general versus specific deficit issue is that this issue is of concern only in certain circumstances. If one's aim is to specify exactly what component of the cognitive system is disrupted in a particular patient, then the general versus specific issue is obviously relevant. However, if the aim is to use patterns of impaired performance to make inferences about the structure of the number-processing/calculation mechanisms, the general/specific issue is often irrelevant.

We suggest, then, that the question of whether a deficit is general or specific is less central than has often been supposed. In the first place one can, independent of this issue, consider what stage(s) of processing within the number-processing/calculation system are disrupted. For example, one can determine that a patient is impaired in retrieving arithmetic facts before taking up the question of whether the retrieval deficit is specific to arithmetic facts, or more general. Further, if one's aim is not to characterize deficits but to elucidate the structure of number-system components, the general/specific issue may often be completely irrelevant. Thus, we suggest that the first step in a study involving number-processing/calculation deficits should be the identification of the disrupted stage(s) of processing (e.g., lexical processing in arabic number comprehension; retrieval of arithmetic facts). Subsequently, if it is relevant, the general/specific issue may be considered. Initially, one may ask whether the pattern of performance within number tasks is consistent with a general deficit. In many instances it may be possible to reject a general-deficit hypothesis on the basis of number-task performance alone. Consider, for example, a patient who fails to carry properly when adding. The hypothesis of a general working memory disorder that renders the patient incapable of holding a carry digit in memory can be entertained only if the addition performance is consistent with the assumption that the patient often forgets carry digits, and the patient also shows deficits in other number-processing/calculation tasks that require temporary memory

(e.g., carrying in multiplication, performing mental calculations in which oper-
ands and/or intermediate results must be maintained in memory). If the number-
task performance is consistent with a general-deficit hypothesis, then appropriate
non-number tasks can be employed to determine whether the deficit is indeed
general. Of course, the general-deficit hypothesis must be sufficiently explicit
that clear predictions can be generated at each step of the process.

CONCLUSION

We have focused in this chapter on the analysis of patterns of calculation impairments as a data base from which to infer the structure of those cognitive mechanisms that constitute the calculation process. The principle guiding our approach
is that if an observed pattern of impaired performance is explicable in terms of a
postulated deficit to a hypothesized model of normal calculation, then the proposed model receives empirical support from the observed pattern of impairment. The data we have reviewed are consistent with the general architecture of
the calculation system proposed in this chapter. We have shown that the component parts of the calculation system proposed—the arithmetic fact system, the
calculation procedure system, and the calculation symbol-processing system—
can be disrupted selectively. Specifically, the fact that it has been possible to
explicate dyscalculic patients' performance by postulating selective damage to
hypothesized components of processing constitutes empirical evidence in favor
of the proposed architecture of calculation.

ACKNOWLEDGMENTS

The research reported here was supported in part by Biomedical Research Support Grant S07-RR07041, Division of Research Resources, National Institutes of
Health. We would like to thank Annamaria Basili, Chief, Audiology and Speech
Therapy Department of the V.A. Medical Center, Fort Howard, the staff of her
service for testing the patients described in this report, and Helen Kahn for
testing patient M.W. We also thank Kathy Sporney for her help in preparing this
manuscript.

REFERENCES

Benson, D. F., & Denckla, M. B. (1969). Verbal paraphasia as a source of calculation disturbance.
    Archives of Neurology, 21, 96–102.
Benson, D. F., & Weir, W. F. (1972). Acalculia: Acquired anarithmetia. *Cortex, 8,* 465–472.
Berger, H. (1926). Ueber Rechenstorungen bei Herderkrankungen des Grosshirns. *Archiv fur Psy-
    chiatrie und Nervenkrankheiten, 78,* 238–263.

Collignon, R., Leclercq, C., & Mahy, J. (1977). Etude de la semiologie des troubles de calcul observés au cours des lésions corticales. *Acta Neurologi Belgi 77,* 257–275.

Dahmen, W., Hartje, W., Bussing, A., & Sturm, W. (1982). Disorders of calculation in aphasic patients—Spatial and verbal components. *Neuropsychologia, 20,* 145–153.

Ferro, J. M., & Botelho, M. H. (1980). Alexia for arithmetical signs: A cause of disturbed calculation. *Cortex, 16,* 175–180.

Grewel, F. (1952). Acalculia. *Brain, 75,* 397–407.

Grewel, F. (1969). The acalculias. In P. J. Vinken & G. W. Bruyn (Eds.), *Handbook of clinical neurology* (Vol. 4). New York: Wiley.

Hécaen, H., Angelergues, R., & Houillier, S. (1961). Les varieties cliniques des acalculies au cours des lesions retrorolandiques: Approche statistique du probleme. *Revue Neurologique, 106,* 85–103.

Krapf, E. (1937). Ueber Akalkulie. *Sweizerische Archiv fur Neurologie und Psychiatrie, 39,* 330–334.

Luria, A. R. (1966). *Human brain and psychological processes.* New York: Harper & Row.

Warrington, E. K. (1982). The fractionation of arithmetical skills: A single case study. *Quarterly Journal of Experimental Psychology, 34*(A), 31–51.

11 The Fractionation of Arithmetical Skills: A Single Case Study[1]

Elizabeth K. Warrington
The National Hospital
London

INTRODUCTION

The component processes of numeracy have been studied in normal adults in whom these skills are well established and in young children in whom these skills are still being acquired. A further source of evidence derives from the neurological literature. It is now generally accepted that acalculia, the impairment of the ability to perform arithmetical calculations, can occur as a relatively selective deficit. Although difficulties with calculation had been previously recorded in the context of more generalized aphasic symptomatology (Lewandowsky & Stadelmann, 1908, Peritz, 1918), Henschen (1919) first identified the syndrome "acalculia," which he described as a disturbance of calculating produced by a focal lesion of the brain. He collated a large series of patients in whom there was a primary impairment of arithmetical calculations, a deficit he considered to be largely independent of the frequent concomitant syndromes, aphasia, alexia, and agraphia (Henschen, 1919, 1920).

Arithmetical calculation is a complex accomplishment and as such is likely to comprise many subcomponents. The neurological case descriptions of disorders of numeracy provide some pointers to the variety of functional systems subserving arithmetical calculation. Henschen (1919) himself drew a distinction between disturbances of number recognition, in which he implicates number sense and number meaning, and a more restricted deficit in carrying out arithmetical operations. Lange (1933) drawing upon the observation that written calculations were

[1]This chapter is reprinted with permission from *Quarterly Journal of Experimental Psychology* (1982) *34A,* 31–51

often performed worse than oral calculations emphasized the patient's inability to manipulate the position or direction of numbers in space. He extended this formulation to single-digit notation; these too were conceptualized as markers on a visuo-spatial scale. Following Lange, Kleist (1934) and Krapf (1937) at much the same time noted the vulnerability of the patient's ability to manipulate spatially (both horizontally and vertically) the position of numbers.

Guttman (1937) described a patient who knew the multiplication tables and could carry out simple arithmetical calculations, yet had an unexpectedly grave difficulty with number estimation and number knowledge. Cohn (1961) distinguished between two quite distinct syndromes in a series of 8 patients in whom acalculia was the major presenting symptom. He tested these patients' knowledge of their multiplication tables and their ability to do written multiplication. Two major types of deficits emerged: (1) the misalignment and misordering of digits and (2) faulty memory of "tables." It is of some interest to note that the former type was in every case associated with a right hemisphere lesion and that the latter type, faulty memory of tables, occurred with either a diffuse lesion or a left hemisphere lesion.

The evidence for selective impairment of arithmetical calculation reported in the neurological literature is at best qualitative and often merely anecdotal. In no instance are control data reported and no study to date reports systematic and quantitative data of a patient's numeracy capacities and incapacities. The aim of the present communication is to report a comprehensive and quantitative investigation of a single patient whose abilities to carry out arithmetical calculations appeared to be selectively impaired. In particular, assessment of the component processes of arithmetical skills is attempted. The findings are considered in relation to current models of arithmetical calculation.

CASE REPORT

DRC, a 61-year-old, right-handed consultant physician was admitted to the National Hospital on 18 October 1979 for investigation of headache and speech disturbance, which had developed suddenly on awakening 3 days previously. On the day of admission he had a further episode of severe headache and transient loss of consciousness, following which there was a significant worsening of his dysphasic symptoms. He had been treated for high blood pressure for the previous 2 years.

On examination he had a macula-splitting right homonymous hemianopia. He was clearly dysphasic, expressive, receptive and nominal speech functions being impaired, and it was noted that he was unable to perform simple calculations; for example when asked to solve 5 + 7 he replied, "13 roughly." The neurological examination was otherwise normal.

The CAT scan (18 October 1979) showed an area of increased attenuation in

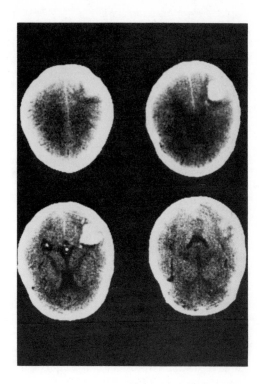

FIGURE 11.1. CAT Scan (18.10.79) showing a left posterior parieto-occipital intra-cerebral haematoma.

the left posterior parieto-occipital region and the trigone was displaced ante-romedially; the diagnosis of an intra-cerebral haematoma was made (see Fig. 11.1). A repeat CAT scan (30 October 1979) showed that there had been a slight resolution of the intracerebral haematoma. There was no evidence of more wide-spread changes and in particular the very mild atrophic changes were considered to be normal for his age. He was treated conservatively and his symptoms improved. DRC was tested once or twice daily, at his own request, between 12 November 1979 and 23 November 1979 (the day of his discharge).

PSYCHOLOGICAL TEST FINDINGS

DRC was first tested on a shortened version of the WAIS on 26 October 1979 and again on 12 November 1979. His prorated IQ scores and the individual age-scaled scores for each subtest obtained on the two occasions are given in Table 11.1. There had been some improvement in all the subtest scores during this period, with the exception of arithmetic which remained at the defective level. During this 2-week period DRC's language functions largely recovered. The following test results were recorded on 12 November 1979: his spontaneous

237

TABLE 11.1
WAIS Intelligence Quotients and WAIS Individual Subtest Scores

	October 26, 1979	November 12, 1979
Verbal IQ	90	103
Performance IQ	97	110
Arithmetic	5	4
Similarities	9	11
Digit span	9	14
Vocabulary	12	14
Picture completion	10	10
Block design	10	12
Picture arrangement	8	12

speech was somewhat ponderous but his sentence construction was almost always correct as to word choice and syntax. On a graded-difficulty naming test he scored 26/30 which is equivalent to a vocabulary age-scaled score within the superior range (see McKenna & Warrington, 1980). On a shortened version of the Token test of comprehension his score was 12/15, which is at the lower limits of normal performance (Coughlan & Warrington, 1978). On the Nelson reading test he read 43/50 words correctly, equivalent to a reading IQ within the superior range (Nelson & O'Connell, 1978). His recognition memory for words, 45/50 correct, was average (Warrington, 1974).

DRC was retested on the arithmetic subtest of the WAIS on 15 November 1979 and he obtained an age-scaled score of 5. However given unlimited time he solved 9/14 problems correctly, including the last three most difficult items. He reasoned aloud while attempting these calculations and it was quite apparent that he knew the appropriate sequence of arithmetical operations for the solution and that his difficulty was one of actual computation. For example, Q.13 (A man earns £60/week; if 15% is withheld for taxes, how much does he receive each week?) was correctly solved in 1 min 10 s. He verbalized as follows: "so we do it 10% first, is £6, half of that is £3, equals £9, 60 minus nine is £51."

He had no difficulty in reading either single numbers or compound numbers. For example, 897,201 was correctly read as eight-hundred-and ninety-seven-thousand, and so on. Similarly he had no difficulty writing similar numbers to dictation. His very satisfactory digit span (eight forward and five backward) could hardly have been achieved if he had not been able to perceive or articulate number names efficiently.

DRC was encouraged to introspect about his difficulties with arithmetical calculations. In his view the process of addition and subtraction were no longer "automatic," and he was adamant that this had been the case previously. He claimed he often knew the approximate solution but not the exact solution and indeed before attempting a calculation he would often say "approximately

. . .'*n*'.'' He would sometimes comment "it must be an odd (or even) number." Given time he could add and subtract accurately by counting forwards or backwards in units of 1 or 2. He himself considered that there was a trade-off between speed and accuracy. In his view if he were to calculate slowly and also check his solution, his performance would be error-free. He claimed that his understanding of arithmetic operations was unimpaired, and indeed his verbalization of arithmetical problems and his definitions of the four basic operations which are quoted below bear this out. Though not strictly correct, they are impressive as definitions attempted without prior warning.

1. Addition—"Adding is a process of, well if I use the word summing, it is a process of summing in which the number of certain magnitude is increased by a number of another magnitude by the numbers which have been defined in the case for each of these magnitudes."

2. Subtraction—"Subtraction is the reduction of the magnitude of a particular number by the magnitude stated of another number and that is it."

3. Multiplication—"The operation of multiplication is to increase by equal magnitudes a stated number."

4. Division—"Division is the apportioning of a number of a certain magnitude into division such as each number is then of the same magnitude, is the same fraction so the number is fractioned and a proportion of that fraction is then removed. I am looking for a number now. A proportion of a fraction is removed, or rather the proportion is fractioned and the fraction is then divided and a decision is made as to which of the fractions is to be kept and which rejected."

In summary, DRC's earlier dysphasic symptoms had almost entirely resolved, the only residual deficit of any significance being an acalculia. This selective impairment of arithmetical calculation is the subject of the following experimental investigation.

EXPERIMENTAL INVESTIGATION

DRC's ability to carry out arithmetical calculations and tests of numeracy was documented as fully as possible. Five matched controls (consultant physicians of the National Hospital, age range 61 to 66) were tested on some of the following procedures. These subjects volunteered to act as controls for a consultant physician whom they knew to have an *acalculia* but they were not given prior knowledge of the tests to be administered.

Test 1—Addition.   DRC attempted to add all combinations of numbers between 1 and 9. This matrix (45 cells) was completed in random order, each addition being spoken by the experimenter at a 1 word/s rate, the larger of the

TABLE 11.2
Distribution of Response Latencies

Latency		0	1	2	3	4	5	6	7	8	9	10	11	12	12+
Test 1 addition															
1-9/1-9	DRC	21	51	21	13	5	4	1	4	2	1	1			2
Test 2 addition															
1-9/11-19	DRC	7	72	55	26	26	12	13	8	10	2	4	2	2	4
	Control (n = 5)	208	151	35	8	1	0	2	0	0	0	0	0	0	0
Test 4 subtraction															
1-9/1-9	DRC	14	46	29	17	2	5	4	1	2	0	0	0	1	2
Test 5 subtraction															
1-9/11-19	DRC	3	34	39	29	34	22	10	10	13	4	4	3	5	37
	Controls (n = 5)	153	149	61	23	6	11	0	1	0	1	0	0	0	0
Test 6 multiplication	DRC	16	73	8	10	3	2	2	6	2	0	1	0	2	2
	Controls (n = 5)	197	99	20	4	2	1	0	0	0	0	0	0	0	1

two numbers being given first (e.g., 4 *add* 2). His accuracy and speed of response (timed by a stop watch to the nearest second) were recorded. "Immediate" responses were recorded as 0" s. (These conditions of presentation and recording were also adopted for Tests 2 to 6). This test was administered on three occasions (15, 20, and 21 November 1979). His overall error rate was 11%. He made no errors on ties (e.g., 5 + 5); his error rate for sums 10 and under was 1.3% and for sums above *10*, it was 23.3%; otherwise there did not appear to be any noticeable pattern of errors. In view of the overall low error rate on this test (and also on Tests 2, 6) a fine grain analysis of the consistency of his error responses over different occasions was not attempted.

His overall average speeds of response for correct and incorrect solutions were 2 and 3.1 s respectively. However there was a wide range of response latencies; from less than 1 s to 14 s for a correct solution and from 1 to 10 s for an incorrect solution (see Table 11.2 for the overall distribution of his response latencies on this test).

Inspection of the response times of the control group on Tests 2, 5, and 6 (described below) indicated that the greater number of response times were "bunched" between 0 and 2 s, the occasional response having a much longer latency (see Table 11.2). In this and in the following analyses, response latencies of over 2 s are called *long* latency responses.

The percentage of long latency responses as a function of the minimum addend, the smaller of the two numbers to be added, are shown for DRC in Fig. 11.2, but no very clear pattern emerges. On the other hand his long latency rate for sums over 10 was considerably higher than for sums up to and including 10 (33.3% and 17.3% respectively). His long latency rate for ties was very low (3%).

An indication of the consistency of the pattern of short and long response

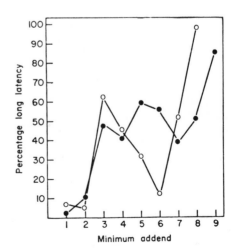

FIGURE 11.2. Addition: The percentage of DRC's long latency responses is shown as a function of the minimum addend for Test 1 (○) and for Test 2 (●).

latencies over his three attempts at this test was computed as follows: First, in this and in the following consistency computations, cells in which there were ties (e.g., $3 + 3$ or $3 - 3$) and cells in which the addend or subtrahend was 1 or 2 were eliminated as the long latency rates were very low; and more important, a solution by counting could be achieved within the time limits of the short latency responses. It was then assumed that his performance on each trial for each remaining cell was independent (his overall long latency rates for each trial of each test were fairly constant). The expected distribution of long latency responses for each cell of the matrix (irrespective of whether the solution was correct or incorrect) was then derived from the overall probability of a long latency response occurring. Thus the chance occurrence of cells in the matrix with consistent responses (three long latencies or three short latencies) and inconsistent responses (one long and two short latency responses or two long and one short latency responses) can be compared (using a Chi-squared test) with the observed occurrence of consistent and inconsistent responses. DRC's consistent and inconsistent response rate together the expected values are given in Table 11.3

It is clear that very simple additions are no longer "automatic" for DRC. A low but not insignificant error rate was observed and his speed of response was slow and variable. It is assumed that the control group, who were not given this test, would have responded accurately, without a significant number of long latency responses.

Test 2—Addition.   DRC attempted to add all number combinations of 1 to 9 and 11 to 19. This matrix (81 cells) was completed in random order, the larger of the two numbers being given first (e.g., 11 *add* 3). His accuracy and speed of response (as for Test 1) were recorded. DRC attempted this test on three occa-

TABLE 11.3
Analysis of Consistency of Short and Long Latency Responses

		Test 1		Test 2		Test 4		Test 5		Test 6	
		E	O	E	O	E	O	E	O	E	O
Consistent cells	LLL (or LL)	2.0	3	12.2	12	1	3	31	35	3.5	3
	SSS (or SS)	3.3	4	5.3	6	5.3	8	0.6	2	37.5	37
Inconsistent cells	LLS (or LS)	7.2	6	25.9	25	5.3	4	24.8	17	22.7	24
	LSS (or LS)	8.4	8	20.4	20	9.2	6	65.0	9	—	—
	χ^2	0.93		0.13		6.8		7.19		0.15	
	P	>0.05		>0.05		>0.05		>0.05		>0.05	

sions (15, 16, and 19 November 1979). The control group attempted this test once. DRC's overall error rate was 8% (the controls made no errors). For sums up to 20 and over 20 his error rate was 10% and 7% respectively. His overall mean speed of response for correct and incorrect solutions was 3.1 and 5.8 s respectively. The distribution of response latencies for DRC and for the control group are given in Table 11.2 and DRC's percentage of long latency responses plotted as a function of the minimum addend are given in Fig. 11.2. Not only is DRC more inaccurate than the control group on this test, but the proportion of long latency responses (which do not conform to any clear-cut pattern) are of a totally different order of magnitude than for the control group.

DRC's consistent and inconsistent response rate together with the expected values are given in Table 11.3. As before, his degree of response consistency does not differ from chance.

Test 3—Addition. DRC attempted to add all number combinations of 1 to 9 and 11 to 19 as in Test 2 except that the smaller addend was spoken first (e.g., 8 *add* 12). His performance on this test can be compared with his performance on Test 2 (on the trial attempted on the same day, 16 November 1979). His error rate was 24.7% when the smaller addend was spoken first compared with 7.4% when the smaller addend was spoken second. The proportion of long latencies on the former task (smaller addend spoken first) was 45.7% compared with 38.3% on the latter task (smaller addend spoken second). DRC appears to be both less accurate and slower when the smaller of the two addends is presented first.

The number of errors on this test together with the errors from the 2nd and 3rd trial of Test 2 (the actual errors on trial 1 of Test 2 were inadvertently not recorded) were sufficient ($n = 32$) to warrant an error analysis. His error responses are plotted as a function of the correct solution in Fig. 11.3, the short latency error responses are indicated separately from the long latency error responses. The correlation (product moment) between the correct solution and the short and long latency error responses was 0.64 and 0.89 respectively.

Test 4—Subtraction. DRC attempted to subtract all number combinations of 1 to 9 from 1 to 9 (calculations with 0 as the remainder were included, negative remainders were excluded). Each subtraction problem was spoken at a 1 word/s rate (e.g., eight take away three) the matrix (45 cells) being completed in random order. This test was administered on three occasions (15, 16, and 20 November 1979). His overall error rate was 8%. The distribution of his response latencies is shown in Table 11.2; his overall mean response time for correct solutions and incorrect solutions was 2.2 and 2.5 s respectively. DRC's long latency rate as a function of the minimum manipulation (that is, the difference between the whole and the remainder or the whole and the subtrahend, whichever is the smaller (e.g., $6 - 2 = 4$ or $6 - 4 = 2$) is shown in Fig. 11.4.

There is a tendency for the long latency rate to increase with the size of the

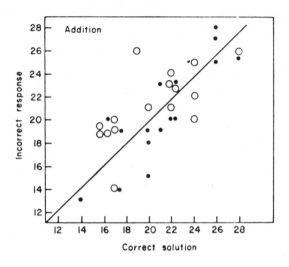

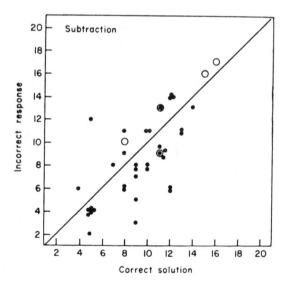

FIGURE 11.3.   Error analysis: The distribution of incorrect responses is shown as a function of the correct solution for Test 2 (addition) and Test 5 (subtraction). The short latency responses (○) are shown separately from the long latency responses (●).

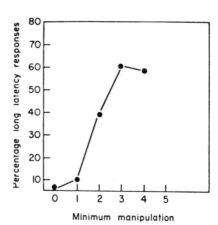

FIGURE 11.4. Subtraction: The percentage of DRC's long latency responses is shown as a function of the minimum manipulation for Test 4 (subtraction).

minimum manipulation (note that with the present procedure the number of data points per condition *decreases* with increase in the minimum manipulation). DRC's consistent and inconsistent response rate together with the expected values are given in Table 11.3, and again his consistency rate is not different from chance.

Test 5—Subtraction. DRC attempted to subtract all possible number combinations of 1 to 9 and 11 to 19 according to the procedure for Test 4. This matrix (81 cells) was attempted on three occasions (15, 19, and 20 November 1979). The control group attempted this test once. DRC's overall error rate was 18% (the control group made no errors). The distribution of response latencies for DRC and the control group are shown in Table 11.2. His average response times for correct and incorrect solutions were 5.5 and 11.3 s respectively. DRC's error rate and long latency rate and the long latency rates of the controls as a function of the minimum manipulation are shown in Fig. 11.5 DRC's performance on both measures deteriorates with the increase in the size of the minimum manipulation. DRC's consistent and inconsistent response rate together with the expected values are given in Table 11.3. The degree of response consistency does not differ from chance.

DRC's error responses plotted as a function of the correct solution are given in Fig. 11.3. All but five of his error responses were of long latency. The correlation between his error response and the correct solution (combining short and long latencies) was 0.72.

Test 6—Multiplication. DRC attempted to multiply all combinations of numbers between 2 and 9. This matrix (64 cells, 4 × 3 and 3 × 4 etc. were both tested) was completed in random order on two occasions (19 and 22 November 1979). The control group attempted this test once. DRC's overall error rate was 8.6% and the distribution of response latencies is given in Table 11.2. His

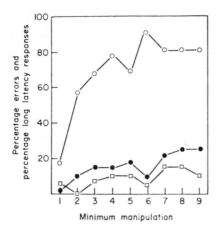

FIGURE 11.5. Subtraction: The percentage of DRC's error responses is shown as a function of the minimum manipulation for Test 5 (●). The percentage of long latency responses for DRC (○) and for the controls (□) is shown as a function of the minimum manipulation for Test 5.

overall average speed of response for correct and incorrect solutions was 2.2 s and 2.4 s respectively. The long latencies rates for DRC and the control group as a function of the minimum multiplicand are given in Fig. 11.6. The long latency response rate for DRC was of a totally different order of magnitude than for the control group, and furthermore his long latency responses did not conform to any obvious pattern of task difficulty. DRC's consistent and inconsistent response rate together with the expected values are given in Table 11.3. The degree of response consistency does not differ from chance.

Number Knowledge

Quite apart from the computations which can be performed with them, numbers have connotations. Consider the number 5, it is a small number, it is the label signifying the number of fingers or toes, it represents the number of units in one

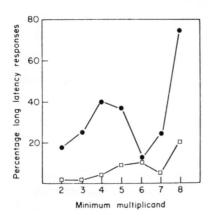

FIGURE 11.6. Multiplication: The percentage of long latency responses for DRC (●) and for the controls (□) is shown as a function of the minimum multiplicand for Test 6.

of the coins, it is the age of a child just starting school. Similarly, 47 represents many, say, family members, but few houses in a street; applied to years it signifies a person of middle age and applied to time it is a post-war year. Two aspects of individual number knowledge can be differentiated, precise quantity numbers and estimated quantity numbers (though whether this is a valid dichotomy is not at present known). Nevertheless, tests were devised to assess both these aspects of quantity.

Test 7—Estimation of Quantity.   In this test the subject was asked to state or estimate the number of black dots randomly arranged on sheets of white paper (8" × 5"). There were 20 stimulus items (2–10, 15, 20, 25, 30, 40, 50, 60, 70, 80, 90 or 100 dots/stimulus) which were presented to the subject in random order. Thus the series comprised quantities which can be readily counted and quantities which could only be estimated. A 5-s inspection period was used in the first trial to allow the subject to become familiarized with the task. Three further trials using a 2-s exposure duration were administered. DRC's results together with the five control subjects expressed as a median value (for the three trials) are shown in Fig. 11.7. DRC's performance is clearly unimpaired either for quantities which could be counted (up to 10) or quantities which had to be estimated (over 10); indeed his number estimation for the larger numbers was marginally more accurate than that of the control group. Response latencies were not recorded on this task, but it was the impression of the experimenter that DRC responded rapidly and as quickly as the control subjects.

Test 8—Rapid Arithmetical Estimations.   DRC appeared to be able to estimate approximate solutions to arithmetical calculations. A test was devised to assess this ability, namely to give the approximate solution to arithmetical problems which for most normal subjects the solution would not be "automatically" known. There were 12 problems (four divisions/fractions, four additions and

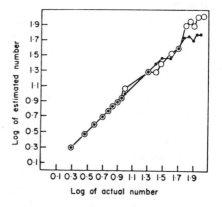

FIGURE 11.7. Estimation of quantity: The log of the estimated number of dots is shown as a function of the log of the actual number of dots for DRC (○) and for the control group (●).

four subtractions), all involving large 2- to 3-digit numbers (see Appendix 1). The subjects were presented with the problem and instructed to respond quickly (within 1 to 2 s) giving an approximate solution. This procedure was not entirely satisfactory insofar as the control subjects would give slow responses apparently attempting a partial computation in the time available. Nevertheless, DRC's responses were within the normal range for 5 of these 12 problems and relatively close to the normal range on the remaining 7 problems (see Appendix 1).

Test 9—Numerical Cognitive Estimates.   Shallice and Evans (1978) de-vised a "cognitive estimates" test in which the subjects were asked to give "reasonable," "sensible" responses to questions for which exact factual infor-mation is not generally known (e.g., What is the best-paid job or occupation in Britain today? How tall is the average English woman?). Following Shallice's technique, a test comprising 10 numerical estimation questions was devised (Shallice's items 5, 6, and 9 were included) (see Appendix 2). DRC's responses were within the range of responses given by the control group for 9/10 questions (see Appendix 2).

Test 10—Number Size Judgements.   A test was devised in which the subject was asked to "circle" the larger of two numbers. 20 pairs of two- or three-digit numbers in which difference in size ranged from 1 to 12 (e.g., 28 to 29, 185 to 197) were typed in a column: there were three sets of 20 number pairs on the page (8″ × 10″). The time taken for the subject to circle the larger of each pair for each of the three sets of numbers was recorded. DRC's median response time for the three trials was 37″ and the median response time for the five control subjects ranged from 18″ to 32″. DRCs median response time is only marginally slower than the slowest control subject and bearing in mind that DRC was handicapped by a resolving right visual field defect his performance on this task is considered to be entirely satisfactory.

Test 11—Number Facts.   Knowledge of exact number facts was assessed, and the five control subjects responded correctly to the following questions (which can be answered using general knowledge available to almost all sub-jects). (1) Boiling point of water, (2) feet and inches in 1 metre, (3) inches in a foot, (4) feet in a yard, (5) ounces in a pound, (6) centimeters in a metre. DRC's only error was on item (5) to which he responded "between one dozen and 20."

Test 12—Numerical Abilities Test.   Hitch (1978a) devised a test of numer-ical ability in which there were three sections:

   (I) A test of speed and accuracy of elementary arithmetic with natural
       numbers. This test comprised six subtests: (1) adding three-digit num-
       bers, no carrying required; (2) adding three-digit numbers, carrying
       required; (3) subtracting three-digit numbers, no carrying required; (4)
       subtracting three-digit numbers, carrying required; (5) multiplication of

digits (max 12); (6) division of two-digit numbers by single digit numbers.

(II) A test of manipulation and conversion of decimals and fractions and percentage where the numerical element was relatively simple. This test comprised four subtests: (1) solving fractions, (2) solving decimal problems; (3) conversions between fractions, decimals and percentages; (4) further long divisions and multiplications. This test was unpaced.

(III) A test of appreciation of the magnitude of numbers and the evaluation of arithmetical expressions. This test comprised four subtests: (1) magnitude judgements; (2) approximation problems; (3) comprehension of numerical expressions; (4) solving ratio, proportion and percentage problems. This test was unpaced.

DRC attempted this test on 21 and 22 November according to the procedure prescribed by Hitch for testing a group of 95 industrial trainee apprentices aged between 17 and 18. The mean and s.d. of this control sample (kindly provided by Hitch) on each of the three sections of Hitch's test, together with DRC's score on each of the 16 subtests are given in Table 11.4. DRC's performance expressed in

TABLE 11.4
Scores on Hitch's Test of Numerical Abilities

	DRC's score	Controls' mean score	Controls' s.d.	DRC's s.d. from mean
Section I				
(1) Addition - no carrying	7	16.66	4.27	−2.26*
(2) Addition - with carrying	5	8.77	2.93	−1.29
(3) Subtraction - no borrowing	8	14.82	3.68	−1.85*
(4) Subtraction - with borrowing	0	4.83	2.58	−1.87*
(5) Multiplication tables	20	23.72	8.71	−0.43
(6) Division	8	24.20	7.93	−2.04*
Total	48	93.00	25.73	−1.75*
Section II				
(1) Fraction arithmetic	8	5.56	3.23	+0.76
(2) Decimal arithmetic	8	7.88	2.82	+0.04
(3) Conversions	9	6.15	3.98	+0.72
(4) Long multiplication and division	2	2.46	1.37	−0.34
Total	27	22.05	9.36	+0.53
Section III				
(1) Magnitude	11	8.59	1.41	+1.71
(2) Approximation	7	5.32	2.02	+0.83
(3) Rules for expression	6	5.40	1.56	+0.38
(4) Ratio, proportion and percentages	7	7.10	1.89	−0.05
Total	31	26.40	5.27	+0.87

*Significant at 5% level.

terms of the standard deviation from the control group mean, together with the significance of the difference is also given in Table 11.4. It is reasonable to suppose that premorbidly DRC's performance would have been superior to Hitch's sample, on all sections of the test. DRC's performance on section I demanding speed and accuracy of elementary arithmetic is significantly worse than that of the control group. In contrast on sections II and III of the test his performance was better (though not significantly) than the control group. Considering the individual subtests, on four out of six of the subtests in section I his performance was significantly worse than that of the control group and in sections II and III his performance was slightly higher than that of the control group on six out of eight of the subtests.

DISCUSSION

DRC lost his ability to perform arithmetical calculations with any semblance of efficiency after sustaining a left posterior hemorrhage. His knowledge of the significance of individual numbers and his concept of quantity appeared to be intact, but simple addition, subtraction, and multiplication were all performed laboriously and inaccurately. Two major questions of interest arise. First, which subcomponent or subcomponents of the processes involved in arithmetical calculation were impaired? Second, do the findings favor any particular model of arithmetical calculation proposed for the normal person?

However, first it is necessary to consider whether it has been established that DRC had a selective impairment of arithmetical skills which was not secondary to any other cognitive deficits. There were only minor degrees of impairment on verbal intelligence tests, on a verbal memory test, and on tests of dysphasia. In particular his word comprehension and word retrieval skills were within normal limits. As his digit span was above average it can be assumed that his ability to perceive and articulate digits was normal; more important, he was not handicapped by a short-term memory deficit for digits on any of the tests of numeracy. Indeed on all the tests of numeracy DRC attempted, it seems clear that it was the demands of the task rather than a non-specific language impairment which determined his performance.

Calculation is a highly complex skill and it will be argued that it was his arithmetical skills not his number knowledge which were impaired, and further that it was his knowledge of arithmetical *facts* not his knowledge of arithmetical *operations* which was impaired.

Two aspects of number knowledge or significance can be differentiated, exact quantity facts and approximate quantity facts. DRC comprehended numbers both absolutely as number facts (e.g., 12 inches = 1 foot) and relatively (e.g., 12 > 11). He could use numbers to make direct estimates of quantity (as in the visual stimulus arrays used in Test 8) and also indirect estimates of quantity applying general principles of numerical knowledge (as in the cognitive estimates used in Test 9). Thus it is argued that the central representations (semantic entries) of individual numbers are intact and accessible.[2]

Consider a simple addition of the form x + y = z. It has been shown that DRC comprehended the numbers (i.e., had knowledge of their absolute and relative quantity). There would appear to be two further stages in achieving a correct solution, first the instruction *add* must be understood, and secondly the *sum* must be computed (whether by counting or direct access will be considered later). It has been demonstrated that DRC's comprehension of the arithmetical operations was intact. He had no difficulty in explaining verbally the appropriate strategy for solving a complex arithmetical problem such as the WAIS arithmetic subtest): he could state the operations required for solution and the order in which they should be performed. In no instance did he produce an impermissible response (e.g., a sum less than either addend) and indeed his incorrect responses were shown to approximate closely to the correct response. There was a very clear dissociation in Hitch's numerical abilities test which specifically compares number operations with number computations. DRC's performance was significantly impaired on the strictly timed tests of arithmetical computations; in striking contrast his performance was slightly (non-significantly) above average on those tests which maximize comprehension of arithmetical operations. Particularly impressive was his good ability to give approximate solutions to more difficult arithmetical problems involving large numbers. These skills could not be achieved were the comprehension and application of arithmetical operations not intact.

The dissociation between arithmetical processing in general and *accurate* arithmetical computations is the main point of interest to emerge from this investigation of DRC's acalculia. This distinction, though implicit in the work of Hitch (1978a, 1978b) is not made explicit in any study of calculation in the child or normal adult.

Restle (1970) has argued that simple addition is achieved in normal adults by an analogue operation. DRC's very satisfactory performance on Test 10, in which he was required to make number size judgments at speed, suggests that such operations may be preserved. If this supposition were correct, then to account for normal calculation in terms of analogue processing would be insufficient, at least it would appear to be insufficient to account for not merely *accurate* calculations but *rapid* calculations. It will be argued that access to arithmetical facts is essential for efficient calculation skills.

Why then is the correct solution inaccessible or only inefficiently accessible?

---

[2]It is not to be assumed that this is a typical feature of all patients presenting with the syndrome acalculia. Shallice and I investigated a patient STH who was unable to comprehend the significance of individual numbers and individual number facts and consequently the simplest arithmetical calculation could not be done. A brief case description of STH is given in Appendix 3.

This can most appropriately be discussed in the context of Parkman and Groen's model of the normal process of calculation. They proposed the "counting" model subsequently elaborated as the retrieval-counting model (Groen & Parkman, 1972; Parkman & Groen, 1971). Their earlier counting model assumed that mental addition consists of two processes; first a counter is set to the larger addend and second a process of incrementation occurs so that the number of increments equals the minimum addend. The strength of this model derived from the observation that in both children and adults response latencies are a function of the minimum addend, but it was necessary to revise this simple counting model to take into account the fact that ties (e.g., 3 + 3) were all faster and equally faster than other single-digit additions (this was also the case for DRC). The radically different slopes of the RT functions for children (400 ms/increment) and for adults (20 ms/increment), as has already been acknowledged (Groen & Parkman, 1972), can hardly command the same explanation. (DRC's unit incremental times are of the same order of magnitude as in young children: for example in Test 1 he achieved an overall unit incremental time of 0.73 s.) Furthermore, it is difficult to encompass multiplication and division within the framework of this model.

Therefore a retrieval-counting model was proposed, which states that most response times reflect direct access to memorised information, such access to each semantic entry requiring an essentially constant amount of time (all entries being equipotential) and on those occasions when direct access fails, the subject reverts to the slow "counting" process observed in children (Groen & Parkman, 1972).[3] Such a formulation would require a bimodal or skewed distribution of response times but this has not yet been reported for normal adult performance. However, inspection of Table 11.2 suggests that this may be a feature of DRC's performance especially in the more demanding tasks, such as Test 11.5. It seems plausible to suggest that in both young children and in DRC there is a failure of direct access in the former because there is not yet a direct semantic entry and for DRC because it is damaged or inaccessible. The observation that DRC's response latencies are inconsistent from trial to trial favors an access deficit, rather than damage to specific semantic entries. Thus for DRC it is suggested that there is faulty access to the semantic entries of the facts of arithmetic (e.g., 2 + 3 = 5), and that when direct access fails he resorts to a more inefficient counting strategy by which means he often arrives at a correct solution, albeit slowly. DRC's performance on the multiplication test, the arithmetical operation which would seem to be most dependent on direct access to arithmetical facts, was inconsistent between the two trials, although his level of performance remained constant. This finding strengthens the present hypothesis that inaccessibility rather than damage to the semantic entries of arithmetical facts is at the core of

---

[3]Modifications of this theory have been suggested, for example, by Ashcraft and Battaglia (1978), but there is as yet insufficient empirical evidence to evaluate their relative merits in relation to DRC.

his acalculia. Thus it is argued that DRC is using the same processing strategies as a normal adult, the crucial difference being that the proportion of access failures is much greater.

There is now accumulating evidence from neuropsychological investigations that semantic memory systems are categorically organized. That broad semantic categories (e.g., letters, colors, words, objects) can be selectively impaired is perhaps not unexpected, but there is now evidence that subcategories within a major system can also be selectively impaired. For example, the double dissociation of abstract and concrete word comprehension impairment and the evidence of selective impairment and selective preservation of the comprehension of object names have been interpreted in these terms (Warrington, 1981). Similarly, it is suggested that numeracy represents a major category of semantic knowledge and that in DRC a subcategory of this system is inoperative, namely the accessibility of arithmetical facts. A more detailed investigation of patients with acalculia could well provide pointers to the more fine-grain organization of arithmetic facts than has been achieved in this investigation.

ACKNOWLEDGEMENTS

I am grateful to Dr. J. N. Blau and to Dr. C. J. Earl for permission to investigate their patients and to report my findings. I wish to thank Dr. G. Hitch and Dr. T. Shallice for their interest in this investigation and for their advice in the preparation of this manuscript. Richard Hutton very kindly undertook the analysis of the results of Hitch's numeracy test. I am particularly indebted to Pat McKenna for her assistance in testing DRC.

APPENDIX 1
Test 8 - Rapid Arithmetical Estimation

Problem	DRC response	Controls response range
(1) $\frac{1}{2}$ of 270	140	135
(2) $\frac{1}{3}$ of 700	180	212–250
(3) $\frac{1}{2}$ of 76	30	23–38
(4) $\frac{1}{4}$ of 270	50	60–80
(5) 634 + 362	900	990–1000
(6) 829 + 328	1200	1150–1200
(7) 704 + 472	1000	1160–1200
(8) 328 + 65	400	381–400
(9) 96 − 71	30	20–25
(10) 73 − 18	60	50–55
(11) 1200 − 450	800	350–800
(12) 3410 − 590	3000	2500–3000

Test 9 - Numerical Cognitive Estimates

Question	DRC response	Controls response range
(1) Age of oldest person alive in Britain	109	106–111
(2) The height of average Englishwoman	5′5″	5′4″–5′6″
(3) The length of an average man's spine	48″	25″–39″
(4) The distance from London to Paris	200	100–500
(5) The distance from London to New York	3000	1500–3000
(6) The distance from London to Edinburgh	400	350–600
(7) The temperature on a hot day in England	80°	80° F
(8) Population of Great Britain	50,000,000	50–70 million
(9) Population of Ireland	8,000,000	1–13 million
(10) The number of people who can board on a double-decker bus	80	60–80

APPENDIX 3 CASE REPORT

STH, a 25-year-old left-handed housewife with a long history of hemiplegic migraine, was admitted to the Middlesex Hopsital one month after an acute episode in which she became dysphasic and hemiplegic. On examination there was a marked right-sided hemiparesis with no movement at all in the upper limb, and very little in the face. Sensation was diminished in the right limbs. There was a dense right homonymous hemianopia. These neurological signs showed gradual recovery over the following 2 months. Her language was severely impaired, her spontaneous speech being restricted to very short non-grammatical phrases, and all other aspects of language function were impaired. Her language skills did not show the same degree of improvements as her other neurological deficits.

A CT scan on 18 March 1980 indicated diffuse isodense swelling of the posterior part of the left hemisphere with compression of the left lateral ventricle. On a repeat CT scan on 22 April 1980, the left lateral ventricle had become normal in shape and in retrospect it was considered that there had been some low attenuation in the posterior temporal lobe and the occipito-temporal gyri of the left hemisphere previously.

Psychological Findings

STH was tested on a shortened version of the WAIS and obtained a verbal IQ of 80 and a performance IQ of 73. The individual age-scaled scores were arithmetic, 2; similarities, 11; digit span, 6; picture completion, 9; block design 7; picture arrangement, 2. Her sentence construction was extremely halting and sparse, but her object naming was relatively well preserved in that she scored

12/15 and 13/15 on tests of naming to confrontation and naming from description (see Coughlan & Warrington, 1978) and on a graded difficulty naming test she scored 9/30 (see McKenna & Warrington, 1980). Her ability to comprehend single spoken words appeared to be intact insofar as she obtained an IQ equivalent of 112 on the Peabody picture vocabulary test. In contrast she was severely dyslexic and dysgraphic. She read only 14 words on the Schonell graded word list (testing was discontinued after 10 consecutive errors). She failed to spell aloud or write correctly any words from the Schonell graded spelling test. Of particular interest in the present context was her apparent greater difficulty in reading single digits (15/24 correct) than letters (23/24 correct). She also had difficulty in writing single-digit numbers to dictation (5/10 correct). The following tests of numeracy were administered:

1. The numbers 1 to 9 were spoken in random order and STH was asked to match the spoken to the written number (3 × 3 random array). Her score was 17/20 correct.

2. A set of numbers greater than 10 were selected (1000, 100, 50, 40, 30, 20, 15, 12, 11) and STH was asked to match the spoken number to the written number (in a 3 × 3 random array). Her score was 12/20 correct. She was only able to read correctly 2/9 of this set of numbers.

3. Pairs of numbers (range 1 to 12) were selected such that one of the pair was larger by either 1, 2, or 4 (e.g., 10–11, 7–9, and 4–8, etc.). There were 10 of each type of stimulus pairs and each pair was *spoken* slowly and STH was asked to name the larger of the two numbers. She clearly understood the task and she was able to repeat the message (note her digit span was five). She scored 23/30 correct and her errors were not obviously related to the magnitude of the difference. With visual presentation, i.e., pointing to the larger of the two printed numbers, her performance was error-free.

4. Cognitive estimates: she attempted a shortened version of the Shallice and Evans (1978) cognitive estimates test; not one of her responses to the numerical items was satisfactory (e.g., Q. What is the average length of a man's spine? R. 6 ft). Her number estimation was clearly very impaired.

5. Number facts: STH was able to count from 1 to 10 fairly efficiently and at reasonable speed. Questions were devised for which there was an exact precise number response. She was able to answer the simplest questions (e.g., How many eggs in ½ doz? How many legs has a bird?), but she was incorrect in stating the number of toes on one foot, the number of days in a week, and the number of fingers on two hands. It seems likely from her performance on the WAIS similarities test that her language comprehension was adequate to the task.

6. Arithmetical facts: In view of STH's impairment in the *comprehension* of spoken numbers, her oral arithmetical skills were not systematically tested. It was noted informally that very simple addition, subtraction, and multiplication were quite impossible for her.

COMMENT

STH has an acalculic syndrome quite different from that recorded in DRC. It would appear that individual spoken numbers have lost their significance for her; the spoken numbers had no connotations. It is assumed that her difficulties with oral arithmetic calculations was secondary to a more basic failure at the level of number knowledge.

REFERENCES

Ashcraft, M. H., & Battaglia, J. (1978). Cognitive arithmetic: Evidence for retrieval and decision processes in mental addition. *Journal of Experimental Psychology, 4*, 527–38.

Cohn, R. (1961). Dyscalculia. *Archives of Neurology, 4*, 301–7.

Coughlan, A. K., & Warrington, E. K. (1978). Word-comprehension and word-retrieval in patients with localised cerebral lesions. *Brain, 101*, 163–85.

Groen, G. J., & Parkman, J. M. (1972). A chronometric analysis of simple addition. *Psychological Review, 79*, 329–43.

Guttmann, E. (1937). Congenital arithmetic disability and acalculia (Henschen). *British Journal of Medical Psychology, 16*, 16–35.

Henschen, S. E. (1919). Ueber Sprach- Musik- und Rechenmechanismen und ihre Lokalisation im Gehirn. *Z. ges. Neurol. Psychiat., 52*, 273–98.

Henschen, S. E. (1920). Klinische und anatomische Beiträge zur Pathologie des Gehirns. *Über Aphasie, Amusie, und Akalkulie*. Stockholm: Nordiska Bokhandeln.

Hitch, G. J. (1978a). The numerical abilities of industrial trainee apprentices. *Journal of Occupational Psychology, 51*, 163–76.

Hitch, G. J. (1978b). The role of short-term working memory in mental arithmetic. *Cognitive Psychology, 10*, 302–23.

Kleist, K. (1934). Gehirn-Pathologie vornehmlich auf Grund der Kriegserfahrungen. In *Handbuch der Arztlichen Erfahrungen im Weltkriege*, Vol. 5. Leipzig: Johann Ambrosius Barth.

Krapf, E. (1937). Über Akalkulie. *Schweiz. Arch. Neurol. u. Psychiat., 39*, 330–4.

Lang, J. (1933). Probleme der Fingeragnosie. *Z. ges. Neurol. Psychiat., 147*, 594–610.

Lewandowsky, M., & Stadelmann, E. (1908). Ueber einen bemerkenswerten Fall von Hirnblutung und über Rechenstörungen bei Herderkrankung des Gehirns. *J. F. Psychol. u. Neurol., 11*, 249–65.

McKenna, P., & Warrington, E. K. (1980). Testing for nominal dysphasia. *Journal of Neurology, Neurosurgery and Psychiatry, 43*, 781–8.

Nelson, H. I., & O'Connell, A. (1978). Dementia: the estimation of premorbid intelligence levels using the new adult reading test. *Cortex, 14*, 234–44.

Parkman, J. N., & Groen, G. J. (1971). Temporal aspects of simple addition and comparison. *Journal of Experimental Psychology, 89*, 335–42.

Peritz, G. (1918). Zur Psychopathologie des Rechens. *Deutsche Ztschr. f. Nervenh., 61*, 234–340.

Restle, F. (1970). Speed of adding and comparing numbers. *Journal of Experimental Psychology, 83*, 274–8.

Shallice, T., & Evans, M. (1978). The involvement of the frontal lobes in cognitive estimation. *Cortex, 14*, 294–303.

Warrington, E. K. (1974). Deficient recognition memory in organic amnesia. *Cortex, 10*, 289–91.

Warrington, E. K. (1981). Neuropsychological studies of verbal semantic systems. *Philosophical Transactions of the Royal Society B, 295*, 411–23.

12 Cross-Cultural Approaches to the Study of Calculation Processes

Jordan Grafman
Clinical Neuropsychology Section
Medical Neurology Branch-NINCDS

François Boller
University of Pittsburgh

The purpose of this chapter is to describe some alternative methods of calculation not frequently observed in the Western world and to see if the information-processing demands of these methods reveal clues about the development and breakdown of calculation abilities in Western man.

We first describe the ability of illiterates to learn to calculate and the effects of cognitive style upon that learning. We next describe a series of investigations of the development of calculation skills in West African societies and compare that development to the ability of schooled Americans. We also examine whether Piaget's steps in development can be used to predict when arithmetic abilities would emerge in African children. Finally, we compare the ability of Asian and American children to learn basic calculation skills. A particular focus of this last section is on abacus proficiency. A discussion follows in which we attempt to interpret cross-cultural variants in calculation ability in information-processing terms. We conclude by speculating whether the patterns of deficits displayed by adult dyscalculics resemble stages of arithmetic ability seen in nonWestern cultures.

INTRODUCTION

Levinson (1977) has recently reviewed a number of research areas in the social sciences that have benefited from cross-cultural surveys. He claims that cross-cultural research has only recently achieved methodological respectability. One reason frequently cited for past failure in examining behavior in nonWestern cultures has been the power of historical myths and the difficulty in understanding the subtlety of communication in foreign cultures (Winthrop, 1980). Reed and Lave (1979) point out that studying a cognitive ability such as arithmetic calculation avoids many of the problems that are pervasive in studying the effects of culture on social science problems. Arithmetic is a "richly analyzed domain" practiced in one form or another in almost all cultures. The formality of arithmetic notation and the nature of its closed system make arithmetic calculation an ideal cognitive process to study cross-culturally. The study of this symbolic or semiotic system (Grewel, 1962) also allows for the development of a model of arithmetic calculation that should be generally unaffected by cross-cultural differences. That is, although cultural idiosyncrasies may be responsible for differing methods of solving a numerical problem, most processes utilized should be able to be represented in a general problem-solving model without weakening the model via parsimony. This method of analyzing a cognitive process is often referred to as componential analysis, and it is not without its critics (Burling, 1964). Nevertheless, it remains the most currently appealing method of analyzing a cognitive process (Fodor, 1983), and we use it in our review.

Saxe and Posner (1983) identify several different ways of representing numerical entities that have been seen in different cultures. These include spatial representation with and without base structures, body parts representing quantities, and formal arithmetic notation. Often, different ways of representing numerical quantities are seen within a single culture, depending on whether a social group is involved in trade or not, whether the social group resides in an urban or rural region, or whether environmental consequences require it.

There have been two major approaches to the development of cognitive processes such as the ability to calculate. One approach, represented by the research of Vygotsky (1962), is concerned with what strategies or representations individuals use to represent the world. This is a very personalized approach and focuses on how the social history of a cultural group determined representational systems and their operations. A second approach was popularized by Piaget (1952), who argued that the origin of cognitive process is sensorimotor in nature, which, through an epigenetic process, is transformed into "mental representations and processes" in development. Thus, Vygotsky (1962) emphasizes sociocultural history, whereas Piaget (1952) stresses developmental steps that all individuals must pass through in order to master a task and, in turn, develop internalized cognitive representations of the act of problem solving (i.e., calculating an arithmetic problem). We believe both approaches can be useful in describing within- and cross-cultural arithmetic problem-solving behaviors.

In examining calculating skills in various cultures, we emphasize the analysis of basic numerical abilities (Gelman, 1982), such as number/symbol transcoding and representation and counting skills (with occasional reference to arithmetic operations such as addition). We would like to address several questions in this area. For example, what allows a culture to produce individuals that master all aspects of calculation as opposed to being limited to simple counting skills? Are there differences in the strategies used by different cultures that allow for more proficient and accurate calculation performance? Are there specific stages that an individual must pass through, regardless of culture, before a more complex operation may be mastered?

Lastly, we have some comments on the difficulty children and adults have in mastering mathemetical concepts (e.g., see Allardice & Ginsburg, 1983). We believe that a careful analysis of why individuals cannot proceed beyond a certain mathematical operation and the nature of that mathematical representation can shed light on both hemispheric specialization for types of arithmetic operations and the patterns of breakdown in calculation ability that have been observed in brain-damaged adults. Before proceeding to a review of some relevant areas of cross-cultural arithmetic research, we offer a rudimentary model of the cognitive operations required for calculation. The model can then be used to test our interpretation of the research described in our review.

A MODEL OF CALCULATION PERFORMANCE

Boller and Grafman (1983) have recently reviewed the development of thought on the nature of dyscalculia (a breakdown in calculation ability that often follows brain injury in adults). They describe several types of dyscalculia that follow brain damage, including problems with writing arithmetic symbols, with alignment of arithmetic symbols, with reading and transcoding individual arithmetic symbols, and difficulty with the actual operations required to perform arithmetic calculations (such as memory for digits, fact retrieval, algorithmic production). Recent attempts to analyze the types of errors made in calculation operations (e.g., Deloche & Seron, 1982; Grafman, Passafiume, Faglioni, & Boller, 1982; Warrington, 1982) have assisted in clarifying at what stage in information processing "operational" errors occur. Using data derived from the performance of brain-injured adults on calculation problems, Boller and Grafman (1985) have suggested how calculation demands on information processing could be modeled. They used a simple addition problem to illustrate the types of processing demands calculation makes upon cognition.

> The subject must initially be able to perceive the spatial alignment of the numbers (i.e., their physical relationship to each other), understand the operation symbol "+," recognize the numerical symbols, and comprehend what is required to adequately perform the task (i.e., the plan of action which must be retrieved in learned subjects from long-term storage and can be considered an automatic process (Schneider and Shiffrin, 1977)). Once these essential initial processing steps are taken, the subject can begin to solve the problem. If the subject has been taught elementary numerical operations such as adding, the additive rule that determines what $7 + 9$ is equal to may be automatized such that the only part of the additive process that necessitates conscious attention and retrieval from long-term store is

the answer itself—fact retrieval (16). If the answer is not automatized, the subject must use a "controlled" (Schneider and Shiffrin, 1977) process, most likely beginning with the number of larger magnitude (Chase, 1978; Katz, 1980) and adding (perhaps by a simple count, i.e., $9 + 1 = 10 (+6) = 16$) upward. The number 16 must be held in short-term store while the partial unit 1 is carried (i.e., either put on paper above the left-hand column, or held in working memory until added mentally). The same process is then repeated for the left-hand column numbers. (p. 475)

Thus, knowledge, stages of memory, stages of lexical access and production, perception, and visual constructional skills are all required for adequate calculation (Hurford, 1975). Following brain injury, one or more stages may be impaired, resulting in errors that are peculiar to the impaired stage of information processing. The errors themselves are particularly helpful in understanding how arithmetic information is lexically represented (Deloche & Seron, 1982).

As we describe calculation ability in various cultures, we occasionally make use of the information-processing scheme briefly presented to explain either the particular cognitive strategy used or why calculation ability may be limited to certain operations. We believe that this approach, in combination with cultural and genetic influences, should have broad explanatory power.

ARITHMETIC ABILITY IN ILLITERATES

Can unschooled illiterates learn to calculate? Rosin (1973) tried to answer this question by describing a study he undertook of an illiterate Indian peasant who demonstrated remarkable conceptualizations independent of writing ability. This peasant was a laborer who struggled for seven years to learn to replace signing documents with an X by a signature. Nevertheless, he was often required to deal with moneylenders, which, in turn, demanded an ability to calculate. By observing his estimation of total counts and recording verbal protocols during calculations, Rosin (1973) was able to explain the peasant's skill. In terms of strategy, each step in the calculation problem was laboriously computed and then stored in memory before proceeding to the next step in the calculation process. Often, he would pause at a particular step to participate in another activity, returning much later to the calculation task. This illustrates the importance of the memorization procedure. As for actual counting, the peasant relied on several strategies, including finger-joint counting. This procedure involves serial counting of the finger joints, with large numbers requiring representation of hands (each representing a count of ten) and individual joints. Eventually, pairs of figures and their solutions are memorized so that fact retrieval is available. This memorization appears painstaking and is dependent on the importance of calculation to a particular individual. Other processes he mastered involve doubling and halving of figures. These operations are often required for agricultural trading and involve purchasing and selling grains or farm animals. These operations are often initially done by visually adding or subtracting physical entities and later by committing the eventual result to memory as a fact. In addition, scales of magnitude are committed to memory for monetary transactions. In summary, the peasant was able to combine a culturally shared knowledge of arithmetic calculation with idiosyncratic methods of memorization and counting to perform the calculations necessary in his society. This combination of idiosyncratic method and the slow operations of primitive counting, scaling, and allied calculations is at odds with the traditional Western way of arithmetic education, which is uniform and designed to be available for a variety of abstract demands and not just cultural requirements.

Laosa (1976) has shown that rural, illiterate Ecuadorian villagers exposed to a nonformal education program designed to increase their numeric and arithmetic skills by emphasizing a Number Bingo game were able to increase their numeric skills significantly. Unfortunately, the learned knowledge was not applied outside the training program. Although not specifically identifying the reason for the improved skill, one can surmise that once again the increased calculation ability was due to fact memorization. The findings of Laosa (1976) and Rosin (1973) point out the importance of sociocultural factors in analyzing the limited calculation ability of unschooled people. If the cultural demands are minimal, less effort will be made to encode arithmetic facts and, in turn, less time will be devoted to discovering creative ways of calculating.

Kulkarni and Naidu (1970) studied the relationship of mathematics achievement to attitudes and other sociocultural factors in Indian society. Surprisingly, they report that their survey indicated that it was, in fact, the poorer students who were often more motivated to achieve arithmetically. They also found that students' attitudes were critically important to learning arithmetic skills and that attitude could be improved by classroom techniques. In general, variables such as age, sex, and socioeconomic factors could be compensated for by classroom teaching. Clark and Halford (1983) discuss the effects of cognitive style on learning arithmetic skills and found that measures of psychometric intelligence were much more critical to the development of calculation skills than cognitive style. Using the results of their study with aboriginal and Anglo-Australian children, they caution against equating cognitive style with cultural and location differences. This is a critical issue for education as psychometric intelligence measures are often claimed to be biased against the nonWestern learning experience. Yet, if the demands of complex arithmetic skills are to be mastered, there may be no alternative to encouraging improvement of psychometric intelligence for the achievement of arithmetic competence. Although we cannot state that limitations in information-processing ability or potential ability account for the arithmetic illiteracy often seen in nonWestern culture, there is some evidence that both sociocultural factors and motivation play an important role in the development of calculation ability.

MATHEMATICAL KNOWLEDGE IN AFRICAN
SOCIETIES

Karr (1983) has recently reported a study of school achievement in the country of Sierra Leone in West Africa. She was particularly interested in the effects of gender and degree of modernization upon Wide Range Achievement Test (WRAT) spelling, reading, and arithmetic scores. Although Grafman et al. (1982) have criticized the use of the WRAT to investigate arithmetic ability, Karr's findings in sixth graders are still of interest. Her results indicated that boys' performance on spelling was significantly higher than girls' performance. In addition, WRAT spelling and reading scores of the most modernized subcultures were strikingly superior to those of three other subcultures. Of more interest was the lack of an effect of either gender or subculture upon arithmetic achievement. Although differentially exposed to technical cultures (students ranged from villagers and tribal members to urban dwellers), all students in this study attended school. It appears then that formal schooling can sometimes override the differing demands of a subculture to provide equivalent arithmetic learning opportunity. It should be noted that spelling and reading may be more important to urban than rural life and that those cultural demands resulted in the significant effects of subculture in those domains.

Posner (1982) also looked at the development of arithmetic concepts in West African children who come from either an agricultural or a merchant society. She studied the children at three age levels: 5–6 years, 7–8 years, and 9–10 years. In Study 1, children were examined in their own language and were asked to estimate relative quantities and recognize equivalent quantities. Posner found that there was a negligible effect of experiential factors like education and cultural background on the ability to rapidly judge the magnitude of numerical quantities. She did find differences on the task requiring estimates of equivalence. Counting was employed in all cases, but younger and unschooled children relied more on size cues for smaller sets. However, when the sets were so large that non-numerical estimates could not be made, a simple counting strategy was reinstated. A second study asked children to solve verbal addition problems. A major strategy difference that emerged in older children was that the children from the merchant culture used memorized facts and regrouping strategies, whereas those from an agricultural community counted more and relied less on memorized facts and occasionally even guessed, which frequently led to incorrect responses. Accuracy on these problems was primarily an effect of age and schooling. The effects of schooling on children from the agricultural community were found to be positive and held to partially offset the advantage of growing up in a merchant society. Finally, counting seemed to be the choice strategy when objects were present, whereas fact retrieval and more complex quantification processes were used for mental addition. These studies provide support for the emergence of counting from knowledge about concrete objects and equivalent numeric entities (same-different tasks). Counting initially appears to be the result of identifying quantities of concrete objects and only later utilizes stored facts and complex regroupings of quantification facts. This later development and its acceleration depends on a combination of demand (culture) and education.

Petitto (1982) sought to examine whether specific mathematical knowledge used by unschooled cloth merchants and tailors could be used to solve arithmetic price problems with both familiar (lengths of cloth) and unusual (oranges) materials involving both measurement and money. Subjects were given the price of a fixed quantity and asked to estimate the price of a smaller quantity. Basic arithmetic knowledge was also tested. Petitto found that scores on abstract arithmetic and meter measurement tests were high across groups and no significant differences emerged. There was no significant effect of materials in the experimental tasks. Cloth merchants, in general, scored higher than tailors, and scores for unfamiliar measurements were substantially lower than for familiar measurements in both groups. For the cloth merchants only, there was a significant correlation between abstract arithmetic problem solving and performance on cloth-pricing tasks. The advantage of the cloth merchants on this type of problem was attributed to fact learning, encoding, and algorithmic familiarity.

Ginsburg, Posner, and Russell (1981a, 1981b) and Petitto and Ginsburg (1982) decided to investigate whether the development of arithmetic knowledge and calculation skills as seen in West African children was comparable to that of children raised in the United States. They found relatively few differences between schooled African and American children in the development of mental addition competence. Similar use of base 10 arithmetic systems may partially account for this finding, as could similar schooling and cultural demands. Both African and American children used regrouping and algorithms in solving standard arithmetic addition problems. However, there does seem to be an early preschool difference between African and American children that African children make up later with schooling. In addition, qualitative similarities in calculation strategy use and types of errors committed by American and African children emerged from these studies. These findings imply similar cognitive processes develop in children from different cultures who are exposed to comparable types of Western schooling and common informal knowledge.

The learning of common informal knowledge often appears as the end result of the application of problem-solving strategies (this may particularly occur in unschooled youngsters; see, for example, Petitto & Ginsburg, 1982). One notable principle of Western arithmetic that unschooled African children do not show is the learning of the principle of commutativity. In addition, they may often rely on nonverbalizable strategies, ignoring more sophisticated notation systems and specific strategies for manipulation of numbers that are typically taught in schools. It is only when *unschooled* African children are compared to American children that striking differences in arithmetic knowledge and calculation emerge.

Omotoso and Shapiro (1976) took a Piagetian approach in examining stages of mathematical achievement in Nigerian children. To assess children, they chose tests of conservation (i.e., the idea of invariance and equality), classification (i.e., the resemblance between members of different classes of symbols or objects), and seriation (i.e., the idea of hierarchical order and reversibility). Piaget (1952) had claimed that the child's ability to understand what the three types of tasks require in order to correctly perform them would be directly related to his ability to understand conventional mathematical concepts. Several Western studies (e.g., Kaminsky, 1970; Nelson, 1969) have indicated high correlations between performance on conservation tasks and arithmetic achievement scores.

Omotoso and Shapiro tested several ethnic groups from Nigeria. All were being taught in English; half were boys, half were girls, from age levels 5, 6, and 7 years. They administered both the Piagetian tasks and two sets of standard mathematics tests. Their results showed that performance on all the Piagetian tasks correlated highly with mathematics achievement, with the test for seriation showing the highest correlations. No age differences emerged. Overall, the performance on the Piagetian tasks predicted mathematics achievement better for boys than girls. Omotoso and Shapiro point out that administering the exams in written instead of oral form and the types of study materials available to the students could have biased the results, allowing seriation ability to have the most predictive power instead of conservation as had been previously reported. Nevertheless, the overall results of this study show the same significant, positive relationship between performance on Piagetian concept tasks and mathematics achievement that exists in studies with American children.

Given the cultural and genetic influences on the development of mathematical reasoning and learning of numerical rules/facts in African children, what can be said about the information-processing strategies they use? Ginsburg (1978) has tried to isolate more general strategies before analyzing their cognitive requirements. He considered tasks such as deciding magnitudes representative of one type of skill, and he considered counting representative of a second type of skill. Judgment of magnitude (i.e., more or less) is solved similarly by African and American children, suggesting somewhat like-cognitive processes are involved. Counting, fact retrieval, and more complex mathematics such as addition may be sensitive to cultural influences but not necessarily formal schooling, suggesting at least somewhat different strategies may be applied by African and American children in solving problems that require these skills.

Gelman (1982) has reviewed the principles of counting and by analyzing error scores (e.g., double counting an item or skipping an item), determined that counting involves maintenance of at least two categories of items in working memory, the "to-be-counted" and "already counted" items, in addition to the summed total of the "already counted" items. This process must proceed in an ordered fashion; plus, when each item represents a single unit, the final sum represented is the total number of items (as opposed to addition of items that have varying unit worth, e.g., $2 + 3 + 6 = ?$). Leaving aside the stages of development when these processes become evident, one could surmise that although magnitude estimation and simple counting are rather basic processes, the complexity of addition and multiplication requires more memorized facts and thus formal schooling.

To summarize, estimates and comparisons of magnitude are developed somewhat preculturally; counting is developed primarily through cultural influence, whereas higher order computations from addition to algebra and geometry probably benefit from formal schooling. Formal schooling induces the fact retainment, rule induction, and problem-solving strategies that we outlined in the introduction when describing a rudimentary model of the information-processing requirements to solve a simple addition problem.

ACHIEVEMENT OF MATHEMATICAL AND CALCULATION KNOWLEDGE IN ASIAN CHILDREN AND ADULTS

Many studies have documented a superiority in mathematics achievement in Asian students over those from the United States (e.g., see Husen, 1967). Stigler, Lee, Lucker, and Stevenson (1982) became interested in documenting when those differences first appear and why. They note that although there is some content overlap between textbooks published in Taiwan, Japan, and the United States, there is a sizable amount of information not shared. For example, Japanese elementary school textbooks often contain information (on such topics as probability or correspondence in geometrical figures) not found until more advanced texts in the United States. Introduction of content areas in school is similar to Grade one, after which Japanese texts more rapidly introduce higher level materials. Taiwan is slowest to introduce high-level materials. Interestingly, both Japanese and Taiwanese (despite the slower introduction of complex materials) children's scores were superior to American children's on culture-fair arithmetic tests. These differences emerged for problems requiring computation as well as those requiring application of arithmetic reasoning. Because both time spent in class and the importance of a child's achievement to the parents is greater in Asian cultures (including actual time spent assisting their child with homework), Stigler et al. attribute their findings to these factors. Tsang (1984) has found this same trend for superior performance even when Asian families immigrate to the United States, reinforcing the importance of cultural factors in mathematical achievement. Arithmetic deficits, when they occur in the immigrant Asian population, appear due to a difficulty in mastering the technical language of the host country (i.e., a cultural bias).

CALCULATION BY ABACUS USERS

As briefly described, Asian and Asian-American children show superior calculation and arithmetic ability when measured by standard base 10 counting systems and Western rules of mathematical operation. A tool for calculation occasionally used in Asian cultures that has been neglected in the United States is the abacus (although the recent introduction of the calculator and computer into elementary education programs may further neutralize cultural differences in calculation ability). Because there may be qualitative as well as quantitatively different information-processing demands required by abacus use when contrasted with other methods of calculation from finger counting (Flegg, 1983; Zaslavsky, 1979) and simple written calculation to fact retrieval, it should be of interest to contrast the calculation performance of subjects when using abacus versus alternative calculation methods.

Stigler (1984) has described the use, proficiency, and information-processing demands of abacus calculation. The abacus is composed of beads that represent place value in the base 10 system of numeration. Each column of beads represents a place value. The beads in the upper portion of the abacus are equal to five times the unit value of the column when pushed toward the dividing bar, zero when pushed away from the bar. Addition with the abacus can be described in terms of bead movement and placement as well as of finger movement. That is, finger movement must co-occur with computational processing steps (and may even become automatic when overlearned). Pattern visualization, similar to that seen in expert chess players, may also play a role in both fact retrieval and decision making within complex computational procedures (i.e., deciding whether a sequence of calculation steps is correct and/or proceeding appropriately). In fact, visualization ability may also allow for "mental abacus calculations." Mental abacus calculation is typically introduced in elementary education following motor abacus proficiency.

Stigler (1984) first tested Chinese children on a range of addition problems with both abacus manipulation and mental addition required. He found that abacus calculation times within subjects were significantly and linearly related to total number of digits in the problem. Mental calculations also showed significant but weaker correlations. Experts were generally faster than subjects with intermediate experience in calculation or novices. Calculation errors were greater with mental calculations than abacus manipulation. There was also a slight tradeoff between speed of response and error rate, particularly with intermediate and novice learners. Experts, however, generally showed a superiority of mental to motor abacus calculation.

Experts relative to intermediate and novice students were also able to accurately distinguish probes representing intermediate stage abacus states versus distractor probes. Whether actually using the abacus or relying on mental abacus calculations, the time required to verify an intermediate stage of computation depends how far down in the sequence of processing steps the stage lies.

Finally, American graduate students were compared to fifth-grade Chinese students on mental addition problems. No American student had experience with the abacus, whereas all the Chinese fifth graders had. Results showed that the American graduate students were slower in calculating answers to mental addition problems than Chinese fifth graders. The addition of addends accounted for a constant increase in computation time for both groups. The longer the total number of digits in the problem, the greater the advantage in response speed for Chinese fifth graders. Accuracy results were similar for experts, intermediate skilled abacus users, and Americans.

Error analyses were interesting. Confusions of "five" occurred significantly more often in the Chinese (regardless of whether they actually manipulated an abacus or used mental abacus calculations). Because the Chinese reported more reliance on visual representation of intermediate state solutions to a mental addition problem, omission of digits in the answer might occur more frequently because of "blurring" together of columns in the mental abacus. This hypothesis was confirmed by the data. American graduate students, using standard mental addition, were much more confident, and commited fewer omissions, in computing the accurate number of digits in an answer. American graduate students who worked from right to left in solving a problem and the Chinese fifth graders who worked from left to right tended to make errors in the most extreme digit positions. No differences emerged for this error type between Chinese using mental abacus computations versus those who had the abacus in front of them. For mental abacus operations only, the width of a problem (i.e., the total number of columns to be imaginally maintained) is a factor in the time necessary to solve an addition problem. An analogy to a spreadsheet that needs image refreshing may be one explanation for this finding.

The time advantage for mental abacus over real abacus manipulation may be due to actual move time. Interestingly, Hatano, Miyoke, and Binks (1977) found that restricting finger movement or requiring finger tapping interfered with concurrent mental abacus calculation, suggesting that covert motor processing in subjects who perform mental abacus calculations may represent mechanisms involved in maintaining a rehearsal loop in working memory. Nonmathematical questions during mental abacus processing did not interfere with solution time or accuracy, whereas responding to mathematical questioning did. Hatano and Osawa (1983) found that mental abacus experts had larger digit spans (but not other symbol spans) than nonexperts. Their digit memory was also more interfered with by visual-spatial compared to auditory-verbal tasks (i.e., digit memory would be visually represented due to mental abacus solution strategies). This storage ability appeared to be responsible for holding several digits just for calculation operations and then, as with a spreadsheet, was erased because nonsolution digit strings used for temporary calculations were not recalled nor even recognized by mental abacus experts who exhibited a superior digit span.

DISCUSSION

This brief overview of selected cross-cultural research on arithmetic and calculation abilities allowed us to discover some general principles about calculation learning and proficiency. It appears that even illiterates who reside in a culture that requires some kind of bartering or merchandising skill are capable of developing both rudimentary and idiosyncratic methods of calculating amounts and magnitudes. Evidence from both adult illiterates and nonschooled children support this finding. As our review indicated, both magnitude estimation and simple equivalence skills appear to develop independent of formal teaching or cultural pressure. Counting skills may require cultural incentive. Some of these arithmetic abilities, although culture-independent, may be object- or trade-specific (i.e., an untaught counting or magnitude estimation ability may be singularly developed for agricultural products, with a particular individual having difficulty generalizing that skill to nonagricultural products). More complex addition and higher order arithmetic skills generally benefit from formal education, regardless of cultural background (e.g., whether an individual is from a mercantile or agricultural society). Strategies in solving arithmetic problems may also vary. Using a visually based pattern (as in the case of an abacus) to represent a numerical amount or figure as an intermediate step to a solution may be faster than conventional Western methods of mental calculation.

Thus, some arithmetic skills appear genetically linked (e.g., magnitude estimation), some culturally linked (e.g., equivalence or certain counting skills), and some educationally linked (e.g., arithmetic calculation and the "tool" used to calculate, be it fingers, strips of paper, abacus, calculator, computer, or brain). This finding suggests that both Piaget and Vygotsky were partially correct in assuming genetic and cultural influences upon number manipulation.

What can be said about information-processing strategies? Some elements appear genetically derived. That is, object recognition, size estimation, simple perceptual discriminations, encoding capability, working memory, and retrieval capabilities all appear along with environment-free and environmentally linked lexical storage elements to develop independently of culture or formal training. Whether environmentally linked or not, there is also an ability to invent mathematical strategies (Smith, 1983) that, although limited, are nevertheless independent of formal education (Hadamard, 1945). Some elements of arithmetic information processing appear culturally linked. This would include type of lexical knowledge, favored calculation strategy, and speed of processing. Finally, some elements of arithmetic information processing must be education linked. These would include the reasoning and schematic aspects of arithmetic processing. Such conceptual entities as problem task environment, heuristic and algorithm generalization, and higher order mathematics are generally seen as requiring formal schooling. This schooling, in turn, will result in greater knowledge, more rapid information-processing speed when computing such knowledge (although speed of processing more basic arithmetic elements may be no faster than that of less schooled cultures), and better ability to generalize and build upon such knowledge (Dinnel, Glover, & Ronning, 1984).

Can cross-cultural research teach us about dyscalculia? We believe that it can. Much of the following is speculative but intriguing. Why are calculation deficits in adult brain-injured patients occasionally accompanied by impaired finger recognition, left-right discrimination impairment, and dysgraphia, among other deficits? It may be that these specific accompanying disabilities reflect an earlier dependence upon such ability to calculate (Menninger, 1977) and that there is some overlap in cortical space reflecting this primitive dependence.

Cultural and educational distinctions in learning arithmetic may help us understand what aspects of information processing may be most sensitive to decay or loss following brain damage. Speed of processing may decay more rapidly in underutilized abilities, generalization of arithmetic strategies may become more limited, and work space may decrease for novel arithmetic problems. It might be suggested that those skills that appear more genetically determined such as magnitude estimation and simple counting, would be the best retained following brain injury. In addition, the scenario in which counting is most frequently used may be better functionally preserved. All of these speculative statements are in addition to what we know about the breakdown of information-processing ability in general, with such deficits as transcoding impairment, specific amnesias, expressive and receptive language disorders, and perceptual deficits playing their usual role depending upon location and type of lesion.

Arithmetic ability in cross-cultural study is often tested by simple problems because speed of response time is the critical dependent variable; thus, error counts are often small and not theoretically significant (i.e., cannot be compared to errors made by dyscalculics). Nevertheless, the use of error protocols and the recording of verbal problem-solving protocols in individual brain-injured cases should assist in the determination of both the cognitive strategy used and the stage of processing where the error was committed.

Cross-cultural research in arithmetic calculation is only now reaching a stage where some of the more important information-processing questions can be asked. Perhaps the most significant one is whether models of arithmetic calculation used in Western cultures that appear in this monograph can be used in all cultures, with only minor adjustment for which routes and stages are most relied on in solving a problem. Except for an occasional reference to learning disability in non-Western cultures, we have virtually no information regarding the effects of brain injury in non-Western and/or illiterate adults upon their ability to utilize whatever cognitive strategies they have adapted to calculate (from abacus use in more advanced cultures to finger-counting strategies seen in the more primitive cultures). We believe that as interest in cross-cultural research continues, these issues will be addressed.

REFERENCES

Allardice, B. S., & Ginsburg, H. P. (1983). Children's psychological difficulties in mathematics. In H. P. Ginsburg (Ed.), *The development of mathematical thinking* pp. 319–350). New York: Academic Press.
Boller, F., & Grafman, J. (1983). Acalculia: Historical development and current significance. *Brain and Cognition, 2*, 205–223.
Boller, F., & Grafman, J. Acalculia. In P. J. Vinken, G. W. Bruyn, and H. L. Klawans (Eds.) *Handbook of Clinical Neurology, (Revised Series) Vol. 45 (J. A. M. Fredericks Ed.), 1985, Amsterdam, Elsevier.*
Burling, R. (1964). Cognition and componential analysis: God's truth or hocus-pocus. *American Anthropologist, 66*(1), 20–28.
Clark, L. A., & Halford, G. S. (1983). Does cognitive style account for cultural differences in scholastic achievement? *Journal of Cross-Cultural Psychology, 14*(3), 279–296.
Deloche, G., & Seron, X. (1982). From three to 3, a differential analysis of skills in transcoding quantities between patients with Broca's and Wernicke's aphasia. *Brain, 105*, 719–733.
Dinnel, D., Glover, G. A., & Ronning, R. R. (1984). A provisional model of mathematical problem solving. *Bulletin of the Psychonomic Society, 22*(5), 459–462.
Flegg, G. (1983). *Numbers: Their history and meaning.* New York: Shocken Books.
Fodor, J. (1983). *The modularity of the mind.* Cambridge, MA: MIT Press.
Gelman, R. (1982). Basic numerical abilities. In R. J. Sternberg (Ed.), *Advances in the psychology of intelligence* (Vol. 1, pp. 181–205). Hillsdale, NJ: Lawrence Erlbaum Associates.
Ginsburg, H. (1978). Poor children, African mathematics, and the problem of schooling. *Education Research Quarterly, 2*(4), 26–44.
Ginsburg, H., Posner, J. K., & Russell, R. L. (1981a). The development of knowledge concerning written arithmetic: A cross-cultural study. *International Journal of Psychology, 16*, 13–34.
Ginsburg, H., Posner, J. K., & Russell, R. L. (1981b). The development of mental addition as a function of schooling and culture. *Journal of Cross-Cultural Psychology, 12*(2), 163–178.
Grafman, J., Passafiume, D., Faglioni, P., & Boller, F. (1982). Calculation disturbances in adults with focal hemispheric damage. *Cortex, 18*, 37–50.
Grewel, F. (1962). Disorders in the use of Semiotic Systems. *Logos, 5*, 43–50.
Hadamard, J. (1945). *The psychology of invention in the mathematical field.* New York: Dover.
Hatano, G., Miyoke, Y., & Binks, M. G. (1977). Performance of expert abacus operators. *Cognition, 5*, 57–71.
Hatano, G., & Osawa, K. (1983). Digit memory of grand experts in abacus-derived mental calculation. *Cognition, 15*, 95–110.
Hurford, J. R. (1975). *The linguistic theory of numerals.* New York: Cambridge University Press.
Husen, T. (1967). *International study of achievement in mathematics: A comparison of twelve countries.* New York: Wiley.
Kamii, M. (1981). Children's ideas about written numbers. *Topics in Learning and Learning Disabilities, 3*, 47–59.
Kaminsky, M. (1970). *A study of conservation ability in relationship to arithmetic achievement.* Unpublished doctoral dissertation, Wayne State University, Detroit, MI.
Karr, S. K. (1983). School achievement of Sierra Leone, West African children from four subcultures. *Perceptual and Motor Skills, 57*, 204–206.

Kulkarni, S. S., & Naidu, C. A. S. (1970). Mathematics achievement related to students' socio-economic and attitude variables—A pilot study. *Indian Journal of Psychology, 45*(1), 53–66.

Laosa, L. M. (1976). Developing arithmetic skills among rural villagers in Ecuador through nonformal education: A field experiment. *Journal of Educational Psychology, 68*(6), 670–679.

Levinson, D. (1977). What have we learned from cross-cultural surveys? *American Behavioral Scientist, 20*(5), 757–792.

Menninger, K. (1977). *Number words and number symbols: A cultural history of numbers.* Cambridge, MA: MIT Press.

Nelson, R. J. (1969). *An investigation of a group test based in Piaget's concept number and length conservation and its ability to predict first-grade arithmetic achievement.* Unpublished doctoral dissertation, Purdue University.

Omotoso, H., & Shapiro, B. (1976). Conservation, seriation, classification, and mathematics achievement in Nigerian children. *Psychological Reports, 38,* 1335–1339.

Petitto, A. L. (1982). Practical arithmetic and transfer: A study among West African tribesmen. *Journal of Cross-Cultural Psychology, 13*(1), 15–28.

Petitto, A. L., & Ginsburg, H. P. (1982). Mental arithmetic in Africa and America: Strategies, principles, and explanations. *International Journal of Psychology, 17,* 81–102.

Piaget, J. (1952). *The child's conception of number.* New York: Norton.

Posner, J. K. (1982). The development of mathematical knowledge in two West African societies. *Child Development, 53,* 200–208.

Reed, H. J., & Lave, J. (1979). Arithmetic as a tool for investigating relations between culture and cognition. *American Ethnologist, 6*(3), 568–582.

Rosin, R. T. (1973). Gold medallions: The arithmetic calculations of an illiterate. *Council on Anthropology and Education Newsletter, 4*(2), 1–9.

Saxe, G. B., & Posner, J. (1983). The development of numerical cognition: Cross-cultural perspectives. In H. P. Ginsburg (Ed.), *The development of mathematical thinking.* New York: Academic Press.

Smith, S. B. (1983). *The great mental calculations: The psychology, methods, and lives of calculating prodigies, past and present.* New York: Columbia University Press.

Stigler, J. W. (1984). "Mental abacus": The effect of abacus training on Chinese children's mental calculation. *Cognitive Psychology, 16,* 145–176.

Stigler, J. W., Lee, S. Y., Lucker, G. W., & Stevenson, H. W. (1982). Curriculum and achievement in mathematics: A study of elementary school children in Japan, Taiwan, and the United States. *Journal of Educational Psychology, 74*(3), 315–322.

Tsang, S-L. (1984). The mathematics education of Asian Americans. *Journal for Research in Mathematics Education, 15*(2), 114–122.

Vygotsky, L. S. (1962). *Thought and language.* Cambridge, MA: M.I.T. Press.

Warrington, E. K. (1982). The fractionation of arithmetical skills: A single case study. *Quarterly Journal of Experimental Psychology, 34a,* 31–51.

Winthrop, H. (1980). Simplifying difficult themes and demythologizing cultural misperception in international studies. *Sociologia Internationalis, 4,* 49–67.

Zaslavsky, C. (1979). *Africa counts: Number and pattern in African culture.* Westport, CT: Lawrence Hill.

Author Index

Subject Index